Radical Volunteers

| POLITICS AND CULTURE IN THE TWENTIETH-CENTURY SOUTH |

SERIES EDITORS

Bryant Simon, *Temple University*
Jane Dailey, *University of Chicago*

ADVISORY BOARD

Rebecca Brückmann, *Carleton College*
Eric Gellman, *University of North Carolina, Chapel Hill*
Charles McKinney, *Rhodes College*
Sarah J. McNamara, *Texas A&M University*
Elizabeth McRae, *Western Carolina University*
La Shonda Mims, *Middle Tennessee State University*
Robert Norrell, *University of Tennessee, Knoxville*
Anke Ortlepp, *Universität zu Köln*
Vanessa Ribas, *University of California, San Diego*
J. Mills Thornton, *University of Michigan*
Allen Tullos, *Emory University*
Brian Ward, *Northumbria University*

Radical Volunteers

DISSENT, DESEGREGATION,
AND STUDENT POWER IN TENNESSEE

Katherine J. Ballantyne

The University of Georgia Press
ATHENS

© 2024 by the University of Georgia Press
Athens, Georgia 30602
www.ugapress.org
All rights reserved
Set in 10.25/13.5 Minion Pro Regular by Kaelin Chappell Broaddus

Most University of Georgia Press titles are
available from popular e-book vendors.

Printed digitally

Part of Chapter 4 has been reprinted with permission from
"Students Are [Not] Slaves": 1960s Student Power Debates in Tennessee,"
Journal of American Studies 54, no. 2 (2020): 295-322.
Copyright © Cambridge University Press and
British Association American Studies 2019

Library of Congress Cataloging-in-Publication Data

Names: Ballantyne, Katherine J., author.
Title: Radical volunteers : dissent, desegregation, and student power in
    Tennessee / Katherine J. Ballantyne.
Identifiers: LCCN 2023043137 (print) | LCCN 2023043138 (ebook) |
    ISBN 9780820366371 (hardback) | ISBN 9780820366456 (paperback) |
    ISBN 9780820366463 (epub) | ISBN 9780820366470 (pdf)
Subjects: LCSH: College students—Political activity—Tennessee—
    History—20th century. | Student movements—Tennessee—History—
    20th century. | Civil rights movements—Tennessee—History—20th
    century. | Tennessee—Politics and government—20th century. |
    Universities and colleges—Political aspects—Tennessee.
Classification: LCC LB3610 .B344 2024 (print) | LCC LB3610 (ebook) | DDC
    378.1/981097680904—dc23/eng/20231214
LC record available at https://lccn.loc.gov/2023043137
LC ebook record available at https://lccn.loc.gov/2023043138

CONTENTS

Acknowledgments vii

List of Organizational Acronyms ix

Introduction 1

CHAPTER 1 Foundations of Student Activism in Tennessee, 1925–1964 10

CHAPTER 2 Kneel, Sit, or Stand: Creating a Student Movement 36

CHAPTER 3 Waging the Labor Struggle in Tennessee, 1964–1968 61

CHAPTER 4 Reforming Administrative Policies: From Protesting *In Loco Parentis* to Student Power, 1968–1970 83

CHAPTER 5 "Deep Division": Tennessee Student Activists and the Vietnam War 120

CONCLUSION The Legacy of the "Prophetic Minority" Within the "Recalcitrant Minority" 144

Notes 155

Bibliography 199

Index 219

ACKNOWLEDGMENTS

As historians, we often struggle to say when something begins. What does the beginning signify, we ask? For this book, the beginning is actually pretty straightforward. Sitting in his college office in 2012, then Mellon Professor of American History Tony Badger listened to me run through a few ideas for my MPhil dissertation. When I reached the end of my list, he paused, and asked: "Have you thought about focusing on Tennessee? What sort of student activism occurred there?" More than a bit surprised, I answered, "Tennessee doesn't have a history of student activism beyond the sit-ins, does it?"

That question has driven this research from the MPhil to the PhD and now in its final form—this book. More than a few archivists looked at me confused and then sympathetically as I went through box after box searching for something they were sure was not there. (It turns out that universities have clever terms for campus activism, but that is a story for another time.) Many archivists and researchers offered invaluable assistance for this project, for which I am extremely grateful. In Tennessee, these individuals include: Kris Bronstad, Sarah E. Calise, Wayne Dowdy, Debra Dylan, Ed Frank, Michelle Ganz, Teresa Gray, Earl J. Hess, Martha Hess, Louis M. Kyriakoudes, DebbieLee Landi, Jennifer Quier, Bill Short, and Kathy Smith. Beyond Tennessee, Allen Fisher, Lee Grady, Ryan Pettigrew, and Stephen Plotkin provided advice and suggestions which greatly helped my research.

I have been lucky to have many historians' thoughts on this work. First, two Mellon Professors of American History, Tony Badger and Gary Gerstle, supervised me at the University of Cambridge. I greatly appreciate their insights into the project and ability to see it for what it could become. For their support and encouragement, my thanks go to the Cambridge American History Graduate Workshop, especially Seth Archer, Hannah Higgin, and Stephen Mawdsley; Andrew Preston at the University of Cambridge; Simon Hall at the University of Leeds; George Lewis at the University of Leicester; Brian Ward at Northumbria University; Emile Chabal, Julie Gibbings, Fabian Hilfrich, Megan Hunt, David Silkenat, and the Centre for the Study of Modern and Contemporary History at the University of Edinburgh; Stephen Tuck and colleagues at the Rothermere American Institute at the University of Oxford; friends at Keele University, especially Rebecca Bowler; and my colleagues at

Liverpool John Moores University and the Centre for Modern and Contemporary History. Much appreciated are the thoughts and feedback from colleagues at the Historians of the Twentieth Century United States (HOTCUS) and British Association for American Studies (BAAS) conferences over the years.

A number of funding grants supported the book's research. My PhD studies were funded by the Cambridge International Scholarship from the Cambridge Commonwealth, European and International Trust. I also received university grants from the Sara Norton Fund and Members' History Fund of the Cambridge History Faculty, the Student Registry Fieldwork Fund, the Clare College Research Expenses Award, and the Prize Research Grant from the Centre for History and Economics. The John F. Kennedy Library Foundation funded my research at the John F. Kennedy Presidential Library with the Theodore C. Sorensen Research Fellowship and I am grateful to have been a participant of the graduate exchange fellowship with the American Political History Institute at Boston University.

Thanks to Nathaniel Holly with the University of Georgia Press for championing this project and his encouragement throughout the process, and to Lea Johnson for seeing the book across the finish line. To Jehanne Moharram for her work copyediting the manuscript and to Ben Shaw for his time indexing the book, thank you—the book is a much stronger product as a result. I'd also like to thank the series editors Bryant Simon and Jane Dailey for believing in this book.

This research has, in one way or another, been a part of my life for more than a decade. From graduate work, several academic jobs, house moves, marriage, and parenthood, researching and then writing this book has been a constant. My parents and family have encouraged me and my daughter has provided constant joy and enthusiasm for life in a way that only she can. I am more grateful for them than they will ever know. The most significant constant in my life during this period, not least for his important role as my coffee maker, has believed in this project and me from the start. This book is dedicated to my husband, whose unfailing support and encouragement has made this work better at every stage. Thank you, David.

LIST OF ORGANIZATIONAL ACRONYMS

AAUP	American Association of University Professors
ACLU	American Civil Liberties Union
AFL-CIO	The American Federation of Labor and Congress of Industrial Organizations
AFSCME	American Federation of State, County and Municipal Employees
ASB	Associated Student Body
AV	Appalachian Volunteers
BLF	Black Liberation Front
BOP	Black Organizing Project
BSA	Black Student Association
BSU	Black Students Union
CIC	Commission on Interracial Cooperation
CIO	Congress of Industrial Organizations
COFO	Council of Federal Organizations
COINTELPRO	Counter Intelligence Program (FBI)
COME	Committee on the Move for Equality
CORE	Congress of Racial Equality
CSM	Council of the Southern Mountains
ERAP	Economic Research Action Project
FBI	Federal Bureau of Investigation
FOR	Fellowship of Reconciliation
FREE	Forum for Racial Equality, Etc.
GMRRC	Greater Memphis Race Relations Committee
GROW	Grassroots Organizing Work
HBCU	Historically Black College or University
JOIN	Jobs or Income Now
JUC	Joint University Council on Human Relations
KCIC	Knoxville Civic Improvement Committee
KKK	Ku Klux Klan
MAP–South	Memphis Area Project–South
MCCR	Memphis Committee on Community Relations
MCRC	Memphis Community Relations Committee

NAACP	National Association for the Advancement of Colored People
NCLC	Nashville Christian Leadership Council
NOP	Neighborhood Organizing Project
NSA	National Student Association
NSL	National Student League
NSM	Nashville Student Movement
OEO	Office of Economic Opportunity
OG	Order of the Gownsmen
PBC	People's Bicentennial Commission
SCCEWV	Southern Coordinating Committee to End the War in Vietnam
SCEF	Southern Conference Educational Fund
SCHW	Southern Conference for Human Welfare
SCLC	Southern Christian Leadership Conference
SDS	Students for a Democratic Society
SEC	Southeastern Conference
SET	Students for Equal Treatment
SGA	Student Government Association
SLAM	Southern Labor Action Movement
SNCC	Student Nonviolent Coordinating Committee
SPC	Second Presbyterian Church
SRC	Southern Regional Council
SSOC	Southern Student Organizing Committee
TVA	Tennessee Valley Authority
UP	United for Progress
VISTA	Volunteers in Service to America
VVAC	Vanderbilt Vietnam Action Committee
WOPC	War on Poverty Committee
WPA	Works Progress Administration
YAF	Young Americans for Freedom

Radical Volunteers

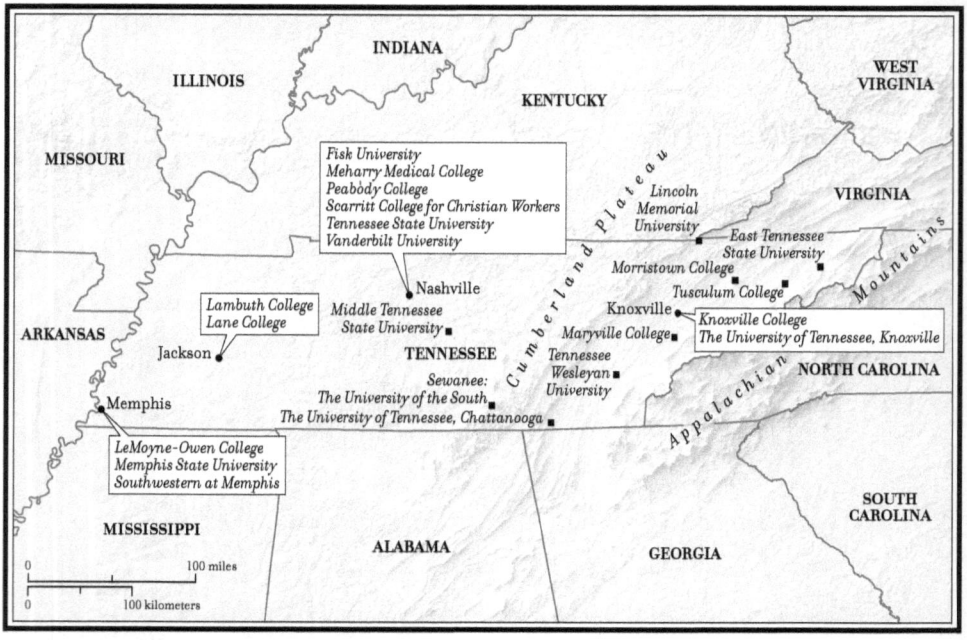

FIG. 1. Map of the Tennessee colleges and universities mentioned in this book. Mapping Specialists, Ltd.

INTRODUCTION

As the tens of thousands of crusade attendees filed past local police and Secret Service to enter Neyland Stadium, they had little idea how the muggy May 28, 1970, evening would pan out. Nor did the few hundred college-age protestors, many of whom walked through security checkpoints outside the football stadium of the University of Tennessee hiding signs stating "Thou Shalt Not Kill" under their shirts and tucked into their waistbands. Rev. Billy Graham and the crusade's organizing committee had anticipated this conflict, however—as had the university. Holding Graham's week-long religious revival at the football stadium presented several headaches for the university; in particular it stoked frustrations of students and staff over the separation of church and state and that the crusade took place during finals. But student unrest had also been at an all-time high on campus that year. It was the announcement that President Richard M. Nixon would be speaking during the crusade's Youth Night that sparked this particular protest. Although surprised by the upcoming presidential visit, the crusade organizers moved forward with their plans, while they, university officials, and the White House anticipated protests but expected them to be small and unimpactful.

They were wrong—to a point. This was Nixon's first appearance at a university campus after the Kent State shootings earlier that month. The White House and Graham's Knoxville crusade committee believed the reception would be overwhelmingly positive, important for Nixon amid the national discord surrounding his Vietnam policies. But Nixon's dissenters, while vastly outnumbered, were loud. Their heckles and chants (including "One-two-three-four, we don't want you anymore") were clearly picked up in official recordings of the event, interrupting Nixon several times during his speech. The protest and subsequent prosecution of several students (named the "Knoxville 22") who attended this event, and indeed the broader student movement in Tennessee, are largely absent from historical accounts, having disappeared from historical understanding of the state. Away from the famous Nashville movement (usually categorized as part of civil rights rather than student activism), the significance of Tennessee's student activism has remained largely unexamined because when it did appear, observers dismissed it as an isolated event rather than as representative of a larger movement.

During a May 1970 news segment for ABC News, Charles Murphy concluded his report on Nixon speaking at the Knoxville crusade with a final word not about the event or its religious attendees, but about the protestors assembled there. "The anti-war demonstrators were a small minority," he stated, "but the fact that they were even here, on a conservative campus in a conservative state, illustrates the deep division even here."[1] While the discovery of the illegal Cambodian bombing and subsequent killing of students at Kent State and Jackson State had catalyzed student activism nationally in May 1970, Murphy's statement overlooked the longer, sustained development of student protest in Tennessee.

The narrative of Tennessee student protest is the story of student activism in much of America during the twentieth century. The notion of the New Left inhabiting only a brief moment in time, rising and falling in the 1960s—"years of hope, days of rage," in Todd Gitlin's influential telling—is problematic in the context of Tennessee.[2] Student movements both developed and fractured more slowly in Tennessee than in the dominant national accounts of student activism. Student activism in Tennessee dates back much further than commonly perceived, as early as the 1920s, and despite the crushing effect of McCarthyism and Communist fears of the 1940s and 1950s, Old Left and New Left activists fostered intergenerational connections based on students' focus on personal autonomy and social welfare.

Furthermore, interracial student activism was evident in the state prior to the start of the sit-in movement in February 1960, dating to collegiate student exchanges and workshops beginning in 1954. White and Black students fought for similar causes pertaining to student life on campuses and community improvement well into the 1960s, and only began to show significant differences around 1968. This is later than the shift in 1964 and 1965 often emphasized by scholars who study student activism elsewhere in the country.[3] The student movement centered on issues related to autonomy and minority rights through the 1960s and reached its peak in spring 1970. From there, while racial inequality and student rights remained prominent focuses, Tennessee student activism evolved on a smaller scale to embrace a broader range of causes, such as women's and gay rights. So while the majority of activism took place between *Brown v. Board of Education of Topeka* (1954) and the national backlash against the May 1970 Kent State University shootings, viewing it over a longer period demonstrates that Tennessee student activism was more than just a flash in the pan.[4]

As the first statewide study of student activism to incorporate Black and white students and their work on campuses and in communities, and one of a growing historiography on southern student activism, this book will broaden scholarly understanding of New Left and white and Black student radicalism from its traditionally defined hotbeds in the Northeast and the West Coast. Previous studies of southern student activism and the New Left specifically detailed the distinctions between activism in the North versus the South. Building on their contributions from the late 1990s to the 2010s, this book draws connections with experiences of students across the South and around the country.[5] In Tennessee, the stifling political and social order forced activism to develop more slowly; for the same reason, the period of mass mobilization among students in the 1960s itself was briefer. Leftist activists in the South had to endure more isolation—and greater risks—than their counterparts elsewhere.

Student activism in Tennessee straddles the historiographies of the 1960s student movement and the civil rights movement. Elements of Tennessee student activism related to one or both of the movements, and many participants did not see themselves as exclusively associated with one or the other. As such, Tennessee student activism makes a significant contribution to studies of the 1960s; previously understood distinctions between the two historiographies are less useful when considering state-level studies such as this one.[6]

Radical Volunteers also departs from existing work in its determination to scrutinize student activism in the communities in which campuses were situated as well as on campuses themselves. Campus-centered research provides deeper insight into specific events and the individuals involved, but by considering student activists alongside community leaders and members, a community-focused approach allows for a more representative accounting of students' initiatives and their effect on their communities.[7] Incorporating primary resources focuses on the students themselves. This, alongside materials that detail the actions of university administrators, faculty, and state and federal actors, reveals a more nuanced story of student activism.[8]

I use a state study of Tennessee to examine the development of student activism in the mid-twentieth century. It is not exclusively a Tennessee story, nor a southern one; in moving across the state of Tennessee from campus to campus, including major cities and rural areas, and contextualizing African American and white student experiences over the long chronological period used in the study, it tells a previously overlooked story of student activism. Focusing on Tennessee specifically, rather than another southern (or non-southern) state, allows for connections to southern, western, and national similarities in my analysis. This is particularly important for context for this period of Tennessee's history given student activism's previously understudied nature outside of the famous Nashville sit-ins. The variety of geographical and demographic settings in Tennessee, as well as its location as a gateway to both the Border South and Deep South, makes the state an insightful case study.

Moreover, Tennessee's student activism is largely representative of most regions of the country, such as the Midwest where studies of Illinois and Oklahoma college campuses and ones in the Appalachian region of Ohio have demonstrated continuities in the focus and development of white student activism. This makes us rethink southern student activism as one not of regional exceptionalism but as a national story with a southern flavor. As much research on southern exceptionalism has shown, when compared with other areas across the country, much of what had been previously understood as exceptionally southern is in fact broadly representative of national trends.[9] Looking beyond one moment or one place, Tennessee can be used to tell the longer, complex history of American student activism.

Framing student activism over a long period of time across the state reveals disjuncture as much as coherence in the movement. Though all case studies contain distinctive and representative features, Tennessee's geographical diversity lends itself well to a study of regional variation. The state's widely recognized West, Middle, and East divisions exemplify different regions of the South.[10] Just as there was no one South, there was no one Tennessee. Political scientist Alexander P. Lamis described Tennessee as "a complex mixture of nearly all of the important elements found throughout the South."[11] Tennessee borders eight other states, with the heavily Black western part of the state bordering the Mississippi River across from Missouri and Arkansas, and the eastern portion running up alongside western North Carolina and the Appalachian Mountains. These geographical differences helped drive the state's economic history, which in turn shaped racial politics in each region. As one visitor claimed in 1962, "It is difficult to believe one state can have such different 'moods.'"[12] Tennessee's seemingly split personality impacted its emergent student movement.

The southern context mattered in shaping Tennessean activism. While for some white activists, their southern heritage molded their work as well as their identity, for others, including the majority of Black students, the region's racial politics were more significant. One white student activist at the University of Alabama during the 1960s quipped, "Living in the South and being a freak isn't like living just anywhere and being a freak,"[13] a feeling many white Tennessee student activists would have shared. This sentiment was a consequence of the region's pervasive political repression of left-wing activism and the small numbers of activists relative to the overall Tennessee student population. The South's political order was more stifling than its counterpart in the North, and could easily turn violent. Student activists in the South grasped these constraints. In pursuing interracial activism, southern students addressed racial issues, but had to do so carefully. Race strongly influenced personal experiences of activism, however. For Black students in Tennessee, the desegregation of public facilities and the integration of higher education institutions was more immediate and personal. They certainly had agency in deciding to organize and participate in activism, but they had more to gain in terms of representation on campus, as well as more to lose; Black student activists were suspended or expelled for their activism in much higher numbers than their white peers. Though not "exceptional," Tennessee student activism certainly had a southern inflection.

Student power emerges as the unifying theme across the decades and racial lines. Defined here as the demand for personal and/or political autonomy, student power was evident as a concept, from the campus-based protests of the 1920s around students' rights through to the 1960s debates over *in loco parentis* campus policy reform. It is also a sentiment expressed by white and Black students alike, and one that unified students of diverse backgrounds on campuses large and small. Both Black and white students viewed attempts to establish personal autonomy within campus and community organizing as vital activities. They understood personal autonomy in a broad sense, conceptualized as student power: it covered immediate concerns over universities' assumption of parental power over students, as well as apparent infringements of civil rights and civil liberties.

By the late 1960s, awareness of continued racial inequalities in education and society drove Black students in larger numbers to demand destruction of the perceived racial "machine" harming African Americans across the country. Many white southern student radicals were sympathetic to this Black quest to uproot the structures sustaining racism, but were less successful in persuading large numbers of whites of its urgency. Meanwhile, a growing majority of Black students no longer believed it was in their best interest to join forces with white New Leftists.[14] The result was a further separation between the initiatives of Black and white student activists. By 1970, the situation in the South mirrored divisions elsewhere, though the split had come later. The Tennessee case adds to the wave of scholarship challenging 1964 or 1965 as the divide between good/bad, interracial/separatist, or successful/unsuccessful categories of 1960s activism.

Student power was not a uniquely Tennessean, southern, or even American concept. Studies of student activism in the Midwest, most notably in Illinois and Oklahoma, highlight similar emphasis on students' personal autonomy as a unifying, pervasive theme. Termed "prairie power," the central organizing concept in these states bore striking similarities to the student power articulated by Tennessee activists, white and Black.[15] Furthermore, as Thomas Weyant's research on Appalachian student activism in Ohio has demonstrated, student activists in that region (including much of East Tennessee) articulated a similar concept to student power, but one that he sees as emphasizing citizenship. Much as the Tennessee case demonstrates, Weyant found that personal ideas of citizenship drove students to be involved in activism around civil rights and the Vietnam War as well as campus reform. In examining why students were drawn to participate in activism, Weyant found that it was their views of themselves as citizens of the region, country, or world that led them to demonstrate despite "limited successes of protest and dissent."[16] Yet unlike Weyant's work on student citizenship, Doug Rossinow's research on "the politics of authenticity" in Austin, Texas, or studies of activism in Oklahoma and Illinois, all of which focus on white student activists, the Tennessee case reveals how both Black and white students in Tennessee embraced student power in their drive for personal and political autonomy.[17] Further studies should scrutinize student demands for power incorporating race as a factor shaping activists' choices.

In order to present the most comprehensive statewide study possible, this book incorporates a broad sample of historically Black and historically white institutions, public and private, in West, Middle, and East Tennessee, combining primary research with more locally focused studies.[18] It concentrates primarily—though not exclusively—on majority-white institutions, largely because they afford a much greater range and depth of archival resources. Highlighting key trends within the borders of Tennessee without losing thematic and narrative focus requires a devotion to discrete events at particular higher education institutions. For example, the section addressing connections between student activists and Highlander Folk School focuses largely on Nashville college students, while sections on demonstrations against segregated public accommodations and on reactions to the Kent State shootings scrutinize major campus protests across different parts of the state.

While many studies on 1960s activism have made valuable historiographical contributions to liberal activity, campus politics of the era in fact was shaped by a more complicated back-and-forth between students on either side of the political spectrum. Not all student activists in the 1960s were radical or even liberal, so focusing exclusively on one side or the other is problematic. Historians such as David Farber have rightly argued for further consideration of the Sixties as "the seed time of conservative populism and religious fundamentalism," while Robert Cohen has stated that in order to "understand the distinctive dynamics of the southern student movement," historians must recognize "that the South's *prophetic minority*—envisioning an America free of racism, sexism, homophobia, and imperialism—faced the daunting task of organizing the region's *recalcitrant majority*: rightward-leaning white students."[19] It is essential, therefore, to analyze the activism by liberal southern students not only within the region's political and socially conservative context, but in direct conversation with conservative student activists.

The following chapters are organized chronologically and thematically. In order to trace the narratives of white and Black student protest, the first chapter introduces the earliest developments of youth activism in the state, which centered on 1920s and 1930s campus activism over student rights, as well as community organizing around Highlander Folk School and its role in fostering interest in activism concerning labor, civil liberties, and later, civil rights. Highlander bridged the gap between the Old and New Left, as well as revealing continuity between the two generations in motivations and thinking. While McCarthyism certainly damaged leftist organizing in the mid-twentieth century, tellingly, in the 1950s and 1960s white and Black students in Tennessee believed that they were connected to the Old Left. Highlander was an important site for mobilizing both Black students and white radicals dissatisfied with the slow pace of racial change. This is where southern student activism really began.

The second chapter places the well-known Nashville sit-ins from February to May 1960 into the context of sit-in movements across the state, and then examines efforts to desegregate public accommodations in other cities across the state.[20] By doing so, this chapter sheds light on the Nashville movement's distinctive elements. It also traces the experiences of students with activism on campuses and in communities, thereby expanding the definition of youth activism and contextualizing radical thought and actions at colleges. Local circumstances mattered, as the contrast between older Black leadership driving activism in Memphis, versus the new, young leadership that emerged on college campuses in Nashville and Knoxville demonstrates. It also scrutinizes university administrators, faculty members, and community leaders. Well before the famous clashes of the late 1960s, these groups harbored anxieties about student unrest.

Chapter 3 traces efforts at economic reform by both white and Black students in the mid- to late 1960s. White student activists believed that labor organizing provided an opportunity for an interracial social movement of poor and working-class southerners. Their Black counterparts were more focused on the rights and needs of Black workers, especially sanitation workers in Memphis. There were evident points of agreement among Black and white students, but forging a common movement proved impossible. Black Power was increasingly influential, and with it a conviction among Black students that the needs of their community required race-specific rather than integrationist strategies. Yet again, the militancy of Black youth brought them into conflict with established civil rights leadership in Memphis and elsewhere.

The fourth chapter assesses the escalating campus activism of the 1968–70 period. It analyzes the tumultuous negotiations among students, faculty, and administration from the mid-1960s for increased student and faculty participation in university governance on the one hand, and expanding the realm of student autonomy on the other. As demands for increased student autonomy intersected with those for eliminating persistent racial inequalities on campuses, universities across Tennessee witnessed escalating tensions that were broadly based and increasingly intractable. These instances of campus unrest were pivotal in guiding how university administrators and politicians prepared for and reacted to demonstrations, particularly later anti-war protests. These episodes were part of a statewide, indeed regional and national (and even international), trend of student activism.

Chapter 5 shows that university students' paths continued along parallel tracks. The Vietnam War increasingly drove Black and white student initiatives in conjunction with continued efforts to gain student power. White activists opposed the war and sought an interracial, anti-racist, anti-imperialist alliance. Their Black peers, on the other hand, increasingly sympathized with other non-white populations worldwide while challenging continued racial inequality at home. Then tensions across the country and in Tennessee exploded following the announcement of President Nixon's escalation of the war in Cambodia and the subsequent Kent State tragedy in May 1970. This moment marked the apex of student activism in Tennessee. While demonstrations showcased anti-war and anti-establishment sentiments, these protests—as the President's Commission on Campus Unrest concluded—in fact built upon tensions over issues of race and personal autonomy long brewing among students, faculty, and administrators. Interest continued in issues that motivated students in the 1960s, namely race, student power, and minority representation.

When placed alongside existing accounts, this largely forgotten story of student activism affirms some aspects of the 1960s student movement and complicates others. Its scope reveals how broad this movement was, and how many different sorts of students—white and Black, private and public, western, middle, and east Tennessean—were involved. Though outnumbered, Tennessee student activists secured significant campus reforms, pursued ambitious community initiatives, and articulated a powerful counter-vision for the South and the United States.

Tennessee student activists built upon relationships with Old Left activists and organizations to create the possibility for radical change in the politically conservative region. For many, Highlander Folk School was both the inspiration and incubator for subsequent organizing.

CHAPTER 1

Foundations of Student Activism in Tennessee, 1925–1964

"Before I'll be a slave, I'll be buried in my grave," shouted students at Fisk University in Tennessee's capital, Nashville, in February 1925.[1] It would be easy to relate this incident to Black intellectual W. E. B. Du Bois's speech at the June graduation months before or as a reaction to an over-zealous college president, but in reality this articulation represents something more. These students were equating their roles as Black students to enslavement decades before Black Power articulations of this.

Students fought for personal autonomy on their college campuses dating back to the 1920s. Similar organizing strategies further tied these earliest episodes of campus-based activism to later demonstrations in the 1960s. Furthermore, Highlander Folk School had a significant influence on the tenor of student organizing in the state from the 1930s, both as inspiration and in educating youth about the Old Left and ideas of welfare and social reform. Highlander also functioned as a site for student activists to meet and organize, which contributed to the success of the sit-in movement later. These meetings, in addition to interracial student exchange programs that brought students from across Tennessee and from outside the state together from the mid-1950s, contributed to the development of the student movement that emerged in the 1960s.

The roots of student power in the state grew from this episode at Fisk. It became a network between campus-based protests, community action efforts, integrated exchange programs, and desegregation. Stretching the focus back stresses the statewide continuities over decades of intergenerational work, and the deep roots of the religious, labor, and race-oriented activism that featured prominently in Tennessee student activism.

Student Power in the Early Twentieth Century

While the term "student power" is not commonly articulated to describe activism pre-1960, the statements and initiatives of students on two campuses in Tennessee in the 1920s and 1930s clearly demonstrate a continuity of ideas, as well as similarities in conditions seen later. Namely, these include students feeling resentful because of a perceived lack of say in administrative decisions, with one particular event setting off protests, most commonly student-body strikes from classes. In terms of locations, Fisk was an urban campus located in the state capital of Nashville, while Lincoln Memorial was in the northeastern area of the state, along the border with Kentucky, in a remote area just south of the Cumberland Gap. While differences exist between the two examples in this section, namely community involvement in campus politics, the protests at Fisk University in 1925 and at Lincoln Memorial University in 1930 demonstrate that there is considerable similarity across racial lines at private colleges. This in turn indicates that conditions for such protest might have more to do with campus circumstances (including student body size and funding) than external forces like politics or social movements.

The student strike at private, predominantly Black Fisk University began on February 5, 1925, and culminated in the institution's white president, Fayette Avery McKenzie, resigning on April 16, 1925.[2] Seemingly spurred on by W. E. B. Du Bois's speech at his daughter Yolande's graduation ceremony at Fisk in June 1924, students organized a number of notable campus-based protests during the following 1924–1925 academic year, concluding with a successful ten-week boycott of classes against perceived autocratic policies put in place by McKenzie.[3] During what historian Ibram X. Kendi has called "one of the most searing face-to-face attacks on a [college] president in American higher education history," Du Bois declared during his speech, "Fisk is choking freedom. Self-knowledge is being hindered by refusal of all initiative to the students."[4] Despite calls among Nashville's Black community for the campus to have a Black president, McKenzie was appointed in 1915 and during his tenure, he brought an astonishing $1 million endowment to Fisk, albeit with strings attached.[5] Described by historian Lester Lamon as "measures taken to ensure student conformity to the southern standard for well-behaved blacks," McKenzie required conservative black clothing, particularly for female students, restrictive policies for student organizations and committees, and censorship of the student paper, the Fisk *Herald*.[6] McKenzie was well-known to reply, "If you don't like Fisk, then get out!" when responding to student frustrations.[7] During a trustees' visit to campus in November 1924, one hundred students greeted them with cheers of "Down with the tyrant!" and "Away with the czar!" and seven students met with the trustees to ask for increased student autonomy on campus. Then in December of that year, groups of students twice disregarded curfew, again emphasizing their personal autonomy on campus to do so.[8] On the eve of the strike, February 4, 1925, more than one hundred male students marched through Fisk's campus. McKenzie responded by having fifty Nashville police officers arrest the seven students who had earlier met with visiting trustees in November, infuriating Fisk students. One of the protestors, George Streator, declared five weeks into the strike that the vast majority of the students were in support of the strike: "We don't need to do anything except tell the students: 'Boycott this, or boycott that,' and believe me they do it to a finish!"[9] Nashville's Negro Board of Trade, in a sign of support for the students' plight and community recognition of campus politics, passed a set of resolutions on the evening of February 9 urging that students be given greater political and personal autonomy at Fisk.[10] McKenzie resigned on April 16, 1925, in a clear acknowledgement of the strike's success.

The student strike at Lincoln Memorial University that lasted for several weeks in March and April 1930 was similarly motivated by a perceived lack of student autonomy, but it was the firing of three teachers and one staff member that tipped the students' sentiments over the edge. One of the students, Hazel Fulton, described the protest as the "fresh uncompromised idealism of youth [set] against an administration which does not measure up to their expectations." She continued, "This idealism of the student body is one of the finest assets of Lincoln Memorial, and should not be crushed in an effort to impose discipline."[11] As resentment grew on campus among students and staff over resources going towards the university's accreditation by the Southern Association to build new facilities and purchase equipment in late 1929, the association rejected the institution's application when inaccuracies in the credentials of university president Dr. Hervin U. Roop and other staff were discovered. This accreditation would have allowed the students' degrees at Lincoln Memorial to be recognized outside of Tennessee.[12] Beginning on March 28, 1930, most of the college's four hundred or so students boycotted classes and chapel services. After a brief break beginning the following day during which students met with administrative officials about how to proceed, the students, disappointed by the lack of progress, started up the strike once again on April 10.[13] On that day, only 102 students attended morning chapel, and twenty-five took down the university's flag as part of their protests. By April 14, fewer than fifty students went to their classes. The strike ended in mid-April when a new president was hired to replace Roop, James Henderson Stuart Morison, who refused to discuss students' demands and expelled twenty-four of the striking students.[14]

Strikingly, the *Knoxville News-Sentinel*'s editors declared that the students had "a truer sense of Lincolnian ideals of justice, democracy and the worth of the individual than the administration which was charged with the responsibility for inculcating them" and the *New Republic* described the strikers as champions for "academic freedom" who were also "naïve, idealistic, [and] simple."[15]

The strikes at Fisk and Lincoln Memorial, while far earlier than other forms of student activism discussed in this book, highlight a few key themes about organizing on college campuses in Tennessee. First, student power is an essential concept both for contemporaries as well as for retrospective analysis of the activism. Students who would otherwise have been unlikely to organize protests were motivated to do so based on a perceived lack of personal and political autonomy on their campuses. They also utilized what power they had (class and chapel attendance in these cases) to demonstrate their frustrations, something that would be echoed in later 1960s protests. Second, while resources available to students mattered (such as the press, sympathetic faculty or community members, etc.), these early episodes of student activism demonstrate the key component to a successful campus protest in this era, as well as later, was a message that reached enough students to have a significant number of activists. Student power is the concept that reached across different campuses irrespective of the racial makeup of the student body, the size of the campus, or the geographical location of the institution within the state.

Highlander Folk School, Incubator of Student Radicalism

The radical Highlander Folk School was founded in 1932 in Monteagle, Tennessee. According to historian Bobby Lovett, Highlander "fostered unionism, individual growth, social change, attacks on southern poverty, the value of complete personal liberty, thoughtful citizenship in community, brotherhood and racial equality, and the full enjoyment of life."[16] Myles Horton, the school's director, created Highlander to educate the poor in the South. A native Tennessean of humble origins, Horton was drawn to community organizing as a mechanism for civic improvement in the southern Appalachian Mountains. When Highlander affiliated itself with the Congress of Industrial Organizations (CIO) in 1937, the school's emphasis broadened to encourage southerners to become local leaders in the labor movement.[17] Horton's own education at Union Theological Seminary in New York and the University of Chicago provided him with "things that would be useful when I returned to the mountains."[18] Up north, he met fellow southern liberals James "Jim" Dombrowski and Don West, who like Horton were interested in bringing radical organizing to the South. While both Dombrowski and West moved on to other organizing endeavors after establishing the school, they remained committed to progressive causes, West as a labor organizer and educator and Dombrowski as head of the Southern Conference for Human Welfare (SCHW) from 1942.[19]

Horton believed that a center of this kind in one of the poorest areas of the country would only succeed if it was seen as an organic part of the local community. Even as Highlander transitioned from identifying as an East Tennessee resource for community improvement to a regional hub for southern labor activism, and then for civil rights organizing, local level organizing remained one of its cardinal principles.[20] This was not a foundational philosophy, however, as the organization's evolution through the 1940s and 1950s demonstrated. For example, Highlander did not include African Americans in its residential programming until 1944, over a decade after its establishment.[21] Nevertheless, from the mid-1940s onwards Highlander became a staunch supporter of civil rights.

Highlander's commitment to local organizing and civil rights made it a crucial link between the activism of the 1930s and later student organizing of the 1960s. No other institution in the South did as much to bring activists, white and Black, together and to transmit the lessons of one generation to another. At Highlander, activists of various ages from across the South could meet others working on similar initiatives. The school enabled these activists to compare experiences, successes, and frustrations. It also provided a space to realize that the races and generations of the South were not as dissimilar as they might have otherwise believed.[22]

The Brotherhood, one group nurtured by Highlander, was a group of Christian youths in Summerfield, Tennessee, a town in Grundy County, which also included Monteagle, where Highlander was located. Tennessee Democratic U.S. Congressman (and later Senator) Estes Kefauver once referred to Grundy as "the problem county" owing to its widespread poverty. Grundy County held the dubious distinction of being the Tennessee county with the highest relief rate at this time.[23] Furthermore, with the exception of a few churches, the area offered little in the way of community social engagement.[24] The Brotherhood grew from a circle of local youths aged fifteen to twenty-four at a local Sunday School into an assembly that met regularly for meetings, elected leadership, and participated in local initiatives. They interpreted their Christianity to mean education, philanthropy, and programs to alleviate poverty and to improve race relations.[25] The group had multiple ties to Highlander: the school's staff spoke at their meetings and Brotherhood members went to socials and informal gatherings at the school. The ideologies of the two organizations became closely intertwined.

Religious conviction spurred The Brotherhood's activism. The group derived its name from the biblical phrase "the brotherhood of the kingdom of God," and framed its mission as exploring "the life of the most powerful man who ever lived to find what meaning his actions have for us today."[26] They saw their work in their local community as central to their faith. In looking around at the many needs of people in their area, members made the following list of economic, educational, and racial problems they saw in their local area:

1) *Not enough jobs* to go around.
2) *Low wages* in those jobs that exist, not giving us enough cash money to buy the things we need or giving other people the cash to buy the crops and other things we want to sell them.
3) *Competition* in selling and buying and getting jobs—which cuts down the prices farmers can get for their crops and keeps wages low.
4) The *poor houses* people live in.
5) *Very little organized play* or recreation for the young people, which causes them to get into trouble.
6) *Lack of educational and cultural advantages.*
7) *Conflict between Negroes and whites.*
8) Poor soil because we don't have the money to buy fertilizer or stock. Coal mines and forests which are rapidly being emptied of their richness so that some day there will be no more mines or lumber mills here to provide work and income for us. *No hope for the future.*[27]

The issues raised in this list bear a striking resemblance to welfare reforms advocated for by 1960s activists, and connect The Brotherhood more closely with later student activists in Tennessee, beyond their association with Highlander. While they were more overtly religious and not affiliated with a college or university like other activists discussed in this book, their approach to societal improvement, focusing on the community around them, would be echoed by groups like the Southern Student Organizing Committee (SSOC) regionally and Volunteers in Service to America (VISTA), Students for a Democratic Society (SDS), and the Black Panther Party nationally. They saw volunteer service in their local area, in conjunction with representation in local political office, as central to their potential success in improving their situation.

When there was a concern or question in the group, they turned to Highlander for advice. The Brotherhood believed that improved living conditions would spur religious observance; they responded positively to a Highlander staff person's observation that "when [people are] poor they have to struggle so hard to make a living they can't think about (or live) brotherhood and love."²⁸ Thus, organizing poor people to demand better wages would persuade them to become more devout in religious observance.

The Brotherhood was interested in representation in local political office, seen in the group's discussion about why "evil conditions" existed in Summerfield. They bemoaned the economic inequality in the community, rooting it in both material and moral shortcomings, namely a "*lack of income* in the hands of the majority of people" and "selfishness, lack of initiative, and laziness in *human personality*," which they viewed as unchristian. Racial intolerance, The Brotherhood believed, further exacerbated the problem of inequality.²⁹ Echoing Highlander, The Brotherhood saw the lack of cooperation between whites and Blacks in economic advancement and community improvement as a missed opportunity. It should be noted that whites heavily outnumbered Blacks in Grundy County; in predominantly African American areas of the South, it is doubtful that white groups would have embraced interracialism so openly.³⁰ Poor white youths in Memphis, for example, would not have considered working with African Americans on shared economic goals in 1938 because to do so would have threatened their social status. They might have shared a low socioeconomic category with Blacks, but their skin color conferred a superiority over Blacks in majority-Black areas that they were loath to sacrifice.

Gaining control of local politics would also provide the group an opportunity to enact change. In 1938, The Brotherhood elected two members to represent the group on the Summerfield Community Council, which had formed to provide a platform for the different organizations in Summerfield to cooperate on local initiatives. Other council members represented Highlander, local churches, Labor's Political Conference, the Workers' Alliance, and the Teachers' Union.³¹ Labor's Political Conference of Grundy County was affiliated with the Democratic Party and strove to elect local officials who would represent "the working people's" interests.³² It formed from ten local unions as well as from four Works Progress Administration (WPA) Common Laborers' Unions in April 1938, and signified, to Horton, a major advance in local community political organization.³³ Highlander was deeply involved in promoting the political conference and asked The Brotherhood to join forces with them.

The Brotherhood's newsletters from the summer of 1938 detail casual gatherings at Highlander, picnics in the surrounding area, baseball games (often playing against the Quakers), meetings of potential interest to members, and personal announcements from the participants. The group also regularly identified needs of the local area to which they could contribute, such as building tables for the nursery school and community center. "It is through such small actions *for other people* that the first steps are taken towards building here on earth the Kingdom of Brotherhood Jesus worked for. There can be no higher purpose in life than to help other people—*to help something better come* into the world."³⁴ In such ways they connected their work with the idea of Christian charity.

Summerfield youth faced limited career opportunities, largely restricted to mining and logging industries with little possibility for economic advancement. Only two out of nineteen families among members in the Brotherhood had fathers who were employed outside of WPA work or subsistence farming.³⁵ Disillusionment was great and added to their interest in education and collaborative activism. Their ideas centered on collective action, an understandable consequence of experiencing the Great Depression and aftermath, but they also believed that as Jesus promoted respect of one's fellow man, alleviating economic distress was one's Christian duty.

Highlander retained a key role in supporting this youth group's focus on local community improvements, an indication of how the school would serve later student activists. The Brotherhood's calls for interracial cooperation and poverty reform intertwined with early Highlander ambitions. In sum, The Brotherhood's emergence demonstrates that youth activism in the 1930s South was more vibrant than previously believed.³⁶

Highlander and the Foundations of the Sit-Ins

Nationally, as well as in Tennessee, campus-based student activism declined in the 1940s, largely due to World War II. Historian Philip Altbach's research has examined the lack of accounts attributing student participation to social movements during World War II. He saw youths as "among the most active proponents of neutrality" prior to World War II and "instrumental in the peace movement of that period," not during the war. Other historians have recently argued that viewing the war as a catalyst for change (citing the "Double V" campaign and return of African American veterans as examples) actually obscures the civil rights efforts that continued locally, as well as white backlashes to changes in race relations.³⁷ However, the issue of Communism came to the fore during the decade, especially as the World War gave way to the Cold War. Conservatives had opposed New Deal programs and leftist politics as communistic even before World War II. After the war, radicals who had either pledged allegiance to the Communist Party or were suspected of affiliation with Communist-front groups were pushed out of public life, and often out of employment as well.

Highlander was subject to red-baiting, threats from the Ku Klux Klan (KKK), and numerous investigations by law enforcement officials well into the 1960s. During this period, the Federal Bureau of Investigation (FBI) put Highlander under surveillance.[38] Some school participants had been Communist Party members, had affiliated with party members, or were suspected of harboring interest in the party. Highlander's staff did not care whether people at Highlander were Communists or not, but whether they were committed to the school's objectives. "If the so-called Communists will respect and help further the organization's goals, then let them in," Horton said. "In the end, it's a question of who can be defined *in*, not who can be defined *out*."[39] In the South, declaring an interest in labor and civil rights as Highlander did was enough to make an institution become a prime target. Highlander further drew the attention of anti-Communists by separating from the CIO in 1949 in reaction to the labor federation's effort to prevent Communist members from holding leadership positions in the organization.[40] Suspicions of Communist sympathies among Highlander staff prompted the state of Tennessee to revoke Highlander's charter in 1961.[41] Highlander responded by renaming itself the "Highlander Research and Education Center" and moving to Knoxville, where Horton and other Highlander officials insisted on carrying on with their work.[42] It survived across the 1950s and 1960s and beyond, despite efforts by opponents to label it a "Communist Training School."[43]

Survival mattered: once the *Brown v. Board of Education* decision invalidated segregated public schooling in May 1954, Highlander again became an important resource for a new generation of college activists. As a leading center for civil rights activism, Highlander was an ideal place for students to learn how to be leaders for racial equality in their communities. As in its relationship with The Brotherhood, Highlander fostered young activists' civil rights initiatives and education by hosting "college weekend" workshops.[44] Ernest W. Burgess, then professor emeritus of sociology at the University of Chicago, wrote in May 1955: "A most significant development in race relations has been the organization in the South of interracial groups of white and Negro university and college students." Highlander was one of the institutions where he saw interracialism flourishing.[45]

Myles Horton was initially unenthusiastic about supporting student groups.[46] He later stated that he had created Highlander as a resource for adults who were out of school, not for students, and he maintained that its importance to the labor and civil rights movements necessitated careful management of Highlander's limited resources. Before the 1960 sit-ins, Horton also could not have imagined a student movement challenging the existing social and political order with such force.[47] Much like The Brotherhood had recognized the potential for New Deal programs and community engagement to effect significant societal change, these students' success in having Horton (and by extension, Highlander) agree to host these college workshops signifies their belief that *Brown* presented an opportunity to challenge Jim Crow segregation.

Beginning in 1954, Highlander's college workshops covered subjects ranging from campus leadership advocating integration to college exchange programs.[48] Sessions discussed contemporary student apathy and why student activism of the 1920s and 1930s had been so much "more pronounced" and "wholehearted." Attendees evidently drew inspiration from New Deal activism, and perceived continuities between 1930s and 1950s organizing efforts.[49] Discussions revealed continued interest in integration, but with an increased focus on how students as campus leaders could promote racial equality in their respective institutions. These workshop discussions anticipated a more general turn within the civil rights movement to university students, a turn that the sit-in movement of 1960 made pronounced.

At the workshops, students learned songs that would come to define the movement, specifically "We Shall Overcome" as taught by Guy Carawan.[50] Beginning as a Highlander staff member in 1960, Guy travelled throughout the South teaching civil rights activists, the majority of them young sit-in demonstrators, songs that would come to be known as "Freedom Songs."[51] Many of the songs that Carawan taught had been labor songs, written to support the labor movement of the 1930s and 1940s. They were an additional reminder for the student activists of the early 1960s of Highlander's longer history of social activism.

Workshop attendees also examined ways for southern white youths to become involved in integration efforts, scrutinized the differences between community and campus activism, and discussed ways that the movement could be one for Black and white students.[52] Highlander's hosting of workshops for college students continued into the early 1960s after it had moved to Knoxville, and included a regular weekly series for students from the nearby University of Tennessee (UT), Maryville College, and Knoxville College.[53]

Prior to the sit-ins, Horton, while pleased that the school offered annual workshops to students, remained firm that student workshops would not become part of the adult program. He told the students, "Look, we've got to talk about serious business.' Horton believed that Highlander's limited resources necessitated that it prioritize its prior commitment to adult-led organizing. He viewed college students as young people, not adults.[54]

The sit-ins in February 1960 changed Highlander's relationship with the student movement in Tennessee, as well as across the South. Once students had participated in sit-in demonstrations in Nashville, where many of them were arrested and jailed, they returned to Highlander and asked Horton, "Are we adults [now]?" He replied, "Well, from now on, anybody that's been in jail is an adult."[55] At a Highlander Executive Council meeting soon after, the school determined that "college students who have participated actively in sit-in demonstrations, thus assuming direct community responsibility, will be included as adults [in future Highlander programs]."[56] That April, the Student Nonviolent Coordinating Committee (SNCC) formed following a meeting at Shaw University in Raleigh, North Carolina. Many of its initial members were veterans of Highlander's programs.[57] Indeed, one Nashville sit-in demonstrator (and later a Highlander staff member), Candie Carawan, recalled that the first assembly of what would become SNCC occurred at Highlander from April 1 to April 3, 1960, prior to the April 15–17 meeting at Shaw.[58] That event, the seventh in its series of annual workshops for college students, "marked a new relationship of Highlander to the students as it marked a new relationship of the students to their society," according to Aimee Isgrig Horton, Myles Horton's wife.[59] In Myles Horton's words, the students' participation in Highlander programs also brought "a new lease on life" to the center as it shifted its work to support the sit-in demonstrations.[60]

Horton saw potential in the Nashville sit-ins and responded quickly. Nashville was the heart of the sit-ins movement in Tennessee, and an essential part of the development of region-wide demonstrations. It was the first location in the state that experienced organized sit-in demonstrations and, with their extensive connections with Highlander, Nashville students greatly impacted the student movement across Tennessee. While Highlander was not seen as representative of the "white liberal intellectuals" in Nashville during this period, largely because of its suspected Communist ties, it retained close links with the student demonstrators as well as the established Old Left and southern organizing networks, which the students utilized to build their movement.[61] An exchange student at Fisk University when she arrived in Nashville in January 1960, Candie Carawan remembered Highlander's role in the Nashville sit-ins: the city "was obviously a very important center for activity.... Myles [Horton] and other staff members [at Highlander] always looked for places where there was the potential for real pressure to be exerted. They were drawn to communities where people were ready to take action."[62]

Highlander supported southern activists and their efforts, providing a safe space to strategize and spend time with other like-minded individuals. Cordy Tindell "C. T." Vivian, an African American adult man studying at American Baptist College in Nashville when the sit-ins began, was a leader of the Nashville movement. Of Highlander, Vivian recalled,

> Going to Highlander and meeting the people who had the same sense of social consciousness that I did, and that we did, made a difference to me ... we'd all

just be joining together having fun on one hand, [and gaining] new knowledge on the other hand: a sense of community, that's what it gave us that was so very, very important.⁶³

The "sense of community" Vivian referred to was shared by many civil rights activists, young and old; as another sit-in protestor noted, Highlander was the place to meet with other movement activists.⁶⁴ Highlander continued its commitment to fostering the student movement after the sit-ins began; it hosted three more workshops for college students between April 1960 and April 1961.⁶⁵ Highlander's college weekends and workshops broadened participants' self-consideration as potential change agents. Meanwhile, several Tennessee colleges and universities ran exchange programs that similarly introduced students to a wider world beyond their campuses and communities.

Interracial Exchange Programs in the Era of Massive Resistance

While activists congregated at Highlander and elsewhere to devise civil rights protests in the 1950s and 1960s, most white Tennesseans opposed changes to the state's racial order. A comprehension of the contemporary racial and political culture is essential for understanding Tennessee student activism. White legislators and community leaders across Tennessee went to great lengths to limit educational integration. Attempting to draft policies that would ostensibly comply with the *Brown* decision without encouraging militant segregationists to organize citizens in opposition, Tennessee's leaders behaved similarly to their peers in other Upper South states.⁶⁶ While they publicly condemned the violence surrounding public school desegregation in the Deep South, they did little to end the threat of violence in their own state.

Different opinions towards interracial education existed across Tennessee in the years after *Brown*. Against the backdrop of violence in Clinton and Nashville directed at school desegregation, three private higher education institutions (Fisk, Sewanee: The University of the South, and Maryville) ran interracial exchange programs with other schools.⁶⁷ In the case of Fisk, the exchange programs actually predated the desegregation of Nashville's public schools. Being private, these colleges were able to operate with greater freedom than others across the state, a freedom that extended to their running of these programs. These two seemingly opposite initiatives, interracial exchange programs and legislative opposition to meaningful integration in Tennessee, coexisted.⁶⁸

Historian William Chafe has argued that the South's history of racial politics featured "a paternalism so unconscious it would never be called such by whites."[69] Rev. Will D. Campbell, a white Nashville civil rights activist and progressive, recalled how the designation of a city as "progressive" often meant little in terms of how its citizens reacted to desegregation pressures: "I think in 1960, Nashville was a progressive city, but so was Little Rock . . . in 1957."[70] Often this supposed "progressivism" reflected commitment to order, more than to racial justice, as in the case of Atlanta, "the city too busy to hate."[71]

The existence of established exchange programs between white and Black colleges in Tennessee appears even more striking against this backdrop of order-focused politics. These programs were important for developing college-aged activists in Tennessee. Their continuation into the 1960s reveals their acceptance by college officials as an acceptable breach of the color line (perhaps owing to the limited extent of desegregation from these exchanges). These programs were eye-opening experiences for the students who participated, while often producing public relations headaches for university administrators. They demonstrated early instances of interracial interaction between college students which, in the case of the oldest program (at Fisk), predated Highlander Folk School's workshops for college students by five years. The Tennessee exchange programs were also undertaken earlier than many others between white and Black colleges nationally, with the programs elsewhere beginning in the mid-1960s.[72]

The exchange program at Fisk was "rather tentatively" undertaken when two Fisk students and two Oberlin College students (from Oberlin, Ohio) switched campuses for a semester of the 1950–1951 school year.[73] By 1958 the program had grown considerably to include exchanges with Pomona College in California and Dartmouth College in New Hampshire. By that year, Fisk already had programs with eleven institutions in Ohio, Indiana, New York, California, Wisconsin, and Idaho.[74] Each of these institutions was a white liberal arts college (while Dartmouth was an Ivy League university), with a majority white student body at the time of the exchange.

The institutions Fisk worked with to establish exchange programs during this period were in non-southern states. For many of the exchange students at Fisk, their time in Nashville was their first experience in the Jim Crow South, and they were confronted with segregation in starker terms than ever before. White exchange students formed relationships with their fellow students at Fisk, and therefore would go into the city on outings. Such public interracialism stirred concern and shock in the broader community. Mike Armer, a white exchange student at Fisk recalled, with humor, that he "feared numerous times that my company with Negro friends as I walked down the campus streets was going to be the cause of an accident if drivers didn't get their eyes off us and on the road."[75] In a more serious vein, another white exchange student named Paul LaPrad recounted, "If I did choose to go Downtown . . . I couldn't do it with my friends from school. And you know, to me, that was a bunch of malarkey."[76]

Some of the Fisk exchange program participants took part in the Nashville sit-ins. Such involvement in civil rights efforts helped to inspire the formation of the New Left.[77] National Association for the Advancement of Colored People (NAACP) executive director Roy Wilkins's April 1960 statement on the white youth participation in the sit-ins as "white student cooperators" indicates the conscious distinction present from the beginning between the two groups; while it is understandable that Black and white students would have different motivations and risks involved in their participation, past research has accepted Wilkins's division, rather than interrogating it.[78] Candie Carawan, Paul LaPrad, Jim Zwerg, and Susan Herrman all participated in the sit-ins as white students of Fisk and there were almost certainly other white exchange students, harder to identify, who participated in demonstrations in Nashville, even across Tennessee, but were not always referred to in accounts as white.[79]

Fisk, however, was not a radical incubator; while liberal students and faculty were on campus, it was a conservative institution overall. Fisk students were divided between feelings of listlessness and a desire for increased campus engagement. The university's newspaper, the *Forum*, described Fisk in a 1957 editorial as having five "liabilities" standing in the way of its continued success: a lack of political effectiveness on the part of its student leadership, a perceived need for additional university support for faculty, a one-person history department, a library with limited resources, and "an overdose of student apathy." The same issue however also included a front-page feature on Fisk student participation at a local boycott in support of eliminating Jim Crow discrimination.[80] The university fostered social engagement by its students, but it did not encourage political action, particularly not with regards to protesting segregation. The Social Action Committee at Fisk held an informational meeting in March 1957 to develop "plans for a boycott of racially segregated places," including downtown movie theaters, and to inform Nashville's Blacks that the municipal bus company had a policy that they would not enforce segregation on buses.[81] These activists at Fisk would continue to mobilize activism efforts, and would feature in James Lawson's nonviolence workshops beginning in 1959.[82]

White administrators within Tennessee (and likely throughout the South) feared exchange programs like Fisk's would lead inextricably to fully integrated campuses. The consideration of exchange programs in 1962 at Sewanee, a private Episcopalian institution, actually came after the university had deliberated over its admission policies, not before. While this decision only applied to the graduate students at its School of Theology, the debate surrounding the issue made the university's administration extremely wary of anything it perceived as promoting undergraduate-level integration. Therefore, the idea that these programs would eventually lead to integration was of paramount concern for the university's administration. Following the provincial synod's resolution in 1951 that its colleges should integrate, Sewanee's Board of Trustees entered into a two-year fight with the church over the issue.[83] In consultation with lawyers in Chattanooga, Nashville, and Memphis, the university argued that as long as Article XXXIV of Tennessee's constitution made interracial education illegal, it would follow the state law, not the provincial synod resolution.[84] This public relations nightmare for the church and Sewanee itself made the administration particularly sensitive to suggestions of integration of its undergraduate program. Sewanee's Board of Trustees eventually passed a resolution to permit the admission of African American students to the university in June 1961, although no Black undergraduates would attend Sewanee until 1963.[85] Perhaps as a consequence of its minimal immediate impact on admissions, this decision was received relatively quietly in comparison with the controversy surrounding the School of Theology's proposed integration nearly a decade earlier.

University administrators threatened Sewanee professor Scott Bates with censure and possible dismissal when he planned a student exchange between Sewanee and the historically Black Howard, Morehouse, and Fisk universities in early 1962 without the support of the administration. The dean of the college, Robert S. Lancaster, accused Bates of putting Sewanee in an uncomfortable position should the exchange not take place. "The institutions with whom you have been discussing the matter may well feel offended and frustrated," Lancaster claimed. "Especially is this true of the universities with whom you discussed the [program]."[86] Lancaster also implied that Bates sought Sewanee's racial integration, as he purportedly discussed the exchange program with the local chapter of the American Association of University Professors (AAUP) prior to discussing it with anyone in the administration or faculty at Sewanee. Bates, in Lancaster's view, had wanted to force Sewanee's hand by presenting an exchange program supported by AAUP and the other participating universities. Lancaster questioned whether Bates should even work at Sewanee: "Even considering your sincerity and zeal for a cause in which you are interested [meaning racial integration], such a manner of proceeding is hardly excusable," and "subversive of good administrative practice and deserving of censure."[87] Given the frequent equation of support for integration with Communist affiliation by opponents of racial change, it seems hardly surprising that Lancaster cast Bates's behavior as "subversive."

The debate over the proposed exchange program continued at Sewanee into the following academic year, with the faculty at Sewanee (with support from the AAUP) recommending that the university participate in the program. The decision then moved to the administration. Bates wrote to the representatives of Fisk, Morehouse, and Howard in November 1962 that despite the faculty's recommendation, Sewanee's administration had decided not to participate in an exchange, "at least for the time being." "They [the administration] expect the first Negro students to come to Sewanee through the normal channels, either as entering Freshmen or as transfer students, and feel that only when this is done will they be inclined to consider adopting the exchange plan." Tellingly, the administration endorsed a conservative color blindness—that is, promoting a nominally race-neutral policy that would create minimal actual integration—once some desegregation became unavoidable. Though Bates "pointed out to members of the administration the advantages of having the Negro university select our first Negro students for us . . . they think that the trustees, regents, alumni, etc., would deem this discrimination in favor of Negro schools, inasmuch as we have no undergraduate exchange programs with any white schools." Defeated on the exchange program issue, Bates noted that should any students from Fisk, Howard, or Morehouse with "good records" like to transfer to Sewanee, the university would be "pleased to consider their applications."[88]

A newspaper article in the files of Sewanee's vice-chancellor, Edward Mc-Crady, from two days after Bates wrote to the Black universities reported Fisk's head librarian Arna Bontemps's announcement that Fisk and Sewanee had agreed on an exchange once each institution lined up "interested students." McCrady circled Bontemps's quotation and wrote, "Now what??" in the margins, in reference to the frustration that Fisk had clearly not received (or had not acknowledged) the letter from Sewanee saying the latter would not, in fact, be participating in an exchange, Bontemps's announcement to the contrary notwithstanding.[89] This measured, reluctant response to token integration on the part of Sewanee was typical of many southern institutions at the time. Very few institutions were willing to challenge politicians, potential donors, and alumni by endorsing desegregation before being compelled to do so. They wanted to keep the desegregation of Sewanee a slow, reluctant process, and in light of the fact that no Black undergraduates had yet been admitted to Sewanee, it seems administrators hoped to continue to control the development.

Unlike Sewanee, Maryville College (which admitted six Black students in the fall of 1954) did not have an exchange program in the traditional sense; instead, its students coordinated a "student exchange" with Knoxville College. Both institutions were Presbyterian, maintained by the United Presbyterian Church of North America. Knoxville College established its exchange program in 1957, with a few white students attending the college from other institutions.[90] By 1960, Maryville and Knoxville Colleges had established an exchange between their two schools, directed by an interracial group of the Young Women and Young Men. The exchange consisted of a monthly meeting between the two institutions, described by Maryville as "a wholesome exchange with the informality of the programs allowing a good freedom of conversation and interchange of ideas."[91] The Maryville College Student-Faculty Senate worried how the surrounding community of Maryville would perceive the exchange initiative. Discussions of an athletic game with Knoxville College, transportation for students to the exchange meetings, and the exchange program itself in the fall of 1960 at the Student-Faculty Senate cited the wider community's response as cause for concern.[92] Dean of Men Frank D. McClellan felt that for the consideration of "public relations," the exchange's "reasons and purposes should be clearly defined." Perhaps alluding to the need to appear respectable and unthreatening, McClellan emphasized that students ought to know that the program was "definitely before the public eye" and therefore "should be constantly open for evaluation."[93]

McClellan's concern was partly due to the KKK's state headquarters being based in the area.[94] Later, in October 1964, Maryville's history of relative tolerance towards integration in its exchange program and the concerns of the non-university community came to a head. At a conference at Maryville between students of the college as well as from Knoxville College and the Knoxville campus of UT, participants discussed how to encourage other southern students to get involved in progressive initiatives.[95] The KKK protested the event. Klansmen were enraged in particular that Dr. Eugene Carson Blake, a leader in the Presbyterian Church and a national civil rights activist, was going to be on campus for the event; wearing their hoods, KKK members picketed outside the campus and distributed leaflets to local residents to encourage them to "fight Godless Communism."[96] As David Cunningham's research on the Klan in North Carolina has revealed, Klan membership in the 1960s was often greater in areas like Maryville, where community leaders and political representatives were less likely to aggressively voice white supremacist frustrations.[97]

The exchange programs involving Tennessee students during this period were sources of pride for liberal groups within these still all-white universities, but they also generated administrators' concerns for potential backlash from the local community. Despite administrative foot dragging, however, the exchange programs showed an interest on the part of students and faculty to be involved in interracial events, or at least to know more about the group on the other side of the racial divide. As the example of Fisk's exchange programs demonstrates, involvement in programs led many to participate in the sit-ins in Nashville and later other civil rights efforts across the region.

Tennessee Higher Education Desegregation

The exchange programs at various campuses set the stage for more concerted efforts at higher education integration in Tennessee, by providing an opportunity to test out interracial education at participating institutions. Though Tennessee politicians offered token compliance with *Brown v. Board of Education*, their reliance on "freedom of choice" to desegregate education ensured that concerns over wholesale integration of education remained prominent before the court-mandated establishment of racially unitary school systems at the end of the 1960s.[98] Freedom of choice policies allowed students to attend the school of their choice, regardless of race, but placed the burden of desegregation on Black students and their parents, and allowed white community pressure to minimize Black requests to attend formerly white schools, the result of freedom of choice was that schools remained largely segregated with white students attending majority-white schools, and Black students going to predominantly Black ones. In higher education, *Brown* certainly pressured administrators to admit Black students, but unlike Governor Ross Barnett's protest on September 29, 1962, at the University of Mississippi or Governor George Wallace's stand at the University of Alabama on June 11, 1963, against the integration of their respective institutions, Tennessee's state politicians never took theatrical public stands against admitting Blacks to white universities. These differences point to the distinctions between racial politics in the Deep South compared with Upper South states like Tennessee. University administrations did, however, adhere to a conservative, deliberately measured pace of desegregation. There are numerous examples of this behavior towards the integration of higher education, from the implementation of racial admittance policies that allowed for token integration over several years, to the complete lack of discussion in the State Board of Education minutes about the subject. The question seems to have been not *whether* to admit Blacks, but rather *how* and *when* to do so.[99] The climate created by the actions of university administrators did as much to foster radicalism in the 1960s as did the early activity of student activists themselves. Consequently, this section focuses on the institutional side of university desegregation.

Tennessee's public and private colleges and universities followed a general trend of gradual, token integration in the early to mid-1960s, with the exception of Maryville College, which voluntarily desegregated in the fall of 1954. The issue of integration was highly contentious for many administrators, whether they felt unfairly forced to comply with the law or were concerned about violent community reactions as a result of integrating. Memphis State University president J. Millard Smith ultimately resigned over the issue. Located in the area with the highest African American population in Tennessee, Memphis administrators faced arguably the most credible fears of a hostile local reaction to desegregation, given the historic preoccupation of Black Belt whites to maintain the color line.[100] In August 1958, Smith asked the State Board of Education to "postpone" its integration plan for the university. Smith and the board had agreed to move forward with plans to integrate Memphis State that coming fall, but in his statement requesting the delay, Smith referenced "tension built up in Memphis" from the Little Rock integration and controversies over the integration of the Memphis public bus system and public libraries as reasons that the plan was now "unacceptable" to Memphis citizens. Smith was "thoroughly convinced that considerable trouble and even violence could occur should we enroll negroes [this fall]."[101] Memphis State delayed the integration of Black students until the following academic year (1959–1960), when eight students entered the university with none of the "problems" that Smith had feared.[102] However, Smith abruptly resigned the presidency in January 1960, and although it was not stated publicly, his choice to leave Memphis State stemmed from the university's integration that past fall. His successor, Dr. Cecil C. Humphreys, later described Smith as a man from "a different era" who was unable to "meet . . . the changes" that he had faced.[103]

Limited integration was also occurring at several other colleges and universities in the state. For these formerly all-white schools, the decision to accept Black students followed the trend statewide of measured, limited integration. In 1951 a federal judge ruled in *Gray v. University of Tennessee* that because the students had been denied admission for graduate education on the basis of their race, they had been denied their constitutional rights provided by the Fourteenth Amendment's equal protection clause. While the case was being decided, the university's president, C. E. Brehm, and the Board of Trustees decided to change the university's admission policy for fall 1952 to admit the graduate students in question, but they continued to resist altering policies to admit African American undergraduates.[104] Vanderbilt Divinity School and the School of Theology at Sewanee admitted Black graduate students to their programs in 1953, and Scarritt College for Christian Workers had Black students beginning in 1952.[105] As historian Benjamin Houston has highlighted, this move by Scarritt was even more striking given that all Scarritt students were allowed to take courses at Peabody College for Teachers and at Vanderbilt; therefore, the Scarritt decision directly impacted two other institutions.[106] Black institutions that decided to admit white students faced very different risks (and rewards). A prominent private school in the area, Knoxville College, had white students attending classes beginning in 1957.[107] Fisk University, in addition to its white exchange students, had fifteen white students enrolled in classes during the 1955–1956 school year, four of whom were undergraduate students.[108] Historically Black Meharry Medical College began to accept white students to its programs in the late 1950s.[109] In January 1962, Fisk president Dr. Stephen J. Wright announced that the university was "considering ways to attract more white students." As part of a series of long-range planning goals for the institution, a committee filled with faculty and trustees was considering ways to "maintain the high levels of excellence to which Fisk aspires," according to Wright.[110]

At public institutions in Tennessee, as elsewhere in the South, a number of Black students enrolled in graduate programs prior to undergraduates being admitted from the early 1960s. At UT for example, Blacks attended graduate programs at its Knoxville campus from 1952.[111] At UT's Nashville branch, sixteen Black students were enrolled in the mid-1950s, but only because they were unable to enroll in equivalent programs at one of Nashville's Black colleges.[112] This distinction was common during this period, a remnant of the earlier Jim Crow legislation to provide "separate but equal" education to Blacks. When the opportunity to study elsewhere was not available, schools were forced (often by court order) to admit Black students, particularly after *Gaines v. Canada* (1938) and *Sweatt v. Painter* (1950). Later, in December 1962, Tennessee State University announced that it had enrolled about six white undergraduate students. The president, Dr. W. S. Davis, guessed that out of 4,130 students at Tennessee State, about twenty non-African American students were enrolled. About one-third of that group were white Americans; the rest were foreign students.[113]

UT, like many public institutions, experienced a continued contestation of students' rights during this period. It was not until Theotis Robinson Jr. from Knoxville applied for a second time in fall 1960 after being denied admission earlier that year that the university voluntarily changed its policy and admitted Black undergraduates: Robinson, Charles E. Blair, and Willie May Gillespie enrolled in January 1961.[114] Demonstrating support for desegregation, UT Vice President Herman E. Spivey wrote to the sitting president, Andrew Holt, in May 1961 urging the Board of Trustees to approve "further integration of qualified Negro students" so that the university could "proceed deliberately and cautiously with the integration of qualified Negro students into the life of the University."[115] Yet Black UT undergraduates did not enjoy equal access to campus facilities because they were forced to eat off campus, an injustice that UT students later protested.[116]

Many private schools in Tennessee, as well as regionally, found an alternative to avoiding taking a position for or against integration. If they had never stated in their bylaws which race of students was welcome to their school, administrators could argue that they welcomed "qualified" students of any race. At Lincoln Memorial University, President Robert L. Kincaid deflected calls for the admission of non-white students from Asian countries as well as African American students by emphasizing the "provincial" nature of the university. The geographical remoteness of the institution, in addition to the small African American population in the surrounding area (and East Tennessee more widely), meant that the school was not confronted with the issue of integration as much as other private universities in Tennessee. Non-white applicants to Lincoln Memorial appear to have been first Asian, then later Black. Indeed, while the university never had racial stipulations for potential student applicants, it is clear from Kincaid's comments that non-white students, whether Asian or Black, were unwelcome.[117] In 1948 when trustees discussed South Koreans coming to Lincoln Memorial, Kincaid deflected the conversation, arguing that foreign students would want more culture and nightlife than the university's rural setting offered. He also emphasized that the university held high academic standards for incoming students, echoing comments by university administrators of all-white institutions against integration.[118] This contrasts with the regional trend for Asian and Asian American students during the Jim Crow era to be considered white in many southern universities, including UT.[119]

"Our college," Kincaid stated, "is for the training of the white boys and girls of the Southern mountains."[120] Kincaid argued that Lincoln Memorial had been established for the purpose of educating southern white youths in Appalachia, while its name affiliation with President Abraham Lincoln led many donors to believe it was a university for African Americans until informed otherwise.[121] His emphasis, therefore, remained focused on the founding ideals of the university rather than addressing whether the institution admitted non-white applicants. After *Brown*, admissions to Lincoln Memorial continued as before. Kincaid stated in 1956 that the school was "not crusading in the present desegregation movement." While they had not yet had any Black applicants, he was "sure in time that will happen and we will meet the situation when it arises." Nominal compliance continued at Lincoln Memorial, but de facto segregation remained until 1968 when the first Black students enrolled in the undergraduate program.¹²²

Sewanee's Vice-Chancellor McCrady discussed "the integration question" with Southwestern at Memphis's president Peyton N. Rhodes in November 1962. Southwestern students had held a meeting with Rhodes that year to argue for integrating the college, but Southwestern did not admit Black students until 1968.¹²³ McCrady stated that Sewanee's Board of Trustees had, in 1961, voted to integrate the university by including a policy stating that no racial qualifications would be used in the admissions process. McCrady explained that the one Black applicant they had had so far was ineligible for admission "irrespective of his color" because his test scores were lower than acceptable.¹²⁴ Like Lincoln Memorial, Sewanee had never instituted an official policy banning the admission of African Americans.¹²⁵ McCrady also defended his school's lack of Black undergraduates in a similar manner to Kincaid at Lincoln Memorial. McCrady emphasized Sewanee's Episcopalian connections and argued that there were very few Black Episcopalians who would be interested in applying, much less attending. "As far as Sewanee is concerned," he wrote, "the whole problem is so highly imaginary as to be trivial as soon as people come to recognize it as such. . . . We are able to accept only a very small fraction of the *large* number of white applicants here. If we accept an equally small fraction of the *small* number of Negro applicants, the number of Negroes in our student body can never be large."¹²⁶ McCrady also mentioned in his correspondence with Rhodes that the president of Randolph-Macon Woman's College in Lynchburg, Virginia, had also contacted him asking about Sewanee's integration policy.¹²⁷

Perhaps the most definitively "moderate" of all Tennessee university presidents and chancellors was Harvie Branscomb of Vanderbilt University. As historian Melissa Kean has described, Branscomb's policy was "moderation with content."¹²⁸ Seemingly straddling two camps, those for and against integration, Branscomb navigated issues as they arose, with care. For the Vanderbilt Board of Trustees, who were majority-conservative well into the early 1960s, Branscomb spoke of moderation as a way to appease major national donors (who he depended on to increase Vanderbilt's national presence as a major university). He argued that when opportunities to proceed with limited integration arose, Vanderbilt would be able to admit a single Black student without too much fuss, and could point out that action to major donors and proponents of integration as an example of the institution's intellectual progress. Personally, Branscomb was "convinced that segregation's days were rightfully numbered; that it was both wrong and a terrible drain on southern society."¹²⁹ He "used nearly every racially pregnant incident" as an opportunity to coax the trustees towards integration.[130] These Tennessee examples were part of a regional trend of strategic resistance to desegregation.

Private, Presbyterian-founded Maryville College held an admission policy of "all races and colors without discrimination" from 1866 until the passage of a state law in 1901 demanding separate educational facilities for whites and Blacks.[131] Maryville's president, Ralph Waldo Lloyd, urged the Maryville Board of Directors to consider its response to the *Brown* decision only two days after it was handed down (on May 19). It was "perfectly clear" that the existing state mandate for racially separated education was now unconstitutional and that "the church college ought to lead, not follow, the secular state colleges in such ethical matters."[132] Maryville College called for a vote by its Board of Directors over the summer of 1954, and by July 19, twenty-six of the thirty directors had returned their ballots by mail. Out of the twenty-six, only one opposed admitting Black students at once, while the rest voted to "[accept] Negro students this year." The college's Committee on Administration met at this time and unanimously adopted a resolution stating that it accepted the directors' vote and "hereby re-establishes the College's policy of accepting qualified students without regard to their race or color."[133] As it had complied with the state legislation in 1901 to segregate its campuses, the college administration argued it was similarly complying with the Supreme Court ruling in 1954.[134] Six African American students were admitted to Maryville College in fall 1954, making it the first of Tennessee's higher education institutions to desegregate following *Brown*, as well as one of the earliest in the South.[135]

The social environment of a college or university is important for any incoming student, but particularly so for a minority student in a recently desegregated institution. These experiences varied by institution, but similarities existed in terms of the social isolation Black students regularly felt. Regulations and customs at UT and Memphis State, like other southern state universities at the time, were a myriad of contradictions where Jim Crow statutes and new administrative policies were concerned. Jimmie Baxter, one of the first Black UT undergraduates in 1961, remembered that despite "many" of its faculty being "openly hostile ... there were a few white students that made a real effort to let black students know, 'look, we're not all like that'. In fact, I would say that white students suffered more than we did from other hostile whites."[136] The students who desegregated Memphis State in 1959 recalled feelings of social isolation, not unlike the majority of their peers throughout the South who were similarly breaking societal norms. Students were allowed on the campus between 8 a.m. and noon, sat in classrooms with seats left empty surrounding them, and were ignored by professors during class.[137]

In contrast, backlash against integration dominated the early post-*Brown* years at Sewanee. Crosses were burned on the campus twice during the 1950s and 1960s, the first of which occurred in February 1957 during a statewide conference of Christian college students; the student newspaper, the *Purple*, described it as an incident by students showing "a very close affinity to the uneducated, bigoted 'Asa Carters' of our country."[138] (Carter was closely associated with the KKK and segregationist John Kasper, and he later wrote speeches for the stridently segregationist Alabama governor George Wallace.) In fall 1963, a cross was burned outside the dormitory of Calvin Kendell Williams, a transfer student from Fisk University who had recently integrated Sewanee.[139] In April 1961, a white student, Blanchard Weber, was taken from his dorm room in the middle of the night and had his head shaved and painted by fellow students wearing white robes with hoods.[140] The students reportedly claimed this was "a lesson to [Weber]," in reference to a rumor that Weber was dating an African American Fisk student, whom he had met at a Highlander Folk School event.[141] This incident brought forth a flurry of letters to the *Purple*. One letter asserted that Sewanee's students must make sure "that such a thing never happens on the mountain again," although it is difficult to establish the overall mood of the student body from the newspaper alone as no poll was taken at the time.[142] The administration appears to have stayed as far away as possible from the episode, as the Board of Trustees meetings in May and June did not mention it nor was there an account of a student being disciplined (or even identified as having been involved).[143] Furthermore, it is unclear whether Weber was pro-integration, though he did attend a Highlander workshop.

Two of the six students who integrated Maryville in 1954, Shirley Carr Clowney and Nancy Smith Wright, had contrasting experiences. Both Clowney and Wright were encouraged, as were many African American students across the South, to apply as part of a group for enrollment in previously all-white institutions. A neighbor and former principal, James Harris Fowler, visited Clowney's father and encouraged him to have Clowney petition for enrollment with the group of local Black students who were applying to Maryville.[144] When she was accepted along with the other five students (including Wright), she received a scholarship from Maryville to attend. Wright had been raised along with her sisters by her aunt and grandmother after her mother's death when Wright was still a child, and so when her Presbyterian minister in Knoxville, Rev. Frank R. Gordon, wanted to "test" *Brown* in 1954, he secured permission from her aunt for Wright to join the enrollment application.[145]

Maryville College limited the impact of integrating students on the college and community as a whole by stating that accommodation would be provided for Black students whose families lived outside Blount County (where the campus was located). Wright, who lived in Knoxville, was allowed to live on campus in a college women's dorm while she attended the college while Clowney, whose family lived in Blount County, had to live at home and commute to class each day.[146] When she received a scholarship to attend Maryville, the college, deeming her home address close enough to commute daily, had made no housing arrangements.[147] Wright was shocked to find that she had been assigned to a single room. "I thought I'd have a roommate and I'd expected to see twin beds and . . . matching spreads . . . they told me I'd have to room by myself and I didn't understand why."[148] The only other student out of the group of Blacks enrolled at Maryville in the fall of 1954 who was allowed to live on campus was a young man named Freeman Wyche, who like Wright was from outside Blount County and therefore was given a room at the college. However, while Wright was given a room in a women's dorm (albeit a single room), Wyche reportedly lived in a room in the gymnasium building.[149] Although Clowney described the integration process as "smooth . . . unlike Clinton [Tennessee] or Little Rock [Arkansas]" and there being "really no clashes," she was nonetheless disappointed. She remarked, "We thought the campus area was going to be more accepting of the integrated situation at that time."[150] While Clowney and the other Black students had been prepared for the city of Maryville to oppose integration, they were still surprised by the number of limitations they experienced off campus. Wright felt the same way. She recalled that while walking to the city from campus with white girlfriends, she felt "uncomfortable . . . and a little afraid." She was told at City Drugstore that she could not be served with her friends. At the movie theater she was told she needed to sit upstairs; her white friend could either go upstairs with Wright or sit by herself on the ground floor.[151]

While Wright recalled some of her best times on campus were while eating in the college cafeteria with her friends, the commuting students like Clowney ate in a separate room in Pearson Hall, apart from the main cafeteria. Clowney was not served at any of the other restaurants on campus, such as the grill.[152] As Clowney and Wright's experiences reveal, while the college treated Black and white students differently, even within the group of Black students admitted in 1954, policies regarding African American students varied.

Perhaps justifiably, given the awkward reception Black Maryville students received in the wider community in the 1950s, Sewanee's Vice-Chancellor McCrady worried as early as 1956 that it would be far more difficult to integrate campus life than to admit Blacks. His concerns occurred years before Sewanee (officially, at least) changed its policy to consider Black applicants, in 1961. In his diary, McCrady envisaged a controlled desegregation approach for Sewanee that was already taking place at Maryville. He wrote that he did not think white southerners were ready to have their children be a part of an integrated campus experience socially, whereas he believed that if integration merely consisted of having Black students attend classes, take exams, and graduate after four years, it would be an easier situation for white southerners to accept.[153]

Personal autonomy, civil rights reforms, economic inequities, and religious concerns inspired early Tennessee student activists. Early progressive youth efforts in the late 1930s and the issues raised by students in the late 1950s spoke to their understanding of how racial segregation reinforced regional economic disparities, and how working within segregated communities as part of an interracial movement might work in the future. Highlander was a vital hub for New Deal–era radicals (including youths) and later activists. The school linked the Old and New Left. Despite the chilling effect of domestic anticommunism on the boundaries of acceptable dissent, Highlander continued to connect older and younger activists, and provided a supportive environment to share organizing strategies. From 1954, the school raised students' racial consciousness through annual college workshops. Highlander built the network from which the subsequent student movement emerged. Simultaneously, the slow desegregation of higher education facilities in Tennessee shaped the context in which student activists operated. While university administrators fretted over the consequences of desegregation, many student interracial program participants (white and Black) became active in civil rights protest. Moreover, the unsatisfying partial accommodation of universities to token integration created the conditions that Black and white student activists would contest in the 1960s.

CHAPTER 2

Kneel, Sit, or Stand

Creating a Student Movement

Southern students' embrace of nonviolent direct action in February 1960 was a turning point in the civil rights movement. In the years following these protests, it would become clear that Black and white students from the South had specific demands for their communities and schools regarding the progress of desegregation. After only two months of protests, sit-in demonstrations had spread to seventy-eight cities in thirteen states across the South.[1] Despite the surge of activism, the institutional change they desired would not be easy to achieve. As the accounts of sit-in demonstrations across Tennessee demonstrate, community leaders and administrators of universities and colleges had vested interests in controlling the pace of change, which led to conflicts with students and community members. Fears of property damage, violence on campus or involving students in the surrounding area, and negative media coverage were strong motivators for administrations to keep a close eye on how demonstrations developed. As the events of early 1960 unfolded, it became clear that the sit-in movement would be much more than just "another college fad of the 'panty-raid' variety."[2]

The sit-in movement also signaled the start of the 1960s student movement, traditionally defined. Whether they sat, kneeled, stood, or sipped in protest, Black and white students who participated in these demonstrations across the state of Tennessee were part of a moment during which students asserted their rights and called for change. Continuing to consider citizenship, human rights and equality, and their place in society as young people before them had, students participating in the student movement of the 1960s seized on the moment of opportunity when they perceived it, both on and off campus. Continued debates over the speed and extent of campus integration and student involvement in campus activities, in conjunction with the sociopolitical ramifications of the sit-ins across the state and region, seemingly encouraged students to organize then. The sit-ins also had a galvanizing effect on other students, besides those discussed in this chapter, who led demonstrations on their campuses; the wave of activism that the sit-ins triggered continued through the decade as students and youth grasped opportunities available to them to assert their personal and political autonomy.

Focusing on the sit-in movement across the state of Tennessee within the context of the student movement more broadly allows connections to be drawn between these protests in the early 1960s and later student protests that emerged throughout the decade. Particularly in a geographically diverse state like Tennessee and part of the Border South, the sit-ins inspired a range of different types of student activism in the early to mid-1960s that would otherwise seem sporadic or unconnected but were representative of increased engagement across the state.

The centrality of the sit-ins built upon the qualified success of mass protest strategies of the civil rights movement. Blacks had used boycotts and marches to challenge forms of Jim Crow segregation dating as far back as Reconstruction.[3] A series of test sit-ins across the region, in Tallahassee in 1956, in Atlanta in 1957, and in Nashville in 1959, preceded the student-led sit-ins.[4] Protestors were not to get themselves arrested, but merely "test" responses of business owners and law enforcement. The sit-ins of 1960 were distinct in terms of the large number of student participants and leaders, and of the possibility for change they inspired throughout the South.[5] Most sit-in participants were college students, supported by community leaders such as politicians and ministers; however, in the case of Chattanooga, high school rather than college students filled the ranks of protestors.[6] Blacks made up the majority of demonstrators in all categories, but white participants played important roles in Nashville and Knoxville. Biracial committees were established in six cities: Athens, Chattanooga, Knoxville, Memphis, Nashville, and Oak Ridge. The success of these groups varied.[7] Protests in each city also featured intergenerational leadership, at times efficient and at others exposing differences in motives and backgrounds. Within a year of the Nashville sit-ins, protests spread across the state to five other cities (Knoxville, Memphis, Oak Ridge, Chattanooga, and Jackson) involving some 16,000 demonstrators and at least 692 arrests.[8]

In Tennessee, where the "politics of moderation" reined in cities across the state, similarities, rather than municipal distinctiveness, were more prevalent across the narratives of Nashville, Knoxville, and Memphis.[9] When it came to racial politics in these cities during this period, particularly in Nashville and Knoxville, white southerners toed the line between limited accommodation of Black demands and continued policies of segregation. In Memphis, Jim Crow segregation was more overt and, with a larger Black population than elsewhere in the state, the politics of Deep South areas were more prevalent. As historian William Chafe has argued, these policies of southern race relations were effectively "a paternalism so unconscious it would never be called such by whites."[10] In his study of Nashville civil rights, historian Benjamin Houston stated, "*Moderation* was used frequently to depict a racial stance that positioned itself between sweeping declarations of vicious racism and the sanctioning of racial equality, defining itself against extremism rather than for a particular racial philosophy."[11] The success of sit-in demonstrations, indeed even the conceptualization of the protest strategy as one that could potentially be effective, happened in the face of such ingrained thinking: white moderates who believed their communities to be racially progressive.

Nashville's sit-ins have shaped histories of civil rights in Tennessee, as well as the national narrative of the sit-ins, with the other cities' protests typically being discussed merely as supporting acts to the Nashville events. Indeed, Nashville student activist and later politician John Lewis would say of the city's sit-in movement that "something happened in Nashville that did not happen any other place in America."[12] Consequently, sit-ins elsewhere in Tennessee have been obscured. By placing the well-known Nashville story into a longer chronology of protest, and into a statewide context, the similarity of Nashville and other self-consciously "moderate" southern locales, the continued cooperation between younger and older activists, and the intensification of student power demands over the early 1960s all become more readily apparent.

The Sit-In Movement Begins in the Athens of the South

Nashville's first sit-in demonstration occurred twelve days after students sat in at a Woolworth lunch counter in Greensboro, North Carolina, but exercised greater influence on the student movement across the South.[13] This prominence was largely due to high participation, strong leadership, and a well-organized effort to begin the sit-ins with people educated in nonviolent direct action. Rev. James M. Lawson Jr., a veteran of the Fellowship of Reconciliation (FOR) and a believer in Gandhian nonviolence, led the Nashville workshops on nonviolent direct action.[14] Lawson had enrolled as a student in Vanderbilt's Divinity School, only the second Black person to have done so, while serving as FOR's southern field secretary.[15] The other significant figure in the origins of the Nashville sit-ins was Rev. Kelly Miller Smith, who was involved in founding the Southern Christian Leadership Conference (SCLC) in 1957, headed by Rev. Martin Luther King Jr. The SCLC model inspired Smith to form a local chapter of the organization in Nashville, which he did in January

1958, when he launched the Nashville Christian Leadership Council (NCLC). The NCLC endeavored to organize Nashville's Black community in the midst of Massive Resistance, as white residents, led by white segregationist firebrand John Kasper, protested the integration of municipal schools and Nashville's public accommodations.[16] Emphasizing Highlander Folk School's importance in the state, historian Benjamin Houston has argued that NCLC was particularly successful largely because its leadership had previous activist experience, including connections with Highlander. The NCLC's initiatives in the late 1950s were so heavily run by adults experienced with activism that the concept of encouraging college students to participate was, according to Houston, "almost an afterthought."[17]

Beginning in fall 1958, with support from Smith and the NCLC, Lawson began holding weekly workshops on nonviolent protest, first for students at Bethel AME Church, then at the churches of First Baptist and Clark Memorial Methodist, since the latter locations were closer to Tennessee State University and Fisk.[18] Unlike earlier workshops, Lawson was teaching those who wanted and needed a way to act, rather than attempting to inspire people to act, and unlike the test sit-ins, this time sit-ins led to the arrests of demonstrators.[19] As former Nashville youth activist Candie Carawan recalled, social change would "come from people who are struggling with the problems reaching inside themselves, analyzing their own experiences and talking with people like themselves."[20] Historian Bobby Lovett has argued that NCLC "had neither a method nor a strategy" for its work before the workshops came about.[21]

The student participants of the workshops, particularly those involved from the beginning, would become central to the movement in Nashville. In October 1959, ten Black college students and attendees of Lawson's workshops formed the Nashville Student Movement (NSM), and encouraged others from the different campuses to attend.[22] From this group, John Lewis, Bernard Lafayette, and James Bevel, students at American Baptist Theological Seminary, Diane Nash, a Fisk exchange student from Chicago, and Marion Barry, a Fisk graduate student from Memphis, led the city's sit-ins through leadership positions in the NSM.[23] Student participation varied across various colleges and universities in the city. While the numbers of workshop attendees rose dramatically from fall 1959, those who decided to attend sessions knew that their colleges might not support their actions, which then made the group that participated a self-selecting one. As February 1960 neared, students from Fisk and Tennessee State in particular were reluctant to join, even with leadership from their campuses in the NSM.[24] While the NSM leadership early on had been all Black, by 1960 the movement included white students at Vanderbilt, Peabody, and Scarritt Colleges, and white Fisk exchange students.[25]

The first sit-in demonstration in Nashville began on February 13, 1960, when 124 people sat in at downtown lunch counters. This continued for two weeks. Students filed in and sat calmly and quietly at the counter. When they refused to leave after being told they would not be served, the store manager would close down the counter.[26] On February 23 however, sit-in protests in Chattanooga at the S. H. Kress & Co. lunch counter broke out in violence, changing the dynamic for subsequent sit-ins, including those in Nashville. On February 27, sit-in demonstrators in Nashville were spat on, kicked, and harassed; an Associated Press article with an image of Paul LaPrad, a white Fisk exchange student, being beaten by white onlookers signaled to the community that the tenor of the protests had changed.[27] The white segregationist youths who came to watch that day's protests at the lunch counters of McClellan's, Walgreen's, and Woolworth's had, in NCLC leader Kelly Miller Smith's description, "obviously previously organized," with some of them wearing jackets with "Chattanooga" scrawled on them. This was a clear reference to the violence at that city's sit-ins a few days earlier.[28] As police arrested sit-in demonstrators in the afternoon, new groups of students arrived to take their seats at the counters, much to the shock and surprise of onlookers. This image of well-dressed students filing into police vans with another group ready to take their place at the counter was particularly provocative, but was made even more so by the news that emerged later from the prisons: the students had refused bail. The move marked a change in the movement, one where students were testing the system to see how much pressure they could exert on the city. The students remained firm in their conviction to stay in prison, even after bail was lowered from one hundred dollars to five. They were released later that evening without any bail being paid.[29]

This change in onlookers' behavior during the demonstrations, and therefore the mood surrounding the movement, also impacted colleges and universities in Nashville. Previously reluctant to speak about the sit-ins, Fisk's president, Stephen J. Wright, gave a speech to students on February 28 in which he voiced encouragement for the student protesters. John Lewis recalled that Wright's speech made him the first Black college president to speak supportively of the sit-ins, which made Lewis and his fellow students "euphoric."[30] Wright's speech was indicative of the movement picking up momentum, yet he seemed to step back from his declaration soon thereafter, issuing a statement that university regulations stipulated that students had to attend class, and therefore those who were protesting during a class they were enrolled in were in violation of university policy.[31] Presidents of Black colleges and universities were under immense pressure both to keep their students on the "right" side of the law and to show support for the issues that students were protesting. Despite this complicated balancing act, however, the majority of Fisk and Tennessee State students believed their presidents navigated the situation well.[32]

The sit-ins exposed tensions in Vanderbilt leadership over the direction of the university in the civil rights era. Following his arrest during the sit-ins and description by the media as the movement's leader, Vanderbilt Divinity School expelled James Lawson in early March 1960.[33] One of the main proponents of the anti-Lawson crusade was James "Jimmy" Stahlman, the publisher of the conservative *Nashville Banner* and a member of Vanderbilt's Board of Trust.[34] This expulsion angered many of Vanderbilt's faculty and students, deeply dividing the student body and bringing Vanderbilt much unwelcome and unfavorable attention. It also provided another instance of university administrators feeling stuck between two potentially damaging options when negotiating student affairs during this period. In an article from the Vanderbilt school newspaper *The Hustler*, a Vanderbilt administrator was quoted as saying, "It is ironic that something like this should happen to Vanderbilt after we were among the first to admit Negroes, after we held to a liberal policy [in its Divinity School]. Now those who didn't will be saying 'I told you so.'"[35] Harvie Branscomb, Vanderbilt's chancellor, held moderately progressive views about racial integration at his institution, but found himself straddling an ever-increasing divide between needing to respond to the concerns of Board of Trust members, and student, faculty, and public sentiment.[36] Black undergraduate students would not be admitted to Vanderbilt until 1964.[37]

Following Lawson's expulsion, student protesters and the NCLC continued to exert pressure on the city of Nashville. Emotions ran high after prominent Black lawyer Z. Alexander Looby's house was bombed in the early morning on April 19. One journalist attributed the Looby bombing to changing public opinion of the sit-ins "more than any other single factor."[38] Later that day, some fifteen hundred pro–civil rights protestors marched from Tennessee State to the Nashville courthouse, their numbers doubling along the way.[39] While waiting for Mayor Ben West to address the crowd, Highlander staff member Guy Carawan led the crowd in a rendition of "We Shall Overcome"; David Halberstam, a young white reporter for the *Tennessean*, stated in his account of the sit-ins that "the students now had their anthem."[40] West arrived, and appeared flustered when criticized for his inaction on behalf of civil rights by Rev. C. T. Vivian. Diane Nash increased the pressure on West during her remarks, thereby compelling him to admit that racially segregated eating establishments should be integrated. West would later say of the admission, "It was a question that I had to answer as a man and not as a politician."[41] A moderate white politician on racial matters, West was more concerned with keeping Nashville open for business than in maintaining racial segregation. In part from the momentum gained by the movement from the events following the Looby house bombing and also from a Black boycott of downtown Nashville businesses, the city's leaders agreed with merchants to integrate the targeted facilities. The desegregation of the city's downtown eating establishments officially began on May 10.[42]

Emboldened by their victory, Nashville activists next decided to shift their energy and attention to the Freedom Riders who were attempting to desegregate buses and bus terminals across the South. When Freedom Riders were attacked in Alabama in May 1961, Diane Nash proposed that Nashville's newly formed SNCC should join the rides. The NCLC's Kelly Miller Smith worried that Nash's plan would be far too dangerous, but "the will of the students prevailed" during a meeting between interested students and the NCLC's executive board that lasted for hours.[43] The NCLC supported the students' efforts financially during the trip, and later retained lawyers for fourteen Tennessee State students who were expelled for their participation in the Freedom Rides.[44]

On May 25, the State Education Commissioner, Joe Morgan, announced that the absentee records of a number of Tennessee State students were under review following their participation in the Freedom Rides. Some of the participants had missed their final exams in order to go to Alabama and had arranged with their instructors to take them upon their return. Intervening, the State Board of Education declared the students to be in violation of the board's absentee policy, and placed fourteen of them on disciplinary probation.[45] Criticism of the university's actions was widespread, including at the Fisk University commencement address by prominent clergyman Truman Douglass in June, by hundreds of protestors demonstrating on the State Capitol grounds, and by Carl T. Rowan, formerly a Tennessee State student, who refused an invitation to speak at the August 1961 Tennessee State commencement in his capacity as a deputy assistant U.S. secretary of state for public affairs. "There is no secret about it—we all know they expelled 14 Tennessee State students for participating in the Freedom Rides," Rowan stated. "I attended school there for one year, but I disagree with their policy. My views are known—I felt no useful purpose could be served at such a time by a speech, which would have embarrassed the [Kennedy] administration."[46] The university declined further comment, except to say "the whole episode is now closed, and we will go on just as if it had not occurred."[47] This incident at Tennessee State was only one of many during this period that illustrates the complex and often difficult position Black colleges and universities found themselves in regarding student protesters. It also demonstrates the risks students were willing to take to participate in activism, despite facing academic probation or expulsion from historically Black colleges for their participation in civil rights protests.

"We don't need to have that kind of stuff in Knoxville"

Student participation in the Knoxville sit-ins involved two different institutions, Knoxville College and the University of Tennessee (UT). The Knoxville movement shifted tactics and participants as it gained success throughout the early and mid-1960s. While the Nashville movement has dominated the historiography of the sit-ins, Knoxville's sit-ins both affirm and complicate the established regional narrative. During the Knoxville sit-ins, communication occurred between students and community leaders, as well as between students and administrators. University administrators are often overlooked in studies of the sit-ins throughout the South, yet considering their role improves our understanding of the various pressures on both parties and how students' efforts for political autonomy on campus impacted the direction of the movement.

Compared to other Tennessee cities, Knoxville's Black population was relatively small. Blacks numbered about 10 percent of the population of this bastion of mountain Republicanism.[48] When racial violence occurred in Knoxville, it was sporadic and riled the Black *and* white community leaders to speak out against the instigators. Those who committed violence were seen as outsiders, evidence of an effort to keep race relations peaceful, if not progressive. While many urban leaders in the South attempted to "keep the peace," Knoxville (like Nashville) was one of only a few cities whose white *and* Black leaders were effective in their preventive efforts.[49] White Knoxville authorities seemed to have prevented violence thanks to what one historian has called its "overriding paternalism."[50] Nevertheless, those participating in desegregation efforts and those speaking up for stronger representation on college campuses and against perceived injustices locally all experienced the local *white* leadership's simultaneous reluctance to alter existing racial patterns, and intolerance of racial violence. The large number of references to Knoxville not being a Deep South city (with the implication that activists were more susceptible to violence there) by Black and white activists as well as civic leaders of both races forces the question of Knoxville's self-professed exceptionalism.

Critics of Knoxville's race relations argued that the city's claimed progressivism inhibited enthusiasm among local Blacks and whites for initiating changes in racial customs. When Martin Luther King Jr. gave the commencement speech at Knoxville College in May 1960, he condemned African Americans in Knoxville as "too passive for the movement to waste valuable time on such a visit."[51] A white sit-in leader, Knoxville College professor Merrill Proudfoot, alleged in his memoir of the movement that "this very indecision as to whether Knoxville is a 'Southern' city has made Knoxvillians extremely timid about suggesting changes in the inherited racial patterns."[52] While white Knoxvillians may not have supported violence against protestors, the majority did not participate in demonstrations nor openly support activist efforts during the 1960s. Understanding the intricacies of Knoxville's contemporary atmosphere is best revealed in how activists, particularly African American activists, negotiated social barriers and saw their potential successes and limitations.

Knoxville College student Robert Booker, a veteran, led the push for protests following the sit-ins in Greensboro; the initial group of demonstrators included other Knoxville College students, community leaders, and local residents.[53] Some Black leaders felt that the sit-ins were a step too far, and that for sustainable progress to be made, community discussions needed to occur before demonstrations were to take place. After Booker's first announcement to community leaders that he and his fellow students wanted to organize sit-ins, older African Americans told them that "we don't have to do that in Knoxville. Knoxville is different. [We have] always had good relations. And if you do that, you would set back race relations in this town. What we think we can do is negotiate with the bus counter operators and open on a peaceful basis."[54] So the students agreed to hold off on organizing, as the mayor's bi-racial committee on race relations held meetings; this committee may have been the first in the South formed in response to the sit-in movement.[55]

Additionally, Knoxville mayor John J. Duncan Sr. took Booker, another Knoxville College student, and the president and executive director of the Chamber of Commerce on a trip to New York to meet with executives of variety stores to discuss the integration of their Knoxville branches.[56] Mayor Duncan took "great pride" in the trip to New York, Highlander Folk School's director Myles Horton told Burke Marshall, head of the Civil Rights Division of the U.S. Department of Justice. In Horton's retelling of a conversation with Duncan, he claimed Duncan also went to Birmingham, Alabama, to try to integrate Knoxville's theaters.[57] When the trip to New York was unsuccessful in terms of getting the stores to integrate, and the negotiations between select community leaders in Knoxville appeared to have stalled by late spring, Booker again began to plan sit-ins in downtown Knoxville.[58] Mayor Duncan requested a meeting with Booker when he heard the news. According to Booker, Duncan said, "I don't know what you people are trying to prove. You know we are in negotiations. We want to do this thing on a peaceful basis, but you people are coming down here creating a disturbance, and what I'm going to do if you do it again, is put you all in jail." In response, Booker refused to delay the protests further: equal rights for Knoxville Blacks could wait no longer.[59]

Initially focused on desegregating the lunch counters downtown and then on movie theaters, the Knoxville sit-ins began on June 9, 1960. They involved Black students from Knoxville College, Black and white ministers, mostly Black community members, four UT students who were also members of the Tennessee Valley Unitarian Universalist Church, and about six UT professors.[60] Other white participants came largely from the local Unitarian congregation, and Black participants came from throughout the city and across different socioeconomic backgrounds. In Booker's words, "the three who really kept the lid on things around here" were ex-mayors George Dempster, Cas Walker, and Mayor Duncan. "They sent the word to the larger community that, 'we're not going to tolerate any foolishness,'" presumably from both integrationists and militant segregationists (as other order-focused southern elites did).[61] Proponents for racial equality from leadership within the African American community included Rev. R. E. James, Rev. W. T. Crutcher, Rev. Frank Gordon, who was a Presbyterian minister and at one time the head of the local NAACP branch, and Dr. James A. Colston, president of Knoxville College.[62] A white Knoxville businessman said of Crutcher and Colston in 1986: "In the tough times, Drs. Colston and Crutcher were there, and we tend to forget that."[63]

While some community members actively supported the sit-in demonstrators from the beginning, other leaders, white and Black, were more concerned with controlling the pace of change in Knoxville. The measured, relatively non-militant sit-in approach to public demonstrations in Knoxville irritated other civil rights activists who had grown impatient with working with "moderate" white politicians.

The sit-ins in Knoxville initially succeeded in integrating the lunch counters of downtown variety stores and movie theaters. By July 9 (one month after they began), five downtown stores in Knoxville agreed to desegregate their lunch counters, leaving only two segregated.[64] Two more facilities voluntarily integrated by July 18, taking the number of institutions desegregated to seven.[65] Majority opinion in the community and on the UT campus was against the protesters and their initiatives. Those sitting-in had given out some 2,500 handbills on a single day (July 7), but the information seems to have mostly fallen on deaf ears.[66] Nevertheless, this first phase of direct action in Knoxville continued when students returned that fall for school; activists sought to integrate the city's theaters in an initiative that continued into fall 1961. When Robert Booker and fifty other Knoxville College students were arrested in October 1961 for picketing a theater, Knoxville College president James Colston spoke in support of the students saying, "They are young people trying to secure their rights and they went about it the way they felt would be best."[67] One of the theater's signs depicted the message "Never Did So Few Cook Up So Much Excitement," and traffic reportedly jammed in the downtown area as a result of the stand-ins, where protestors stood in place to block normal service at the ticket counter.[68]

After some successes in 1960 and 1961, the sit-in movement in Knoxville stalled. Highlighting tensions among Knoxville Blacks over protest strategies, Avon Rollins, a SNCC field secretary from 1961 to 1965 and an active demonstration leader in his native Knoxville, was unconvinced of the success of these early direct-action protests.[69] Speaking of the later demonstrations of which he was a leader, Rollins recalled that "things were not really accomplished until we started having mass demonstrations which were pretty much organized by the University of Tennessee students and who were getting involved with the Knoxville College students [beginning in 1962]. Well, after some time we came from different sides and converged together in terms of community, when we opened up the theaters and restaurants, and we even demonstrated at hospitals."[70] Other members of the Black community similarly saw the earlier desegregation efforts as ineffective.[71]

Booker saw the change between the two phases of demonstrations differently. "There was a lull . . . but I think the larger community saw what was going on and they said, 'we don't need to have that kind of stuff in Knoxville,'" seemingly a reference to the violence inflicted on sit-in demonstrators elsewhere.[72] Other activists, white adults who participated in the sit-in organizing, recalled other difficulties, such as keeping all participants fully trained in nonviolence, getting the national media's attention despite the local media's decision to ignore the sit-ins, and the lack of involvement by local ministers.[73]

Beginning in 1962, this second phase of civil rights direct action in Knoxville involved students from UT and Knoxville College. More significantly, as an example of inter-institutional collaboration by activists, during these protests activists stretched the definition of "the campus" to include restaurants near the university (not on its actual property). Three student organizations originated around this time in Knoxville and worked together to push through direct action initiatives within the community; while they included student leaders, the organizations were not directly affiliated with UT or Knoxville College. Described by local media as a "pro-integration group," the Knoxville Civic Improvement Committee (KCIC), of which Rollins was president, conducted sit-ins.[74] KCIC was an affiliate of SNCC, most likely the result of Rollins's leadership in both SNCC and local initiatives: KCIC ran local and regional projects, such as a clothing drive for families in Mississippi that two Black high school students coordinated in Knoxville.⁷⁵

In spring 1962, an interracial group of UT students formed Students for Equal Treatment (SET) with the intent of leading demonstrations at segregated restaurants around the UT campus. Marion Barry, a Black graduate student at UT who had been a leader in Nashville's sit-in movement, and Harry Wiersema, a white UT student who participated in Knoxville's sit-ins along with his parents, led the group while Rollins and several other young people involved in the civil rights movement in Knoxville were active in it (most of the group were graduate students).⁷⁶ After UT's administration banned SET from gathering on campus, Barry, Wiersema, and other SET members organized a second group, called Forum for Racial Equality, Etc. (FREE), which being a "discussion group" was allowed to meet on UT's campus as a student group. FREE operated in a sense as the "recruiting arm" for SET by hosting various meetings where civil rights issues could be discussed. Meanwhile, Rev. Ewell K. Reagin gave SET space to meet at the Presbyterian Center just off campus.⁷⁷ Wiersema recalled that "we talked about why all the students should join SET at the FREE meetings and gave out literature on FREE at SET meetings. So [FREE] was our sort of recruiting wing."⁷⁸ According to Nashville-based white student activist Ed Hamlett, the group had proposed a statewide assembly of activists on "Peace, Civil Liberties and [C]ivil [R]ights" but their plans "fell through" because "they couldn't get recognition on their own campus." While leaders such as Wiersema discussed the qualified success of FREE's collaboration with SET, other activists like Hamlett believed the arrangement was indicative of leadership problems. In Hamlett's view, "A structure aimed at drawing in larger numbers of students around broader issues than civil rights . . . could not be set up on one campus, [because] those key students at U.T. were demoralized."⁷⁹

With the help of campus ministers at UT, SET was able to negotiate agreements with five establishments to integrate.⁸⁰ However, when SET students returned to Knoxville that fall, two of the restaurants reneged on their agreement. SET then again utilized the assistance from campus ministers and Herman Spivey, the white academic vice president at UT.⁸¹ Spivey stated that his involvement was not tied to his position at the university but was instead motivated by a personal conviction to assist the students. Spivey recalled telling proprietors that student-led demonstrations would continue unless they desegregated their facilities. Despite his assurances to the contrary, many restaurant owners interpreted this as a veiled threat within the context of Spivey's administrative role at UT. Consequently, his involvement became a complication for UT. "The worst part" of the period, Spivey later stated, "was the mixed public reaction in which it became a cause for some anxiety among the trustees and some anxiety within the community because it appeared as though the University was using threats in trying to exert pressure."[82]

SET faced additional administrative problems. SET attempted to gain support from UT's Student Government Association (SGA) in early 1963, but the organization, in SET's words, "refused to act and passed a motion saying, in effect, 'There is no problem [which we can be involved in],'" implicitly, no race relations problem.[83] In an article for the *Orange and White*, a university publication, one UT student was unsympathetic. "This picketing of restaurants is totally unnecessary," he said. "It is a plea for sympathy and the picketers definitely don't need sympathy."[84]

In an early 1963 statement of their position, SET detailed the various groups they had worked with to negotiate their integration agreements, only to have them reneged upon, while trying "to proceed in ways which would not reflect [badly] upon the University or the city of Knoxville," including "the Church, the city government, the University Administration, the faculty, and the student government." "These efforts have met with some measure of success," the announcement concluded, "but we have come to the point where we feel that a new form of action is dictated."[85] This "new form of action" involved picketing restaurants that failed to comply with the group's request for integrated service, including the Tennessean Restaurant and Byerley's Cafeteria, which were the two that had refused to integrate from the beginning of SET's efforts.

Up to this point, UT students involved in protests at Byerley's had faced some legal concerns, such as arrest warrants for three UT students being issued but not served. Later, Avon Rollins was arrested in October 1962 along with a local minister, Rev. Matthew Jones. A proprietor at Byerley's claimed that Marion Barry had kicked him during a demonstration, while Barry alleged that he was the one who had been assaulted. By early 1963, all SET members were included in a suit in chancery court for their disruption of the establishment not being "in good faith."[86]

Escalated demonstrations outside Byerley's and the Tennessean were exactly what community leaders (white and Black) and the university administration had hoped to avoid; not only were they disruptive to service and the public, but they demanded action from the university administration, which had wanted to evade controversy but also did not support this minority of the student body's actions. Administrators generally wanted order over change, and their selective support of protestors reflected this. In the midst of this conflict, *Look* magazine named Knoxville the "All American City" in April 1963, which led to "mass arrests" when students protested the moniker. These demonstrations put further pressure on Byerley's and the Tennessean, as well as UT administration officials to avoid further negative media attention.[87]

Facing charges in chancery court, Harry Wiersema called his father, Harry Wiersema Sr. Wiersema Jr. worried about his future at UT after he and Marion Barry (as leaders of SET) both received notices to appear before the dean and assistant dean of students. Wiersema Sr. was a senior engineer with the Tennessee Valley Authority (TVA) and had been an integral part of the Knoxville sit-ins' success as a member of the local Unitarian church. Wiersema Jr. recalled telling his father, "This is obviously over us getting arrested and looks like they're going to try and kick us out of college."[88] The April 8 meeting for Wiersema and Barry was held in Spivey's office with Dean of Students Ralph Dunford and Assistant Dean of Students Charles Burchett.[89] According to Wiersema, after Dunford and Burchett argued for Barry and Wiersema to be "disciplined" by the university for their recent arrests, which "[reflected] very badly on UT," Spivey spoke in favor of the students, saying: "From now on the subject of this meeting will be how you two deans can assist these fine young men in achieving the laudatory goal of assuring that all students who attend the University of Tennessee will have equal treatment in all the nearby restaurants. Now I'm not asking you to sit-in yourself, but when we meet again, I'll be asking you what you're doing to help make this come about."[90] Spivey's support of the students "flabbergasted" administrators and the Board of Trustees. His behavior placed him and UT president Andrew Holt in a difficult situation when Holt stood behind Spivey.[91] With Holt's defense of his actions giving him the necessary support, Spivey continued to negotiate with restaurant owners on the condition that SET would "tone down" their demonstrations.[92]

Spivey and Holt's intercession was partly responsible for the success of the sit-in movement. SET continued to picket the restaurants that spring, with Spivey assisting in negotiations, and no UT students were arrested in connection with the demonstrations.[93] SET-led efforts continued, with the biracial committee now making inroads with the desegregation of three hospitals as stand-ins at the movie theaters persisted.[94] Tensions between the university, students affiliated with (or suspected of holding associations with) SET, and the local police remained high. Knoxville police searched a graduation party on May 31 hosted by, according to Wiersema, a SET "hanger-on," and forty of the attendees were arrested as a result; most of those arrested were UT students, while reportedly no Knoxville College students were among the group.[95] The police reported that they saw "a drunken sex orgy," interracial couples "lying all over the front yard and throughout the house" with open liquor bottles strewn about, descriptions that reached the local newspapers.[96] According to one attendee, "the only 'crime' committed was having whites and blacks together at the party." UT put several students on probation following an investigation into the "wild party."[97]

SET's later activity mirrored the goals of other southern student activists, such as integrating the school's athletic teams. Noting that the University of Kentucky had integrated their program, SET called on the university's Board of Trustees in March 1964 to "immediately authorize the Athletic Department to recruit and play athletes regardless of race, creed or color."[98] Marion Barry, in the statement, clarified that UT should desegregate both because Kentucky had done so and because it was the university's "moral responsibility."[99]

This situation highlights an important change in the UT student body. Both SGA presidential candidates "pledged their support" for the integration of UT's athletics program, indicative of a significant shift in popular opinion among students.[100] University of Kentucky President Frank G. Dickey received limited but quiet support from a handful of southern university administrators, including those from UT and Vanderbilt, for his efforts to desegregate football programs of the Southeastern Conference (SEC) by example; Kentucky's first Black player (and the first in the SEC) was Nat Northington, who was signed in 1965 but played his first game in September 1967. UT was the next after Kentucky to desegregate its athletics program when it signed Lester McClain in 1967, who played his first game in September 1968.[101] While there may have been private acknowledgement on the part of administrators that desegregating athletic programs had merit, the process of incorporating Black players remained contentious and resulted in most keeping their thoughts on the subject private. Leadership mattered; General Robert R. Neyland, the director of UT's athletics department, was less inclined towards desegregation of the university's sports programs. Student activist Theotis Robinson Jr. recalled that Neyland had Avon Rollins thrown out of the event when Rollins attempted to try out for the basketball team in 1961. Robinson also alleged that Neyland cancelled a track meet at UT because the coach of a visiting team would not exclude his Black athletes.[102]

The Knoxville story of African American youth activism enriches the established narrative of student participation in the civil rights movement. It presents an episode of protest more representative of areas of the Border South or outside the South where racial politics were less entrenched. Local student activists negotiated with white political elites even before beginning protests. They then focused on specific integration initiatives throughout the city after reaching swift agreements to desegregate five of the seven downtown lunch counters. Not wanting to "graduate from college into second-class citizenship," Knoxville students organized sit-ins in the downtown area to desegregate public accommodations and improve minority employment opportunities.[103] They viewed their behavior as both civil rights activism and as part of the emerging student movement. In particular, the push for administrators to support protesting students evolved into a drive for greater student influence over administrative issues later in the decade. Even though it did not have a history of entrenched racial violence, and despite white citizens imagining their city as un-southern (with "southernness" indicating entrenched racial discrimination and antipathies), persistent racial inequalities remained in Knoxville. Though little known, the Knoxville case furthers historians' understanding of southern student organizing and racial change.

"The day has finally arrived"

Unlike Nashville and Knoxville, student participation in the early stages of Memphis's civil rights movement was almost exclusively Black, drawing students from the city's two historically Black colleges, LeMoyne College and Owen Junior College. Collaboration also differed from Nashville, where a number of established African American leaders within the middle and upper middle classes assisted students, and from Knoxville, where Black students and a handful of ministers (Black and white) and community leaders led the movement. Integration of public facilities was achieved through the efforts of the city's strong NAACP chapter and Black leadership, in conjunction with strong Black youth activism and pressure from the federal government and alongside assistance from Memphis's business leaders, who wanted to open the city's public services to all residents.[104] In Memphis, the city's larger African American population provided more potentially sympathetic activists, and a greater threat to white businesses' profits. Exploiting this opportunity, the city's local NAACP chapter and Black leaders formed the Memphis and Shelby County Improvement League in late January 1960, led by Rev. Benjamin L. Hooks and attorney R. B. Sugarmon Jr.[105] The NAACP chapter in Memphis, combined with the strong adult leadership of the Black community, spearheaded civil rights advancements in the city. Whereas the Nashville and Knoxville sit-in movements were largely student-led with assistance from adult leaders and local organizations like the NCLC in Nashville, Memphis's sit-ins were organized by students with considerable involvement of the city's Black leadership through its active NAACP chapter.

The demonstrations for the integration of public accommodations in Memphis built more significantly upon the racial initiatives of the city's civil rights groups. Furthermore, Memphis's sit-in movement took longer to desegregate local businesses. Given the unwillingness of local whites to change racial practices, strong Black leadership in Memphis played an important role in negotiations with the city's white power structure. Elected in 1959, Mayor Henry Loeb, a self-professed "good segregationist," was representative of the city's white leadership on the eve of the 1960s. Mirroring beliefs in other southern localities with sizable Black populations, most white Memphians treated white power as essential and maintained it through strict ordinances.[106] In the fall of 1947, students and faculty at LeMoyne College and Southwestern College had formed the Memphis Community Relations Committee (MCRC), which held discussions over human rights and hosted visiting academics presenting on related topics.[107] This interracial group existed partly due to community-wide discussions at the time over whether the Freedom Train, an integrated Cold War–era interstate travel initiative to unite the country in favor of democracy, would travel through Memphis in January 1948 as scheduled, and because unlike other interracial civic groups, it was not intended to promote policy, but rather functioned as a discussion group.[108] A 1956 effort to improve race relations, the Greater Memphis Race Relations Committee (GMRRC), was quickly disbanded when its members failed to meet and discuss issues together. The GMRRC formed two subcommittees (for Black and white members) in an effort to correct this, but because the two groups met separately, discussion over the issues stalled.[109]

Prior to the sit-ins, some of the initiatives led by Black leaders in Memphis included a city bus court case in the spring of 1956, a lawsuit against the whites-only public library in late 1957, a desegregation case against the city's Overton Park Zoo in early 1959, a garbage workers' strike beginning in January 1960, and an ongoing campaign to register the city's Blacks to vote.[110] Aimed at furthering integration in the city, these attempts by Black leaders demonstrate the vitality of the civil rights struggle in Memphis before the 1960s. After the failure of both the GMRRC and subsequent biracial efforts to negotiate Memphis business integration in 1959, local Black political power and federal intervention converged to produce a sustainable, significant movement.[111] The city's NAACP chapter was the largest in the South, and included local leaders such as Vasco and Maxine Smith. Vasco was the president of the chapter from December 1960, while Maxine oversaw the chapter's daily activities; in 1962, she became the chapter's executive secretary.[112] By May 1960, after the sit-ins had begun in Memphis, one single membership drive increased the local NAACP chapter membership by 1,500 to 6,750, 655 of whom were student members.[113]

Collaboration between Memphis NAACP members and youths pointed to subsequent developments in the civil rights movement, and in the post–sit-in student movement. The first occurred during the Tennessee Conference of the NAACP, held in Memphis from September 25 to September 27, 1959. College chapters from LeMoyne College in Memphis, Lane College in Jackson, Fisk University in Nashville, and Knoxville College attended, along with city chapters from across the state: Memphis and Jackson in West Tennessee, Nashville and Clarksville in Middle Tennessee, and Knoxville, Oak Ridge, and Chattanooga in East Tennessee.[114] In March 1963 Maxine Smith and thirty students from Memphis State University, LeMoyne, Owen, and white Southwestern at Memphis established an NAACP intercollegiate chapter.[115] This group indicated further interest, both from Black Memphis leadership and some college students, in continuing intergenerational civil rights efforts.

Building upon the adult-led movement against segregation in Memphis, the student-led initiative, referred to as the Memphis Freedom Movement, began on March 18, 1960, when twelve students from LeMoyne visited the McLellan's lunch counter.[116] LeMoyne graduate and later UT graduate student Marion Barry and Nashville's James Lawson had educated the students on nonviolent direct action prior to their first sit-in.[117] The following day, on March 19, students from LeMoyne went into two white branches of the Memphis Public Library, saying they "needed some more books for their term papers and [to] study." In the following days, students from Owen joined those from LeMoyne to tackle additional locations, including the Brooks Memorial Art Gallery.[118] Speaking of the community support he felt in the initial days of the movement, Evander Ford recalled, "From that moment on, from that day on, it was just lightning fire."[119] Johnnie Rodgers Turner compared the feeling to "like being in a revival," adding, "You got so much support and you got thousands of people, whole lives and generations of injustices, and I guess they said it's too late for me. And here they see these young people have put their lives on the line."[120] From early on in their protests, the Memphis movement targeted a greater variety of locations than other movements in the state, where students typically first tackled lunch counter integration, then moved on to other public accommodations. In Memphis, the downtown lunch counters became the focus in mid-May 1960, after the initial wave of sit-ins at other municipal facilities.[121] Why exactly this is the case is unclear, but it could be that in an area of such significant and entrenched racial segregation like Memphis, a broader approach towards desegregation seemed stronger, or it could also speak to the strategies of the NAACP. It could also be that students in Memphis were particularly focused on continuing with their momentum; Elaine Lee Turner recalled, "There was no way we would just stop and say that maybe they're going to change everything else. . . . Just because they desegregated the buses, then they're going to desegregate everything else? No."[122]

Memphis students recognized the pitfalls they faced for protesting. Students at LeMoyne College recalled being informed by college administration, including the college's president, Dr. Hollis Price, that in addition to their financial aid being rescinded, they risked jeopardizing their future career prospects as well as their parents' jobs.[123] Approximately thirty-six students were subsequently arrested for their participation in the sit-ins and jailed, with charges including breach of peace, disorderly conduct, and loitering.[124] Having been arrested and facing trials, the students reached out to the local NAACP chapter.[125] The students clearly felt that they were participating in something so different from previous activism that they contacted the city's adult Black leadership only when they needed financial and legal assistance, not before. As much as it appears in retrospect that they were building upon the foundations of a civil rights movement in Memphis, students saw their actions at the time as distinct. The trial for the forty-one individuals arrested during the McLellan's sit-in and for protesting at the library branches was set for March 21, 1960. The forty-one included several members of the press and bystanders who were arrested for simply being present during the demonstrations.[126] Those arrested for protesting at the Brooks Memorial Art Gallery faced trial on April 6. Members of the Black community contributed thousands of dollars that spring for the legal defense of the protestors, indicative of widespread support for the sit-ins.[127]

While students and their sit-ins were part of a larger movement in Memphis, their participation revealed an acceleration in the pace of change. In witnessing the community rallying around the sit-in demonstrators on trial on March 21, Vasco Smith proudly exclaimed, "The day has finally arrived."[128] Later, on March 30, the local Black newspaper the *Memphis World* declared with pride, "It was inevitable that the student sit-downs throughout the South would [finally] come to Memphis."[129]

In May, the NAACP's Memphis youth chapter put pressure on the city by picketing establishments in downtown Memphis. Their strategy was one of economic boycotts, as they carried signs stating, "This store integrates your money and segregates you."[130] Black leaders in Memphis appear to have seized the opportunity provided by student activists. That same month Black residents brought a legal case to integrate all of Memphis's public recreational areas. *I. T. Watson et al. v. City of Memphis et al.* was ultimately appealed to the U.S. Supreme Court.[131] That August, in an effort led by Maxine Smith, the local NAACP chapter pressured Memphis radio station WDIA to discontinue programs that the chapter saw as "[encouraging] segregation." The station was white-owned but run by and marketed to Memphis Blacks.[132] The tactic to focus on WDIA demonstrated an understanding that radio programming could be influential to the movement. The city's biracial committee on race relations, the Memphis Committee on Community Relations (MCCR), contributed to these successes as well.[133] The MCCR, which included four Memphis NAACP members, had worked behind the scenes with the municipal government and business owners to negotiate the desegregation of city buses (September 1960), the public library (October 1960), and Memphis's public zoo (December 1960). The MCCR largely achieved these changes in light of student sit-ins in Memphis, amid concerns that they, like demonstrations had elsewhere in the South, would escalate quickly.[134] Although the specific individuals from the MCCR or white business community responsible for the desegregation are unknown, downtown establishments took such actions voluntarily.[135]

Protests continued through the spring and summer of 1961. City leaders and the NAACP chapter activated the young, preachers, many women, and all societal groups in the initiatives, which included a series of sit-in demonstrations at downtown department stores in late June.[136] Legal challenges to segregation policies—many orchestrated by the NAACP—were argued in courts, with little to no support from state officials.[137]

Another major student protest in Memphis took a different target: organized religion. On consecutive Sundays between March and May 1964, groups of Black and white students participating in the NAACP intercollegiate chapter attempted eight times to integrate Memphis's white churches, including a prominent church with connections to Southwestern: Second Presbyterian Church (SPC).[138] SPC gave large donations to Southwestern, making the church an important institution to Southwestern's president at the time, Peyton Rhodes.[139] Southwestern was the last place many Memphis residents would have expected a protest, but students organized a demonstration to urge U.S. Senator Herbert Walters (D-TN) to vote for the 1964 Civil Rights Act when he visited the campus in January 1964.[140] Startled by the reaction to his visit, Walters exclaimed, "Well, this is certainly a surprise . . . at such a sedate place as Southwestern . . . wow . . . what is this world coming to?"[141]

The tactic would be a kneel-in. Small groups of students, Black and white, would attempt to attend the service, and would report their success or failure back to the group.[142] Students had in fact attempted this elsewhere in the South before 1964, and in Memphis on two Sundays in late August 1960. Black students had tried to attend church services both times. They were either received with suspicion and directed to sit in a roped-off area of the church, turned away, or the service itself was suspended.[143] Instead of turning away Black students from their church doors, in 1964 congregations now confronted Black and white students who also had the support of the NAACP as members of its collegiate chapter.[144]

Following the participation by Southwestern students in the kneel-ins at SPC, church leaders and Southwestern administrators held a meeting in late spring of 1964. Despite pressure and suggestions from church officials that the church's usually significant amount of funding to Southwestern would be withheld if the college did not punish the protesting students, President Rhodes refused to bend and took the stand that "the College is not for sale."[145] Rhodes's refusal to bend did not mean, however, that he gave the students carte blanche. In one letter to a prominent Memphis businessman and college alumnus, Rhodes wrote, "Personally I deplore any sort of picketing, demonstrating, lying down, sitting down, standing up, or anything or [sic] the sort, and I think the students, . . . who elected to attend worship at a place where they were not wanted, were exhibiting bad manners and poor taste." The college, he claimed, did not support the students' efforts. Rather the administration was simply not punishing the students because it would create a storm of bad publicity directed at the college, particularly as the Presbyterian Church's General Assembly had already urged integration.[146] Students, specifically those at Southwestern, stopped kneeling-in at SPC when the academic year ended, but resumed in January 1965.[147] The protests continued for three weeks that month, and this time forced an official change in the church's segregation policy.[148]

Protests by Memphis students were more drawn out and from the beginning focused more on a variety of public accommodations and stores than in other cities in Tennessee, demonstrating the complexities of direct action in a more racially divided city. The level of entrenched racial segregation in Memphis necessitated different strategies than in Nashville and Knoxville, for example. In those cities, Blacks and whites shared, to varying extents, some measure of physical space, whereas in Memphis public areas were even more strictly designated as Black or white.[149]

The Southern White New Left

Black students made up the majority of sit-in participants, but there were a number of white students involved in the demonstrations as well. The development of campus-based initiatives on white campuses across the country in the early 1960s was a direct result of the widespread impact of the Black-led nonviolent participatory democracy from 1960. As Michael Kazin has argued, white student organizations like SDS and SSOC held an idealistic view of participatory democracy in which they could join Blacks (principally SNCC) in their freedom struggle, for mutual benefit. This belief marked an important difference between the Old Left and the New Left, as leaders of the Old Left rarely considered Blacks as equal agents, while New Leftists did.[150]

The awakening of white students occurred across the South, and as news continued to spread throughout the country, students became aware of the youth-led initiatives in the civil rights movement. Many white students who participated in civil rights projects, like the Freedom Rides in 1961 and Mississippi's Freedom Summer in 1964, were fundamentally changed by their experiences. Tom Hayden, an author of SDS's founding document, *The Port Huron Statement*, and later member of the Chicago Eight following the protests during the 1968 Democratic National Convention, became an important leader of the New Left after he participated in the Freedom Rides.[151] Similarly, Mario Savio led students on the Berkeley campus of the University of California in protest against perceived infringements of students' freedom of speech when he returned to school after Freedom Summer.[152]

SSOC was formed at a meeting in Nashville in April 1964, where forty-five representatives from fifteen campuses across ten southern states attended to discuss the role of the white southerner in the civil rights movement.[153] Including students from Vanderbilt, UT, and Maryville College, this group signified the first organized (and leftist) white student movement in the South since the 1930s youth groups discussed in the previous chapter.[154] While SDS had established several collegiate chapters on southern campuses, including at Vanderbilt in early 1964, SDS agreed to leave the South to SSOC.[155]

Like SDS and SSOC, the National Student Association (NSA), an interracial organization of students, was interested in the growing student activism on college campuses in the early 1960s; the NSA had a presence in Tennessee when students at Memphis State University formed a NSA chapter in 1963. The organization's members had telling debates over the direction of and support for the sit-ins.[156] The sit-ins created conflict for the organization as its members debated whether or not to publicly support them at the fall 1960 NSA Congress.[157] The NSA decided to support the sit-ins by the end of its 1960 convention.[158] Arguments in the NSA mirrored those discussed by adult civil rights movement leaders. It was clear that students, Black and white, were growing in consciousness and were inclined to act, but disagreements over what forms of protest could be considered legitimate dominated the discussion. Also, debates emerged as to whether Blacks and whites should belong to the same organizations or to separate ones. As SNCC moved in a direction of racial separatism, southern white students founded a white organization, SSOC. SNCC's John Lewis recalled, "The very fact that it [SSOC] was formed was much more significant than anything the group ever accomplished.... That an all-white shadow of SNCC was created in 1964 was an indication of the intensity of the racial issues that were brewing within our own organization."[159]

For white students in the South, participation in civil rights initiatives most often began with local efforts; they saw news reports of protests happening near them and responded with a desire to get involved. The NSA's Southern Student Human Relations Project director, Constance "Connie" Curry, compiled a list in the early 1960s of a number of southern student organizations focused on resolving racial injustice, which included the Joint University Council on Human Relations (JUC) in Nashville, and SET in Knoxville.[160] In Nashville specifically, the JUC and its precursor PROD were the campus groups that led to the organization of SSOC. In the aftermath of the sit-ins, students at Vanderbilt University created PROD in the spring of 1963. Its participants made the desegregation of the nearby Campus Grill restaurant its main issue after they joined some divinity students from Vanderbilt who had been boycotting the restaurant. PROD encouraged Vanderbilt's student senate to pass a resolution in favor of Nashville restaurant desegregation. Following these efforts however, PROD split after its members disagreed over the group's intentions. Many of its former members joined JUC and later SSOC, both intercampus organizations that organized across university lines.[161]

Sixty students from Peabody, Vanderbilt, and Scarritt founded JUC on April 21, 1964, in a demonstration of intercampus collaboration, two weeks after SSOC was organized. Many of the same SSOC students also participated in JUC. As JUC membership overlapped with individuals involved in SSOC such as Archie Allen, Sue Thrasher, David Kotelchuck, and Ron Parker, JUC quickly affiliated itself with SSOC and within a week of forming similarly joined with the Nashville Leadership Council and the local SNCC chapter in Nashville to protest for the desegregation of downtown restaurants.[162] Sue Thrasher, one of the founding members of SSOC, later recalled the denial of service at a Nashville restaurant to an exchange student from Fiji and the subsequent picketing of the offending establishment by white Nashville students as the catalyst for founding JUC.[163] Thrasher remembered that the idea to combine the various Nashville student groups under the umbrella of a single organization came from this incident, and resulted in SSOC's creation in 1964.[164] JUC's major success was during a sip-in at Morrison's in downtown Nashville on May 3, 1964, planned to coincide with a visit by Martin Luther King Jr.[165] A sip-in, as the name implies, was similar to the sit-in as a form of nonviolent direct action, but one that was conducted at a soda shop where customers would "sip" their drinks.

These efforts led by white students, predominantly for Vanderbilt, once again placed Nashville at the center of southern student organizing. White activists had viewed Nashville's sit-ins as indicating the potential successes of youth-led initiatives. As Thrasher recalled, "There was something very powerful in the act of confronting segregation, in standing up and saying, 'No more,' with the body. It was very different than the endless talk about interracial gatherings and working behind the scenes."¹⁶⁶

According to one Vanderbilt student and SDS member, Lee Frissell, the conception of membership to one or more of these student organizations at Vanderbilt was a fluid one. "Actual membership in organizations was pretty lax, in fact relatively irrelevant.... I don't think any of us really thought of ourselves as 'members.' We were supporters, followers."¹⁶⁷ The result, therefore, was a series of small student organizations based at Vanderbilt, which, while relatively insignificant on their own, were influential in the formation of a nationally recognized student organization based in the South, SSOC. SSOC also conceived of organization and student participation loosely; Sue Thrasher remembered that it was not established to be a separate organization for southern whites, but rather a way to involve more of them into the movement. "It wasn't so much about creating an organization," she stated, "[but instead] about how you involve more whites in the civil rights movement."¹⁶⁸

Finally, contrasting with Doug Rossinow's research on white students at the University of Texas at Austin, affiliation with Christianity does not appear to have been a strong motivation for white Vanderbilt students to participate in progressive efforts. Indeed, Frissell believed that most of the Vanderbilt SDS members were atheists.¹⁶⁹ Given the deep symbolism of Christianity for Black sit-in protestors in Nashville, this factor of white student organizing, if true for most Vanderbilt participants, points to a significant difference between Black and white Nashville student activists.

SSOC turned to organizations established by progressives the generation before, as well as to SNCC, for financial assistance in getting on their feet. In fact, both SNCC and SSOC received funding from the Southern Conference Educational Fund (SCEF) when they first began. Anne Braden, an established white civil rights activist from Kentucky, ran SCEF and vocally opposed racial segregation, along with her husband Carl.¹⁷⁰ SCEF had provided the funds for a white field secretary for SNCC's White Southern Student Project, while Anne Braden corresponded with SNCC activists as they organized the inaugural program in mid-1961.¹⁷¹ When SSOC formed in 1964, the group solicited and received grants from both SNCC and SCEF. SSOC asked for donations in the first issue of its publication, the *New Rebel*, a name reflective of SSOC's attempt to fuse interracial collaboration with southern pride.¹⁷² Anne Braden was perceived as a link between the Old and New Left by 1960s southern activists; SSOC founder and Tennessee student activist Sue Thrasher recalled a conversation she had with Braden: "[Anne] told me ... in no uncertain terms that my generation was not the first actively to oppose segregation and that I owed it to myself to find out more about the radicals of the 1930s."[173] Historians Catherine Fosl and Anne Stefani have also argued that Braden's place in the movement bridged the two generations.[174]

SSOC benefitted from the financial and networking assistance provided by SCEF and the Bradens, but it also had to contend with lasting anti-Communist fears within the Old Left as a result. When the Southern Regional Council (SRC) gave SSOC a grant for operating funds in 1964, Leslie Dunbar, SRC's director, was initially concerned with SSOC's relations with the Bradens, with whom he and other southern liberals in SRC had strained relationships given the latter's potential Communist affiliations.[175] Leaders of progressive reform groups feared being viewed as sympathetic to Communism, a concern that at times complicated southern New Leftists' organizing.

Beyond demonstrating the similarity in the approaches self-consciously moderate white politicians in different locales took to limit racial change, viewing the Nashville sit-ins in a broader geographical framework and within the other student protests of the early to mid-1960s demonstrates the centrality of student power across different groups and organizations. Students across Tennessee were building on existing networks and, in some cases, momentum from campus chapters and groups, but they recognized there was something unique about the particular moment in early 1960 when the sit-in movement began. In joining together in this movement, Tennessee students conceptualized themselves as activists and leaders in larger numbers than previously seen. These examples of successful student organizing remained in popular memory, and as their demands for greater autonomy and racial equality grew over the decade, students drew upon lessons from the sit-in movement in later campus protests.

CHAPTER 3

Waging the Labor Struggle in Tennessee, 1964–1968

SSOC was an idealistic organization that believed its work could help to repair hundreds of years of racial oppression with well-intentioned policies. SSOC consciously sought to appropriate southern imagery for its avowedly interracial purpose. Its emblem featured a white hand and a Black hand embracing, with the Confederate flag in the background. This was very similar to SNCC's logo, which depicted a handshake between a Black hand and a white one on a blank background; SSOC's adoption of this symbol was most likely an intentional reference to SNCC, with the flag giving it a white southern inflection.[1] SSOC members believed that this symbol signified their commitment to build an interracial southern coalition for social change and would inspire other white southerners to join. Members saw the civil rights movement and especially 1964 (with the passage of the Civil Rights Act) as a turning point in history when the opportunity for poor whites and Blacks to unite for socioeconomic and political improvement was possible. While this moment of potential unification passed, Tennessee student activists remained busy building their coalitions.

Unlike previous iterations of student activism, Tennessee student activists found themselves operating on parallel tracks between 1964 and 1968. White students reckoned with their heritage as southerners and Black students increasingly found their voices in the language of Black Power. Both groups moved from sit-ins and campus-based protests to community-based activism during this time, bringing them into contact with labor activism.

Tennessee in the late 1960s witnessed two major interrelated, but distinct, student labor-organizing initiatives. Many white student activists, epitomized by SSOC, viewed labor as a means of uniting poor and working-class whites and Blacks in political action. Shared interests, they believed, would overcome racial divisions and produce sustained, community-driven initiatives. SSOC's connections to its southern cultural roots and the Populists, however, emphasize the idealism (if not naiveté) that compromised the group's work, and stretched the organization too thinly between campus and community organizing, and anti-Vietnam War initiatives. Contrasting with SSOC's ultimately futile efforts to create an interracial alliance, Black students in West Tennessee also viewed economics as central to their struggle, but within a Black Power–inspired, racially separatist context. Black Power concepts held currency among Black Tennessee students at least as early as 1963. The Memphis Sanitation Strike exposed generational divisions among Black youth and adult activists in Memphis, particularly with regards to perceptions of Black Power. Black students and youth in Memphis became integral to protests related to economic disparities and desegregation during the late 1960s. In addition to these motivations, students' pre-existing concerns over personal autonomy and racial inequality on university campuses, as well as the Vietnam War draft, influenced their approach to demonstrations in Memphis.

Sixties Populists: Nashville's SSOC and Southern Labor Organizing

The students who developed SSOC in 1964 wanted to connect their activism to the civil rights movement, specifically the student activism that SNCC represented so prominently. Their motivation for forming SSOC was to give white southern students a way to participate in the movement; they viewed their place within the period's activism as supporting the Black-led engagement. Unlike SNCC and SDS, which had defined themselves and their roles in student activism as the majority-Black and white counterparts of the New Left, SSOC attempted to forge an identity as an exclusively southern, majority-white organization. In terms of its conceptions of labor and race in the mid- to late 1960s, SSOC's unclear straddling of the existing SNCC and SDS organizations foreshadowed the eventual division that split its membership. SSOC's difficulties with intellectually conceptualizing its members as crusaders for progress was indicative of the challenging position many southern white activists encountered during this period. As will be discussed, the organization's membership included people who wanted to focus on ending the systemic economic inequality that they believed had created a rift between working-class whites and Blacks, but many others believed the organization's limited resources should go towards supporting civil rights protests and organizing white college students across the South. SSOC also believed that they were connected to the longer history of southern radical organizing, particularly the Populist movement.

Robb Burlage, a founding member of SDS and a graduate student at the University of Texas, wrote SSOC's founding statement, "We'll Take Our Stand," for the group's first meeting in the spring of 1964,[2] a direct reference to the Southern Agrarians' 1930 "I'll Take My Stand." SSOC's acceptance of "We'll Take Our Stand" as their manifesto as well as their founding in Nashville, where the Southern Agrarians had been based, reworked the original document and its message. Angered by essayist H. L. Mencken's criticisms of the South in his 1917 "The Sahara of the Bozart," which alleged that the region was "almost as sterile, artistically, intellectually, culturally, as the Sahara Desert," the Agrarians' statement asserted their intellectual pride in the South.[3] Burlage saw the Agrarians as radicals in their stance against southern industrialization, but also as racist products of their time period and place. He wanted SSOC both to connect to earlier organizing in the South and to stake out a new commitment to interracialism. Part of the manifesto read, "We as young Southerners hereby pledge to take *our* stand now together here to work for a new order, a new South, a place which embodies our ideals for all the world to emulate, not ridicule."[4]

Ironically, the dissolution of SSOC five years after its founding mirrored the short-lived Populists. References to the Populists appeared throughout the organization's literature as well as in retrospective accounts by former members, largely related to their attempt to politically unify working-class whites and Blacks under common goals. SSOC activists believed that, like the Populists, they had an opportunity to succeed by not "[fleeing] back to the false glory of [their] white skin" when things became difficult.[5] At a 2002 reunion of SSOC, member Lynn Wells recalled, "We were all [progressives]; those well-meaning people the Agrarians warned of. If SSOC did [represent a missed opportunity] perhaps it might have provided an independent place for young, idealistic Southern college students to have genuinely pondered the South's fate."[6] Furthermore, SSOC activists were inspired by activists of the earlier generation, particularly the Bradens of the SCEF and Myles Horton and Jim Dombrowski of Highlander; this influence reinforced SSOC's commitment to organizing workers into an interracial crusade based on shared economic interests.[7]

SSOC members' work in labor activism and intellectual ideas around labor organizing were informed by previous social movements. A former SSOC member recounted that SSOC participants "developed an appreciation of the relationship of the Civil Rights Movement to the history of labor organizing in the South and what was going on with people who were disadvantaged, who were being discriminated against, who were being exploited."[8] For SSOC activists, the late nineteenth century Populist Movement, the Great Depression–era Southern Tenant Farmers Union, and the CIO's organizing campaigns of the 1930s and 1940s demonstrated that biracial labor organizing could achieve significant social change.[9] This type of activism also compared to what historian Thomas Kiffmeyer has described as the post–World War II "cooperative, New Deal, top-down approach" where activists focused on "impoverished areas" like the Appalachian region.[10] While Populists had (at length) endeavored to gain control over their lives through political participation and many progressives sought a greater government presence in business practices, New Dealers attempted to combine the two concepts for social reform.[11] SSOC activists took this concept of socio-political activism and applied it to organizing on college campuses and communities alike. While the distinction between these two locations caused trouble for the organization later on, initially SSOC viewed organizing in both environments as different but complementary arms of the movement. SSOC's initiatives illustrate its belief that if it addressed the common issues facing workers in labor unions, then the racial differences between individuals would prove surmountable. SSOC activists believed that once labor problems were resolved, the cooperation that resulted between Blacks and whites in labor unions would spread biracial collaboration throughout the South.[12]

SSOC organizers initially distinguished themselves from SNCC and SDS as a regional, rather than national, organization. SSOC considered its role as, in large part, endeavoring to bring southern whites into the movement, and therefore it focused on the South, not the United States as a whole. That said, SNCC and SDS still viewed the South and its college campuses as potential spaces for expansion, despite SSOC's presence in the region. SNCC conceptualized southern universities as venues for continued public accommodations integration following the 1964 Civil Rights Act and for "recruitment" of new members.[13] SDS had strong economic principles and believed fervently that union organizing benefited society, but, with the exception of a few SDS chapters, its reach did not extend into the South.[14] SDS developed an agreement with SSOC to allow the newer organization to work in the area without impeding its efforts to organize campuses in the North. This arrangement, however, broke down during SSOC's existence.[15] There were SDS chapters on southern college campuses, but they were widely regarded as radical and contrary to the majority of students' opinions. SDS chapters existed at some southern campuses, such as Memphis State University, University of North Carolina-Chapel Hill, and the University of Texas at Austin.[16] SSOC explicitly claimed to represent the interests of more southern students than SDS. Administrators, including those in Tennessee, saw SDS's presence on campuses as a threat; they viewed the request by students to set up an SDS chapter as a sign of unrest. Debates over the right for SDS to be recognized concerned administrators at the

Knoxville campus of the University of Tennessee (UT) and Memphis State, as well as the student body and surrounding community members.[17] Neither was SSOC immune to the concerns of administrators. At UT, students questioned the Administrative Council's non-explanation of its vote to deny SSOC official recognition on the campus; the *Daily Beacon* described the situation as "a shining example" of "the highly infamous 'communications gap'" between students and faculty and administrators.[18]

In the words of a former participant, SSOC had, by 1966, "fashioned itself as a uniquely Southern group and had begun to grow as a membership organization—pro-civil rights, pro-labor, anti-Vietnam war."[19] The first edition of the *New Rebel*, SSOC's newsletter published in 1964, included an essay by Robb and Dorothy Burlage that contended that a successful southern progressive movement had to convince white southerners that economic issues overrode racial differences.[20] A draft proposal to SSOC written by a member in 1967 about her upcoming employment as a student worker in North Carolina included the following list of initiatives: "a) students and labor, b) students and community organizing, c) fostering of on-campus activities at individual schools and d) servicing of all these activities and tying them into SSOC."[21] SSOC focused on two types of labor organizing: assisting strikers in various locations across the South, often through educating fellow students on their campuses, and also running community-based programs that focused on improving material conditions for lower-income families.

SSOC's direct involvement with labor activism included participation in union efforts across the South and providing support for white workers. The main person behind SSOC's work with southern labor unions was Gene Guerrero, who was also influential in Emory University's attempt to support local unions, and was SSOC's first chairman in 1964.[22] Guerrero helped to organize an April 1966 SSOC conference at Durham's historically Black North Carolina College, on students' participation in labor issues.[23] Beginning in the fall of 1966, Guerrero worked with Textile Workers Union of America organizers to unionize textile workers in North Carolina.[24] SSOC organizers worked with the American Federation of Labor and Congress of Industrial Organizations (AFL-CIO) to support migrant farm workers' attempts to unionize in 1966, which resulted in the 1967 creation of a local chapter of the United Packinghouse Workers of America in Belle Glade, Florida.[25] SSOC also participated in several strikes in 1968: sanitation workers in Memphis (discussed later in this chapter); textile workers in Dayton, Tennessee; meat cutters in Tennessee, Florida, and Virginia; tobacco workers in Virginia and North Carolina; mine workers in West Virginia; and even the work of the United Farm Workers Organizing Committee for California migrant workers.[26] SSOC's work with striking unions involved publicity about the event on college campuses, occasionally boycotting the company's product, and contacting the strikers and assisting in various ways such as standing on the picket line or making coffee for the strikers.[27] As historian Gregg Michel has noted, while these campaigns had been largely unsuccessful, they were not without promise. "SSOC had shown that white students were capable of connecting with working whites." Moreover, "the union campaigns represented a moment of possibility, a point in time when it seemed conceivable that workers and students, black and white, could unite in common cause."[28]

SSOC activists also worked to create sustainable societal change through grassroots organizing among southern whites. SSOC's rationale was that if poorer whites received similar educational advantages to those the civil rights activists attempted to give African American communities, these individuals would realize how much they had in common with disenfranchised southern Blacks and might join in support for civil rights reforms. While different from labor union organizing, these projects demonstrated another side to the effort to unite the South along class lines. One of SSOC's earliest attempts to organize within the South was the White Community Project (otherwise known as the "White Folks Project") that focused on organizing working-class whites in Mississippi on economic issues, beginning in the summer of 1964. This project's approach mirrored the grassroots organizing that SNCC had earlier employed while promoting Black voter registration throughout the Deep South during Freedom Summer, but focused on local whites.[29] Sue Thrasher, one of the Nashville founders of SSOC, wrote of the project in the *Southern Patriot*, the SCEF newsletter, that "it was hoped that work in the white community would closely parallel that in the Negro community—freedom schools, community centers, voter education and registration."[30] The project exposed several key tensions: disagreements regarding the extent to which the organization should be invested in community organizing as opposed to campus-based activities and whether project workers should focus on working-class or middle-class Mississippians were front and center. The project ultimately sought to persuade middle-class Mississippians to support the civil rights movement, but with very little success.[31]

The Southern Labor Action Movement (SLAM) was a SSOC-affiliated initiative that represented SSOC's regional focus on labor, but by specifically focusing on organizing white blue-collar workers.[32] SLAM emerged from a cohort within SSOC that believed earlier work with local whites, largely the White Community Project, could have been successful if focused on working-class, rather than middle-class, whites. It aimed to help students educate strikers about their rights, inform white community members about the long history of labor organizing, and to lead other students in demonstrations for labor efforts.³³ Sam Shirah, a white SNCC field secretary who had been part of SSOC's founding, conceived of SLAM after working with the International Ladies' Garment Workers Union in Atlanta, Georgia, where he came to believe that workers' needs were not being addressed.³⁴ Like some of the Populists who had attempted to unite working-class Blacks and whites, some SSOC activists believed that organizing poor whites over labor issues would unite white and Black workers by class and similar, shared economic initiatives.³⁵ Not all SSOC members agreed that white labor organizing was a direction the organization should go in, demonstrating the diversity of opinions in an activist organization like SSOC and illustrating the difficulties in deciding the best approach to southern reform. In one SSOC proposal from May 1967, the feelings of some members of SSOC were articulated as: "Our work is with the campus, not with labor ... It is valuable for us to relate students to the sufferings of some of the workers in the South, but we should not turn into a southern labor organizing committee."³⁶ This concern mirrored Highlander's emphasis on regional interracial labor organizing.³⁷

SLAM was a short-lived initiative, lasting only three months; its single enterprise was providing support for a wildcat strike at a Levi-Strauss Co. plant in Blue Ridge, Georgia, an Appalachian town in the northern part of the state. According to SSOC members reflecting retrospectively, SLAM's support for workers striking against their own union drove a wedge between it and SSOC.³⁸ Regarding the AFL-CIO, a prospectus for SLAM stated that "the AFL-CIO must shoulder its share of the blame [for the failure of southern labor organizing in the past, for] ... the narrow materialism of its goals [and] the authoritarianism of its structure".³⁹ SSOC members tended to be more deferential to established unions than were SLAM activists.

Two further projects led by and involving white southern student activists were indicative of the move to focus on community organizing of working-class and poor white southerners, and had connections with Tennessee. They speak to the centrality of ideas around anti-poverty reform during the mid-1960s across the South and the country more generally, as well as the interest young activists had in projects like these. The first project was the Appalachian Volunteers (AV), which was created by the Council of the Southern Mountains (CSM) in 1964. Oak Ridge, Tennessee, native and AV participant George Brosi recalled that his next step into community organizing, after participating in the civil rights movement on a local level, was picketing a segregated laundromat in Oak Ridge in 1961. Brosi participated in the first AV project, a trip to Harlan County, Kentucky, where college students and CSM staff repainted a schoolhouse over the holidays in 1963–1964.⁴⁰ The majority of the CSM's (and by extension, AV's) focus geographically was on eastern Kentucky, but the project drew interest from Tennessee student activists, and its existence speaks to the regionality of similar reform efforts.[41] The CSM, like SNCC and indeed The Brotherhood mentioned in the first chapter of this book, saw a clear connection between their work and their religious convictions. CSM executive director Perley Ayer described the CSM as "[serving] the Appalachian South in a religiously motivated fellowship which has united leaders and efforts of almost every conceivable interest and diversity in one common cause."[42]

The second project, SSOC's North Nashville Project of 1966, demonstrated an effort to organize "blue-collar whites on such issues as poverty, unemployment, and economic empowerment," with a particular focus on neighborhood white youth who were either employed in the workforce or unemployed non-students.[43] The program attempted to work within the lower income, working-class community of North Nashville, much like the earlier White Community Project, but with a greater understanding of the challenges and dangers of working as organizers in such an environment. North Nashville, a predominantly Black area of the city, included Tennessee State and Fisk University. Urban renewal and increasing suburbanization in the 1960s led to the neighborhood gradually becoming more segregated.[44] The project was also controversial in the eyes of many white political leaders in Nashville because it received federal funds from the Office of Economic Opportunity (OEO) and because of SSOC's connection with SNCC. The skepticism of and paranoia towards community organizations like the North Nashville Project for their perceived Black radical connections and federal funding was part of a region-wide white reluctance to support anti-poverty programs.[45]

Similar organizing efforts focused on community welfare development of working-class whites outside the South, demonstrating the continuity of these community-based initiatives during the era. Working with whites, white student activists believed, would help garner support for civil rights issues along class lines. Community action groups elsewhere in America operated in similar ways to SSOC. An arm of SDS for example, the Economic Research Action Project (ERAP), worked within communities to unify Blacks and whites politically along economic lines.[46] According to historian Jennifer Frost, ERAP "challenges the emphasis" in past accounts of student participation in 1960s activism that have privileged campus and anti-war aspects of this activity.[47] One ERAP program, Jobs or Income Now (JOIN), was based in Chicago beginning in 1963. JOIN endeavored to lay the groundwork for student activists to continue participation in reform efforts in poor neighborhoods. In contrast to SSOC, which attempted to combine its focus on community organizing with college campus activism, JOIN's purpose was to take students off campus and into local workplaces.[48] As one of several groups that viewed class-based and racial organizing as two integrally tied initiatives, JOIN and other similar groups operated as many New Leftists did: they formed connections with established organizations like SCEF and a New Orleans–based group, Grassroots Organizing Work (GROW), political parties such as the Black Panthers, and labor unions.[49]

Working-class white southerners who had relocated to the North were also the focus of some New Leftist organizing, demonstrating the continuity of these ideas around community activism as well as the prevalence of systemic economic inequality. By this time, Chicago's poor neighborhood Uptown had large numbers of poor whites from Appalachia living there, making this group an unusual example of a southern white ethnic minority in the North.[50] Pushed out of the region by the coal industry's shift to increased mechanization and changes to demands for coal on the global market, Appalachians moved out of the South into areas of the North and Midwest in unprecedented numbers.[51] CSM was concerned about this significant migration of Appalachians out of the area, both in terms of the "'brain and talent' drain" that the region was left with as well as how to assist these former southerners in adjusting to urban life in the North.[52] Another Chicago-based group that emerged out of the city's Appalachian white migrant population in conjunction with the New Left, the Young Patriots Organization, redefined the symbolism of the Confederate flag, much as SSOC did. The Young Patriots wore the flag on their clothing as a symbol of their cultural identification with an oppressed group.[53]

SSOC's work in labor activism was part of a broader trend of white activists to work within their own communities organizing southern whites. In early 1967, SSOC activists participated in a conference with "mostly civil rights movement veterans . . . to discuss community organization and [how] their attention was turned toward trade unions" in Washington, D.C. The Conference on Radical Vocations in the White Community was unique because of the strong southern presence. "When compared to the multitude of 'new left' activists' conferences over the past few years, what was new about this meeting was the accent on labor," stated one account of the event.[54] In his correspondence with historian C. Vann Woodward in March 1967, SSOC and SDS organizer Ed Hamlett discussed the Washington conference. "Very much in response to their request [from SNCC] that we go build the other part of that great coalition that everyone dreams of," Hamlett wrote, "there was a meeting of a lot [of] people who once worked in the black community to talk about vocations in the white community. . . . It turned out pretty good . . . [and] indicated that a batch of folks are thinking seriously of white community organizing."[55]

As the decade drew to an end, students began to discuss more radical considerations tied to institutional racism in the economy and labor. SSOC youth activists were still focused on traditional labor issues throughout the South, particularly in Tennessee, West Virginia, and Mississippi, as students took part in manufacturing strikes and spoke out on their campuses about these topics.[56] Historian Terry Anderson has argued that on a national scale, Vietnam acted as a wedge between union workers and student activists, such as in 1967 when SDS activists failed to form an alliance with the Progressive Labor Party over the issue of the AFL-CIO publicly supporting U.S. involvement in Vietnam.[57] While the Progressive Labor Party, the Black Panthers, the Socialist Workers Party, and SDS (which all had student participation in their organizations) called for the death of capitalism, they were a very small minority of the larger student movement during the late 1960s.[58] At a May 1967 SSOC conference entitled "The Role of the Southern Radical in the American Left," an SDS member proposed that SDS and SSOC merge over their shared labor interests, but SSOC rejected the proposal.[59] Many SSOC members perceived SDS's Marxist notions of organizing the world's workers into a racism-free fight against capitalism as too extreme to work within the South.

SDS and SSOC coexisted in a complicated relationship until 1969, a mere ten weeks prior to SSOC's own dissolution in June of that year.[60] While a number of factors contributed to the dissolution, the increasingly radicalized discussion over capitalism and race played a significant role. SSOC's dissolution document was one of the few examples of white southern radicalism to put racial liberation in a global perspective.[61] The document stated, "The basis of white racism in this country is both of a class and a colonial nature. . . . Black and brown peoples are oppressed both as a caste of a class and as a people. We see that contradictions among the people are used by imperialists against the people. White racism serves to divide black and white workers, and allows the capitalists to engage in super-exploitation and oppression of black workers."[62] In fact, these ideas of global racism and capitalism were present in New Left organizing as early as the 1964 Free Speech Movement in Berkeley. One participant claimed the movement "should be . . . an impetus to American radicals to finally kick the labor metaphysic and drop the vulgar Marxist belief . . . that men must be hungry or unemployed or discriminated against to participate in radical political action."[63] What is clear, however, is that the New Left had not found a way to incorporate these ideas into the mainstream movement. Instead, by the late 1960s, many within the white New Left had become less interested in labor, but instead viewed Black militancy as the new source of revolution. From this perspective, it was less important for the New Left to "understand labor."[64]

SSOC members' self-assessment of the organization's dissolution presented two main reasons: SSOC's broad (and numerous) initiatives and the difficulty it encountered in presenting itself as progressively southern while appropriating "Old South" cultural references. These methods, while ambitious, ultimately brought the group's downfall as SSOC stretched itself too thinly and too ambiguously on its core principles and initiatives. Indeed, their idealistic belief in appropriating regional symbols of secession and the Confederate flag as a means to inspire white college students to join SSOC and participate in the civil rights movement had little chance of working on a large scale. Moreover SSOC also had difficulties including multiple college chapters' different needs and initiatives under one organizational umbrella.

Identity as a regional organization aside, many of the problems SSOC encountered were administrative as the campus/community-focused initiatives put forward by each chapter presented too many varying directions for the organization to sufficiently cover. Former members criticized SSOC on multiple grounds, largely centered on the perceived failings of its economic initiatives, but also on its New Left origins. In SSOC's dissolution statement, members proposed that because "liberals see social problems as soluble within a capitalistic framework," SSOC, having bought into this liberalism, would never be able to achieve its goals because it did not view "social problems as symptoms of class antagonisms under capitalism." It suggested that grassroots programs such as VISTA and the War on Poverty in general were doomed to failure like SSOC because they operated within this capitalist structure rather than being truly radical and outside capitalism's parameters.[65] Community action programs, as evidenced by numerous personal accounts, presented different challenges from campus organizing in that tangible results were slower to emerge and therefore more difficult to advertise as evidence for the value of the work undertaken.

The final reason for SSOC's demise, as evidenced by the organization's dissolution document, was its intention to help build an interracial coalition that would spread outside the South. As stated in the document, "No mass-based white student organization, regardless of its structure, can keep going as a regional one because our struggle is not a regional one."[66] SSOC's strength, its members contended, was also its Achilles heel; SSOC idealistically believed that it could remake the South into a place of interracial cooperation and economic progress by empowering the lower classes, just as Populists had believed. Increasingly divergent focuses for white and Black activists, as well as the Vietnam War, presented challenges to this attempt at an interracial, equal organization. However, it is important to note that notions of interracial civil rights–based and class-conscious organizing did not end with the dissolution of SSOC and SDS. A student organization based out of Atlanta, Georgia, and Los Angeles, California, named the October League, "arose," in one historian's words, "from the ashes" of SSOC and SDS.[67] The October League is evidence of the salience of the radical, interracial organization SSOC members envisioned, and indicates that while SSOC may have dissolved in 1969, its vision did not necessarily die with it.

While there still remains a great deal to discover about the depth and expanse of labor connections with respect to student activism in Tennessee, it is clear that the southern student movement of the 1960s clearly drew connections between itself and the Populists, as well as unintentionally emulating their trajectory as a short-lived, idealistic social movement. As a former member of SSOC recounted, the organization "brought together... people who had initiated or been involved in civil rights activities at the local level... [with] the history of labor organizing in the South and what was going on with people who were disadvantaged, who were being discriminated against, who were being exploited, including Appalachian Whites."[68] As Thomas Kiffmeyer's work on Appalachian student activism focused on poverty reform has demonstrated, however, it mattered where the reformers were from. Southerners working in the South, and specifically in Appalachia as seen in Kiffmeyer's research, were seen as less threatening than people from outside the region. "In short, the War on Poverty magnified the social, political, economic, and cultural problems precipitated by the collision of class, culture, urban and rural values, and corporate domination—and not just in Appalachia, but nationwide."[69] These tensions were evident most clearly in white southern student activism, throughout Tennessee as well as regionally. The radicalism of the white Tennessee students during the mid- to late 1960s, specifically those in SSOC, occurred in parallel with Black activists' escalated organizing with Black Power–influenced principles.

Civil Rights, Labor, Anti-Poverty Initiatives, and Black Power Converge on Memphis

Conceptions of Black Power percolated on college campuses in the late 1960s. As with many other advocates of the ideology, Black Tennessee radicals rarely presented a concise version of what they meant by Black Power. These students articulated multiple, at times seemingly contradictory, versions of the concept. Broadly, they promoted Black economic and political empowerment and greater cultural awareness for African Americans. They also rejected total nonviolence in favor of armed self-defense. Nonetheless, individuals and groups—notably the Invaders—promoted a mix of pluralism (the belief that peaceful coexistence with other groups in the United States was achievable once proponents had secured greater Black Power, and, to a lesser extent, revolutionary nationalism (the notion that one group would inevitably dominate others, so Blacks should use violence to advance their goals).[70]

As the 1968 Memphis Sanitation Strike demonstrated, Black students organized around these concepts and significantly impacted the strike's development. Narratives of the strike have, until very recently, been dominated by the roles of the strikers, municipal leadership, union organizers, and civil rights activists.[71] Black college students in Tennessee justified armed self-defense at least as early as March 1963, when Fisk University student Ray Hanson wrote an article for the *Fisk University Forum* questioning the successes of nonviolent protest, and vocalizing support for Robert F. Williams, a Black advocate of armed self-defense. Hanson asked, "Can American Negroes be expected to sit tight and let the cigarettes burn out on their backs while other dark-skinned peoples the world over are daily shattering the myths of white supremacy?"[72] Unlike white activists who saw organizing working-class whites as a tactic to promote racial change, Black student activists in Tennessee (and particularly those in Memphis in 1968) brought Black Power concepts to their participation in the sanitation strike. To them, race was central to the workers' struggle.

Memphis, in the years after President Lyndon B. Johnson's Great Society pledge and the passage of major civil rights legislation, witnessed a convergence of politics and labor initiatives. Almost 60 percent of Black Memphis families lived below the poverty line in the mid-1960s, a figure that far exceeded both the local white poverty rate and national Black poverty levels.[73] Following poor rural migration into the city and continued economic polarization, national headlines described in detail the violence and community tensions of the Memphis Sanitation Strike in 1968. The protests that surprised the city's whites arose from the economic plight of the city's poor. Grassroots activists sought to bind together labor and racial issues and to involve students and youth as well as adults within the wider community. These efforts built upon years of social activism locally. Speaking to the strong network of grassroots activism in Memphis, historian Harry Holloway has speculated that Memphis saw more sit-ins and boycotts than any other American city during the 1960s.[74] For Black Memphis college students in particular, the alignment of Black Power and student power was clear.

Federally funded efforts to reduce economic disparities in Memphis drew on the Economic Opportunity Act's "maximum feasible participation" qualification to involve many poor Black residents in community action programs. Racial issues defined differences between Black youth and adults involved in the Sanitation Strike. The young Black activists were frustrated by what they perceived as the slow racial progress Memphis Black leaders presided over, and alternatively, the adult leaders saw the younger protestors as instigating violence with their interest in Black Power activism.

As with elsewhere across the country, in Memphis there was overlap between anti-poverty initiatives, civil rights activism, and Black Power in terms of leadership, participation in organizations, and in white leadership's concerns about the groups.[75] The 1968 Sanitation Strike originated from frustrations and concerns among local minority residents over poverty and racial discrimination, spurred by a tragic accident after municipal sanitation workers had endured years of financial hardship. Students and community organizers interacted during Memphis protests to lead the demonstrations, which exposed tensions within the African American community regarding the ideals and perceptions of Black Power and anti-poverty programs, as well as concerns over the direction of the national civil rights movement.

Several organizations were central to this activism, and their participants represented the varying backgrounds and initiatives tied up in the effort. Two that represented the older generation of Blacks in Memphis, the NAACP and the Committee on the Move for Equality (COME), led by Rev. James Lawson, frequently considered younger Black activists too radical and inclined towards violence. The Neighborhood Organizing Project (NOP), a War on Poverty grassroots anti-poverty and civil rights program active in the city, included both older and younger Black activists among its participants, which, in addition to the difficulties it faced in warding off accusations of exploiting federal funds as an anti-poverty program, complicated its direction at times. Finally, the Black Organizing Project (BOP), an "umbrella organization" for Black youth groups in Memphis, included members of the Black Student Association (BSA) at Memphis State, as well as the Invaders, a local Black Power group under surveillance by the Counter Intelligence Program of the FBI (COINTELPRO).[76]

War on Poverty projects first arrived in Memphis in 1965 with the influx of $46,500 from initial applications by city officials to the OEO. The funds went to the local War on Poverty Committee (WOPC), which distributed them to programs seeking to reduce the city's economic disparities. The WOPC was composed of sixty-six individuals who represented various community organizations and the city government.[77] Of these Memphis programs (numbering over twenty by mid-1967), the NOP best represented the coordination between adult community leaders and youths within OEO-funded programs.[78]

Other organizations took the lead, most notably Lawson's group, COME, and another Memphis WOPC-funded program, Memphis Area Project-South (MAP-South). MAP-South was a community program in South Memphis that, in its 1965 constitution, affirmed it would work "to develop the economic, environmental, and social conditions of the citizens of the area."[79] Many of the strikers were members of MAP-South through their families.[80] It had initially welcomed Black Power supporters, hiring local Black Power leaders Coby Smith and Charles Cabbage to work with poor, Black youths in South Memphis. But pressure from WOPC forced MAP-South to fire them in 1967.[81] Still, MAP-South retained a connection with poor Blacks, particularly youth who were increasingly frustrated by the lack of opportunities for economic advancement.

A contemporary of MAP-South was the NOP, another Memphis WOPC program, with canvassers who were simultaneously members of the BOP and the Invaders; the latter group voiced the need for racial equality in terms similar to the national Black Panther Party in Oakland.[82] The NOP attempted to educate community members about voting rights and working together to affect political change, as well as providing education about Black culture more broadly. Its nonviolent initiatives, however, clashed with public perception of the Black Panther Party and Black Power more generally. The association of the BOP with the Invaders presented significant challenges for WOPC programs throughout Memphis as the jarring rhetoric of the most militant Black Power advocates encouraged the popular belief among the white and Black middle class that young Black activists wished to achieve equality through any means, including violent ones, in direct contrast to the WOPC's mission. The NOP's association with the Invaders damaged the former's credibility.[83] The head of the NOP was fired in 1968 following the discovery that the Invaders had been holding meetings at one of the project's offices in Memphis.[84]

The BOP was a Black Power group that functioned as an "umbrella" for Black student organizations on campuses as well as Black youth community groups. In addition to the Memphis State BSA and the Invaders, it also included other campus organizations and the LeMoyne College's Intercollegiate Chapter of the NAACP, which demonstrated further generational divisions within the city's Black community as the NAACP was particularly strong in Memphis.[85] Charles Cabbage and Coby Smith formed the BOP in the summer of 1967. According to Smith, the BOP "organized in the streets, in the schools, in the churches, in the pool rooms" for members, targeting young Blacks who had, in his words, never had anyone "communicate with them . . . you've got to be able to relate to them and to understand their problems."[86] Representatives from each organization affiliated with the BOP sent their leader to BOP meetings, and that smaller group of the BOP would discuss issues and make resolutions for the individual organizations to pursue.[87] Cabbage described the BOP as a way for younger Black activists to "control their communities" through "control of economics, the politics, the social life as well as the cultural life."[88]

Black Memphis State students regarded the development of Black studies programs and the BSA at their university as a promising, if long overdue, step towards their equality with their fellow students. Black activists were angry about widespread student apathy (among fellow students, Black and white) towards their concerns. The chairman of the Memphis State BSA in 1968, Ronald Ivy, identified a significant difference between organizing at Memphis State as opposed to at LeMoyne or Owen Colleges, namely that the LeMoyne and Owen students were more politically aware and less apathetic. Political organizing on these all-Black campuses with established NAACP campus representation differed from the experiences of Memphis State students. "When I first came out here, I saw something lacking. . . . Memphis State students always seemed so backwards," Ivy recalled. "They knew what was in the books . . . but they didn't know anything about what was happening in the world."[89] The strike became one of the tactics used by Black student organizers at Memphis State to animate their peers. Indeed, one BSA member, Eddie Jenkins, recalled that the strike—unlike other unifying points for Black students—was an "issue to rally around and not just a cause."[90] Dismayed at student apathy and Black campus life, another African American student at Memphis State in 1968 declared the university "a wet noodle." He claimed that "there won't be any real integration at the university . . . until a black student can be involved in campus activities and still maintain his identity as a black student who has black characteristics and a black culture."[91] This was almost a decade after the school's token integration. Evidently, resentment among Black students over conditions in newly desegregated higher education lingered well beyond desegregation.

Members of the Memphis State BSA also wanted to be taken seriously in the community, and articulated their desire to be considered different from white youth activists in Memphis. During a demonstration in 1968, a BSA member at Memphis State declared that "black people can organize for better black people and for a better America. We don't want what you've got. We want to get something for ourselves."[92] Memphis State BSA members also articulated their reluctance towards outright violence as a means to achieve political authority, which differentiated them from other Black activists as well as more radical white student activists. David Acey, a leader of the Memphis State BSA, recalled, "We never wanted them [the Memphis SDS] involved because we knew white boys were crazy. They're blowing shit up. We couldn't have that because we didn't know what they were going to do."[93] Highlighting differences between competing strands of Black Power ideology, students who affiliated with the BSA were generally less inclined towards a violent overthrow of the system, which the Invaders seemingly advocated.

The Memphis State BSA encouraged the university to hire more African American faculty and staff, to create scholarships for deserving Black students, and to provide part-time jobs for Black students at the university to help them attend school.[94] African American student demands on Memphis campuses, however, lacked unity, mirroring more general African American debates over Black Power. While general Black Power concepts remained at the forefront of discussions of students' roles on campuses and in the city, many students were reluctant to self-identify as followers of Black Power. Memphis State BSA chairman Ronald Ivy said that the reactions between Black and white students on the campus to expressions such as "black power" and "black revolution" were equally negative.[95]

While the BOP focused on political representation as a means for organizing Black youths, the Invaders were known as the "military end" of the BOP. As one member recalled, the Invaders were "responsible for security, for putting out sheets on guerrilla warfare, [and] training people in liberation tactics."[96] Accounts from former members presented conflicting descriptions of the organization. A BOP leader and member of the Invaders, Calvin Taylor, described the members behaving as "everyday, ordinary people act," in order to hide their true objective. "If you saw me downtown, I'd look like any other shopper downtown and you wouldn't know if I was . . . a black man . . . getting ready to bomb your place or just a black man in the city."[97] However, once the sanitation strike began, the Invaders were adamant that, while their language may have indirectly encouraged younger Blacks unaffiliated with the group to riot, the Invaders themselves had not told anyone to behave violently. Taylor recalled, "We represented the [frustrated] element that really did break it [the windows of storefronts during the riots], but these people were not controlled by us."[98] Memphis police and the FBI blamed violence in Memphis during the period on the Invaders, and by extension the WOPC programs, but the size of the Invaders' membership remains uncertain, putting in question the group's actual influence. Historian Laurie Green has estimated that only about 100 African American youths participated in the Invaders, but one of the leaders claimed the group numbered over 300 at its peak, and another account estimated membership between 1,500 and 2,000 in early 1968.[95] According to the FBI's COINTELPRO, the Invaders had disintegrated by 1970.[100]

African Americans in Memphis were far from unified over the best strategy to improve the economic and political future of the city's Blacks. Oftentimes differences in opinion on this subject were divided along age lines. Older people largely viewed Black Power cautiously and with reservations about its effectiveness, but younger activists also split on the subject. Speaking of the Invaders in 1968, an older Memphis radio station disc jockey, Nat D. Williams of WDIA, claimed their militancy would be better directed towards education and job training. He exclaimed, "The Invaders ought to lead their followers into an invasion of night schools . . . such an invasion should be a major program of their black militancy. Then will begin the real 'march' to the realization of the black 'man' image . . . rather than the 'boy' designation."[101] For Williams, and many older African American leaders, the Invaders were nothing more than a rebellious group of youths who were misguided in their beliefs that violence was the answer to resolving the inequalities they experienced every day.

These three forces—established Black leadership, community-based antipoverty programs, and Black students inspired by Black Power—converged in Memphis during the late 1960s. A "vacuum" of activism, created by the two very different influences of former mayor and political boss E. H. Crump's political machine and strong NAACP leadership in Memphis, existed among working-class individuals and younger Black activists in the city.[102] Many Black youths and laborers found themselves without "representation" in political leadership in Memphis after the sit-in demonstrations, and so when the sanitation strike occurred, both groups, searching for a cause, seized the opportunity to act. While Black workers across the city, from public school teachers to janitorial staff, were barred from skilled job opportunities and job advancement, historian Michael Honey has argued that conditions for sanitation workers in particular "exemplified" the worst position for Blacks, given the meagre wages and hard labor.[103] Therefore, when the tinderbox of frustrations and desperation the city's sanitation workers felt was lit at the beginning of February 1968, the resulting strike gained the support of the majority of the city's African Americans, and consequently became more than just a strike; it grew into a movement for civil rights reform in Memphis unlike the city had ever seen.

On February 1, 1968, two Memphis sanitation workers, huddling inside the back of their garbage truck to wait out a rain shower, were crushed by a faulty mechanism in the truck. The men who were killed, Echol Cole and Robert Walker, and their fellow workers routinely worked long hours doing physically demanding tasks for little pay, coped with old, faulty equipment that the city refused to replace, and faced the constant threat that a rainy day meant they would not be paid, and that the Department of Public Works could fire them at any time.[104] Led by fellow sanitation worker T. O. Jones, almost 1,300 sanitation workers went on strike on February 12, 1968.[105] Of the period prior to the strike, Jones's son recalled that Jones told him, "They don't realize that if they come together, that they can overcome these things." This concept of uniting together to overthrow "the system" would seem like a rallying call for young Black activists who were looking for their chance to enact real political change.[106]

The striking men were supported by the union American Federation of State, County, and Municipal Employees (AFSCME) in terms of advice, but they chose to perform a "work stoppage" rather than an official strike, in Jones's words. This meant that they participated in the strike without the certainty of financial support during the strike, until they would be able to form a union on their own.[107] When Henry Loeb, the mayor of Memphis, and the Memphis city council refused to acknowledge the strikers, and declared the strike illegal, marches that would continue through March began.[108] Friction existed between the Black workers and majority-white Memphis labor officials and union members; as Rev. Harold Middlebrook recalled, "labor was not used to having 1,300 black men out on strike, on a strike that labor did not call, and on a strike where there was no contract, there was no recognition of the union."[109] Many African Americans in Memphis were angered by what they viewed as the white municipal leadership's disregard of Black complaints related to the sanitation strike. When Blacks denounced Mayor Loeb's hiring of non-union workers to replace strikers, Loeb appeared confused as to why the reaction was so negative, saying, "We're not trying to break the men. We want them back."[110]

Several demonstrations around the strike turned violent; the most notable of these occurred on March 28. Prior to the scheduled demonstration on March 28, COME and BOP leaders went to high schools and colleges throughout Memphis to encourage students to march with them downtown that day. At majority-Black Hamilton High School in South Memphis, students who wished to attend the march clashed with police who were stationed at the school to maintain order. Out of the three thousand to five thousand marchers on March 28, a majority were students from high school and college.[111] In addition to the chaos created by the rioting, one Black sixteen-year-old was killed, sixty-two people were injured, and 218 people were arrested. The looting that day resulted in an estimated $400,000 in damages.[112]

One Invader said of the riot, "Man, if you expect honkies to get the message, you got to break some windows."[113] Yet the Invaders seemed to lack a unified plan; would they instigate violence, or would they distance themselves from the event as much as possible? It appears that the Invaders as well as the BOP were split on this point. BOP leader and Invader Calvin Taylor described a significant difference between himself and those Black youths who participated in the riot, calling them "Stokely Carmichaels who wanted to see their names in the paper the next day" who therefore "decided that this was the moment to make the trouble."[114]

FIG. 2. College workshop at Highlander Folk School, April 1959. Courtesy of Wisconsin Historical Society.

FIG. 3. Founding members of the Southern Student Organizing Committee (SSOC) at a committee meeting. Seated on floor, left to right: Dan Harmeling, Harry Boyte, Sue Thrasher, Cathy Cade, Marjorie Henderson. Top row, left to right: Sam Shirah, Jerry Gainey, Roy Money, Gene Guerrero, Ed Hamlett, Jim Williams, John Shively, Bob Potter, Bob Richardson, Marion Barry Jr. Courtesy of Wisconsin Historical Society.

FIG. 4. The UT Vietnam Moratorium office depicting the poster declaring "Students Are Slaves!" October 1969. Courtesy of University of Tennessee, Knoxville Libraries.

FIG. 5. President Cecil C. Humphreys talks to student demonstrators, May 1970. Courtesy of University of Memphis Libraries.

FIG. 6. Carroll Bible, dressed in a robe, holds up a sign saying "Let Our People Go" at the Nixon/Graham protest, May 1970. Courtesy of Betsey B. Creekmore Special Collections and University Archives, University of Tennessee, Knoxville.

FIG. 7. Memphis businessman Ned Cook hangs in effigy as Sallie Broshears and Tom Wells, members of the MTSU People's Bicentennial Commission, man a table at an event, October 1975. Courtesy of the Albert Gore Research Center, Middle Tennessee State University.

James Lawson encouraged Martin Luther King Jr. to come to Memphis to help the strikers gain control over their demonstrations. Once he arrived, King was dismayed when the debate over Black Power became, in his view, central to the protest. Marking an unusual instance where he appeared shaken (from fear of escalating violence as a result of the demonstration), King led the march.[115] One protestor remembered King saying that he was led to believe the demonstration was nonviolent. But the involvement of Black Power advocates made him realize that the commitment to nonviolence was tenuous.[116] He did not consider Black Power activists as responsible for rioting; instead, King attributed civic unrest to conflicts over War on Poverty programs and the reluctance of Memphis whites to improve conditions for Blacks.[117] Still, tensions escalated between King and the Invaders and other younger Black Power protestors. Corroborating King's concerns over the limited commitment to nonviolent protest, Coby Smith recalled that "most of us who were considered to be militants were trained in the nonviolent movement, so it was not a question of us not believing in nonviolence, it was that we saw nonviolence as a tactic and a tactic alone."[118] King wanted no association with Black Power in Memphis. In contrast, adult Black leadership in Memphis were inclined to use the Invaders as a threat. Smith remembered the threat as, "Either you deal with us [ministers] or you have to deal with the violent mob."[119] The sanitation strike demonstrated that a shift in the civil rights movement had indeed occurred, with King seemingly unable to keep the young Blacks from rioting, and labor becoming even more central to the region's civil rights movement.[120]

Memphis Blacks were angry not just about local Black poverty, but also unfair Vietnam War draft policies. Realizing that the poorest young men, disproportionately Black, were being drafted for the war in greater numbers than their white counterparts infuriated Black and white student activists alike.[121] One LeMoyne College student wrote during the strike that "many youths are afraid of being drafted and are tired of being discriminated against in job opportunities. In short, they do not care [whether] they die here or in Vietnam—either way they will die a useless death."[122] In August 1968, the city's underground newspaper, *The Liberator*, further revealed the extent of perceived economic injustice among Black Memphis students:

> Oh, there ain't no flies on Memphis, and there ain't no rats on Loeb;
> And our troubles are not piling up (are they?) like the trials of fabled Job.
> The garbage dumps: they aren't stinking. And the Wolf: smells like French perfume.
> And the ghettos, they ain't crowded; with only 10 to a room! . . .

Explain that HOLLOMAN'S POLICE FORCE won't harm a hair on your head
If you're dressed in a silk tuxedo, and can prove that you're dead & not red!
Cause their tanks & their clubs & their tear gas, make it easy for you and me
To attend brother Billy LOEB'S PARTY (during curfew!) to drown our ennui![123]

Another underground newspaper, *The Apex*, written by Memphis State University students, proclaimed, "A garbage pile-up is an odd punishment for the Negroes and other poor people of Memphis. They have lived with garbage all their lives and a little more here or there is not going to affect them."[124]

These sentiments from Black students starkly contrasted with the views of most white Memphis State students. In a class on American labor history, when asked whether they supported Loeb's administration or the strikers, eleven of the twenty-one students expressed support for the city government's actions. Their views stressed how entrenched racial divisions were within Memphis, yet the closely divided white students indicated that white student opinion was far from unanimously opposed to Black economic demands by the late 1960s. While some of the students mentioned it was "unfair" that Black sanitation workers earned less than their white peers, they felt the workers were putting the city at risk of civic unrest or public health crises.[125]

In the aftermath of King's assassination, Memphis's entrenched racial inequalities continued to fester in the strike discussions. On April 5, 1968, the day after King's assassination, a meeting was held in Loeb's office between strike organizers, Memphis ministers, and Loeb. With a loaded rifle hidden under his desk for protection, the mayor insisted that, despite the tragic circumstances surrounding King's assassination, the city was in no position to meet the demands of the strikers. Angered by Loeb's dismissal of the strikers' demands, the Presbyterian chaplain at Memphis State, Dick Moon, led a sit-in outside Loeb's office for over a week. The group of five protestors fasting in city hall and in support of the strike included Memphis State student Jimmy Gates and Memphis State instructor Richard Geller.[126] In the days after King's assassination, urban unrest and racial fears ignited throughout Memphis.[127] Following a rumor of a planned bombing at Memphis State, the annual Memphis Cotton Carnival parade was cancelled. This event's participants were white and its attendees Black. Given the event's openly segregated appearance and its activities, which "romanticized slavery and the virtues of the plantation," its organizers worried that it would incite further violence.[128] Similarly, Humphreys at Memphis State was so concerned that campus unrest would develop after King's assassination that the university's spring break vacation was moved up a week.[129]

Riots continued in Memphis after King's assassination and caused enough damage to property that Loeb and the state governor, Buford Ellington, requested federal tax relief to pay for recovery from the riots.[130] While Loeb and Ellington requested relief for the damage caused by the riots, Washington Butler, the executive director of the WOPC of Memphis-Shelby County, asked for additional funds to continue the committee's work in Memphis, which he felt could reduce poverty among the city's Black community. Butler wrote to the Johnson administration twice in April 1968 with an "urgent appeal . . . for emergency funds to assist in dealing with the root causes of poverty which led to the recent slaying of Dr. Martin Luther King, Jr. in our community."[131] In Nashville, students at Tennessee State also rioted after King's assassination.[132]

King's assassination "galvanized" national organized labor support for the strike, which ended on April 16.[133] The strikers secured recognition of their union, agreement that promotions would be determined by "seniority and competency" only, and a non-discrimination clause in the agreement itself. Securing this deal had taken sixty-five days and represented a significant attack on the city's established white supremacist order.[134] As an additional part of their settlement with the city, the strikers agreed to take Social Security benefits in place of a municipal pension, but as time passed, the pensions offered by Memphis became more valuable than Social Security. In July 2017, Memphis attempted to redress this gap between the strikers' Social Security benefits and city pensions with $50,000 grants for the fourteen surviving strikers. Memphis's mayor, Jim Strickland, described these grants, which went towards the workers' retirements, as "a major step toward the financial security they deserve."[135]

As the decade drew to a close, white and Black student activists were pulled in opposite directions. While Vietnam and the civil rights movement were contributing factors to the wedge forcing the two groups' initiatives apart, different perspectives on how to organize around labor initiatives were central. White students in SSOC believed it was possible to create an interracial labor movement, harking back to the Populists' attempts. They attempted to both assist strikers on the front lines as well as encourage southern college students of the need to support labor, with campus organizing, education, and work within local communities to organize whites around civil rights. For Black students, particularly those in Memphis, the realities of economic relief and racism were far starker. The city became a convergence point of federal funding, civil rights reform, and a major labor strike in 1968. The strike exposed differences in rhetoric and perspective between older Black leaders in Memphis and the younger Black Power-inspired activists.

CHAPTER 4

Reforming Administrative Policies

From Protesting *In Loco Parentis* to
Student Power, 1968–1970

The 1960s saw a major shift in the role students played in establishing new administrative procedures, many of which are still in practice and which influenced the policies in place at institutions today. Students throughout the country sought a greater say in their lives while in college, which meant confronting the established practice of *in loco parentis*, the policy of universities and colleges to act as guardians for students in place of their parents or guardians during their time on campus. Furthermore, university administrations as well as the students themselves played key roles in campus protest during the academic year. Following urban riots in the summer of 1967 and the anti-war movement's escalation during this period, the likelihood of a campus erupting in unrest, even in the politically conservative state of Tennessee, seemed highly probable to university administrators and student activists alike. This chapter demonstrates that small campus-based protests over issues surrounding *in loco parentis*, when combined with continued concerns surrounding racial inequalities in higher education, polarization in the civil rights movement, and the developing anger towards the U.S. military involvement in Vietnam, transformed those demonstrations into large-scale attacks on the establishment broadly defined. Student power during this period truly came into its own, unifying student bodies across the state as students related personally to the issues raised related to *in loco parentis* and their personal and political autonomy. These included matters such as traditional student decorum, as well as students' efforts to increase student government's presence in administrative issues amid concerns of student apathy, invitations for speakers to visit universities in Tennessee, and issues surrounding the establishment of Black studies programs and the hiring of African American staff. As debates raged over the extent of student power and racial inequality on campuses, administrators were forced to contend with this changing environment.

Student Life Renegotiations, 1968–1970

As the 1960s dawned, campuses were forced to make changes in their accommodation for the Baby Boomer generation. With such a large increase in student enrollment, many colleges felt the strain on existing facilities, such as dormitories and cafeterias, which in turn encouraged student resentment of university administrations owing to overcrowding. For example, as enrollment at the University of Tennessee (UT) increased by 61 percent between 1964 and 1969 (and by 75 percent across the South between 1960 and 1965), students demanded improved facilities.[1] The issues students raised in the early 1960s over their right to improved facilities, and the debates over these demands, are echoed in contemporary conversations over the impact of capitalism on higher education.[2]

Increased student numbers in the post–World War II and GI Bill era brought the subject of women attending college to the fore. The majority of universities and colleges in Tennessee arranged for either admitting women or increasing their female student attendance. Educating both sexes on campus necessitated additional funding for new dormitories, larger cafeterias, and new campus facilities, as well as new or revised policies for visitation and student life.

In light of women's increased college attendance, dormitory curfews were a common flashpoint for renegotiation between students and campus administrations. Almost every campus dormitory in America was segregated by sex, with strict visitation rules. By the mid- to late 1960s, most campuses had seen some kind of push against these visitation policies, particularly evening curfews, which were especially stringent for female students. Throughout Tennessee, college administrators became aware of demands for reconsidering dormitory curfews beginning in 1968. While most of the campuses had already had women attending the institutions for some time, the strain for additional facilities for women as well as for the burgeoning student population as a whole forced dormitory curfew discussions to the forefront of campus administrative policy. An analysis of student-led renegotiations and campus administrations' reactions demonstrates the centrality of protests over curfew rules to student activism in Tennessee in the late 1960s. In a traditionally conservative area like Tennessee, activists had to reach a critical mass with issues that drew support from across the student body on their campuses; student rights (or the perceived lack of them) were the causes that unified students across the state.³

Dormitory curfew protests at Tennessee's colleges progressed differently at private and public institutions. Private colleges and universities operated with more freedom than public institutions, largely because their financial support came from endowments built by alumni donations in larger proportions than state universities, which relied more heavily on federal and state funding. The comparative autonomy many private institutions enjoyed compared with state-run colleges allowed for more flexibility in negotiating between administrators and students over student autonomy.

Students' tendency to voice their grievances partly resulted from the increased visibility of youths as political activists from the early 1960s. In Tennessee, each campus protest occurred after disaffected student numbers hit a critical mass; while they most often remained in the minority, there needed to be enough students participating to organize a demonstration. Prior to the shift in majority student opinion for greater personal autonomy, Nancy Smith Wright, one of the first Black students to attend Maryville College in the 1950s, recalled that while the private, religiously funded college was "very strict," "we didn't think anything about it" because most of the students had grown up in households with strong Presbyterian values.⁴ Policies that were widely accepted in the 1950s were increasingly seen as unsustainable by students of the 1960s, particularly in the latter years of the decade.

Women were not the only ones frustrated by dormitory policies, as the reaction from one Sewanee male in October 1958 demonstrated. Ruffled at new regulations barring female dates from visiting male students' rooms, the student stated for the student newspaper, "I do not believe that we are the kind of men for whom an authoritarian government is a necessity. We can, if we so desire, reclaim our status as gentlemen in addition to our present scholarly pose."⁵ His words emphasized his resentment at not being considered a "gentleman"; the university's visitation policies, in his opinion, stripped him of this right. Sewanee students proposed an open dorm policy in late 1970 that the university's administration vetoed.⁶

These debates over dormitory regulations on Tennessee campuses were part of a larger, national development. UT students held a rally calling for the elimination of dormitory curfews in early February 1969 simultaneous with protests at five other campuses nationally: the University of Chicago in Chicago, Illinois; Wiley College in Marshall, Texas; the University of Notre Dame in Notre Dame, Indiana; Stillman College in Tuscaloosa, Alabama; and American University in Washington, D.C.⁷ All of the other institutions were private, and two, Wiley College and Stillman College, were historically Black. UT's rally on February 6 was organized by the campus's ad hoc Committee for Student Rights, and the thousand students who attended heard speeches from the SGA president, Chris Whittle, and university professor Dr. Richard Marius in favor of students organizing for their rights; in this case, more relaxed dormitory regulations. Whittle encouraged female students to lead the fight to change visitation hours, while Marius likened the negotiation students had to hold with university administration officials to the pressure coaches faced from community members. "Maybe the only language they [the administration] understand is the language of football," Marius stated. "In football when the team loses, you fire the coach."[8] Football was a major athletic sport in the South, particularly in Tennessee.

White and Black students felt similar tensions over dormitory curfew policies, although the administrative response at Black campuses was often harsher. Morristown College was a historically Black college located in the Appalachian region of East Tennessee that witnessed similar protests by its student body. At Morristown, however, the administration expelled the students, and the FBI's COINTELPRO noted the unrest. In May 1968, the college president, Elmer P. Gibson, expelled eleven co-ed students following a meeting with the college's Board of Trustees because they "rebelled" when they were reminded to clean up their dormitory rooms and to follow the check-in and check-out procedures when going off campus.[9] Some one hundred female students were involved in the protests, spurred on by an institutional order to "improve their housekeeping and to observe sign-in sign-out regulations," while the eleven who were expelled were seen as leading the protests. The campus unrest entailed a boycott of classes for one day, as well as a march and a meeting inside their dormitory.[10] The eleven expelled students were reportedly allowed to complete their final exams from home.[11] Gibson, an African American, was far from alone in acting autocratically as the principal of a historically Black college or university (HBCU), but it is unclear whether appeasing white board members of the college or white community members played a role in his dismissal of these students.[12] Nonetheless, the Morristown College case—as with the later expulsion of the Lane College student body in March 1969 after arson attacks on campus buildings—showed how harshly some HBCU administrations would react to campus-based protests.[13]

At some historically white universities, administrators chose conciliation over expulsion in the late 1960s. Notably, Memphis State University's president Dr. Cecil C. Humphreys visited campus dormitories regularly from 1968 so students would consider him available to negotiate with and thereby prevent demonstrations from occurring. This tactic was conspicuously successful.[14]

College administrations at private, religiously founded campuses viewed dormitory curfews as a necessary part of managing coeducation in campuses, but they too witnessed significant student-led efforts to eliminate the policies in the late 1960s. At Maryville, dormitory regulations also dictated that female students were only allowed to visit the city of Maryville and that dates were only allowed during specific hours of the evening and weekend.[15] At private Southwestern, male students needed to know the details of parietal dormitory visitation before going off campus for a date with a female student, as returning late had negative consequences for both students.[16] Female Southwestern students were expected to sit an annual curfew rules exam on the university's parietal policies. When twenty-one women walked out of the exam on October 11, 1968, many other students on campus took the opportunity to voice their dislike of the current policies and demand the administration heed their concerns. Some one hundred male students joined the protest, several of whom attempted to disrupt the proceedings "by creating a furious din outside the testing room," while others erected signs across campus questioning the need for such restrictions. At the time, female students who either failed the exam or were unable to take it were forbidden to leave campus, so it is unlikely they would have taken the step of walking out of the exam room lightly. Some of the women who left the exam felt the rules for visitation hours and off-campus privileges were outdated; others argued that parietal exams were redundant as they had already pledged as Southwestern students to follow the student handbook, which required them to behave in a manner that would reflect well on Southwestern.[17] Students from Vanderbilt University and Tusculum College, a private Appalachian East Tennessee institution, also protested dormitory regulations. The Tusculum students also wanted the university administration to acknowledge their SGA as students' "sole representative."[18]

Not all students across Tennessee were in support of loosening campus policies. Efforts to change dormitory curfews at UT exposed divisions within the student body over issues of increased autonomy and politics, and encouraged the establishment of a conservative student organization chapter on campus as well. Writing in March 1965, Stanton Evans, conservative columnist and associate editor of the *National Review* at the time, described a growing period of backlash against New Leftists on campuses across the country. Evans noted that conservative student groups had organized "counter-movements" led by Young Americans for Freedom (YAF) at the University of Tennessee, the University of Wisconsin, the University of Texas, Columbia University, and Stanford University.[19] The UT-based group, called the Majority Coalition, opposed "student government members battling the school administration" in terms of a student-led effort to remove dormitory curfew hours. While they aligned themselves against the liberal students' tactics, Majority Coalition members were not necessarily opposed to eliminating dormitory hours. The Majority Coalition chairman, Jim Duncan (the son of conservative Republican Tennessee congressman Jim Duncan), stated that its members wanted to "demonstrate support for the UT administration in its efforts to maintain a truly free academic environment on the campus. The small minority of students who have been extremely critical of the administration lately is definitely not representative of the student body as a whole . . . and [the majority does] not support efforts to tear it down."[20]

Private institutions had stricter policies for students' attire, making dissent from these codes easier to identify than at larger, public universities. Male students at Southwestern, Sewanee, and Maryville were expected to dress neatly around campus and to wear a coat, shirt, and tie for chapel services, while it was mandatory for female students to dress smartly in skirts.[21] Students who were members of the Order of the Gownsmen (OG)—Sewanee's honor society for upperclassmen with excellent academic records—could wear gowns around campus, although the student body's relative noncompliance with this rule further demonstrated students' general reluctance to dress formally; the administration, however, successfully fought to continue the gown tradition.[22] The student newspaper, the *Sewanee Purple*, had hosted debates over the relevancy of Sewanee's dress code as far back as March 1956, indicating the long pedigree of this particular disagreement between some students and administrators.[23]

Mandatory chapel attendance was a feature of life at many small colleges during the 1960s. At Southwestern, chapel services were compulsory, with Sunday and Wednesday services as well as the choice of a Tuesday or Thursday morning session that could either be educational or religious. Chapel attendance was required until 1968, when the college rescinded its policy.[24] The Presbyterian Church ran Maryville College through the 1960s. Consequently, this campus community was more socially conservative than state-run and larger universities in Tennessee (although the university's leadership was more liberal on race than almost all other southern universities).[25] Maryville College students were expected to attend church, although attendance was not mandatory as it was at Southwestern. The women's handbook from 1963–64 listed Sunday as "a special day set aside primarily [for] worship," and "urged" students to attend a church regularly in the community.[26] Students at Sewanee were frustrated in October 1966 when the administration allowed OG members to attend fewer mandatory chapel services than the rest of the student body.[27] At Tennessee Wesleyan College in Athens (located in the southeastern part of the state), the administration responded quickly to students' urging for a reformed chapel attendance policy in the fall of 1968. The school changed its earlier policy of required chapel attendance (tallied up each semester) with a proposed list of twenty convocations per semester that would be a combination of religious, educational, or fine arts events. Students still had to attend a certain number each semester, but the college chaplain believed that providing a choice of events would prevent a student boycott.[28]

Some institutions in Tennessee were slow to accommodate female students. As late as 1968, Sewanee's trustees had considered building a separate college exclusively for women in an effort to admit women without changing the campus environment. They decided instead to admit women in the fall of 1969.[29] While this occurred after the rest of the state's institutions had admitted women, negotiations concerning dormitory curfews and the dress code soon followed Sewanee's transition to coeducation, as they had elsewhere in Tennessee.

Universities responded to protests in various ways. Southwestern formed the Social Regulations Council as the executive branch of the college's dormitory board.[30] The council discussed disagreements over parietals and, in collaboration with the college's administration, adopted solutions. Despite the attempt to include students in the process (and thus potentially find a resolution more quickly), students and administrators continued to negotiate dormitory rules into the spring of 1971. It was evidently difficult to enact policies that would gain both student and administrative approval.[31] Administrators at Tennessee Wesleyan avoided campus unrest by giving students representation on faculty committees through the 1960s and on the board of trustees from 1973. The college president, Charles C. Turner Jr., also held what he called "rap sessions" with students to hear their concerns and answer questions.[32] Essential to this tactic's success, however, were administrative flexibility and the accommodation to at least some student demands.

Some protests over campus policies had little to do with traditionally defined *in loco parentis*. Instead, they demonstrated a growing student interest in personal and political autonomy. Protests on smaller campuses and larger public universities shared similar traits. At Sewanee, an increased student body size put pressure on the dining facilities during the 1960s, building to student disorder in February 1967. Following complaints from March 1963 of poor food quality at the campus cafeteria, Gailor Hall, an editorial in October 1966 connected the "expanding student body" with the cramped situation in the dining hall and unappetizing food.[33] The administration met with student and faculty representatives over rioting that had occurred in Gailor in December 1966, but at least some students remained unappeased by the gesture from the administration. In an editorial, one student stated, "The riots in Gailor should cease, that goes without argument. But if a man is fed as if he were in a kindergarten class, he will probably use the manners of a preschooler. If he is fed like a gentleman, he will undoubtedly employ the manners of gentility."[34] The student's argument blamed the rioting squarely on the administration for not resolving the overcrowding in Gailor.

The administration's apparent unaccountability continued to frustrate Sewanee students. When the dean of men, John Maurice Webb, asked OG members to sit at the heads of the dining hall tables in an effort to have them police mealtimes at Gailor, non-OG students were offended at the accusation that they needed peer supervision, while OG members were angered about the absence of student consultation prior to Webb's announcement. A group of students gathered in front of Vice-Chancellor Edward McCrady's campus residence on February 23, 1967, to protest the administration's "autocratic" behavior. The demonstration numbered 150 or 200 and the crowd chanted "Let them eat cake" and "Down with Gailor," and sang "We Shall Overcome."[35] Sewanee students clearly felt their civil liberties had been infringed, as the singing of "We Shall Overcome" demonstrated; invoking the civil rights anthem in 1967 suggested that students associated their struggle for personal and political autonomy with earlier civil rights struggles, much as Berkeley students had done during the 1964 Free Speech Movement. Frustrations at Knoxville College over limited library hours in February 1965 similarly revealed the sorts of campus issues that student activists found pressing. The students wrote to SSOC asking for a survey of two hundred other schools, particularly ones in Tennessee, to determine the standard hours of a campus library; students wanted Knoxville College's library to stay open for two more hours each evening.[36]

UT administrators worried about students' next target. Not alone in their concerns, UT's staff was troubled with the threat of an overly active student body. In October 1970, in his annual address, Chancellor Charles Weaver stated that the university evidently needed to "move as rapidly as possible to separate itself from control of students' private lives" while still providing dormitories. He stressed the importance to "diversify" the choices of housing available to students and noted that any student who chose to live in campus accommodation would be under civil law, "with additional rules and constraints" applying to only individual cases where the student or their guardian had requested them.[37] What had been an accepted part of university life, the protection of students' interests by the institution, had become a major potential liability for the administrators. The university administration would continue to fear potentially violent demonstrations into the 1970s as the student body and many faculty members continued to call for a stronger voice in the university's decisions.

While university administrators statewide were concerned about student unrest, students on campuses lacking substantial liberal or radical student activism routinely decried these apparently apathetic student bodies. These condemnations emerged in both private and public Tennessee universities in the mid-1950s. Maryville College, Vanderbilt University, and Sewanee in particular saw student activists on their campuses call for greater student participation in activism. These students' complaints revealed their awareness of, and disappointment at, the general absence of like-minded students on their campuses. Denunciations of apathy, then, served as calls from more radical students for greater student involvement in dismantling the limitations university administrations placed on students' personal autonomy on campuses. Moreover, complaints about student apathy became increasingly frequent in campus publications in the late 1960s, coinciding with the period of greatest organization over students' personal and political autonomy on Tennessee campuses. The student newspaper *Vanderbilt Hustler* published two articles in February 1967 in reaction to perceived diminished student political involvement. Entitled "Why The Campus Sleeps" and "Apathy Invincible: Activist Vs. Vandy," these articles demonstrated that some students were becoming disillusioned with their peers' limited interest in campus activism.[38]

Although determining the impact of these condemnations on previously apathetic students is difficult to gauge, demands for greater student engagement at least reached a wide potential audience through publication in student newspapers. The similar word usage and subject matter in editorials and articles of student newspapers suggests that even if the students who professed these ideas of their peers as apathetic were a minority on campuses across Tennessee, these more radical students felt similar concerns across the state.

At Maryville College, student concerns about a lack of wider student engagement seemed to have inspired the largest proportion of students to organize. Unlike elsewhere in the state, students raised their concerns over apathy with university leadership. At the Student-Faculty Senate in February 1966, student members wanted to find out why the student body was "dead." One student even asked, "What is [Maryville College] to do to direct the student to live *now*?"[39] When students held a "Demonstration Week" in May 1969 to protest apparent underrepresentation in college affairs, students initially praised the university's board members for listening to them. When changes failed to materialize, students were again frustrated. As one student declared, "Paternalism is dead as a doctrine for decisions, and all have to acknowledge that.

This includes not only faculty and administration who would like to paternalize, but also students who are willing to sit back and be paternalized."⁴⁰ These students believed that the student body needed to involve itself in college matters or risk their wishes going unrecognized in this notionally post–*in loco parentis* period. Later, at the biannual Board of Directors meeting in spring 1971, the co-chairman of the All-College Council (a committee formed of students, faculty, and staff at Maryville College that operated similarly to the Student-Faculty Senate) brought up the issue of "student disenchantment" with the council. According to the complaint, students believed the council did not deal with the problems they highlighted, and that council members did not truly respect the students.⁴¹

These southern student activists were stating ideas similar to those espoused by the leaders of the Berkeley Free Speech Movement in California in 1964. Both emphasized student autonomy and free speech within the university system as a political strategy. Historian Robert Cohen has argued that the movement in Berkeley was the first 1960s demonstration to bring strategies from the civil rights movement, namely civil disobedience tactics like the sit-in, to university campuses, and that these approaches "[set] the stage for mass student protests against the Vietnam War."⁴² While southern campuses did not, in general, see anywhere near the level of anti-war demonstrations that occurred elsewhere across the United States, southern student activists used civil rights movement methods at their campuses. Berkeley's activists described students as being a part of the machine of university life, as when Mario Savio declared that "the battlefields [college campuses and the South] may seem quite different to some observers, [but] the same rights are at stake in both places."⁴³ Berkeley movement leader Steve Weissman even spoke at Memphis State in May 1965 to a crowd of several hundred students, a move that shocked the university administration and underlined the continuity of ideas between the liberal California campus and even a conservative southern campus.⁴⁴

Some two years later, in June 1967, southern student radicals had seemingly adopted the equation of student rights with civil rights. Lynn Wells, a member of SSOC, discussed the growing "intensity" of "student power protests" on campuses like Berkeley and "black campuses in the South." She looked forward with hope to a time when college students nationally, "for the most part apathetic," would rise up against their collegiate systems where they were "'forced' to consume facts like machines."⁴⁵ While Wells was referring to college students across the country, the UT SGA's presidential election in 1969 showed that student demands for greater power gained traction in Tennessee too.

Student Power's Electoral Victory

Every spring, UT's SGA held its election for the following year's officials. The May 1969 election began like others before it. Yet by its close, it had changed how future elections would be held on the campus in two ways. In a literal sense, the election changed future electoral procedures. Beyond that, the SGA election demonstrated a significant, explicit victory for student power at a major state university. Students turned out in larger numbers than ever before in the university's history to vote in favor of change: for the removal of the remaining *in loco parentis* policies, an end to student apathy, more diversity in elected representation, and more student representation in university decisions.

There were originally five candidates running for SGA president. Jim Hager, co-leader of the Majority Coalition and Tennessee chairman of the YAF, ran for the United for Progress (UP) party, John R. Long, for the Challenge '69 party, James "Jimmie" Baxter, for the Student Coalition party (originally the Student Power Coalition), Jay Austin, for the Why Not? party, and Robert Webb, who ran as an independent.[46] By the time of the rescheduled election, three remained: Hager, Long, and Baxter.[47]

While they promoted different platforms, each candidate's party representation revealed the general interest in change; UP with its literal implication of moving upwards towards something better, the connotation of Challenge '69 as questioning the student's acceptance of the status quo, and Student Coalition representing a unified student body all signified elements of activism. All three parties agreed on the main idea of increased student representation in university affairs, while Challenge '69 and Student Coalition also agreed on removing existing *in loco parentis* policies (namely adopting an open speaker policy and removing dormitory hours); UP also wanted reform to the speaker policy but more in line with existing procedures whereby student polls would influence the speakers chosen rather than a wider pool of invitations in an open speaker policy.[48]

The three parties spoke of better representing students on the campus, but differed slightly in who they targeted and their plans for how to do so. Their statements also made reference, whether overtly or more subtly, to more radical students on campus. UP advocated for "[representing] the entire student body" through the use of opinion polls to see how students felt about various campus issues. Alluding to campus protestors dominating discussions on campus, one UP supporter and captain of the football team the previous year said, "We have been silent too long . . . [w]e need to voice our opinions and make something happen."⁴⁹ Student Coalition called for "radical reform" of the SGA, arguing that the government had "lost its relevance" but that "there is nothing radical about democracy. There is nothing radical about modernization.... What we seek is the betterment of this university through needed reform; and we seek it not by means of disruption and destruction, but by rational means."⁵⁰ Challenge '69 spoke of "winds of change [that] are sweeping the UT campus" but that they offer "neither reaction nor revolution, but the promise of rapid reform."⁵¹ While all three took relatively moderate political stances, UP was on the more conservative end, Challenge '69 followed the middle lane, and Student Coalition took a more liberal approach.

The election was held as planned on May 7, 1969, but by the end of the day a student had submitted a lawsuit to the SGA Tribunal (the acting body that investigated SGA issues like complaints or accusations). The plaintiffs questioned the legitimacy of the election given that the requirement to write in their Social Security number on their ballot denied them a secret vote.⁵² Used on everything from class attendance rosters to student identification cards, the Social Security number was the established method for the university to track every student. Students accused the university of "an infringement on [the student's] rights of secrecy."⁵³ Following the SGA Tribunal's May 10, 1969, ruling that the election was void and needed to be held again, the election was rescheduled for May 23.⁵⁴

As the second election drew near, campaigning for SGA president intensified. John Long and Jim Hager criticized each other in campaign events and the newspaper, indicating their awareness that they were after many of the same voters. In the original election, Long had won narrowly against Hager, with Baxter coming in third.⁵⁵ According to the university newspaper, the *Daily Beacon*, Long dismissed Hager's central focus on campus violence as a scare tactic. Long argued that Hager's membership in a student group, Let's Talk Sense, which opposed an open speaker policy, and Hager's opposition to a rally for open hours at women's dormitories on campus earlier that year demonstrated how conservative Hager's presidency would be.⁵⁶ Hager argued for students to be realistic about their expectations, saying it was necessary to work with "the Administration, the Legislature and the people of Tennessee."⁵⁷ And Baxter continued to advocate for uniting the campus around students' rights, saying, "It makes no difference what you believe—whether you are a revolutionist or a racist. We [students] are all out there in the cold."⁵⁸ Even prior to the second election results, Baxter's message seemed to resonate; some 550 students attended a Student Coalition rally the night before.⁵⁹

In the second May 23, 1969, SGA presidential election, Jimmie Baxter, the African American candidate, won. Formerly all-white universities occasionally elected Black student body presidents in the late 1960s but it was rare, particularly in the South.[60] Baxter was a twenty-five-year-old Air Force veteran, so perhaps had a leadership edge over his college peers.[61] The vote tallies from the first election were reversed. With a larger number of votes tabulated than the first election, which itself was "a record-turnout," Baxter came in first with Hager and Long claiming second and third place respectively.[62] Following the election, Baxter claimed that the large turnout "demonstrated the [students'] concern with their role in the University." Long agreed: evidently "the student body wants far-reaching changes on campus."[63] Voters and candidates alike recognized that this election reflected growing student interest in the university and the desire for greater involvement in governance. Following the election, Baxter contended that "[UT] students should be concerned more about making sure they really have a voice here intellectually."[64]

UT's 1969 SGA presidential election reflected ongoing changes on campuses across the country, particularly students' increased desire for greater personal autonomy. In his post-election interview with the *Daily Beacon*, Baxter focused mainly on UT students redefining *in loco parentis* in the upcoming academic year. His "primary concern" was with "student power" and the student body's ability to increase student involvement in campus decision-making through an expanded SGA role. UT's student body, Baxter argued, needed to "demonstrate to the Administration that we are really not satisfied and won't just step by and accept our role as children."[65] In a later oral history he claimed, "We needed to have a legitimate say in running the affairs of the University, particularly regarding the affairs of students. . . We had to be recognized by the University and given some authority."[66] The strategies Baxter had in mind to gain this power for students included "economic and class boycotts" as a way to "convince the University, through rational discourse, of the reality of our requests."[67]

In winning the election, Baxter defied many of his fellow students who 'assumed that I didn't have a chance of being elected, because I was black. Their theory was 'white students just won't vote for you, because this is a racist campus.'"[68] In making student power his central focus, Baxter sought to make race a nonissue in his campaign. The second SGA campaign was largely free of explicit racial animus, with the only instance of potentially open racial antagonism occurring when someone "slashed" Baxter's campaign posters the night of May 21, shortly after the SGA Tribunal had demanded another election.[69] Nonetheless, white supporters of Jim Hager, Baxter's conservative opponent, employed more implicit racial campaigning tactics. Before the second election, they showed Baxter's photograph to local business owners and managers and then solicited campaign donations, a staple political tactic of conservatives running against Black candidates or white candidates who allegedly promoted Black interests, particularly once explicitly racist or segregationist campaigning became politically unprofitable.[70]

While Baxter attempted to frame the election around student rights, the fact that he was Black remained a concern for many in Knoxville; white UT student Barry Bozeman recalled that Baxter's election "[scared] the crap out of the fathers."[71] Ultimately, Baxter's campaign platform of representation for all UT students successfully crossed racial lines, which brought his election from a student electorate that remained overwhelmingly white. Elsewhere in Tennessee, issues of race and student power continued to intensify campus-based demonstrations, many of which concerned demands for the creation of educational and social programs for Black students.

Student Autonomy and Race

In the late 1960s Tennessee student activists focused on issues both on campuses and in the communities surrounding universities. Along with wanting involvement in campus administrative issues, many students felt compelled to work in their communities as well. Whether in favor or opposed to student protest, civic responsibility motivated many students to act. Prominent among motivations for students to organize, particularly for Black youth, were frustrations in witnessing examples in their daily lives on and off campus of the limitations of desegregation. Feelings of inequality experienced during this formative period of their lives were emotionally resonant, and combined ideas of gaining equality as African Americans along with power as students.

The intersections between racial justice and student power, which would continue to develop throughout the decade, were clear from the mid-1960s in Tennessee. At a student-organized conference at Fisk University in May 1964, participants raised the "clarion call for the radical Black Student movement," according to Black Power movement scholar Peniel Joseph.[72] The conference was organized by the Afro-American Student Movement (described as a "radical affiliation of SNCC" by historian Ibram X. Kendi).[73] The event fostered discussions about developing Black studies programs and curriculum reform nationally. According to one participant, the conference "was the ideological catalyst that eventually shifted the Civil Rights Movement into the Black Power Movement."[74] Later on in 1968, some Fisk student activists even went so far as to call for the expulsion of white students.[75]

As discussions moved to action, student and faculty strikes were extremely effective in securing greater influence over administrative policy-making in the late 1960s and 1970s. In nearly every case in Tennessee, extremely concerned administrations initially sought to cooperate with the strikers. Administrators were understandably worried given the national (and international) flurry of strikes and protests in universities and colleges in the late 1960s, the threat of violence and damage to property, and the prospect of losing funding from donors for apparent mismanagement of protests. Strikes were the most common type of protest against higher education administrations in Tennessee, regardless of the cause of unrest.

As more attended formerly all-white universities throughout the country in the late 1960s and 1970s, African American students demanded a greater incorporation of Black interests and culture into campus life. This increased interest in African American history, as well as a nationwide Black Power–derived emphasis on Black empowerment, brought the establishment of Black studies programs across the country.[76] In petitioning for these programs to exist, many students and faculty members had to argue against the established curricula at their respective institutions. Perry Wallace, the first Black varsity athlete to play basketball in the SEC at Vanderbilt, spoke of his time at the university in 1970 as "lonesome." "Over the years many people knew my name but they were not interested in knowing me," Wallace said. "On the dormitory halls I got to know some people but there were others who condescended, people who were used to blacks who cut the grass and who swept the floors. They respected my basketball ability but they still consider[ed] me a person who [swept] floors."[77] Despite Black student admissions to formerly all-white institutions, Blacks encountered segregation in campus-based social groups like fraternities and sororities. Their feelings of isolation and desires to have social activities on campus resulted in some Greek organizations admitting Black students. But most national Greek organizations remained uninterested in actively seeking Black members, causing Black students to form their own Greek organizations and Black student unions.

Demands by Black students for more inclusion and representation generated strife at Memphis State and other state university campuses.[78] Giving Black student groups recognition also required administrators to respond directly to student demands or demonstrations. Administrators were generally reluctant to appear too accommodating to student activists, but the optics of Black campus radicalism in Tennessee, particularly at Memphis State and UT, occasionally forced student activists and administrators into conflict. Disagreements over race and student power came to a head at these Tennessee institutions in the late 1960s, namely Memphis State and UT, mirroring trends nationwide.

At Memphis State, Black students were a much larger percentage of the student body than at other Tennessee universities. Consequently, there were stronger demands for both Black studies programs and Black student groups, while the university administration had greater concerns over potential student unrest. In 1967, Memphis State's enrollment was 15,914, of which 7 percent were African American students, while UT's respective figures were 20,111 and 2 percent.[79] In March 1968, a Memphis news reporter claimed that Memphis State authorities maintained social segregation once Black students had desegregated the university. One African American Memphis State law student, Isaac Taylor, lamented Black students' inability to participate in social organizations on campus. Instead, one section of the university's student center was "the ghetto" where Black students could socialize with each other. Unable to join other university social activities, another Black student stated: "You go to class, you sit in the Student Center, you go home—that's it."[80] Despite the formation of a Memphis State BSA in 1963, many Black Memphis State students still felt isolated.[81] Memphis State's BSA issued a March 23, 1969, statement with several demands. It called for starting a Black studies program, hiring more Black instructors and administrators, creating a budget for Black student events (including a proposed "Black Extravaganza"), recruiting Black student athletes, and ending anti-Black discrimination in campus fraternities and sororities.[82]

In April 1969, Memphis State BSA members occupied university president Cecil C. Humphreys's office to demand funding to invite Congressman Adam Clayton Powell, an African American, to speak at Memphis State for the Black Extravaganza program, scheduled for May 16–17.[83] (UT students had invited Powell to speak in 1967, but university administrators refused to let him talk on campus.)[84] In a morning meeting on April 23, Humphreys told two BSA representatives that the university had no additional funding in its student speakers' budget to pay for Powell's attendance; the students had earlier unsuccessfully requested the necessary $1,750 from the Dean of Students' office.[85] Shortly after noon, over seventy-five African American students arrived at Humphreys's office, again requesting funding for Powell to speak on campus. In a thirty-minute meeting, BSA members also raised the same issues cited in their March 23 statement, before Humphreys asked them to leave to allow him to meet subsequent appointments that day. The students refused, even after Humphreys told them of the university and state's policy to call the Memphis Police Department to end university building occupations.[86] Police soon removed the students without arresting them, and law enforcement remained on the campus as a precaution at Humphreys's request.[87]

Following their sit-in, the BSA students went to the Memphis State University Center where Dr. H. Ralph Jackson, the vice chairman of Memphis's COME, and Maxine Smith, executive secretary of the NAACP Memphis chapter, assured them that both organizations supported the students' efforts.[88] The following morning, four BSA members delivered a list of issues they wished to discuss with Humphreys, and arranged a meeting with two representatives from the Dean of Students' office for the next day.[89] During this session the BSA students requested the removal of police from campus. The administration refused to do this, and in fact kept them on campus over the next two days (during the weekend). "Because of additional threats to University property, the attempt to recruit people from other cities to come to Memphis, and newspaper statements attributed to certain student leaders," Humphreys claimed in a subsequent public announcement, "Memphis Police Department assistance was continued over the weekend."[90]

Perceiving the threat from BSA students to be low, that Monday, April 28, the university decreased the police presence on campus. After a BSA meeting that day, 115 students occupied Humphreys's office shortly after noon while he was not present. They intended to occupy the office, according to Humphreys, "until police were removed or they were arrested."[91] The administration notified the students that they were in violation of Memphis State's Student Conduct and Disciplinary Proceedings; those who remained would be suspended from Memphis State. Most of the students stayed, and were subsequently driven to jail.[92] A total of 109 students were arrested and charged with trespassing on university property; of that group, 103 were Black, and 104 were Memphis State students. The "BSA 109," as the group became known, were suspended from Memphis State as a result of their arrests, but were given the chance to appeal this decision.[93] In his statement on the situation, Humphreys cited his compliance with three "directives": Section 39-1214 of the Tennessee Code Annotated, which stated "any person who trespasses in the building of any public school and who there engages in any disorderly conduct is guilty of a misdemeanor"; the State Board of Education's August 9, 1968, directive that each institution it governed, including Memphis State, create policies against campus unrest including "unauthorized occupancy of University facilities"; and Memphis State's own Student Conduct and Disciplinary Proceedings, which forbade "any interference with functions or activities of the University."[94]

There was considerable local support for the university to appear strong against Black student unrest, a common event in the late 1960s. More than 250 Black student-led demonstrations occurred on campuses across the country during the 1968-69 academic year.[95] Furthermore, by May 15, 1969, seventy-two university presidents resigned following that academic year's campus protests.[96] On April 29, 1969, the day after BSA members were arrested, some 870 Memphis State students signed a petition in support of the university administration's actions.[97] Humphreys received dozens of letters from Memphis State students and Tennessee residents in support of his behavior, seen as a strong stand against student unrest and Black radicalism. Humphreys, however, sounded a conciliatory tone. "I hope," he remarked, "that everyone realizes that we don't need a strong polarization. I hope we all realize we are trying to present an educational opportunity for everyone."[98]

When the Memphis State BSA sit-in protests occurred, Humphreys and other administrators knew of unrest at two historically Black colleges in West Tennessee, where students at LeMoyne-Owen College in Memphis, following the colleges' merger in 1968, and Lane College in Jackson had held similar disagreements with their college administrations over the students' role in institutional decisions. While the tenor of the protests was tenser than at predominantly white campuses like Memphis State or UT (as Black students were an overwhelming majority of enrollees at Lane and LeMoyne-Owen), the issues these students raised mirrored the concerns Black and white students voiced elsewhere in the state. Indeed, the administrative and governmental responses to these protests were far more reactionary than other campuses, specifically those at more racially mixed institutions. Demonstrating continuity between West Tennessee and other areas of the Deep South in particular, these two incidents (at LeMoyne-Owen and Lane) are regionally comparable to other occurrences, in particular the violent reaction to student protest at South Carolina State University in February 1968.[99]

Following the merger of LeMoyne College, a four-year institution, with Owen Junior College, a two-year college, in 1968, students voiced resentment over the campus resources available to students.[100] LeMoyne-Owen College students held a symposium, Inquiry Week, from November 11 to November 15, 1968, which according to their Student Government president, Charles Diggs, sought to "open the minds of the students."[101] The speakers referenced protests on Black campuses across the country, and some urged students to report their grievances to their administration. Students subsequently listed nineteen demands for the university administration to address. These included a curriculum that was more tailored to Black history and culture, additional work-study options, opening of the campus gym to students, more student access to health services, and lower tuition costs. The students also wanted to be involved in the selection of the college's next president, as the current president, Dr. Hollis Price, was retiring at the end of the year. This final request, to have a say in the next president's hiring, foreshadowed similar demands by UT students in 1969.[102] When the students felt their issues were ignored by

Price, a group seized the campus administration building, Brownlee Hall. Students held it for two weeks.[103] Diggs argued that this protest was in fact carefully planned to increase their authority on campus. "Our particular grievances have always been here," said Diggs. "You can ask any alumnus and he'll tell you that the problems he had as a student are still prevalent today. But before now there has never been the strength to change those problems. Now it's different."[104]

The situation at Lane College mirrored that at nearby LeMoyne-Owen, with a list of student demands and discussions with administration officials, but the reaction to the protests from administrators and students alike differed greatly. Developing from student grievances, student leaders and activists from the Black Liberation Front (BLF) organized a sizeable protest at the end of February 1969. From February 26 to February 28, the campus experienced general "unrest," including a class boycott that resulted in 1,000 students, out of a student body of 1,100, not attending classes.[105] The BLF, which was not a college-sanctioned group, had organized the boycott, and also presented a list of fourteen demands to the administration.[106] This list, which echoed the students' rights asserted by students across Tennessee at the time, included extending the campus grill's hours, ending mandatory chapel attendance, allowing women to wear pants to class, allowing all students to style their hair in Afros, adding Black studies courses to the curriculum, and students gaining greater say in administrative affairs of the college.[107] The college president, Dr. Chester A. Kirkendoll, met on March 1 with a group made up of eight BLF members, eight administrators, and four students for five hours to discuss how to proceed. Describing the meeting to the media, Kirkendoll emphasized that "respect for law and order must prevail."[108] The meeting did not resolve the issue fully however, and several different fires were set on the campus in the first few days of the month. The Jackson Fire Department was called to campus six times to attend to fires, including in the library, a men's dormitory, and the gymnasium.[109] Concerned for student safety and wanting to gain control of the situation, Kirkendoll closed campus dormitories and shut down the campus from March 3 for nine days. "Lane College is going through one of the worst experiences in its 87-year history," he stated.[110] Little did he know at the time that things would escalate. Soon after the campus reopened, the science building on campus burned to the ground from a suspected arson attack on March 20, causing half a million dollars in damages and leading Kirkendoll to request law enforcement's presence on campus two days later. A curfew was put in place for campus as well as one for the surrounding area, Governor Buford Ellington declared a civil emergency in Jackson, and local police were joined by 125 "riot-trained state highway patrolmen."[111] The end of the protests was attributed to a rain storm on March 23, with the aftermath of the unrest resulting in the arrests of some eighty-five Lane students at the end of the period.[112] Some of the students convicted of offenses such as inciting to riot were suspended from Lane, while others faced lesser disciplinary action.[113]

Black students organized at predominantly white institutions over similar issues. Emphasizing a feeling of not belonging at UT, which echoed sentiments of Memphis State Black students, the Black Students Union (BSU) student handbook, issued in the fall of 1969, referred to Black UT students as "a fly in the buttermilk."[114] Frustrations over the Black studies program at UT in fall 1969 resulted in the BSU considering a boycott of all Black studies courses but one (a course taught by a professor of both UT and Knoxville College, the city's historically Black college). Students were angry about the lack of consultation for the new program's curriculum, and the paucity of African American professors involved in the program. One BSU member argued that "a white man cannot possibly have an understanding of the black situation, so he can't very well teach a black studies course" and later, "black students are fed up with the hiring of the Negro for purposes of tokenism and we will not tolerate inter-department racism disguised as an Afro-American Studies Program."[115] Notably, a Black student at Vanderbilt University in Nashville also charged that university with "tokenism" in its Black studies courses. When congressmen (including white Tennessee Republican congressman William Brock) asked Black Vanderbilt students about their impressions of the campus, to investigate the likelihood of future student protest on the campus, Brock recalled them saying that "a white man can't teach Soul courses." Brock agreed.[116] Other statements by Black Tennessee students concerned issues of inequality that were less visible to white students, staff, and faculty. Echoing the disillusionment of many Black Americans with the reality of desegregating, Maryville College freshman Larry McDowell remarked that his experience on the campus was of being "practically unnoticed." "Many people will boastfully say that Maryville College is an integrated institution," McDowell wrote in February 1970. "They think this statement is true because there are sixteen black students enrolled here. Sixteen black students in comparison to the number of whites here on campus is not integration, it is a form of tokenism." McDowell urged the college to not only increase their Black student enrollment and Black faculty and staff hiring, but to also rework the curriculum to include more Black studies. "Believe it or not there is more to black people than riots, revolution, and demonstrations," McDowell stated. "I am asking that Maryville College let me graduate a satisfied well-educated Black man, instead of a well-conditioned Uncle Tom."[117] Coming from arguably the state's most racially liberal institution, McDowell's comments highlighted the breadth of Black student anger over limited racial change, even among those who renounced radical alternatives.

Members of UT's newly created BSU generated a list of further changes they wished to see at the university in the spring of 1969. The official request for university recognition of the BSU and Black studies programs came on May 8, 1969, when fifty Black students "peacefully picketed" UT's Administration Building for the whole day. The group listed seven "demands" for the university's administration to address. In addition to wanting reconsideration of a Black cheerleader's application, they sought the funds they had applied for from the Student Activities Office to be paid to the group as a student organization, more Black counselors, more scholarships for all students, Black recruiters as part of the university's application process (for both students and staff members), and an investigation of classroom discrimination. Howard F. Aldmon, UT's vice-chancellor for student affairs, responded to these demands by providing information to the demonstrators on how to move forward with their various requests through existing university administrative procedures.[118] Peaceful demonstrations involving seventy-five students took place over the next few days.[119] A lone reactionary counter-protestor, who held up a sign reading "White Student Union," failed to goad the demonstrators into a fight.[120] Following these demonstrations, BSU members met with university president Andrew D. Holt, Howard Aldmon, and Chancellor Weaver.[121]

The Adawayhi Pep Club's elections in 1969 were another instance where the BSU demanded UT's administration address racial prejudice. Following the pep club's annual auditions for cheerleaders, three unsuccessful male applicants brought a case to the SGA Tribunal for review in May 1969. They claimed that the club's president, Robert E. Briggers, demonstrated "bias" in choosing three of his fraternity brothers from Pi Kappa Alpha over them.[122] Then, on May 2, Shirley Majors, a Black UT student from Nashville, filed a request for a hearing that charged the pep club with "racial discrimination" in selecting cheerleaders. She claimed that the club had recorded an incorrect grade point average (GPA) for her. The club claimed to have taken Majors's GPA from the administration, but when her adviser said this was untrue, Majors filed for a hearing. While the SGA Tribunal did not find any racial or non-racial bias in the pep club's auditions process, it did find that five of the selected finalists did not meet the minimum GPA requirements necessary to participate (the ostensible reason for Majors's non-acceptance). Despite the GPA violations, the Tribunal cleared the club of all charges on May 6, a decision that suggested most UT students did not view the pep club's actions as racially biased.[123] UT's Administrative Council then ruled on May 19 that the club had to rescreen all of its applicants. While the issue began as one calling for administrative reform within the university and later evolved into one related to racial discrimination, it revealed one of the many ways white students could use apparently non-racial rationales to exclude Black students from campus organizations. Meanwhile, the administration addressed merely the pep club's contravention of GPA requirements for cheerleaders, without tackling Majors's more damaging claim of racial discrimination.

To further demonstrate that the administration took these students' requests seriously, Aldmon wrote to the BSU president, Johnny Pierce, in September 1969 to follow up on progress towards the seven demands the BSU had presented in the spring. Aldmon listed numerous improvements in conditions for African Americans at the university: the Adawayhi Pep Club's second election for new cheerleaders, the university funds the BSU received, the five Black students employed in dormitories as assistant head residents or resident assistants for the 1969–70 school year (three more than the previous year), the new Black counselor hired to the admissions staff, and a promise from Lawrence Silverman, vice-chancellor for academic affairs, to make a "concerted effort" to hire more Black faculty. The university also declared openness to establishing a Black fraternity or sorority and agreed to stop playing "Dixie" (a Confederate anthem) at home football games. Finally, it had hired forty-two more Black employees for university staff positions.[124] The university clearly felt it was important to demonstrate its cooperation with the BSU's demands. The BSU continued to challenge administrative policy into 1970 with calls for new courses, a separate Black studies library, and reorganizing the Black Studies Committee of the College of Liberal Arts to include appointing a Black chairman, with a two-week deadline for these changes. BSU president Pierce remained skeptical of the administration's intentions. "Black students on this campus," he noted, "have been continually told that the University and the faculty are sincere in their efforts to create a viable and strong Black Studies program. Well, it's time that some substantial results of this 'sincerity' are seen."[125]

As the comparisons between Memphis State's and UT's Black student organizations and programs demonstrate, many of the issues of student power were tied to concerns over racial inequalities. While both Memphis State and UT administrations cooperated with the BSA and BSU respectively, Black and white students continued to feel underrepresented by the administrations.[126] In light of the widespread campus protests across the country during the 1968–1969 academic year, administrators took steps to accommodate student activists to prevent greater unrest on their own campuses. As the Memphis State and UT cases reveal, these measures were often limited and, in the minds of student activists, did little to tackle the root issue—their feelings of not being heard by university administrations. With student disaffection having developed from small protests over student rights, and from mostly Black demands for greater attention to racial inequalities on campus, by the 1969–1970 academic year, Tennessee's campuses seemed on the edge of all-out protest.

The Apex of Student Unrest, 1969–1970

After visiting campuses in Nashville for a congressional investigation into campus unrest, specifically historically Black Fisk University and Tennessee State, and predominantly white Vanderbilt University, Pennsylvania congressman Lawrence Coughlin wrote to Tennessee Republican William Brock about the congressional participants' impressions of campus dynamics in May 1969. According to the congressman, many of the college administrations had "very poor communication with their students, if any." To resolve this problem, Coughlin noted that "where there is ample communication, the problem of violent confrontation appears considerably reduced."[127] Although college administrators and politicians feared student protests, contrary to Coughlin's suggestion (and the Memphis State and Maryville examples), rather than communicating more with disaffected students, the major Tennessee state university system adopted a more adversarial approach to campus unrest, as the events surrounding Edward J. Boling's appointment as UT president demonstrated.

When UT President Andrew D. Holt announced his retirement in June 1969, many students on campus felt they should have more input in the Board of Trustees' choice of a successor.[128] Demands for greater student and faculty influence over the presidential appointment grew louder amid speculation that the Board of Trustees favored Edward J. Boling, vice president of development, whom many students and faculty did not respect.[129] Many students and faculty wanted an academic as university president; Boling's previous work in the university development office was deemed insufficiently scholarly.[130] Tensions rose throughout the fall semester as students and faculty heard rumors that Boling was favored for the presidency. Despite administration-led efforts to include students and faculty in the decision-making process, students and faculty grew increasingly concerned that their opinions were not taken seriously. One article in the *Daily Beacon* in August 1969 addressed the Board of Trustees directly, calling for "this damn monkey business to stop,' and asserted that "students are *not* little children, and faculty members are *not* intellectual day-dreamers." The article concluded with the demand to "give students and faculty a significant voice, not token toleration, in selecting UT's new president. *You may be sorry if you don't*."[131] While the article's author may have been angrier than most students about this issue, the article and the tension on campus impacted university administrators' preparation for and later reaction to the announcement of Boling's appointment in January 1970.

Students called for a demonstration on January 15, 1970, where some 2,500 students attended a five-hour protest as participants or spectators. Classes continued throughout the demonstration. At the demonstration, protestor Peter Kami challenged President Boling to a duel. It was to be an arm-wrestling match, but the choice of the term "duel" was significant.[132] Though many students present that day viewed the challenge as a joke, largely due to Kami's thin shape and small frame, the university administration interpreted it as an advance warning of trouble.[133] One of the few who knew Kami then even described him years later as "the frail Brazilian," as students believed—erroneously—that he had been born in Brazil.[134] Centering the issue of student power in the demonstration, one of the speakers had called for students to give administrators "a taste of student power."[135] Despite efforts by administration officials and protest leaders to negotiate, with mediation help offered by an American Civil Liberties Union (ACLU) representative, Harry Wiersema Sr., after several hours the university and Knoxville police arrived. Following Knoxville police threats to use tear gas, they arrested twenty-two protestors, an incident Chancellor Weaver termed "most distasteful."[136] UT YAF members and policemen in plainclothes assisted in the arrests.[137] Those arrested became known as the "Knoxville 22." An FBI memorandum filed on the event described the participants as a group of "discontented students" and "hippie-type individuals."[138] One Black student activist, James "Sparky" Rucker, argued that the police, by wearing riot gear, had already determined that there would be violence, despite protestors' nonviolent intentions.[139]

Jimmie Baxter, SGA president, told students at the demonstration that he would call for a general student strike the next week if the administration did not approve the demonstrators' proposed reforms.[140] Baxter did not articulate what these particular suggestions were, but he stated that if these demands were not met, UT students would have "to prepare to shut the system down" with the strike. "If we play this game—the game of violence—then I'll start taking bets on who will win," Baxter said, explaining that he believed the police would triumph.[141] Almost a month after the January protest, sixty students gathered in front of the university's administration building in support of the Knoxville 22, then being charged with felony to incite a riot. Some five hundred spectators watched.[142] While the student newspaper, the *Daily Beacon*, seemed to congratulate the campus on the peacefulness of this demonstration, the student-faculty strike later that spring revealed that the major disagreements between the students and faculty and the administration remained unresolved.

Other UT campuses besides Knoxville protested Boling's appointment. Prior to the January 15 Knoxville demonstration, there was a large-scale protest at the satellite Chattanooga campus when the university's Board of Trustees scheduled its meeting there in early January 1970. Amid about thirty protestors screaming "Fascist pig" at security policemen guarding the building where the meeting was taking place, the student government president, Russell King, told the trustees that they had "disregarded student rights and ignored the feelings and opinions of students across the state."[143] Governor Buford Ellington was so frustrated by the public animosity towards the administration that he "expressed fears that their juvenile behavior might result in great harm to the institution" to a local Chattanooga newspaper. The article reporting on the incident cited "some [university] officials" who feared the students' improper behavior could lose the institution more than $1 million in state funding for the next year.[144] For his part, King accused the administration of attempting to keep the students from protesting that day by having a man water the grass on a hill leading to the building where the meeting was meant to take place, even though subfreezing temperatures were forecast that evening. When he asked the man why he was watering the grass on such a cold night, the man reportedly told King, "It's the craziest thing I ever seen. They just told me to come out here and water down the hill."[145] Neither King nor the newspaper discovered who "they" were, but implied it was university officials. The Chattanooga incident showcased the university administration's failure to communicate with students and faculty or to relate to the concerns of those for whom they were responsible.

Subsequent events at UT in May 1970 "struck deeper into the emotions of the people of the state more than anything [else] that's happened" and "hurt the image of the University [deeply]," according to Chancellor Weaver. He was referencing the student and faculty strike that followed the news of the deaths of students at Kent State University during a May 4, 1970, anti-war protest.[146] The three-day strike of classes resulted in a 50 percent drop in class attendance. Many professors joined in. In reaction to the strike, the Army Reserve National Center and the Music Annex Building on campus were firebombed as "mass demonstrations" occurred across the campus.[147] While this may seem to have been just an anti-war demonstration, the strike drew on deep campus grievances at UT.

Following the SGA election controversy of May 1969 and the conflicts surrounding Boling's elevation to the UT presidency in January 1970, the university's administration hoped the atmosphere on campus would cool after the official announcement of Boling's appointment. The revelations of secret U.S. military activities in Cambodia and the violent suppression of a subsequent protest at Kent State exacerbated existing tensions at UT. The student-faculty strike of May 1970 in reaction to the Kent State tragedy began the month on tense terms. Then, President Nixon's surprise appearance at the Billy Graham Crusade held on campus in late May 1970 and the ensuing anti-Nixon protests led university administrators to devise plans for managing future campus demonstrations.[148] At the same time, disagreements arose over invited speaker policies that exposed underlying conflicts over race and student power.

University and College Speaker Policies

Looking towards the future, UT's SGA president Jimmie Baxter said in his post-election interview in May 1969 that if the university adopted an open speaker policy, he wanted speakers who "would at least make a contribution to the student body. I think it would be good if we could bring, [not] so much the has-beens but the young activists."[149] An open speaker policy would allow students to choose anyone to talk on campus, without university administrators having veto power. In the late 1960s, many universities and colleges in Tennessee and across the country were changing their speaker policies. As with other issues concerning student power in the late 1960s, the behavior of university administration, students, and faculty shaped how these policies changed on individual campuses.[150]

Controversies over speaker policies at Tennessee campuses began in 1967 with SNCC chairman Stokely Carmichael's proposed visit to Vanderbilt.[151] In Nashville, the issue soon involved the entire city and multiple campuses. In April 1967, the Vanderbilt University Impact Symposium invited Carmichael to speak, alongside the vocally segregationist Republican senator from South Carolina, Strom Thurmond, and civil rights leader Martin Luther King Jr. Carmichael scheduled speeches at Tennessee State and Fisk Universities for his time in Nashville. A few days before Carmichael's scheduled appearance, the Nashville-based newspapers *Banner* and *Tennessean* began to attack Carmichael as a radical activist. The day before the scheduled event, the typically more moderate *Tennessean* repeated a local businessman's slur that Carmichael was "more Red [Communist] than black."[152] Incidentally, Malcolm X was reportedly invited to the small, private Tennessee Wesleyan College campus in Athens around 1964, so Vanderbilt's invitation to Carmichael was perhaps not as radical as many Nashvillians perceived it.[153]

As the Tennessee General Assembly discussed whether to ban Carmichael's visit to Nashville, officials at Tennessee State and Fisk debated whether to prevent his presence on their campuses, but soon faced opposition from their student bodies. Despite the uproar at his scheduled visit, Carmichael arrived in

Nashville two days earlier than planned and spoke at Fisk University that day (April 6), as well as to SCEF board members the next morning and at Tennessee State that evening, much to the disgust of the *Banner*.[154] Despite Carmichael's speech being relatively tame compared with local white expectations, the North Nashville neighborhood around historically Black Meharry Medical College, Fisk, and Tennessee State witnessed violent incidents as police raided buildings claiming to search for marijuana. Nashville experienced riots from April 8 to April 11, 1967, centered around Fisk and Tennessee State's campuses. Accounts of Molotov cocktails, looting of businesses, and heavy gunfire featured in reports, as well as estimations of participant numbers somewhere between 150 and 300 individuals, mostly of college age.[155] Bottles, bricks, and firecrackers were thrown at police and protestors alike. The commotion restarted the next evening. On Monday the *Banner* covered the disturbances and blamed Carmichael for inciting the violence, despite the fact that Carmichael had actually left Nashville prior to the violence occurring.[156] SNCC members were widely blamed for the unrest in Nashville in April 1967, to the extent that FBI reports and testimony by the head of the Intelligence Division of the Nashville-Davidson County Metropolitan Police Department, Captain John Sorace, implicated the organization as a whole as well as specific members.[157] Part of this focus on SNCC owed to the local SNCC chapter holding the National Black Power Conference a few weeks before the civil unrest, while it also related to SNCC's connections with SSOC and SCEF. Captain Sorace testified afterwards that the riot would not have taken place in Nashville without the influence of outsiders. He mentioned secret meetings between these groups in planning the riot, and said local white officials had a "good rapport with the legitimate [Black] civil rights leaders in the community."[158] College administrators were not free from condemnation either, even those who had presided over campuses that had experienced no violence. An editorial from the *Banner* featured in the *Tennessean* years later condemned Vanderbilt chancellor Alexander Heard for allowing university students to invite Carmichael. It claimed, "Nothing that could be said by way of public apology . . . can remove the stench of the Stokely Carmichael visit to Vanderbilt University."[159] In a subsequent phone conversation with Heard, *Banner* editor and Vanderbilt trustee James Stahlman told Heard that he would "reap the whirlwind" of his choice to support the students' invitation of Carmichael to campus.[160] Heard would later recall that the episode was the "most overt friction" he experienced as chancellor.[161] Following several days of discussions between civil rights leaders, organizers in the community, and municipal staff, the groups remained at odds.[162] African American community leader Avon Williams partially blamed Carmichael for the violence but also said, "Part of the trouble was the result of the blindness of the white people who have refused for months to see trouble coming," a critique applicable to both the wider community and local university campuses.[163] In light of the surveillance and blame for inciting the riot directed towards them, SNCC and Carmichael filed a complaint in U.S. District Court in Nashville on April 21, 1967, where they accused Nashville officials (including the mayor) of "[engaging] in a plot to deprive [them] of their rights." The court decided in favor of the city.[164]

Nashville rioting, in which college-age individuals participated, and the subsequent paranoia of city officials in particular towards Black youths with potential New Left connections, contributed to continued white establishment distrust of protestors. This lack of faith, seemingly understandable given Captain Sorace's anti-activist witch hunt, contributed to the resentment of older white Nashvillians toward anti-Vietnam protestors, and also towards civil rights protestors. One of Sorace's examples of alleged New Left subversion was a meeting on Fisk University's campus of a Freedom School where Diane Nash, famous for her leadership in the Nashville sit-ins a few years earlier, had shown the schoolchildren a film that supported the anti-war movement.[165]

Nashville was not the only Tennessee city to experience a riot during 1967. There were riots in Jackson and Memphis on July 17 and July 27 respectively, Knoxville on July 28, and Chattanooga on August 12.[166] City-wide rioting was a statewide and nationwide concern in the late 1960s, and led to the creation of the National Advisory Commission on Civil Disorders. This commission, established on July 28, 1967, by President Johnson, was commonly known as the Kerner Commission after the chair, Otto Kerner Jr., governor of Illinois. The commission's final report, released on February 29, 1968, found the cause of civic rioting across the nation to be anger among African Americans over a lack of potential economic advancement.[167] The unrest in Tennessee, however, which the commission's report analyzed, also revealed the disillusionment felt by many youths, mostly Black, across the state; this resentment shaped both the reactions to Vietnam in the state as well as continued student attempts to attack perceived racial inequalities. Rather than stemming from Black economic frustrations, many white leaders saw urban unrest as either Black-led disorder or protests by "psychedelic kooks of the campus New Left ... [whose behavior could be described as] subversive organizational deviltry," as an article in the conservative *Banner* put it.[168]

At Vanderbilt, Carmichael's speech struck a chord with Black students who had been discussing whether or not to form their own organization; from fall 1967, they applied for the Afro-American Association to have university status as an official campus organization, and held informal gatherings on the eleventh floor of one of the Carmichael Towers buildings on campus. Vanderbilt basketball player, editor of the university's free newspaper *Rap from the 11th Floor*, and president of the Afro-American Association Godfrey Dillard recalled of the period, "We are not going to sit back and be stagnant until the white student decides to hand us our freedom."[169] Vanderbilt's university chaplain, Rev. Beverly "Bev" Asbury, recalled of Dillard that "all of Vanderbilt's Black students in those days were basically middle-of-the-road, [t]here was not a radical among them." Asbury continued, "But there were people of conscience and deep conviction, and he was one of them."[170]

Within the UT system, administrators worried in the late 1960s that a lengthy debate on the rights of students and the university to invite speakers to campus would threaten the institution. If the administration took a firm stance on the issue, the university feared facing increased violence, public campus demonstrations, media coverage of protestors, and general unrest on the campus. If they gave more control to the student body, however, giving invitations to controversial individuals might create bad publicity for the university, threaten the funding it depended on from state and national-level politicians, and anger conservative alumni and private university donors. After controversy between students and the administration over a prospective visit from African American congressman Adam Clayton Powell, the university administration created a joint faculty-student-administration body, the Student Rights and Responsibilities Committee, to review the incident and potential solutions for future disagreements. The committee was charged with considering speaker policies and making recommendations regarding student life on campus. This committee's existence (with the administration's approval) demonstrated the administration's intent at least to hear the reforms students wanted.[171] In addition to Powell, UT students invited speakers such as lawyer William Kunstler, political scientist Hans Morgenthau, *New York Post* columnist Max Lerner, LSD researcher Dr. Timothy Leary, and southern civil rights leader and Vietnam War opponent Julian Bond during the late 1960s and early 1970s.[172] In connections with campuses and regions outside of the South, speaker invitations during this period were part of a national trend, with particular speakers being of such notoriety and popularity that student bodies across the country wanted to have them speak. Similarities between UT and two universities in Oklahoma, the University of Oklahoma and Oklahoma State University, points to the lack of regionality in speaker invitations at state universities of the time; Leary, Ginsberg, and Powell were invited by students at Oklahoma State University, but Powell's offer was denied by the administration (much like the initial actions by UT officials), and Bond was invited to speak at the University of Oklahoma.[173]

When the student-run lecture series *Issues* sought approval in the summer of 1968 for its upcoming fall semester speakers through the administrative channels outlined in the university student handbook, Chancellor Weaver told *Issues* executive committee members and SGA president Chris Whittle in a meeting that one of the invited speakers, Dick Gregory, could not attend the series because "Gregory's appearance would upset the outside community, including the legislature, and could potentially result in a cut in the University's state appropriated budget."[174] Governor Ellington's recommendation of a lower financial appropriation for the UT system in 1969 seemed to validate Weaver's concern for the university's financial wellbeing.[175] The ensuing conflicts between students and the administration from Weaver's actions led the university president, Andrew D. Holt, to ask the Board of Trustees to review the speaker policies on other campuses in the region and to consider alternative policies the university could adopt. Ranging from not changing the current policy at all to giving administrative approval to university students for all future speakers, Holt's list of options demonstrated an effort to accommodate all interests and keep the university's policy transition private.[176] Contrasting with Holt's seeming encouragement for the Board of Trustees to adopt an open speaker policy (allowing students to invite outside speakers without prior administrative approval), Chancellor Weaver announced his opposition to the policy in September 1968 on the grounds that administrators should have the right to refuse speaker requests, given their need "to supply appropriate security and in effect, appropriate financial aid."[177] At its October 1968 meeting, rather than adopting an open speaker policy for the UT system, the Board of Trustees ordered chancellors on each campus to devise a speaker policy, and then return general guidelines for later board consideration.[178]

With the Board of Trustees making no decision on the speaker policy at its February 1969 meeting, impatient students filed suit in a U.S. District Court three weeks later. The students' suit, alongside Julian Bond's refusal to speak at Knoxville owing to UT's denial of an invitation to Dick Gregory, and the university's 1969 blocking of Timothy Leary's speaking, kept the dispute well publicized through early 1969.[179] In the court case, the judge ruled that the university had violated the freedom of speech guaranteed to all citizens, but he refused to issue an injunction, which the students and faculty who had sued the university had requested. A restraining order, the judge contended, was unnecessary.[180] The university developed a new speaker policy by June 1969, seemingly as a consequence of sustained student pressure. The new policy created a fifteen-person committee with final authority over the granting or denial of invitations from groups that requested funding aid to bring speakers to campus. Making up the committee (reappointed annually) were five faculty members, the SGA president, the senior class president, presidents of five other student organizations appointed by the chancellor, two chancellor-designated campus administrators, and a university system representative chosen by the president. The policy further specified that speakers would be held to standing local, state, and national laws and that it would be the sponsoring organization's responsibility to ensure the speakers' awareness of this condition.[181]

On May 14, 1970, the civil rights activist and lawyer William Kunstler spoke at UT to a reported crowd of fifteen hundred students. Kunstler was famous for his widely publicized defense of the Chicago Seven, anti-war activists charged with conspiracy to incite a riot in the aftermath of the violence surrounding the 1968 Democratic National Convention in Chicago.[182] The speech was originally scheduled for April 2, 1970, followed by another speech on April 10 in Nashville as part of Vanderbilt University's Impact Symposium, where Kunstler would speak along with conservative columnist James J. Kilpatrick.[183] The arraignment for the Knoxville 22 was scheduled for the same day as Kunstler's Knoxville engagement. While he was not expected to offer legal advice to the group, Kunstler's anticipated presence in town at the same time was notable; Lonnie Kaufman, one of the Knoxville 22, reportedly contacted Kunstler for legal assistance after the speech had been scheduled.[184]

The news that UT students intended to invite Kunstler to speak on campus enraged conservatives across the state. With Kunstler's larger-than-life personality, his public statements that students should organize against oppressive campus administrations, and his committed defense of the Chicago Seven (whom many Americans saw as ridiculous and disrespectful of the justice system), many of the state's leaders would not support funding his visit. The governor and ex officio chairman of UT's Board of Trustees, Buford Ellington, said he would "put up a strong fight to see that no state funds or student fees go into financing speeches by men like Kunstler."[185] Knoxville mayor Leonard Rogers and Republican congressman John Duncan Sr. joined Ellington in opposing Kunstler's visit.[186] The local paper's editorial section mocked the event for weeks leading up to the speech; one state resident even suggested that Kunstler give the speech at the city dump rather than the UT campus. "It shouldn't be too hard to provide him with a soap box," the man argued, but if it should take place at UT, the campus "should be fully fumigated following the long hair and hand waving affair."[187]

Kunstler's speech in Knoxville for April 2 was cancelled at the last minute due to travel complications, but the local newspaper covered his subsequent speeches at the University of Kentucky (UK) and later at Vanderbilt in detail.[188] UK students invited Kunstler to speak on campus on April 4, 1970, and despite expressing concern and frustration over his invitation, University of Kentucky president Dr. Otis Singletary allowed Kunstler to speak. Singletary stated that the lawyer's presence on campus "does not imply university approval or disapproval" of his views. Nonetheless, the Kunstler function had to be "peaceful and orderly." A group of two hundred attendees listened to the speech, during which Kunstler reportedly told students that they "have the power to turn this university upside down, as they did at Columbia, if you really want to," a reference to that university's 1968 student uprising.[189] Two of the Knoxville 22, Peter Kami and Carroll Bible, had organized a "statewide student alliance" to demonstrate at Centennial Park in Nashville in conjunction with Kunstler's April 10 speech, with the event set for April 12. Pledging to "fight" government "repression," Kami stated they were "interested in making an alliance between students, poor people, blacks, labor unions and other minority groups."[190] This alliance is reminiscent of the intentions of radical student groups like SSOC and SDS, and highlights that white Tennessee student activists hoped to organize minorities to advance progressive political ideals. Jerry Rubin, one of the Chicago Seven defendants, was scheduled to speak at the rally at Centennial Park, as was Rev. James Lawson and AFSCME representative Joe Paisley, both of whom had played active roles in the 1968 Memphis Sanitation Strike.[191]

Kunstler's speech at UT's Circle Park on May 14, 1970, concerned the UT administration because he encouraged the students to continue their protests until the university met their demands. A report on the speech filed by the local branch of the FBI included the following underscored sentence: "He [Kunstler] stated students should not worry about getting jobs, getting degrees, getting into law school, but should worry about rights and, if necessary, occupy buildings and destroy property."[192] In his speech, the lawyer urged UT students to strike for greater student political power and in solidarity for the antiwar movement. While Kunstler claimed not to advocate rebellion per se, he contended that "we're beyond the point where conventional protest is called for."[193] Kunstler's words did nothing to assuage the already-apprehensive university administration's fears of further student protests. Following Kunstler's speech, UT student Carroll Bible led an impromptu march, where students chanted "strike" with raised fists as they walked across the campus to the Humanities Plaza.[194] With professors Dr. Richard Marius and Dr. Charles Reynolds in attendance, a group of seventy-five students debated the idea of a strike later that evening in the University Center. As UT students had just held a strike the week before, the leaders of the earlier strike did not feel another one so soon afterwards was viable.[195]

The socio-political environment on campuses shaped what student activists stated, and how they behaved. Meanwhile, as concerned as they were to enact change, administrators and politicians feared the implications of unrestricted, student-led campus unrest. These worries impacted how protests developed on campuses across Tennessee.

Administrative and Political Responses to Student Unrest

College administrators in politically conservative communities—like East Tennessee—fretted that local residents would harm student protestors. In a 1987 interview, Chancellor Weaver recalled that in 1969 and 1970, the university was "living with protests every day ... [including] bomb threats at football games]... There were constant protests and threats of protests ... so there was a period there where the protests were the style."[196] Speaking specifically of the protest during President Nixon's speech at the Graham Crusade, Weaver remembered being concerned about the general public's "revulsion" towards student demonstrators.[197] Still treating the university as responsible for students' wellbeing (reminiscent of the *in loco parentis* measures students were fighting against), Weaver retrospectively claimed that the university needed to protect student protestors from potential backlash from local residents. Following Kent State, Weaver recalled that the university had "lots of problems ... from conservative activists saying, 'if you're not going to control it [likely liberal activism or campus disruptions] then we're going to come in and handle it.'"[198] Following the campus protests, the university issued statements denouncing the demonstrations.[199]

UT's administration was well aware of ongoing nationwide student-led protests. Earlier university efforts to resolve problems before they escalated waned in the mid-1960s as most campuses across the country now did the reverse, seeking to defuse protests only once they occurred. The state legislature also developed legislation to crack down on campus protests. Between 1967 and 1969 the state legislature made non-student incitement or participation in riots at schools a felony, and obstructing access to any campus buildings a misdemeanor.[200] Efforts by the state legislature in April 1969 to curtail potential campus disorders on state-funded campuses involved the introduction of House Bill Number 86 and Senate Bill Number 376. While the House bill was believed to be unconstitutional by SGA representative Gary Crawford and future UT president Edward J. Boling because it limited access to assembly through permits, both men supported the Senate bill, which allowed a protestor refusing to leave the campus or preventing the "normal use" of campus buildings to be charged with trespassing, a misdemeanor under Section 39–105.[201] Chancellor Weaver revealed his awareness of this non-conciliatory trend in a letter to university personnel in September 1969, discussing the state legislature's recent legislation regarding the appropriate measures campuses could take against demonstrators. It was, Weaver stated, "important" for university members to know the new legislation's guidelines and particularly the "penalties faced by those who violate them."[202]

Before Weaver acknowledged the possibility of campus disturbances, President Holt dismissed concerns about student unrest in his biennial report for 1968–70; while UT campuses "felt the impact of the 'student unrest'" seen at other institutions, "99 per cent of UT's students have conducted themselves with maturity" while only a "small" minority "resorted to disruptive measures in attempting to make themselves heard."[203] Holt also discussed the creation of university-wide efforts to incorporate more student and faculty participation into administrative decisions. One of these methods was the adoption of student and faculty counselors to the president, with representatives from each campus giving the president "direct communications" with students and faculty.[204] While the university administration certainly wanted to preempt demonstrations, and student unrest defied simple resolution, the administrators' misinterpretations of the causes of unrest and their unwillingness to meaningfully incorporate student-faculty input in decision-making led to unprecedented disruption by early 1970.

In response to student agitation in the 1969–70 academic year, the university established the Committee to Develop Guidelines on Appropriate Use of Force on UT Campus. The committee presented its final report to the university senate on June 17, 1970. The committee's first goal was to "develop approaches which would minimize the probability that the use of force will be necessary in the event of campus disturbances . . . and to determine the point, if any, at which force should be used." The report called for establishing an Advisory Committee, with three students and three faculty members, to "consult with and advise" the chancellor "as to the use of force when disruption and violence may occur or has occurred." It also set up a Faculty Observer Corps of three Advisory Committee-elected faculty members to "provide visual coverage of campus demonstrations and protest activities" as well as compile a "visual and written record of incidents associated with demonstrations and of the behavior of individuals, students-staff-non-university, who may become involved in such demonstrations."[205] The administration was evidently developing a plan for dealing with potential demonstrations in response to events from the previous academic year. In doing so, the university acknowledged that student demands may have merited consideration before protests occurred. By establishing the protocol for the Faculty Observer Corps to watch peers' behavior, the committee (and by extension the university) demonstrated that its primary concern was to identify potential problematic situations and instigators prior to any activism.

Administrative decisions such as this often were a reflection of the university president's personal commitment to the subject. In public statements, Edward Boling's central concern was protecting academic freedom. He spoke of "the ideal of academic freedom" that the university president must uphold, and that his "moral obligation" was "not to pronounce a position for or against" any "current political, economic and social issues."[206] Boling argued the university president needed to protect academic freedom in its highest ideal, if only because expressing differing views formed the core of academic discourse. By presenting the university as an institution formed on ideals of free speech and simultaneously responsible for protecting those ideals, Boling invoked ideas of constitutional democracy. He also appeared to suggest why the university took the positions it had in 1970 immediately following his appointment, namely opposing campus disruptions (detrimental to Boling's notion of academic freedom) while not engaging with the complaints of the disaffected students.

In his role as university president, Boling's rhetoric was similar to Tennessee congressman William E. Brock. While he was running successfully for Senator Albert Gore Sr.'s Senate seat in 1970, Brock discussed campus demonstrations and particularly the youth of the participants. Brock was one of several United States congressmen who sent President Nixon a report on "campus unrest" in June 1969, which they regarded as a problem of "critical urgency."[207] Similar to Boling, Brock used constitutional language to invoke ideas of traditional democracy and the contemporary ideals of the Republican Party. Speaking about campus riots in October 1970, Brock conflated student unrest with violent 1960s upheavals, a tactic numerous conservative politicians employed. It was, he claimed, a "tragedy" that so much of the country "chose to turn a blind eye while the epidemic of violence and anarchy reached the boiling point." He lamented that the majority of American college students "respect America" while a vocal "minority of trouble-makers among these must be taught that they can't spit in Uncle Sam's face and pick his pocket at the same time." To resolve this situation, Brock called for stricter university administration policies.[208] In a separate address, Brock contended that "violence on the campus is just as immoral . . . as violence anywhere else in America . . . [it] simply means that one individual is taking away the rights of another."[209]

Both Chancellor Weaver and Congressman Brock used the term "sanctuary" to describe the university administration's responsibility to protect students' and faculty interests. For Weaver, UT was not to be a "sanctuary of any sort for those who break the law," while Brock referred to campuses as "not a sanctuary where violence will be tolerated."[210] It is also worth mentioning that both of these usages of the word "sanctuary" occurred in June and July 1970 respectively, indicating the parallel shift of opinion after the May 1970 UT protests. Boling and Brock's ideological justifications for opposing campus protests suggested they saw protestors as rabble rousers, and mirrored the national-level shift towards "law and order" promotion, rather than considering the merits of protestors' demands. In their views, those students and faculty who did not participate in demonstrations were the law-abiding, ideal Americans. While UT administrators in 1969 and 1970 generally saw nonviolent demonstrations as valid expressions of opinion, Boling, Weaver, and Brock's remarks indicate that by the end of 1970 this viewpoint had shifted.

Maryville College marked a major exception to UT's adversarial approach towards student protests. The Board of Directors at Maryville began developing a campus plan in the spring of 1969 to deal with potential demonstrations, prior to any campus disruptions. After the American Council on Education published a "Declaration on Campus Unrest," Maryville's Board approved the declaration as an action plan on April 4, 1969.[211] Much as Boling argued, the declaration considered the college as a "part of the greater democratic society," where "the philosophy of academic freedom and individual freedom" must be protected.[212] Nonetheless, the college's declaration definitively gave college members the right "to criticize, to protest, to petition, to suggest, and to attempt by orderly, constitutional, peaceful, and legal means, any rule or regulation of the College with which they do not agree."[213] Very likely a product of the college's Presbyterian founding, which emphasized the rights of individuals, this statement was more affirmative of campus demonstrators' rights than other Tennessee institutions during this period. This behavior fits with the progressive position the college administration took towards *Brown v. Board of Education*, in integrating the college two days after the decision.[214]

In summary, the operation of Tennessee colleges and universities changed significantly between 1968 and 1970, as leftist students and faculty sought greater control over university policies and their personal lives, while administrators sought to limit student protest, and occasionally student complaints. The reformation of university administrative policies occurred on campuses across the country, catalyzed by increased student enrollment in the 1960s. Throughout Tennessee, demands for greater student autonomy often overlapped with concerns over racial inequalities, as the push for greater sensitivity to Black students' academic and extracurricular lives on campus demonstrated. As disputes over university speaker policies showed, disagreements between students wanting greater control and worried administrators proved intractable. Fearing student unrest, many universities devised policies for dealing with student demonstrations, although with few exceptions these approaches sought to contain protest, rather than resolve the causes of student dissatisfaction. The few instances of successful administrative management of student unrest in the late 1960s—notably Maryville, Memphis State, and Tennessee Wesleyan—were characterized by administrators' willingness to communicate relatively openly with students and incorporate several student demands. At the time Tennessee student activism peaked in 1970, universities—notably the UT system—shifted from a relatively conciliatory approach to student protestors to denying the right to demonstrate at all. Simultaneously, disillusionment over the Vietnam War brought a crest in student activism on campuses.

CHAPTER 5

"Deep Division"

Tennessee Student Activists and the Vietnam War

Tennessee campuses, like the state's politics, were conservative in the late 1960s, as were the majority of their student bodies. Students were aware of major issues that activists across the United States organized around in the latter part of the decade, verbalizing their opinions in newspaper editorials and articles and sometimes organizing protests of their own. In general, however, the trend across the state and the South more generally was that anti-war protests were smaller and received growing attention from campus and community as the decade grew to a close.[1] Those who demonstrated in anti-war protests were a minority of their student body, with remaining students either in support of U.S. involvement in Vietnam, in favor of trusting those in leadership (either in government or campus administration), or politically apathetic. On Tennessee campuses, the peace movement—which was so prominent among college students nationally by the late 1960s—was not a strong motivator of student protest. In scrutinizing the actions of the minority of students and faculty who organized anti-war protests leading up to May 1970, however, a picture of smaller, yet equally symbolic events correlating with the national anti-war movement emerges. The draft, the morality of the war, and continued racial inequalities inspired campus discussions over the roles of students and "the machine." There were activist tendencies among larger groups of southern students regarding campus rights, so southern anti-war activists connected Vietnam with student power in an attempt to garner more support for their efforts. This also related to the national debates around African Americans drafted into the war and the calls for Third World liberation. Nonetheless, mobilization of the region's college students never matched their expectations. Conservatism and apathy remained problems; so did racial division in the ranks of the students themselves.

In the years prior to Vietnam, Tennessee student activism had been limited to two student groups, divided by race and social background, whose collaborations with each other produced significant albeit small-scale protests. But these protests remained local and episodic. With the national civil rights movement radicalizing and the anti-war movement gaining momentum, student activists who had previously organized their peers in campus-based demonstrations for student rights now built larger, albeit more fractured, student coalitions around issues of race, war, and power. David Acey, a Black student leader at Memphis State University, declared during the campus protest following Kent State that, "Four white students had to die before other whites understood what black people had known all of their lives."[2] He was probably referring to the role of government authority as an oppressive force.

While the Tennessee anti-war student protestors were in the minority, their behavior still broadly followed the arc of national anti-war activism. Unlike other universities where student body anger over the draft and corporate funding from Dow Chemical and others inspired large, long-lasting protests that took over the entire campus, southern campuses experienced smaller, seemingly isolated protests. Across the South, protests peaked in May 1970; only the universities of Texas and Florida saw later student-led protests on a May 1970 scale, in April and May 1972 respectively.[3]

Differences in the perception of student activism nationally and in Tennessee speaks to contemporary distinctions drawn between protests on the state's campuses and the national anti-war movement. Despite concerns from East Tennessee university administrators and politicians representing the region that the New Left would organize a significant movement, however, local intelligence officers initially doubted that radicals could present a substantial threat. The Knoxville division of the FBI's COINTELPRO, for example, perceived its surveillance of New Leftists in the area as unnecessary, as it suggested to the FBI director's office in June 1969 to close down its operations.[4] The Bureau disregarded this recommendation, however, "in view of the serious [campus] violence" nationwide during the previous academic year, which was largely "spontaneous," and directed the Knoxville division to continue its counterintelligence work. "During this period of abated activity by the New Left," J. Edgar Hoover counselled, "you should prepare for and seek new ways of arresting the attacks by the New Left which will, in all probability, develop during the coming academic year."[5] Despite the FBI's apprehension about campus activity and the lack of concern from the Knoxville division about future protests, the 1969–70 academic year *was* in fact the most explosive during this period, with Kent State acting as the spark.

"The student movement may, indeed, have flown South—and landed. There is even the possibility that it will stay awhile and flourish."

In fall 1965 it seemed possible that a substantial anti-war movement would develop, distinctly southern in its approach and concerns, but despite several campus protests across the South, a widespread movement failed to emerge. The main reasons for anti-war activism fizzling were the expanding divide between Black and white students and the fading sense of urgency that had permeated the conservatism of the region. Sustained racial inequality in higher education threatened the limited biracial campus activism under the auspices of "student power" that followed demonstrations against segregated public accommodations earlier in the decade; Vietnam proved more divisive than unifying for Black and white students. Ed Hamlett, a Nashville-based white activist, recalled that "you couldn't fight poverty, you couldn't fight racism ... 'cause everything was being poured into ... this damn war over in Vietnam."[6] Fighting racism, in his eyes, should have remained paramount, an approach that the government's military expenditures threatened nationally. White Tennessee activists could never quite overcome the non-liberal majority's patriotism and reverence for the military to persuade them to sympathize with their cause. Meanwhile, while Black students recognized their disproportionate military burden, they proved more concerned with domestic racial inequalities than foreign interventions.[7] When they did protest the war, most Blacks focused their efforts primarily on measures to assist other African Americans and non-white people worldwide, rather than seeking interracial collaboration with their white activist peers.

The number of anti-war actions on southern campuses grew from the fall of 1965. Mirroring questions of focus and direction from previous organizing, including around labor and student rights on campus, SSOC activists debated whether or not the group should become involved in anti-war protests, and to what extent these protests should be part of the movement, if at all. This issue was divisive enough that it threatened to break the organization apart in 1965, but SSOC remained unified and supported the recently created Southern Coordinating Committee to End the War in Vietnam (SCCEWV), which styled itself as the first southern anti-Vietnam War protest group.[8] During the fall and winter of 1965 and 1966, SCCEWV brought together five hundred people in Nashville at Vanderbilt University to hear SDS founder and anti-war activist Tom Hayden speak about his recent trip to North Vietnam, and also held events in Atlanta, Georgia, and Richmond, Virginia.[9] In addition to Tom Hayden's speech at Vanderbilt, the university also held a debate around the same time between Vanderbilt physics professor, civil rights activist, and SSOC supporter Dr. David Kotelchuck and political science professor Dr. John T. Dorsey.[10]

Black student activists also contended with issues surrounding Vietnam from 1965, but in ways that divided the civil rights coalition. SNCC, like other major civil rights organizations, was forced to take a stand on the anti-war movement. They did so publicly in a statement on January 6, 1966, declaring that they did not agree with the United States' involvement in Vietnam, and connecting the unjust treatment of Black draftees to African American oppression in the segregated South.[11] Former Nashville student sit-in leader Diane Nash, by then a national figure in the civil rights movement, visited North Vietnam in December 1966.[12] Nash's public statements about the visit reiterated the direction many civil rights activists in Tennessee took towards Vietnam: she emphasized that she was there solely to promote the interests of African Americans, victims, as were the Vietnamese, of American imperialism.[13] She offered few words on which to build a united front with southern white anti-war protestors. Historian Clayborne Carson argued that SNCC's opposition to the war "obscured a growing gulf" between Black SNCC activists and white New Leftists, but this division was already apparent in Tennessee. The racial divisions among southern student activists were widening.[14]

The war also exposed issues concerning the assertion of manhood for young Black men. These ideas were present among African Americans long before Vietnam, as the Memphis Sanitation Strike in 1968 demonstrated with the images of protestors carrying signs declaring "I AM A MAN." Steve Estes has demonstrated that Blacks historically viewed military service as a "rite of passage into manhood."[15] Conflicts surrounding the U.S. involvement in Vietnam, however, amplified tensions in how African Americans, particularly those who were of enlistment age, viewed military service. James E. Westheider's research has shown that while many African Americans had previously viewed military enlistment as an opportunity for societal advancement and recognition, the Vietnam War was different.[16] Part of this variance can be attributed to the emergence of student power politics on college campuses, as well as the racial discrimination evident in the draft. In Memphis, Terry Whitmore graduated from high school in 1966 and considered the military as the only option available to him for social advancement. He felt like a "dumb motherfucker," who upon graduation pondered what "[Uncle] Sam [would] want with me. A nobody. Just a poor-ass on the block. Sam doesn't even know I'm alive." When he enlisted, Whitmore chose the Marines in an effort to assert his manhood. The Marines, he claimed, were "the *real* military," not any "cheap imitation."[17] Even in his decision to enlist, Whitmore referenced his feeling of being unknown, with the implication that participation in the Marines would give him recognition.

A significant feature of the Vietnam anti-war movement, and indeed the changes seen to the student movement from 1965, was the draft. White and Black activists alike viewed the draft as part of a racist machine, a prominent example of a system constructed and run by powerful white elites to keep young people in their place.[18] The Selective Service System, which oversaw the draft, was not intended to be racist, but the differences between white and Black young men in the mid-1960s in terms of education, access to legal aid, and even health resulted in the shocking differences in the military burden experience by the two races. As the United States' military involvement in the war intensified from 1965, larger percentages of young men were called up for the draft.[19] At this point, draft deferments were available for a number of reasons, including enrolment in higher education. These college deferments were more available to whites than Blacks, given the high cost of education and the higher standard of historically white secondary education. White men who were not in school and were called up for the draft were also more likely than their Black peers to have the financial resources for a lawyer to argue their cause or a doctor to provide a medical excuse for their unsuitability to fight. For example, the national median income in 1967 for an average Black family was $5,141, versus $8,274 for whites.[20] All of these reasons contributed to more Blacks than whites being drafted, which led many young activists to portray the draft as part of a "sinister attempt to murder young African Americans."[21] The Selective Service System was also focused on using a "device of pressurized guidance" to "channel" students with deferments into careers that contributed to the "national interest," as a July 1965 memo sent to local draft boards across the country explained.[22] This indicated that the military intended to press college students not only to excel in their studies, but to pursue nationally "beneficial" careers after graduation, instead of dropping out of school or becoming activists, for example.[23]

Further concerns about the draft for Black youths regarded racially discriminatory local Selective Service System draft boards. These boards were made up of local officials tasked with overseeing the classification of potential draftees, and therefore decided who would be drafted.[24] One of the methods of classification was the Selective Service College Qualifications Test, an aptitude test on which those who wished to hold a 2-s deferment, or students enrolled in school, needed to make a score of 70 or higher out of 150.[25] The test, introduced in March 1966 but not undertaken until May 1966, was voluntary for students to take, but failing to sit the exam would put the student in a precarious position if he was called up for the draft.[26] SSOC collaborated with

SDS in its attempt to counter the test by handing out their own exam at the testing centers nationwide. In doing so, they recognized the continued injustice an aptitude test posed to youths, particularly those who were Black, and many who were civil rights activists. Those taking the SDS/SSOC exam would assess themselves, deciding whether they "know enough about the Vietnamese to take some day the personal responsibility for their death."[27] Blacks were underrepresented on the draft boards themselves, notably in areas with higher white populations resistant to desegregation, which led SNCC activist Cleveland Sellers and others to contend that the boards were racially discriminatory.[28] There is some debate about whether the draft boards intentionally enlisted civil rights activists and radicals, but as white New Left activists more frequently scored above-average grades, when the Selective Service changed its policy of conscription to include those university students with below-average grades, Black activists remained more vulnerable to conscription than their white peers.[29]

Given the deployment of Black men at much higher rates than their white peers, civil rights leaders in areas with little or no African American representation on draft boards sought remedies from the federal government. In Memphis, the local NAACP chapter's executive secretary, Maxine Smith, wrote directly to President Johnson's administration in September 1966 following the "token" appointment of a Black individual to each of the six draft boards. This recent appointment was a step in the right direction, Smith argued, but out of twenty-six draft board representatives, having six Black members would still greatly underrepresent African Americans in Memphis and Shelby County. As approximately 50 percent of Shelby County residents who were drafted were Black, and as at least 50 percent of those from Shelby who had been killed in the war were Black, there needed to be more Black representation on the local draft boards. Smith also advocated employing "a comparable percentage" of African Americans on the local Appeal Board (which was then all-white) as on the boards themselves.[30] Smith's demands were rebuffed. The director of the Selective Service System, General Lewis B. Hershey, replied that the president could not handle this request. Rather, because members of the draft boards were appointed by the governor of Tennessee, Smith and the Memphis NAACP branch needed to contact the governor or state director of the Selective Service of Tennessee.[31]

The national draft program transformed dramatically beginning in 1967, as it implemented changes intended to resolve at least some racial and class discrimination. At this point, deferments for students enrolled in graduate school were phased out, alongside later deferments for those in undergraduate education and the exceptions for those with children.[32] These alterations to the draft system affected young men across the country and catalyzed the anti-war movement's growth nationally.

In spring 1967, anti-war protest moved from discussions at campuses and draft centers to public demonstrations. A group of SSOC activists, including Vanderbilt students, protested a speech President Johnson gave on the Vietnam War in Nashville on March 15, 1967. During the speech, forty demonstrators carried signs, one of them reading, "WE NEED BLACK MEN HERE TO FIGHT WHITE RACISTS."[33] The sign indicated activists' understanding of a racial aspect to the draft selection process, and that SSOC activists believed issues of domestic racial inequality trumped any imperative of fighting in Vietnam. As the president's motorcade drove past the state capitol building after the speech, three SSOC activists protested Johnson's appearance by falling to the ground in front of cars in the motorcade. They were subsequently arrested. The following day, the district attorney worked with the activists' lawyer to arrange an out-of-court settlement, so as to "not make martyrs out of you."[34]

Similar anti-war protests occurred at other large southern universities, demonstrating the continuity of objectives and tactics regionally. When General William Westmoreland came to the University of South Carolina in Columbia to receive an honorary doctorate in April 1967, a group of thirty students protesting his presence on campus were hit with "projectiles" and had their protest signs ripped by a mob of over four hundred students who supported Westmoreland.[35] That same month, the University of Texas SDS chapter picketed Vice President Hubert Humphrey's visit to Austin, Texas. After the university condemned the SDS chapter's demonstration, several thousand students organized a rally in support of the SDS members' efforts.[36]

Some activists struggled to understand why southern support for the war was so strong. In his March 1967 correspondence with the historian and public intellectual C. Vann Woodward, SSOC member Ed Hamlett wrote: "I've thought about what you said concerning the South's fervor for the holy war in VN; it seems to me that this arises partially out of guilt—the guilt that comes from rebeling [sic] over rights for Negroes—so they try to make up for it by beating the war drums even harder. Does that make sense?" Americans, in Hamlett's view, needed to break away from the "oppression our country is practicing" including "the racism and exploitation of the poor at home and the Selective Service System."[37]

Continued U.S. military activity in Vietnam over the summer and fall of 1967 significantly impacted the national anti-war movement, while activism in Tennessee continued its incremental progression. The commander of the U.S. forces, General William Westmoreland, publicly stated that the war was being fought with "no end in sight," and although Westmoreland later changed his view, claiming in late November 1967 that the United States was winning, the quote indicated uncertainty over the war's progress. In August 1967 the *New York Times* similarly described the war as having reached a "stalemate."[38] Frustrations and fatigue over U.S. involvement in Vietnam were turning popular opinion against the war: one Gallup Poll from October 1967 estimated that over 40 percent of those aged twenty-one to twenty-nine years old considered the Vietnam War a mistake.[39]

With war-weariness spreading nationally, SSOC doggedly pursued its antiwar campaign in the 1967–1968 school year, with mixed results. While its earlier Peace Tour through Florida in February and March 1967 had been moderately successful, the organization's efforts to expand the program across the South were not well received. Subsequent Peace Tours in Tennessee, Arkansas, North Carolina, South Carolina, and Virginia were met with antagonism and spurred little support.[40]

Two protests on Tennessee campuses in November 1967 did draw some support from college students and faculty. During a visit by General Maxwell Taylor, the chair of the President's Intelligence Advisory Board, to UT in Knoxville on November 1, 1967, fifteen demonstrators gathered outside the Alumni Memorial Gymnasium while Taylor spoke inside the building. They were met by seventy-five to one hundred egg-throwing pro-war activists.[41] In Nashville, Vanderbilt University welcomed campus recruiters from the Dow Corning Company, the U.S. State Department, the Central Intelligence Agency (CIA), and the U.S. Naval Reserve Officers' Training Corps (ROTC) in November.[42] Dow Chemical Company was invested in the Dow Corning Company, which produced napalm, a highly flammable gel used by the U.S. military in Vietnam. In reaction to its production of napalm, Dow had begun to see large-scale protests against their presence on college campuses in fall 1967, most notably at the University of Wisconsin in Madison, where a demonstration had ended with physical confrontations between police and students, and the arrests of hundreds of protestors.[43] The Vanderbilt Vietnam Action Committee (VVAC), a group of students and faculty united in anti-war efforts, protested each of these campus recruitment visits. The day after Dow Chemical's planned visit was announced for November 9, fifty VVAC members marched from the campus chapel to the Science Center carrying posters and handing out fliers. The VVAC protestors wore "lab coats stained with a rusty red and with 'DOW' printed on the back" and carried a grey coffin.[44] In a VVAC account of the protest, the group declared that with this demonstration, "the student movement may, indeed, have flown South—and landed. There is even the possibility that it will stay awhile and flourish."[45]

The Tet Offensive in January 1968 belied official accounts that the United

States was winning in Vietnam and caused a marked shift in public opinion across the country. A *Wall Street Journal* editorial on February 23 stated that "the whole Vietnam effort may be doomed," while in a February 27 broadcast from Vietnam, CBS News anchor Walter Cronkite said the United States was "mired in stalemate" and had no other option but "to negotiate, not as victors but as an honorable people who ... did the best they could."[46] In part a response to these public representations of Vietnam, the national anti-war movement continued to gather momentum, simultaneously shaping students' political identification. National poll results showed the proportion of those describing themselves as "radical or far left" and "liberal" rose between spring 1968 and spring 1969.[47] Furthermore, the assassination of Martin Luther King Jr. in Memphis on April 4, 1968, and subsequent nationwide urban unrest further spotlighted the persistence of racial discrimination and disproportionate levels of poverty among Blacks across the country. The campus takeover of Columbia University in New York City in April 1968 and the protests (and subsequent televised violence) during the Democratic National Convention in August 1968, as well as the trial of student activists named the "Chicago Seven," indicated an escalation of potentially hostile events involving students. By September, an Army intelligence briefing to Johnson's administration stated its expectation that "student agitation ... [would] follow previous motivational and action patterns ... [including] opposition to U.S. presence in Vietnam, opposition to the military draft, dissatisfaction with school administrations, support of 'black power' racial concepts, and a general expression of societal alienation."[48]

While Tennessean proponents of the anti-war movement remained small in number in late 1967, the Tet Offensive in January 1968 spurred an escalation in anti-war protests on college campuses across the South.[49] From early 1968, college administrators in Tennessee became increasingly concerned that the various tensions existing on each campus from earlier in the decade would combine with anti-war sentiment to create full-scale campus unrest. Administrators at Memphis State University and Vanderbilt University were well aware of these national protests and were determined to keep similar incidents from developing on their campuses. Cecil C. Humphreys, president of Memphis State University, took steps to clarify the state Board of Education's position as well as that of his university regarding student demonstrations. In August 1968, Humphreys proposed a set of guidelines that the board passed unanimously, which outlined the rights of students to protest policies and politics on campus, local, state, and national levels. These guidelines also protected the university's interests by prohibiting demonstrations that prevented students from attending classes, using college facilities, and those that involved illegal activity.⁵⁰ Humphreys later referred to the late 1960s as "the best of times and the worst of times," during which he and other administrators made it their goal "to not over-react."⁵¹

Alexander Heard, president of Vanderbilt, urged his Board of Trust to consider "how Vanderbilt should conduct itself" in "the light of the intensified social activism throughout [America]."⁵² Heard was sympathetic to student concerns but also identified their frequently contradictory character. He stated that "a student ridicules the concept of *in loco parentis* . . . [saying] 'Our personal lives are not your concern' . . . [then the same student] pleads that the university has an obligation, in the name of intellectual freedom as one of them said to me, to protect students against the requirements of the Selective Service system."⁵³

The two years following Tet witnessed a gradual escalation of protests on campuses, rather than a marked spike. When General Lewis Hershey of the Selective Service System spoke at UT on March 28, 1968, between 500 and 1,000 demonstrators wore black armbands and stood outside the University Center, waiting for him to leave the building after his speech. Three students burned their draft cards before the crowd. As violence was feared, campus police wearing crash helmets surrounded the protestors, whose ranks included students from UT as well as from other East Tennessee institutions like Knoxville College, East Tennessee State University, Tusculum College, and Milligan College.⁵⁴ UT's Vietnam Education Group organized the event and stated that its presence at Hershey's speech was in opposition to President Johnson's administration and its involvement in Vietnam, not Hershey personally. The protest remained peaceful. Hershey was escorted out of the rear of the building without incident after his speech. UT's vice president for student affairs said the event was conducted in a "seemly" manner and that "the entire student body [would] gain in stature by their actions."⁵⁵ On November 21 that year, two students from Southwestern and Lambuth College burned an American flag in protest of the war. The demonstration took place on Lambuth's campus in Jackson. The Lambuth student, Robert Dickerson, was suspended from the college, while Southwestern took no formal action against its flag burner, John Finis Smith. Both students were charged with flag burning and released from jail on a $1,000 bond.⁵⁶ The high bond amount was likely in response to the amended Flag Desecration Act, which Congress passed on July 5, 1968; the act intensified the penalties for anti-war protests in an effort to curtail civic unrest.⁵⁷ A jury later acquitted the students of the charges after deliberating for only fifteen minutes; the students had said the episode had followed a "beer-drinking spree" and likely the jury was convinced that this was at most a youthful indiscretion.⁵⁸

Regionally, the anti-war movement became more vocal as white New Leftists emphasized American racism domestically and in foreign policy. Joining with SDS's International Student Strike on April 26, 1968, SSOC called for a ten-day national protest against the war from April 20 to April 30, called the Southern Days of Secession.[59] They declared that as "young Southerners we hereby SECEDE" against "THE WAR AGAINST THE VIETNAMESE, RACISM AND EXPLOITATION OF THE POOR, [AND] THE SELECTIVE SERVICE SYSTEM." They further stated the desire to disconnect from the "tools" the United States used to "implement its attempts at global domination, especially the draft law and the use of our universities for military research, investment, and training."[60] This attempt to appropriate the South's Civil War history in support of SSOC's resistance to oppressive authority sprang from the organization's previous efforts to "rewrite" their identity as southerners. Secession, SSOC members argued, was in fact, "a radical tradition in the South."[61]

Students linked their anti-war protests to longstanding campus-based efforts to gain greater student representation in university affairs. So did faculty members. UT's AAUP campus chapter stated in a March 1969 letter that it condemned violence on campuses and believed that being a student at UT was a privilege, "not an inalienable right," yet they "[approved of] these responsible student leaders on this campus who have labored so hard this year for an open speaker policy and for relaxed dormitory hours for women."[62] The reference to the open speaker policy and parietals at UT clarifies that faculty members perceived these campus protests as part of a broader range of student complaints. The letter also referenced several times the democratic nature of the protests in an attempt to counter accusations from "many people, both inside and outside our academic community, [who] have equated the proper efforts of our students to achieve reform with the nefarious violence of nihilists on other campuses across the country."[63] The faculty members who signed the letter expressed disappointment that UT's administration did not respond more positively to UT student proposals.

Prior to the national October 15, 1969, Moratorium (a day of awareness and education in protest against the Vietnam War), UT students were deeply divided on whether the university should hold an event in support of it. Knoxville was the most logical site for the protest within the state, given that support and plans for the moratorium on other smaller campuses across the state were "limited, if at all existent," according to the moratorium's southern coordinator, Jean Libby. Efforts focused on campuses in Knoxville, Nashville, and Memphis because they "[had] large numbers of students and big, well-organized plans backed by hard working students"; by October eleven campuses had committed to participating, with four still considering involvement.⁶⁴ Tennessee's event organizers sanctioned boycotts of classes to minimize disruption for the general student body, in contrast to the national plans.⁶⁵ Organizers considered having participants skip their classes, a less confrontational (and more feasible) alternative to holding physical demonstrations to block other students from attending.

Student activists at UT denounced the wider student body's supposed apathy in the context of Vietnam, echoing back to previous criticisms of supposed lack of political agency on Tennessee campuses. In an October 1969 article in the *Daily Beacon*, UT's student newspaper, a photograph of the university office used to organize the campus's Vietnam War Moratorium showed a poster stating, "Students Are Slaves!"⁶⁶ Student activists at smaller schools complained of student apathy as well, notably at historically Black Fisk, and historically white Sewanee, Southwestern, and Maryville.⁶⁷ The week before the moratorium, the *Highland Echo* featured an article announcing the events at Maryville College with the following call to action for the student body: "There's no excuse for remaining passive—except, of course, the same insane apathy which has already slaughtered millions of innocent people."⁶⁸ Two years earlier, the newspaper had published a poem needling apathetic students. It referenced Che Guevara's death, the peace movement, Albert Camus's novel *The Rebel* (in reference to existentialism), whether one could support those troops who fought in Vietnam but also be against the war, and ended with the hook, "Do we really give a damn?"⁶⁹

On October 15, 1969, moratorium events took place at Sewanee, Vanderbilt, Southwestern, and Tennessee Wesleyan College.⁷⁰ Regionally, other moratorium-related events in Austin, Little Rock, Atlanta, Tallahassee, and Chapel Hill had between three hundred and seven thousand attendees, while the one in Memphis reportedly had two thousand participants.⁷¹ In an interview shortly before the moratorium, Libby, the event's southern coordinator, said she was "really surprised we're getting so much support from a state with a conservative reputation like Tennessee."⁷²

The reaction from conservative students and the state's Republicans was hostile. The state chairman of the YAF, UT student Jim Hager (who also ran unsuccessfully for the SGA presidency in 1969), publicly described the moratorium as "rather phony pacifism that points to the fact that we are the ones in the wrong here and makes no acknowledgement of North Vietnam, China, Russia, and various Communist satellites," and condemned the moratorium supporters as "new left nazis" [*sic*].⁷³ Fred Berry, a Republican state senator, echoed Hager's condemnation, and recommended that UT refuse to pay the salaries of any faculty who participated in the moratorium.⁷⁴ Republican congressman Bill Brock denounced the national moratorium as an attempt to "demoralize our men in Vietnam [and] weaken President Nixon's efforts" while Congressman John Duncan, another Tennessee Republican, encouraged Americans to "boycott the boycotters," and said that the moratorium would be "a big day for some but . . . will be a day of shame" for the country as a whole.[75]

As these protests revealed, conservative student activism had become well organized by 1969.[76] In addition to the YAF college chapter at UT, the Majority Coalition emerged to counter the student body's perceived radicalization. The Majority Coalition first criticized the efforts of fellow students during the debates over dormitory hours. The group was not against eliminating campus dormitory hours per se but condemned the rhetoric liberal students used to attack university administrators. Jim Duncan, the UT Majority Coalition's chairman and Rep. John Duncan's son, contended that "our group is composed of concerned students who wish to demonstrate support for the UT administration in its efforts to maintain a truly free academic environment on the campus. The small minority of students who have been extremely critical of the administration lately is definitely not representative of the student body as a whole. Most UT students are proud of their school and do not support efforts to tear it down."[77]

Reactions to Kent State

The shock of the Kent State shootings changed the tenor of Vietnam demonstrations in Tennessee. Student newspapers and oral histories confirm a marked change in perceptions of the war after Kent State; while student bodies of campuses across the state increasingly opposed the war by 1970, the tragedy at Kent State personalized the war for many students. The idea of their peers being shot for exercising their right to free speech was shocking enough to spur white and Black students alike into action.[78] Students across the country were furious after Kent State, with President Nixon's approval rating on college campuses dropping as low as 31 percent in some polls.[79] Across the country, two million university students went on strike following Kent State, with hundreds of universities and colleges ending the academic year early.[80] National Guardsmen were called onto a number of campuses to maintain peace after Kent State, although only one of those campuses was in the South, the University of South Carolina.[81]

The Kent State tragedy occurred during an anti-war protest on the campus on May 4, 1970. The next day, a group of students gathered at Memphis State University's campus flagpole at noon and lowered the flag to half-mast as a memorial to the students who had died the day before at Kent State.[82]

Within minutes, another group of students reached the pole and raised the flag back up. Several minutes later a crowd of more than a thousand students had amassed around the flag. Fighting ensued, and the staff in the Administration Building (which faced the flagpole) became concerned about the fights spilling into the building.[83]

President Humphreys stepped out onto the steps at the front of the Administration Building and attempted to reason with the crowd of students. "We have a strong difference of opinion here which could lead to direct confrontation, which leads to bloodshed," he told the students. "I know you don't want that. If you get nothing else from education you should get the ability to discuss in a rational manner a difference of opinion. Intelligent people do try to resolve those differences."[84] Humphreys's intervention failed to quell the anger both groups felt, and the crowd continued to fight for control of the flagpole. Humphreys left the steps of the Administration Building at this point and made his way through the crowd, stopping at the crowd's center with his back to the flagpole. Changing his approach, Humphreys spoke of the American flag's symbolic importance to the thousands of young men and women who had died protecting the country from "brutal dictators and tyrants."[85] Recalling the situation years later, Humphreys said, "I took the position that even if there had been bad national decisions . . . It was still the same flag that former students had given their lives for."[86] Humphreys convinced both groups to nominate six representatives each to meet in his office. Following these discussions, students agreed to raise the flag to full staff, but the university would organize a memorial service the next day, with the flag at half-staff during the service.[87]

While Humphreys recalled his actions during this period with pride in resolving a potentially major conflict on the campus, some contemporaries disparaged his behavior. Responding to criticism from one Memphis resident, Humphreys denied that students had "intimidated" him. "We [wanted] to avoid increasing the tension of the situation, which could . . . give the antiwar militants something . . . they could use to inflame the minds of . . . young people. . . . It takes a great deal of patience . . . but . . . we feel we have exercised strong and firm judgment in not backing down from certain basic principles."[88]

UT's chancellor, Charles Weaver, recalled that both he and Humphreys knew their responsibility for the safety of all students and that post–Kent State protests had antagonized some local residents. Weaver said that pro-war locals in Knoxville told him that if he did not control the anti-war students, then they would violently end the protests. Weaver later argued that Humphreys was similarly concerned about some Memphis pro-war activists, and that he had heard Humphreys say the "people who supported him scared him much, much more than any protester did... [because their ideas] were so outrageous and so wrong that it was frightening."[89] Violent reactions to anti-war demonstrations were plausible concerns for Weaver and Humphreys, particularly given the widespread news coverage of the Hard Hat Riot in New York City on May 8, 1970, where unionized construction workers attacked anti-war protestors.[90]

"Idealism at its worst"

Despite efforts by university administrators to quell anger on campus, post–Kent State student unrest at UT continued to mount. Student demands for greater autonomy contributed to demonstrations during the late 1960s that had focused on continued racial discrepancies and gaining a greater voice in university affairs.

Shortly after the Kent State shootings, SGA president Jimmie Baxter, the first African American elected to the position, called for a student strike of classes at UT for the remainder of the week.[91] Speaking at a rally of around three thousand students after the memorial, Baxter said, "Yesterday four students were killed because they were in the process of protesting something we probably should have been protesting long ago.... We have an obligation to speak out... we can't wait until it comes to UT."[92] A student editorial in UT's *Daily Beacon* written just after Kent State described UT as "a relatively conservative school in a conservative state" and called for support of the strike. "Allow this force—these deaths—to bring about the needed reforms in government and its military policy."[93] During the strike over half of students were estimated to have stayed away from class, although it is unclear how many supported the strike versus those who used it as a pretext to skip lectures.[94] Contrasting Baxter's measured response on May 5, 1970, the bombing of the UT campus ROTC building the same day provided a more militant reaction to the tragedy.[95] Black student activist "Sparky" Rucker recalled of the moment, "it was the first time I felt the University of Tennessee was united in the struggle against this war."[96]

Students at private Tennessee campuses used the strike as a tactic in reaction to Kent State. Knoxville College students held a strike, blocking professors from the campus. Cynthia Fleming recalled of why she participated in the strike, "When people your age get killed, [activism] means something different to you."[97] Sewanee suspended classes following a vote by faculty and student governing bodies for most of May 8 and the morning of May 9 (a Friday and Saturday). Perhaps with the potential reaction of conservative local community members in mind, a university administrator later denied in a press release that the administration had mandated a suspension of classes.[98] Maryville College similarly cancelled classes on May 8, following a large meeting of students and a prayer service for the victims earlier in the week.[99] Southwestern College's students and faculty declared on May 15 that the institution would organize a strike of classes for one day in order to hold an educational day on the war in Vietnam as well as in support of the Kent State victims.[100] During the nationwide student strikes precipitated by the Kent State shootings, nearly half of the undergraduate population participated nationally.[101]

The most public manifestation of student frustrations over Kent State occurred during President Nixon's surprise appearance at Rev. Billy Graham's evangelical crusade in Knoxville. The Graham Crusade Committee of Knoxville had secured Neyland Stadium, UT's 65,000-seat football venue, for the event, planned for May 22–31, 1970.[102] UT student activists claimed to have had no complaint with Graham's presence on campus. Kathleen Anderson, for example, was a psychology major who had not previously participated in any protests. When recalling her feelings about Graham's anticipated visit to campus, she stated "I didn't really have much feeling about it," although she "certainly wasn't a Billy Graham supporter." Rather, the announcement on May 27 that President Nixon would be speaking the next day during the crusade inspired her and her fellow students' actions. Anderson called the idea that Nixon would make his first campus appearance after the Kent State shootings at UT "an insult," adding that was "the main reason" she demonstrated.[103] Historian Steven P. Miller argued that Graham's Knoxville crusade was different: unlike the southern desegregated services Graham had held throughout the South in the 1950s and 1960s, including services in Chattanooga and Nashville in 1953 and 1954 respectively, the Knoxville crusade "indicated the momentary alignment of his domestic crusades with the Nixonian political style."[104] One of the faculty members who participated in the protest recalled, "Nixon was certainly the main target of our resentment for his showing up, he was not seen in a very favorable light."[105] Jimmie Baxter, by then the departing SGA president, declared that the majority of the student body and faculty opposed Nixon's policies, and that his appearance on the campus "could incite violence."[106] Nixon's decision to attend surprised the university administration; Chancellor Weaver recalled that UT had extended several unsuccessful invitations to Nixon to visit the campus in 1970 before his May trip.[107] To Weaver, Nixon's speech could not have been planned for a worse time for the university, given the significant campus unrest the school had weathered earlier in the 1969–1970 school year.[108]

It is unclear why the White House decided that Knoxville would be a good location for Nixon to speak, although Republican congressman John Duncan's May 23 conversation with fellow Tennessean and White House staffer William E. Timmons likely contributed. In his report of the conversation, Timmons ended with the statement, "I doubt that there would be any problem of student demonstrations in Tennessee."[109] Prior to Nixon's visit, a rumor spread throughout the campus that Nixon's administration had chosen UT for his first public speech on a university or college campus following Kent State because it believed he would be speaking to an audience of supporters.[110] This frustrated students, faculty, and administrators alike at UT. The head of the psychology department, Dr. William Verplanck, described the campus as being in "constant turmoil" after word got out that Nixon was going to visit.[111] Administrators like Chancellor Weaver feared the potential for campus protest with the announcement of Nixon's appearance, particularly given the presence in Knoxville of journalists from around the country and the three major news broadcasting networks (CBS, ABC, and NBC) to cover both the crusade and Nixon's speech.[112] While protests earlier in the academic year had drawn only limited local media coverage, Nixon's presence on the campus ensured both a reason for student protest as well as an audience of national television and print media journalists.

Unknown to UT's administrators, the White House and Graham had discussed the president visiting Knoxville since February 1970, with initial discussions concerning the tone and avowed purpose for the visit. According to a White House memo from February 1970, Nixon was originally merely "*considering* the *possibility* of attending" the Memorial Day service during the Graham crusade, which would have been May 30, two days later than was eventually agreed upon.[113] White House correspondence reveals that the Nixon administration did not fear his reception at UT, but rather that the president's appearance would seem to interfere with the state's upcoming political primaries.[114] Communications regarding the visit emphasized the administration's concern not to "get involved" in the senatorial and gubernatorial nominations (Tennessee's filing deadline for the upcoming elections was June 4, and its primary was scheduled for August 6, 1970), as well as keeping the tone of the visit as "going in for a 'church service,'" not to "build a political rally out of it," however unrealistic that goal might be for a presidential visit.[115] Similarly, Nixon's chief of staff, H. R. Bob Haldeman, opposed Graham's suggestion to sing "God Bless America" after Nixon's speech, on the grounds that the audience would view the song as too political.[116] Despite this concern, the audience sang "God Bless America" after the president's address anyway.[117]

By May 25 the White House and Graham had settled on May 28 for Nixon's speech. A White House official stated on May 25 that Graham did not want

Nixon's speech to be related to Memorial Day (May 25) at all, likely due to the political implications that would arise from such an association. Instead, the evening was to be a "Youth Night" for the crusade. Graham "[felt] the President should concentrate on saying something to the youth of the country" and on "the importance of religion to the moral fiber of the nation" given that the speech was taking place on the campus and that the crusade had anywhere from ten to fifteen thousand UT students in attendance each evening. Graham expected even more to attend the Youth Night on May 28.[118] Graham reportedly also wanted Nixon to emphasize "that the youth are the leaders of tomorrow and that their lives must be balanced—and part of that balancing is the acceptance and belief in religious values."[119] Of course, a speech by Nixon on a college campus shortly after Kent State could not possibly be perceived as apolitical. Thus, it fueled protest at UT among student activists.

Graham and White House officials soon became worried about the possibility of protest and made efforts to frame the event differently. Graham requested that Nixon's visit to Knoxville not be announced until the evening of May 26 or the morning of May 27, and be phrased as "the President is just dropping by the Crusade on the way to California." Graham's reason for suggesting this late statement was the alleged presence of some 140 "radical students" at UT who "will probably try to cause some trouble," though he believed "the bulk" of student attendees "will behave themselves properly."[120] In the hours prior to the speech, the White House expected only twenty to thirty students to be involved in protests. Intelligence reports described protesters' plans to hand out leaflets outside the stadium but not to enter Neyland Stadium itself.[121]

While a growing minority of the student body was frustrated by Nixon's appearance, some of their peers welcomed Nixon's upcoming speech. On May 27, the incoming SGA president, John Smith, requested a "hand-shake meeting" with Nixon during his visit to Knoxville. With the help of Congressman Duncan, Smith met with Nixon on Air Force One after the crusade.[122] Smith asked for the meeting in order to "solve the problems facing the universities today" and to get Nixon's opinion on "what other students can do to become better informed" citizens.[123] In official correspondence, Nixon described his conversation with Smith as one of the "most interesting aspects of the trip," but Chief of Staff Bob Haldeman wrote in his diary that Nixon "was very *un*impressed."[124] To news media after his talk with Nixon, Smith said that while he had articulated his opposition to the Vietnam war, he felt Nixon was "a very strong man to face the dissent within and the dissent without and still say I am the President."[125] Given Smith's comments, it seems that Nixon's impression of the meeting centered on Smith's disagreement with American involvement in

Vietnam. Smith attempted, unsuccessfully, to meet Nixon again in July 1970, in Washington, D.C.[126]

Whatever the expectations or plans for the protests, a small yet vocal group of students and faculty protested Nixon's presence inside Neyland Stadium. One UT student protestor described the scene as "250 Lions to 90,000 Christians."[127] The protestors numbered between 300 and 500 and were outnumbered between 100-to-1 and 250-to-1 by crusade attendees. The differences in estimations are partly due to whether or not the source took into account the crowd gathered outside the stadium. Contemporary sources estimated 55,000 to 100,000 people in attendance overall. The higher figures must include those outside Neyland Stadium, as the stadium's capacity at the time was 65,000.[128]

Student and faculty protestors carried signs stating "Thou Shalt Not Kill" and attempted to enter the stadium for Nixon's speech.[129] A crusade attendee reportedly told one of the student protestors holding a sign "to stick it up [their] a—."[130] The Secret Service and local law enforcement standing outside the stadium confiscated these signs but members of the group were still able to enter Neyland Stadium, some with their signs hidden on their persons.[131] In a possible reference to students' apparent serfdom, student protestor Carroll Bible wore a robe, and held a sign demanding "Let my people go," echoing Moses's remarks to the pharaoh in Exodus, as he led the Israelites out of slavery. There appears to be a question among protestors, however, as to who Bible represented; fellow student Barry Bozeman remembered him dressing up as Jesus, not Moses.[132] Once inside, however, the plans for silent protest fell apart as several members loudly interrupted the religious proceedings as well as Nixon's speech.[133] The expectation that they could maintain such a disciplined approach was, as a protesting faculty member later remarked, "idealism at its worst."[134]

Instead of simply protesting Nixon's speech and otherwise remaining quiet during the rest of the crusade proceedings (or leaving the stadium after Nixon's speech), protestors chanted, booed, and heckled loudly throughout the entire program. Graham warmly introduced Nixon and referred to previous presidents' controversial decisions that nonetheless, in Graham's opinion, demonstrated their leadership and commitment. Graham said, "I know all Presidents have had to make hard, agonizing decisions that are often unpopular—but which they think are in the best interests of our country."[135] Graham's implicit backing of Nixon's war policies in the environment of a mostly supportive crowd cheered Nixon. Haldeman noted in his diary that Nixon was "really cranked up as a result" and that it "did him [Nixon] personally a lot of good."[136]

During his speech, Nixon spoke about the importance of this generation of youth and the honor of speaking at such an event. Protestors interrupted

Nixon enough that at one point he stopped speaking and gestured to them. Chants of "One-two-three-four, we don't want you anymore" could be heard at times until the crowd drowned it out with either cheers and clapping for Nixon or with boos towards the protestors.[137] Pleased, Nixon told the crowd that he was "just glad that there seems to be a rather solid majority on one side rather than the other side tonight."[138] Gospel singer Ethel Waters chided the protestors by saying,

> Now you chillun listen to Mom . . . when you know him [Nixon] you'll love him and that includes you chillun over there who I love and if I was close enough to yuh I'd [makes smacking noise with her hands] I'd smack yuh! [cheers from the crowd and she laughs] But I love yuh and I'd give yuh a big hug and a big kiss![139]

Haldeman called Waters's comment "a spectacular put down."[140]

National media also analyzed the event, as it was Nixon's first campus appearance after Kent State, and highlighted his domestic agenda of appealing to southern and youth voters.[141] In the ABC News report on the event, which unlike NBC and CBS focused on the presence of anti-war demonstrators rather than Nixon's speech, reporter Charles Murphy stated that within Neyland Stadium "the anti-war demonstrators were a small minority, but the fact that they were even here, on a conservative campus in a conservative state illustrates the deep division even here."[142] Echoing Murphy's comment, one UT student recalled "the connections between University of Tennessee and other campuses where demonstrations were taking place made me . . . proud that there was enough here for people to do something."[143]

Chancellor Weaver defended the university's position soon after the event. "The University of Tennessee is not now and will never be a sanctuary of any sort for those who break the law. . . . There is never any excuse for the disruption of speakers on any platform at the University of Tennessee."[144] Photographs of protestors taken during the event assisted with the arrests of over forty people for violating Tennessee Code Annotated 39-1204, which criminalized the disruption of religious services.[145] Several of the participants in the January 1970 demonstration against Edward Boling's appointment as university president were also present at the crusade to protest Nixon's speech. Many UT student activists believed that those arrested in January had been unfairly treated by the administration and local officials; the charges against their peers for disturbing a religious service at the crusade seemed to be yet another example of the system's injustice.[146]

The Nixon administration knew of the demonstrators' arrests In a letter to a concerned citizen in Knoxville, a Nixon staffer noted that the president had urged local authorities to be "firm but carefully judicious" and to allow the arrested students to finish their exams before facing prosecution. Knoxville mayor Leonard Rogers did not attempt to stop the arrests and later faced anger from UT faculty members for not controlling what they viewed as overzealous police action.[147] The FBI's COINTELPRO Knoxville division also pursued surveillance of the charges and trials of the protestors, signifying both the organization's reach as well as the perceived threat of student protest towards the president, even in a city that Bureau officials had considered insignificant enough to recommend ceasing surveillance of New Leftist activities there a year earlier.[148]

The protest at Neyland Stadium was, at its core, an anti-war, anti-Nixon event. Student unrest, however, was not confined to Nixon's visit, the Cambodian bombing, or Kent State. As reports to the president from the Scranton Commission and Vanderbilt chancellor Alexander Heard highlighted, contrary to many administrators' prior beliefs, students in Tennessee and elsewhere had long become disenchanted over issues of student power, race, and broader societal injustices.

The Scranton Commission

President Richard Nixon publicly announced the establishment of the President's Commission on Campus Unrest on June 13, 1970, a little over a month after the Kent State shootings and the killing of two Black students at Jackson State College, in Jackson, Mississippi.[149] University administrators across the country had worried for some time about the growing resentment among their students but these two events forced the issue to the forefront. Higher education administrators became deeply concerned that unrest in surrounding communities could spread to their campuses, or that these riots would inspire their own student bodies to organize.

The President's Commission on Campus Unrest was a nine-person panel that included collegiate administrators and faculty and individuals representing the press, law enforcement, and the judiciary, with the members hailing from locations across the country. The commission was commonly referred to as the Scranton Commission after its chairman, William Scranton, former governor of Pennsylvania. When Nixon established the commission, he called for the group to: "[identify] the principal causes of campus violence and the breakdown in the process of orderly expression of dissent on the campus"; "[suggest] specific methods and procedures through which grievances can be resolved by means other than the exertion of force"; "[suggest] ways to protect academic freedom, the right to obtain an education free from improper interference, and the right of peaceful dissent and protest"; and "[propose] practical steps which can be taken by government at all levels, by the administrations of institutions of higher learning, and by students, through student governments or otherwise, to minimize dangers attendant upon expressions of dissent."[150] After months of hearings and investigations into campus disorder (including two reports specifically on Kent State and Jackson State as well as an interim findings report), the commission concluded in September 1970 that, while rioting and looting of any public or private property warranted condemnation, university administrators should also respect students' demands for greater personal and political autonomy. The commission further concluded that campus unrest was bound up with growing resentment and frustrations over the Vietnam War.

Alongside the Scranton Commission's investigations, in May 1970 Nixon appointed Vanderbilt chancellor Alexander Heard as a special advisor to the president. Heard was to keep the president "fully and currently informed on the thinking of the academic community and especially the young," and suggest how he could become "better advised on campus affairs." Heard worked in concert with Howard University president James E. Cheek, who held a similar position.[151] Heard's peers respected him for his handling of the April 1967 Nashville riots, during which he took a moderate approach to campus activism, and kept the university free from violence.[152] In 1966, an early example of such moderation from a southern administrator, Heard observed, "The university's obligation is not to protect students from ideas, but rather to expose them to ideas, and to help make them capable of handling and, hopefully, having ideas." By 1970, Heard had already served as chairman for President John F. Kennedy's Commission on Presidential Campaign Costs in 1961 and 1962, and on President Johnson's 1964 National Citizens' Committee for Community Relations, 1966 Task Force on Education, and 1967 Advisory Commission on Intergovernmental Relations.[153]

If Nixon and his administration expected Heard's report to reinforce their condemnation of student unrest, they were sorely disappointed. The report, delivered to Nixon and his administration in July 1970, articulated Heard's findings on campus unrest, derived from considering campus surveys, some eleven hours of meetings with Nixon, conversations with members of the federal government including Vice President Spiro Agnew, and discussions with Cheek. Instead of describing the previous few months of dissent as a passing instance of protest limited to universities, Heard argued that this was instead a "*national* crisis." The Cambodian invasion and Kent State, Heard wrote, "triggered a vast pre-existing charge of pent up frustration and dissatisfaction" among students nationally, which was not just a result of U.S. involvement in Vietnam, but also from "fears . . . of repression," frustrations towards university administrations, and "the political system itself." Students' "idealism," Heard argued, came from "human concern for victims of racial discrimination, for those who suffer in the urban ghettos, for the poor in Appalachia, and for those who die—under whatever flag—in Southeast Asia." Heard and Cheek agreed that southern Black students experienced "frustration, anger, outrage, fears, and anxieties" that mirrored those of the Black community nationally.[154]

Nixon, as well as Haldeman and Daniel Patrick Moynihan within his administration, were sharply critical of the position Heard and Cheek had taken in writing the document, and they simultaneously released the report to the media alongside their condemnations of it. Nixon publicly attacked the Heard report. He argued that "responsibility [for campus unrest fell] . . . squarely on the shoulders of the disrupters" and that college administrations, not the federal government, were responsible for maintaining control of activity on their campuses.[155] Moynihan took particular offense to the report's contention that reconsidering the federal government's policies at home and abroad were necessary to calm tempers on college campuses; he declared this observation "a breathtaking form of political blackmail."[156] Despite the Nixon administration's harsh response, Heard stood by his conclusions. Speaking later in July 1970, Heard acknowledged his surprise that the administration had published what he felt had been a "private" report, but stated, "when one accepts an invitation to walk in the political forest, he must be prepared to be snagged by a few brambles."[157]

Despite criticism and skepticism from members of the Nixon administration and Congress, the Scranton Commission released its report on September 26, 1970.[158] Writing to Nixon, Scranton argued that while campus violence "must be met with firm and just responses," to prosper, universities "must be prepared to institute needed reforms in their administrative procedures and instructional programs."[159] The commission had held hearings in Washington, D.C., Los Angeles, Kent, Ohio, and Jackson, Mississippi, and sent a survey regarding student unrest to each of the country's 2,789 higher education institutions.[160] The surveys were to be filled out by the institution's president, the head of the faculty or comparable representative, and the student president. The commission received at least one response from 1,890 institutions.[161] It is unclear how many of these surveys were received from Tennessee, but the president of Southwestern, William L. Bowden, kept a copy of his responses to the survey in his files. His responses correlated with the commission's findings nationally, in that he was most concerned by the Vietnam War, demands by Black students for greater minority representation on campus, and underlying student frustrations regarding campus regulations. Bowden emphasized the college administration's efforts to accommodate the desires of students to protest while keeping classes open to all students. He noted, "We find that if we can get to the student groups first when something like Cambodia or Kent State happens, we are able to steer some of the energy, static and emotion into rational activities." He felt it was important for administrators and faculty to "take the initiative of communicating daily" with student leaders "to help channel energies, emotions, and plans along constructive paths."[162]

Anti-war demonstrations in Tennessee were almost entirely the product of earlier conflicts for greater student autonomy and remedies for racial inequalities. There was anti-war activism in the state before 1970, but the war's opponents were heavily outnumbered in Tennessee, and across the South. White and Black students feared the draft, although the Selective Service's racially discriminatory impact made the war more immediately pressing for Blacks. While the Tet Offensive was an inflection point for public support for the war nationally, anti-war activism in Tennessee built more gradually to the 1969 War Moratorium and the 1970 Kent State shootings, which motivated the largest number of Tennessee youths to protest. The limited organizing about Vietnam prior to May 1970, and the general lack of student consciousness about the issue until the war intersected with underlying resentment over unresolved demands for greater personal autonomy, points to the Vietnam War acting as a spark rather than a larger contributing factor to student unrest. While the protests that occurred were not as violent as others nationally, Tennessee's student activism during this period exhibited what the Scranton Commission was formed to investigate: preexisting volatile tensions between university administrators and students and faculty made explosive by political events, namely Vietnam and campus unrest nationally.

CONCLUSION

The Legacy of the "Prophetic Minority" Within the "Recalcitrant Minority"

The sound of students' voices filled the air as they stood around a large bonfire in protest. As they gathered around the fire for warmth on a cool November evening, students at Middle Tennessee State University (MTSU) roasted marshmallows over the ashes of a burned effigy. An international political controversy had drawn them to the campus parking lot, but the broader forces surrounding the event were rooted in continuing debates over student power.[1]

This episode of guerrilla theater was notable for several reasons. First, although it took place at an institution that experienced a drawn-out debate over the university's Confederate symbolism, a controversy that continued beyond the burning, this effigy had no connection to this Confederate past, nor a racial angle. Second, the burning of the effigy was actually sanctioned by the university; Dean of Students Paul Cantrell reversed his initial opposition after student pushback.[2] The student newspaper and the unanimous support of the student government organization, the Associated Student Body (ASB), promoted the burning (and perhaps more significantly, opposed the university's initial lack of support for the event).[3] One editorial declared that the fact the burning had even become an issue was "a pitiful comment on the university administration." "Hopefully, the administrators have learned a lesson," the article continued, "that you can only step out on a limb so far before it breaks—that the students of this university can no longer be treated like children. Also, hopefully, the students have realized the potential they have by asserting their rights."[4] As this November 1975 editorial highlighted, students' fight for personal autonomy continued beyond the 1960s. And third, the event took place in 1975, a good five years after the state's most significant student activism.

With the advent of the country's bicentennial in 1975, the People's Bicentennial Commission (PBC) emerged on the national stage, fostered by continued interest on the left in political organizing and guerrilla theater, and frustrations over the anticipated depiction of American life in 1975 as worthy of decorating in proud red, white, and blue at the national bicentennial celebrations. These events' commercialization and the anticipated depiction of the country as unified and its citizens as unabashedly proud to be American hit a nerve for New Leftists.[5] The PBC was a "radical, populist organization that sought to promote fundamental economic change during the mid-1970s," according to historian Simon Hall.[6] Founded in 1971, the PBC had a national membership of twenty thousand and by 1975, when the Murfreesboro protest took place, had organized protests across the country advocating for economic reform away from corporatization towards more centrist, populist policies.[7]

For MTSU students, PBC's proposed economic reforms had a clear appeal, as the subject for the effigy demonstrated, but on the surface, it may seem surprising that the PBC attracted such a large following in a place like Murfreesboro. Guerrilla theater occurred sporadically across Tennessee college campuses in the 1960s and early 1970s, but on a limited scale and without major student support. Part of the PBC's appeal locally may have been its youthful membership; according to its own internal analysis, its members tended to have some college background and were between the ages of twenty-four and thirty-four.[8] The greater draw for MTSU students was likely the relevancy of the protest; the Tennessee General Assembly had voted to override Democratic governor Ray Blanton's veto of tax breaks to grain executives like Ned Cook, chairman of Cook Industries, who had made profitable exports of wheat to the Soviet Union. These sales, the national PBC alleged, led to increased prices for bread and other wheat products.[9] "Cook has accumulated more than $55 million in untaxed profits from foreign grain sales over the past two fiscal years," local PBC chairman Rick Edmondson alleged in 1975. "This is nothing more than government welfare for the rich, and an insult to everyone who has to work for a living."[10] The local PBC described Cook as their "Tory of the Month," with clear connections to the British government and the bicentennial, and alleged he was representative of "corporate tyranny" that flew in the face of "the founding principles of our republic," which the PBC encouraged citizens to "measure . . . against the authoritarian financial institutions that [ruled] America."[11] With the reluctant support of the administration and rare support from the student body, Cook's effigy was burned at MTSU in November 1975.[12]

After the statewide activism of spring 1970, the division between white and Black Tennessee student activists was evident. The increasingly divergent paths that activists had navigated by the end of the 1960s were clear from the summer of 1970 as white students focused on political protests like the MTSU

PBC episode, as well as other causes such as women's rights, gay rights, environmentalism, and conservative anti-leftist activism. In Tennessee, students connected these topics to their continued demand for greater student power. After spring 1970, Black student activists in Tennessee continued to fight for racial equality as white students largely moved on to other issues. The impact of the 1960s was clear, however, in how Black students framed the issue: they continued to discuss the racial discrimination they experienced on campus as an infringement on their student rights, asserting their personal and political autonomy.

Following the significant numbers of students involved in campus protests in spring 1970, the campus unrest in Tennessee during the 1970s was on a much smaller scale. Fewer students were involved in protests, and reactions to demonstrations both on campus as well as in surrounding areas were smaller. The moment of substantial student activism may have passed, but tactics and areas of focus present in 1960s activism were visible in the 1970s.[13]

Black student activists on college campuses across Tennessee continued to negotiate racial inequality after May 1970. In October 1970, Morristown College, a historically Black campus in East Tennessee, was the site of a shooting following a class boycott and sit-in protest of the administration building involving one hundred students. Three students—Derrel Jay, Ozzie Jones, and Benny Derrico—were hit by gunfire as they stood outside on the building's balcony. The protest had come about after students felt their demands for relaxed dormitory hours for female students, longer library hours, an end to curfews for male students, and better cafeteria food had not made enough progress in a week-long period of negotiations with campus administration officials.[14] Two months later, in Murfreesboro, after comedian and political activist Dick Gregory spoke on the campus and during a basketball game at MTSU, a cross was burned on the campus. Students had organized "Get Hip Whitey Week" and in reaction to the burning, some sixty Black students demonstrated in front of the university president's home on campus.[15] Months later in March 1971, it appeared the students were correct, at least concerning local indifference to racial injustice; the Tennessee Bureau of Criminal Identification had still not identified anyone who had participated in the cross burning. In the immediate aftermath of the burning, the university president M. G. Scarlett made a radio address that echoed previous administrative statements urging calm. Encouraging students to not overreact, he appealed to students' understanding and referred to the university's prior "excellent race relationships." The president of the campus BSA, Gerald Edwards, remarked that the incident gave him "mixed reactions." "Perhaps they have tried [to prosecute those responsible], and perhaps they can't get a definite prosecution," but that did not change the fact that the burning had occurred.[16]

The cross burning at MTSU did not occur in a vacuum. From the 1960s as the institution slowly integrated and well into the 1970s, students and administrators argued over the university's official mascot, the Blue Raiders, and its unofficial (albeit longstanding) associations to the Confederacy, particularly the Confederate General Nathan Bedford Forrest. Forrest, a slave trader before the Civil War, gained notoriety for overseeing the massacre of surrendered Black Union soldiers after the Battle of Fort Pillow in Henning, Tennessee, in April 1864 and for his leadership in the KKK after the war.[17] The Blue Raiders were selected as the institution's mascot in 1933 as part of a contest.[18] It was during President Q. M. Smith's tenure (1938–58) that Forrest became associated with the school as part of a public relations drive to sell merchandise; decals sold in the campus bookstore and promotional literature drew the connection between the institution's mascot and Forrest, whom Smith referred to as "the First with the Most."[19] As a student explained in 1961, Forrest was "the symbol for the leader of the student body" and "a reminder of those qualities of leadership, ingenuity, honesty, vigor of thought, and strength of character that are part of the Southern tradition." "GET OUT AND GET BEHIND THE BLUE RAIDER CONCEPT!" the writer urged, encouraging fellow students to follow Forrest's example of rallying others by reminding them of his nickname as the Blue Raider, supposedly earned "because he constantly raided the Yankee Blue lines and camps."[20] As with many other southern Confederate imagery revivals during the 1950s, MTSU's campus most significantly adopted Confederate imagery (with campus fundraisers selling Confederate flags and the Confederate anthem "Dixie" proudly being played during sports events), at a time of increasing desegregation pressures.[21] By the late 1960s, a growing student minority challenged MTSU's Confederate embrace.[22] The Blue Raider evolved into an increasingly bizarre list of mascots from 1968 when the university officially discontinued Forrest as the mascot, the first few involving a St. Bernard dog in various identities.[23] The numerous changes to MTSU's mascot in the late 1960s and 1970s, in an effort to soft-pedal its Confederate associations, revealed the administration's difficulty in adopting an inoffensive mascot while not angering alumni. Unlike SSOC activists who had attempted in the 1960s to rewrite the racist history of the Confederate flag as a tradition of radical resistance, the politics surrounding the flag on campuses were more complicated. As administrative policy committees navigated local politics centered on the meaning of the flag, some higher education institutions like MTSU decided to abandon the flag altogether.

Demonstrating the continuation of direct action strategies, a protest organized by the BSA at Southwestern in April 1972 reportedly began after a Black student's suspension for cheating. Student activists argued that their problem did not lie with whether he was guilty or not, but instead the harsh punishment issued by the student-controlled honor council. After the verdict was delivered on Friday, April 21, twenty-nine BSA members protested the next day by disrupting an invitational track meet at Southwestern, urging reconsideration of the student's suspension.[24] The students organized a lie-in over the track, which brought the meet's cancellation. On the Sunday (April 23), some twenty-five BSA members hand-delivered a request for a meeting to the president, and later that evening about 250 students met in the campus amphitheater to discuss the issue.[25] A month later, frustrations were evident between the BSA and the administration when nineteen of the lie-in participants were still under academic probation; Southwestern decided that the lie-in was "unacceptable action" because it "disrupted a college function, [and interfered] with the freedom of other members of the college community and of the college's invited guests."[26] Much like earlier protests on small, private campuses like Southwestern, the fact that the protests occurred is more notable than any lasting policy changes that did not.

Other issues related to identity and sexuality, namely feminism and gender activism, would pierce the South's largely conservative sociopolitical landscape in the early 1970s, but built into larger, significant social movements later on that decade. Evidence of changing mores and discussions of these ideas on Tennessee campuses suggest first, that ongoing campus organizing was successful in giving more-liberal activists a platform to express themselves, and second, that their efforts to associate their activism with broader notions of student power were effective. Institutions continued to loosen campus policies on women's hours, sometimes explicitly framed as a result of the national women's liberation movement. Following a 1969 rally at UT, an April 1970 rally organized by a group of students calling themselves the Women's Action Movement drew a crowd of 1,500 to push for additional liberalizations of dormitory hours.[27] This echoed earlier protests on campuses across the state around the same issue, but here they were explicitly framed as an issue of gender equality rather than as one of student power.

On small campuses in particular, it was no small feat for student activists to achieve increased student autonomy, but some gains were made in women's rights.[28] One editorial urging the administration to eliminate women's hours at Maryville College argued, "College females from eighteen to twenty-one are, on the whole, more sophisticated and versed in the ways of the world than ever before. Generally speaking, they do not wish to be shielded or protected from the reality of day to day existence."[29] Female students at Maryville were polled in September 1970 and even in a small poll of twenty-five freshmen and twenty-five senior girls, the poll's creator declared that it seemed "to indicate that members of the Women's Liberation Movement might feel very much at home on our campus and might gain some support with the exception of the one question, 'Should the Miss America Pageant be abolished?.'" The results were four to twenty-one in favor of abolition for the freshmen and six to thirteen (with six unsure) for the seniors. "Perhaps most women get a little secret pleasure," the student mused, "from seeing those all-American girls on stage and maybe wishing that they might be there too."[30]

In a similar tone, nine female East Tennessee State University students questioned whether women's rights had come to the region in October 1970. "I have mixed emotions," one student explained about the women's liberation movement. "I'm afraid women may lose more in a fight for equality than they would gain. I'm afraid the women pushing this movement aren't going about it in the right way."[31] By May 1976, the Maryville student body seemed to have moved closer towards embracing second-wave feminism, with a campus poll showing that 83 percent of the student body supported passage of the Equal Rights Amendment (ERA).[32] Notably, support of feminism appears to have gained more traction on the campus than busing; in the same poll, 70 percent of respondents opposed busing to integrate school systems.[33] Unlike busing, which had grown unpopular even among southern Blacks by the 1970s, an equal rights amendment held broader appeal in Tennessee; unlike all former Confederate states except Texas, Tennessee's legislature ratified the ERA, though it later rescinded its approval. Southern college students seemed more open than other southerners: in the 1970s and 1980s, it was more typical for southern feminists to couch their demands within prevailing notions of white southern womanhood, or to advance feminist initiatives while simultaneously downplaying their feminist content.[34]

Maryville students discussed the gay rights movement, too, with a November 1972 guest editorial declaring it was time for accepting homosexuality on the campus. "Homosexuality is neither better or lesser than heterosexuality," the author explained. "Gay Liberation isn't freedom to hang out our hang-ups, but a chance to lose them. . . . We all stand to gain. Gay or straight. Freak or 'straight'. Black or white. Genital male or female 'Chick'. Nigger. Queer. The terms are all the same. Sexism equals racism. Think about it."[35] While certainly the author was making a point about the relevancy of gay rights, it is doubtful how many other Maryville students, including female and Black students, agreed with his equation of women's rights and civil rights with gay rights.

Tennessee students were also aware of environmental conservation and the social movement surrounding it in the 1970s. As with gay rights, there was more student newspaper discussion about the topic rather than calls for organized activism. In particular, Maryville College, in its close proximity to the Great Smoky Mountains National Park, was a center of these student reflections on human impact on the environment from higher education institutions across the state. The campus held a discussion in February 1970 on "'the danger from the three swords of Damocles': pollution, population, and the threat of nuclear war," as well as organized events of litter pickup and cleanup programs on the campus as well as the nearby mountains that spring.[36] Maryville students continued to discuss ecology in their surrounding area through the 1970s. A September 1972 article depicting a cartoon owl named "Woodsy" gave a list of 104 ways for students to help reduce pollution, with the closing statement, "Give a hoot! Don't pollute!"[37]

Some of these students expressed their dissatisfaction with the 1960s cultural revolution with sardonic humor. In May 1972, one Maryville College student expressed, ironically, his frustrations that "ecology, racism, women's liberation, war and the rest of the list" were too often expressed in a way that made people "feel guilty if we're not doing what's Right, and we feel Wrong if we're not feeling the guilt." "Too often the Relevance Regalia focuses only on what's not there rather than what exists," he continued, espousing his love for the television show *All in the Family*, running the water while he brushed his teeth, using Tide laundry products, and having "blazing fires in [his] fireplace."[38] He described elements of environmental activism, the main focus of his ire, with humor, but was likely parodying a majority-student viewpoint that 1960s sociocultural changes had gone far enough. In a similar tone, one MTSU student argued in 1971 that if the university mascot's similarity to Forrest was upsetting to some, a new mascot that would be completely noncontroversial should be chosen; he suggested Bambi, the Disney deer character. "In choosing any symbol for such a wide diversity of people it has always been the rule to choose something ferocious and overwhelming such as rigers [sic], bears or lions," he wrote. "Bambi, Peter Pan, Mickey Mouse, or even Bullwinkle Moose (especially for the highly scholastic universities) could be the wave [sic] of the future. The aggressive menagerie of university animals must cease.... Bambi implies no racial overtones, yet he remains native to the South, a factor which should please many unreformed confederates."[39] If the mascot was seen as offensive, the student reasoned, why not choose something so clearly innocuous that no one could find an issue with it?

The student activism of the early 1970s in Tennessee marked a shift from the student movement of the 1960s, but built upon the earlier student power focus that had united Black and white students. Student activism did not end in May 1970. Instead, post-1970 student activism was on a smaller scale and resembled pre-1968 activism in that small protests dotted the landscape, although still connected by the concept of student power.

◉ ◉ ◉

Student activists discussed in this book came from different backgrounds, with varied expectations of their higher education experiences. Whether they were white or Black, students at a large state university, small private college, or a historically Black institution, they articulated elements of student power as an organizing principle. This central idea, focused on the personal and political autonomy of students, was evident at least as early as 1925 at Fisk University, reemerged in the 1950s, and grew slowly in popularity and intensity to 1968. From there, the concept of student power dominated campus-based protests until May 1970. Later activism incorporated a broader range of concerns, but student power remained a lens through which many activists understood their work.

Tennessee student activism, broadly speaking, was representative of national trends of student activism of the era, more than it was regionally distinctive. While elements of the activism had a southern flair, activists' personal reflections of themselves as activists working in the South were more representative of activists outside the exceptional hotbeds of the West Coast and northeast. The individuals discussed in this research reveal the complexity of societal dissent within the once "Solid South" (admittedly somewhat less solid in Tennessee than elsewhere), and present variations of the "student activist" from the stereotypical idealistic, long-haired, hippie protestor. Susan Carver, a UT student activist on her campus in 1969, reacted negatively to an accusation from Congressman James "Jimmy" Quillen (R-TN) that she and her fellow students were "campus radicals." "Am I pictured as a stringy-haired girl, covered with flower stickers and smoking pot, taking over the Administration Building?" she questioned. "I sincerely hope not, for I find the prospect as disgusting as members of the 'unhip' generation do!"[40] Largely because these students did not easily fit into one description or view of activists at the time, they have been overlooked in the regional and national narrative.

Student activists on southern university campuses in the late 1950s and 1960s were well within the minority of the student population on campus. Unlike many institutions across the country, southern colleges maintained a semblance of continuity in terms of student behavior for much of the 1960s. Traditions from the 1950s such as fraternity and sorority parties and football games pageantry held strong, and rules dictating dress and decorum remained well established. Historian Dan Carter recalled that registering at the University of South Carolina in 1960 brought him a "gift pack" from textile magnate and major Republican donor Roger Milliken that included, in addition to basic toiletry items, an anti-union pamphlet from the National Right to Work Committee, and a copy of FBI director J. Edgar Hoover's anti-Communist tract *Masters of Deceit*.[41] The symbolism of new students receiving these two items was clear: radicalism was unacceptable, "un-southern," beyond the pale. Well into the 1960s, students at historically Black colleges faced remarkable restrictions on their personal autonomy; beyond 10:00 p.m. dormitory curfews and restrictions on women's attire, students at Grambling College in Louisiana in 1967 ate breakfast at 6:00 a.m. surrounded by signs demanding they "take bite-size mouthfuls."[42] Southern college students during the 1960s were well aware that furious resistance would meet radical political action on campus.

As this book has demonstrated, Black and white student experiences, and their activism, differed. The radicalization of Black students from the *Brown* decision in 1954 and the subsequent debates over university desegregation created divisions between students and faculty and administrators over racial issues, which continued to grow throughout the 1960s. Simply put, racial discrimination remained a far more pressing concern for African American students. The administrative responses to student dissent also differed between majority-white and predominantly Black campuses. Awareness of potential repercussions for activism had a significant impact on a student's decision to participate in protests, as well as on the unfolding of these demonstrations. Nonetheless, there were similarities between white and Black student experiences on southern university campuses, especially in terms of the desire on the part of both groups for political and personal autonomy. Broadly speaking, Black students were largely involved in public accommodations demonstrations off campus to integrate businesses frequented by students; on-campus efforts to gain equality for African American students, faculty, and staff; and in the creation of Black studies programs and minority clubs at their schools. White students, while involved in these anti-segregation efforts, often concentrated more on anti-war demonstrations and *in loco parentis* protests later in the 1960s. Many Black and white student activists diverged over Vietnam, with Blacks seeking solidarity with non-white colonized peoples worldwide rather than with whites at home. There remained some Black-white student collaboration in the state through the 1960s, especially on majority-white campuses in Middle and East Tennessee. This was most apparent in the late 1960s protests across the state over student power, and a war that students increasingly viewed as immoral and illegal. But by 1970, the two groups had, by and large, succumbed to the imperatives of separate trajectories, while separately continuing to articulate student power as their individual driving principle.

Tennessee's history of student activism depicts a slower, gradually growing movement that begins from an earlier date than classic SDS-centric accounts of 1960s student activism. This trajectory differed significantly from the traditional historiographical narrative derived from focusing on several notable protests and major organizations. As previous studies in Tennessee and across the South have shown, despite being part of a growing historiographical field, incidents of southern student activism have largely appeared intermittent and unconnected with events and concepts regionally, much less nationally. This study encourages future scholarly work on these overlooked areas of activism. With further research conducted on these less famous locales, a clearer picture of American student activism during this period will emerge.

Tennessee student activists and their student groups organized grassroots community programs and campus organizations that sought to gain power for Black students and other student minorities. They fought for greater political autonomy and rights on campus. They enjoyed some successes; even when they failed, they forced a reckoning with major issues of American life: how racial equality was to be achieved, how universities were to be governed, under what circumstances America ought to involve itself in foreign wars. These issues are still with us. The southern student activists who raised them with such urgency in the 1960s deserve our attention.

NOTES

Introduction

1. Richard M. Nixon Presidential Library, (RNPLM) The White House Communications Agency, Weekly News Summaries, File 3737, May 29, 1970.

2. Gitlin, *The Sixties*. For critiques of this organization-centric analysis and its impact on New Left studies, see, for instance, Hunt, "How New Was the New Left?" in *The New Left Revisited*, eds. McMillian and Buhle, 139–55; Anderson, *The Movement and the Sixties*.

3. Historiographically, this book departs from the influential periodization frameworks for 1960s radicalism put forward by historians such as Van Gosse and Ibram X. Kendi (Rogers took the name Kendi in 2013). Gosse contends that various 1960s social movements originated at the beginning of the decade and moved in a unified trajectory, reaching their peak in the mid- to late 1960s, and then fracturing over a myriad of issues (such as Vietnam and federal counterintelligence subversion). See Gosse, *The Movements of the New Left, 1950–1975*. Kendi has argued that the arc of campus activism across the United States began later—around 1965—and ended later—around 1972. Rogers, *The Black Campus Movement*; Rogers, "The Black Campus Movement."

4. This point has been extensively discussed within civil rights historiography. Stephen Tuck describes this as viewing the shorter civil rights movement within the longer freedom struggle. See Tuck, *We Ain't What We Ought To Be*, 8. For a sympathetic account of the "long civil rights movement" paradigm, see especially Hall, "The Long Civil Rights Movement and the Political Uses of the Past." For critiques, see Arnesen, "Reconsidering the 'Long Civil Rights Movement'"; Cha-Jua and Lang, "The 'Long Movement' as Vampire." For a recent study that employs a long movement framework, see, for instance, Gilmore, *Defying Dixie*.

5. The historiographical field of southern student activism and the southern New Left began with Rossinow, *The Politics of Authenticity*, and Billingsley, *Communists on Campus* in 1998 and 1999 respectively. Michel, *Struggle For a Better South*, Williamson, *Radicalizing the Ebony Tower*, Turner, *Sitting In and Speaking Out*, and Cohen and Snyder, eds., *Rebellion in Black and White*, followed.

6. Simon Hall made a similar argument about civil rights, New Left, and antiwar movements. See Hall, "'On The Tail of the Panther': Black Power and the 1967 Convention of the National Conference for New Politics," *Journal of American Studies* 37, no. 1 (April 2003): 59–78, especially 60.

7. Michael S. Hevel and Heidi A. Jaeckle made a similar argument relating to recent scholarship in higher education. See Hevel and Jaeckle, "Trends in the Historiography of American College Student Life: Populations, Organizations, and Behaviors," in *Rethinking Campus Life*, eds. Ogren and VanOverbeke, 24. For campus-centered studies that have influenced this work, see Rossinow, *The Politics of Authenticity*; Sprayberry, "Student Radicalism and the Antiwar Movement," 148–70; Hess, *Lincoln Memorial University*; Akins and Wiggins, *Keeping the Faith*; Smith and Williamson, eds., *Sewanee Perspectives on the History of the University of the South*; Williamson, *Sewanee Sesquicentennial*

History; Heineman, *Campus Wars*; Billingsley, *Communists on Campus*; Turner, *Sitting In and Speaking Out*; deGregory, "Raising a Nonviolent Army"; Lorenzini, "'Power concedes nothing without a demand'"; Mariner, "'People Who Look Like Me'"; Lesesne, *A History of the University of South Carolina, 1940–2000*; Michel, "It Even Happened Here." For community studies that have been particularly central to this book, see Chafe, *Civilities and Civil Rights*; Fairclough, *Race & Democracy*; Kinchen, *Black Power in the Bluff City*; Kinchen, "'We want what people generally refer to as Black Power'"; Favors, "Shelter in a Time of Storm"; Saunders, "Encouraged By a Little Progress"; Sumner, "The Local Press and the Nashville Student Movement, 1960"; Lee, "The Nashville Civil Rights Movement"; Harris, "Unfamiliar Streets."

8. On parallel top-down versus grassroots-focused debates in civil rights historiography, see especially Lawson and Payne, *Debating the Civil Rights Movement: 1945–1968*. For works emphasizing a grassroots-approach to analysis of activism (specifically of SNCC), see Dittmer, *Local People*; Payne, *I've Got the Light of Freedom*; Thornton, *Dividing Lines*. For similar grassroots approaches, see Anderson, *Little Rock: Race and Resistance at Central High School*; Crosby, ed., *Civil Rights History from the Ground Up*; Greene, *Our Separate Ways*.

9. For recent works that address southern exceptionalism (or its absence), see, for instance, Lassiter and Crespino, eds., *The Myth of Southern Exceptionalism*; Lassiter and Kruse, "The Bulldozer Revolution"; Edwards, "Southern History as U.S. History"; Carter, "More than Race" in *Unlocking V. O. Key Jr.*, eds. Maxwell and Shields: 129–60; Cobb, *The South and America Since World War II*, esp. chapter 12.

10. Lamis, ed., *Southern Politics in the 1990s*, 4.

11. Lamis, *The Two-Party South*, 163.

12. Houston, *The Nashville Way*, 3.

13. Sprayberry, "Student Radicalism and the Antiwar Movement at the University of Alabama" in *Rebellion in Black and White*, eds. Cohen and Snyder: 148–70, esp. 149. For a former UT student discussing being a "freak" on campus in the 1960s, see the interview with JoAnn Alspaugh for "A Sense of Revolution," *The Vietnam War: East Tennessee* series, East Tennessee PBS, 2017.

14. See for instance Rogers, *The Black Campus Movement*; Joseph, ed., *The Black Power Movement*; Rogers, "The Black Campus Movement and the Institutionalization of Black Studies, 1965–1970"; Rogers, "The Black Campus Movement."

15. For studies on "prairie power," please see Janda, *Prairie Power*; Lieberman, *Prairie Power*. For relevant analysis from the Midwest but on Kansas, see Bailey, *Sex in the Heartland*.

16. Weyant, "'We Will Be Heard'", 25.

17. Rossinow, *The Politics of Authenticity*.

18. For a complete list of the institutions mentioned in the book, please see the map. The institutional names used in the book acknowledge changes during the period.

19. Italics in original; italicized terms are from journalist Jack Newfield as quoted in Cohen. Farber, introduction in *The Sixties*, 4; Cohen, "Prophetic Minority versus Recalcitrant Majority," introduction in *Rebellion in Black and White*, 16.

20. Lovett, *The Civil Rights Movement in Tennessee*, 124–40.

Chapter 1. Foundations of Student Activism in Tennessee

1. Rogers, *The Black Campus Movement*, 40.

2. Lamon, "The Black Community in Nashville and the Fisk University Student Strike of 1924–1925," 225–44, 225.

3. Rogers, *The Black Campus Movement*, 39–40.

4. Ibid., 40.

5. Lamon, "The Black Community in Nashville," 230; Rogers, *The Black Campus Movement*, 39.

6. Lamon, "The Black Community in Nashville," 232.

7. Rogers, *The Black Campus Movement*, 39.

8. Rogers, *The Black Campus Movement*, 40; Lamon, "The Black Community in Nashville," 235–36.

9. Rogers, *The Black Campus Movement*, 40.

10. Lamon, "The Black Community in Nashville," 241–42.

11. Hess, *Lincoln Memorial University*, 135.

12. Ibid., 136.

13. Ibid., 142–44.

14. Ibid., 145, 149–50.

15. Ibid., 150–51.

16. Lovett, *The Civil Rights Movement*, 135.

17. Horton and Kohl, *The Long Haul*, 60; Sullivan, *Days of Hope*, 95, 150–51.

18. Horton, *The Long Haul*, 46.

19. Dombrowski was originally from Tampa, Florida, living in New Orleans, Louisiana, and met Horton at Union. West was from north Georgia. Dr. Will Alexander, head of the Commission on Interracial Cooperation (CIC), introduced Horton to West after Alexander met Horton at Union. See Horton, *The Long Haul*, 58 and 63; James J. Lorence, "Don West (1906–1992)," *New Georgia Encyclopedia*, December 17, 2015, http://www.georgiaencyclopedia.org/articles/arts-culture/don-west-1906-1992; Sullivan, *Days of Hope*, 152–53. For more on West, see Don West, Interview E-0016, interviewed by Jacquelyn Hall, January 22, 1975, Southern Oral History Program (SOHP). For more on the three and their Union Theological Seminary days, see Altman, *Socialism before Sanders*, esp. chapter 3.

20. Horton, *The Long Haul*, 63.

21. Sullivan, *Days of Hope*, 151. The event in 1944 included Black laborers, and was the first time Highlander had allowed Blacks to reside overnight at the site.

22. Rossinow, *Visions of Progress*, 2.

23. Horton, *The Highlander Folk School*, 33–34. See also Adams with Horton, *Unearthing Seeds of Fire*, 28.

24. Horton, *The Highlander Folk School*, 35.

25. The church was the Summerfield Methodist Church. See Wisconsin Historical Society (WHS), Highlander Research and Education Center Collection (MSS 265), Part 1, MSS 265: Original Collection, 1917–1973 (HRECC), Series: Subject Files, Box 84, Folder 6, A-6, *Brotherhood* 1, no. 2, June 30, 1938.

26. WHS, HRECC, Series: Subject Files, Box 84, Folder 6, A-6, *Brotherhood*, newsletter week of June 19–25, 1938.

27. Italics in original. WHS, HRECC, Series: Subject Files, Box 84, Folder 6, A-6, *Brotherhood* 1, no. 2, June 30, 1938. For more on the logging and mining problems the area faced, see Horton, *The Long Haul*, 71; Horton, *The Highlander Folk School*, 33; Adams, *Unearthing Seeds of Fire*, 28.

28. WHS, HRECC, Series: Subject Files, Box 84, Folder 6, A-6, *Brotherhood* 1, no. 6, July 26, 1938.

29. Italics in original. WHS, HRECC, Series: Subject Files, Box 84, Folder 6, A-6, *Brotherhood* 1, no. 7, August 5, 1938.

30. *Statistical Abstract of the United States: 1938*, http://www.census.gov/library/publications/1939/compendia/statab/60ed.html.

31. WHS, HRECC, Series: Subject Files, Box 84, Folder 6, A-6, *Brotherhood* 1, no. 10, August 26, 1938.

32. WHS, HRECC, Series: Subject Files, Box 84, Folder 6, A-6, *Brotherhood* 1, no. 5, July 20, 1938.

33. Horton, *The Highlander Folk School*, 68.

34. Italics in original. WHS, HRECC, Series: Subject Files, Box 84, Folder 6, A-6, *Brotherhood* 1, no. 4, July 13, 1938.

35. WHS, HRECC, Series: Subject Files, Box 84, Folder 6, A-6, *Brotherhood* 1, no. 3, July 7, 1938. For more on Tennessee's history with the WPA, see Minton, *The New Deal in Tennessee, 1932–1938*, 70–77.

36. Robert Cohen argued that student radicalism was insignificant outside of the northeast. See Cohen, *When the Old Left Was Young*.

37. See Altbach, *Student Politics in America*, 11; Kruse and Tuck, eds., *Fog of War*. For reference to "black activists" and "student intellectuals" being "ready and able to express a new form of dissent," see Gosse, *Rethinking the New Left*, 15.

38. See the FBI's files on Highlander Folk School, https://vault.fbi.gov/Highlander%20Folk%20School.

39. Italics in original. Adams, *Unearthing Seeds of Fire*, 170.

40. Horton, *The Long Haul*, 96.

41. Blum, "Everyone You Don't Like," 58; Horton, *The Long Haul*, 108–12.

42. Cotham, *Toil, Turmoil & Triumph*, 222–23. See also Raines, *My Soul Is Rested*, 400.

43. Horton, *The Long Haul*, 121; Adams, *Unearthing Seeds of Fire*, 126; Cotham, *Toil, Turmoil & Triumph*, 223; Blum, "Everyone You Don't Like," 60. Highlander moved to New Market in 1972.

44. For more on these college workshops, see Horton, *The Highlander Folk School*, 240–42, and Adams, *Unearthing Seeds of Fire*, 143.

45. Library of Congress (LC), "Other Developments," *Southern School News* 1, issue 9, May 1955.

46. John Glen argues that the school "maintained flexibility" when it came to including students in its programs, and that Horton was quickly supportive of their participation at Highlander. See Glen, *Highlander*, 144. Horton's autobiography contradicts this view. See Horton, *The Long Haul*, 186.

47. Horton, *The Long Haul*, 186.

48. WHS, HRECC, Series: Subject Files, Box 78, Folder 8: College Weekends, 1954–1959; Horton, *The Long Haul*, 185; Horton, *The Highlander Folk School*, 240.

49. WHS, HRECC, Series: Subject Files, Box 78, Folder 8: College Weekends, 1954–1959, "Report of 1959 College Workshop," n.d.

50. Nashville Public Library (NPL), Civil Rights Oral History Project (CROHP), oral history interview of Guy Carawan and Candie Carawan, interviewed by K. G. Bennett, January 17, 2003. See for example Lewis, *Walking With the Wind*, 81–82; Weisbrot, *Freedom Bound*, 27; Lawson and Payne, *Debating the Civil Rights Movement*, 118; Horton, *The Highlander Folk School*, 242–43; Farrell, *The Spirit of the Sixties*, 76–77.

51. NPL, CROHP, Carawans oral history, January 17, 2003.

52. For more on the place of southern whites in the movement, see WHS, HRECC, Series: Administrative Files, Sub-Series: Annual Reports and Related Materials, Box 1, Folder 7: 1960–1973 (Incomplete), "College Workshops, Nov. 11–13, Apr. 7–9," *Highlander Reports*, 29th Annual Report, October 1, 1960–September 30, 1961; WHS, HRECC, Series:

Administrative Files, Sub-Series: Annual Reports and Related Materials, Box 1, Folder 7: 1960–1973 (Incomplete), "The New Agenda," *Highlander Reports*, 28th Annual Report, October 1, 1959–September 30, 1960. For more on the differences between community and campus activism, see WHS, HRECC, Series: Administrative Files, Sub-Series: Annual Reports and Related Materials, Box 1, Folder 7: 1960–1973 (Incomplete), "College Workshops, Nov. 11–13, Apr. 7–9," *Highlander Reports*, 29th Annual Report, October 1, 1960–September 30, 1961; WHS, HRECC, Series: Subject Files, Box 78, Folder 10: "College Weekends," 1960, November. For more on an interracial movement, see WHS, HRECC, Series: Administrative Files, Sub-Series: Annual Reports and Related Materials, Box 1, Folder 7: 1960–1973 (Incomplete), "The New Agenda," *Highlander Reports*, 28th Annual Report, October 1, 1959–September 30, 1960.

53. Vanderbilt University Special Collections and Archives (VUSCUA), Nelson and Marian D. Fuson Collection, Box 2, Folder 21, *The Voice of the Movement*, n.d.; VUSCUA, SSOC Reunion-2002-Box (SSOC), "SSOC," interdepartmental memo from SSOC to members regarding Christmas Workshop on the New South at the Institute for Policy Studies, n.d. [likely fall 1965]; LC, "Highlander Meeting," *Southern School News* 6, issue 11, May 1960; Blum, "Everyone You Don't Like," 64–65.

54. Horton, *The Long Haul*, 186.

55. Ibid.

56. Horton, *The Highlander Folk School*, 249.

57. Horton, *The Long Haul*, 186.

58. Candie Carawan, correspondence with author, February 5, 2013; "The Founding of SNCC (From SNCC 50th Anniversary Conference)," http://www.crmvet.org/info/snccfoun.htm. For more on Highlander and this founding meeting of SNCC, see Horton, *The Highlander Folk School*, 245–46.

59. Students from the following Nashville colleges and universities attended: Tennessee State, Vanderbilt, American Baptist Seminary, Fisk University, and Meharry Medical College. See Horton, *The Highlander Folk School*, 241–42.

60. Glen, *Highlander*, 145.

61. Jackson, "White Liberal Intellectuals, Civil Rights and Gradualism, 1954–1960," in *The Making of Martin Luther King and the Civil Rights Movement*, eds. Ward and Badger, 99.

62. Guy worked for Highlander from 1960 to 1965. See Carawan, correspondence, February 5, 2013.

63. NPL, CROHP, oral history interview of C. T. Vivian and Octavia Vivian, interviewed by Kathy Bennett, May 12, 2003.

64. NPL, CROHP, oral history interview of Matthew Walker Jr., interviewed by Kathy Bennett, September 3, 2004.

65. Horton, *The Highlander Folk School*, 246–50.

66. See for instance, Bartley, *The Rise of Massive Resistance*; Kirk, "'Massive Resistance and Minimum Compliance'", in *Massive Resistance*, ed. Webb, 76–98; Chafe, *Civilities and Civil Rights*; Walker, *The Ghost of Jim Crow*.

67. For more information on school integration controversies at Clinton and Nashville, Tennessee, please see Webb, *Rabble Rousers*; Houston, *The Nashville Way*; Lovett, *The Civil Rights Movement*; Ramsey, "'We Will Be Ready Whenever They Are'".

68. See for example, Bartley, *The Rise of Massive Resistance*; Badger, *New Deal/New South*, chapter 11, esp. 212; Badger, "Lyndon Johnson and Albert Gore," in *Poverty and Progress in the U.S. South Since 1920*, eds. Jones and Newman, 117.

69. Chafe, *Civilities and Civil Rights*, 8. See also Chappell, *Inside Agitators*.

70. Interview with Reverend Will Campbell, for *Eyes on the Prize: The Complete Series*, November 3, 1985, Washington University Film and Media Archive, Henry Hampton Collection, http://mavisweb.wulib.wustl.edu:81/mavisDetail/TitleWork/key/1033.

71. See Kruse, *White Flight*; Cobb, *The Selling of the South*.

72. These programs were formed with the intention of providing educational resources to southern Black schools and existed between the following institutions: the University of Michigan and the Tuskegee Institute, Indiana University and Stillman College, Brown University and Tougaloo College, the University of Wisconsin and North Carolina College, and Southern Illinois University and Winston-Salem State University. Faculty exchanges between Michigan and Tuskegee began in 1963 and ran until 1974. See Park, "Planting the Seeds of Academic Excellence and Cultural Awareness," 117, 126.

73. Fisk University Special Collections and Archives (FUSCA), Arna Wendell Bontemps Collection Papers, 1934–1965 (AWBCP), Box 102, Folder 3, "Student Exchange Program," *Fisk News*, March 1957.

74. The other institutions that had exchange programs with Fisk during this period were: Denison University (Granville, Ohio), College of Wooster (Wooster, Ohio), Oberlin College (Oberlin, Ohio), DePauw University (Greencastle, Ind.), Skidmore College (Saratoga Springs, N.Y.), Occidental College (Los Angeles, Ca.), Beloit College (Beloit, Wis.), the College of Idaho (Caldwell, Idaho), San Diego State College (San Diego, Ca.), Whittier College (Whittier, Ca.), and Manchester College (North Manchester, Ind.). See FUSCA, AWBCP, Box 102, Folder 3, "Exchange Colleges," November 24, 1958.

75. FUSCA, AWBCP, Box 102, Folder 3, Mike Armer, "A Combination of Thoughts on Fisk," May 29, 1958.

76. Amber [no last name given], "Paul LaPrad: Civil Rights Activist," 9 March 2015, Nashville Public Library Blog, https://library.nashville.org/blog/2015/03/paul-laprad-civil-rights-activist.

77. Rossinow, *The Politics of Authenticity*, 1. For further discussion of what white students of the New Left gained from the civil rights movement, see Farrell, *The Spirit of the Sixties*, 106–9.

78. Hall, "The Sit-Ins, SNCC, and Cold War Patriotism," in *From Sit-Ins to SNCC*, 135.

79. David L. Chappell articulates this point in reference to white southern SNCC members. See Chappell, *Inside Agitators*, 274–75n3. While a member of SNCC, Paul LaPrad was "more prominent" in the local Nashville efforts than in the national organization of SNCC. See Ling, "SNCCs," in *From Sit-Ins to SNCC*, 89. Candie Carawan was another exchange student who participated in the sit-ins, from Pomona College in Claremont, California. See NPL, CROHP, Carawans oral history, January 17, 2003.

80. Turner, *Sitting In and Speaking Out*, 24–25.

81. LC, "Community Action," *Southern School News* 3, issue 10, April 1957.

82. Lovett, *The Civil Rights Movement*, 121–22. The sit-ins will be discussed in greater detail in the following chapter.

83. Roberson, "The Problem of the Twentieth Century: Sewanee, Race and Race Relations" in *Sewanee Perspectives,* eds. Smith and Williamson, 503.

84. Sewanee: The University of the South, University Archives and Special Collections (SUASC), University Records, Executive Offices, Vice-Chancellor Edward McCrady, 14. 1951–1971, (E08.04.14) (UR), Box 81, Negro file—official and miscellaneous, Letter to R. Bland Mitchell, Chancellor of the University of the South, from Cecil Sims, law partner at Bass, Berry & Sims, Nashville, Tennessee, May 13, 1952; SUASC, UR, Box 81, Negro file—official and miscellaneous, Letter to R. Bland Mitchell from J. S. Allen, law partner at Armstrong, McCadden, Allen, Braden & Goodman, Memphis, Tennessee, May 22, 1952;

SUASC, UR, Box 81, Negro file—official and miscellaneous, Letter to R. Bland Mitchell from S. Bartow Strang, law partner at Strang, Fletcher & Carriger, Chattanooga, Tennessee, June 2, 1952; Roberson, "The Problem of the Twentieth Century," 503.

85. The date of the board's resolution was June 7, 1961. SUASC, UR, Box 100, Folder—Letters Concerning Admission of Negroes to Seminary Sept–Oct, 1952, "Resolution Passed By the Board of Trustees of the University of the South," June 6, 1952; SUASC, UR, Box 100, Folder—Segregation correspondence, Letter to President Peyton N. Rhodes, Southwestern at Memphis, from McCrady on November 14, 1962; Roberson, "The Problem of the Twentieth Century," 508; Williamson Jr., *Sewanee Sesquicentennial History*, 312.

86. Bates was a professor in the French department. SUASC, UR, Box 100, Folder—Segregation correspondence, Letter to Scott Bates from Robert S. Lancaster, Dean of the College, May 28, 1962.

87. Ibid.

88. Handwritten note on letter states that the same letter was sent to Fisk and Morehouse on the same day. See SUASC, UR, Box 100, Folder—Segregation correspondence, Letter to Prof. Annette H. Eaton, who was in charge of the Student Exchange Program at Howard University, from Scott Bates, Assoc. Prof. of French at Sewanee, November 23, 1962; Roberson, "The Problem of the Twentieth Century," 508.

89. SUASC, UR, Box 100, Folder—Segregation correspondence, John Hemphill, "The College Scene: Fisk Has Largest Student Swap Plan," *The Tennessean*, November 25, 1962.

90. Maryville College Archives (MC), Reports of Board Directors, 1946–1950, 1950–1957 (RBD), "The President's Annual Report, Part II, October 11–12, 1957."

91. MC, Box—Ledgers, File—Student-Faculty Senate Minutes 1960–1967, November 25, 1960. This exchange is comparable within the region to when students from Agnes Scott College and Emory University "expressed an interest" in discussing race with Black Atlanta college students. See Fleming, *Soon We Will Not Cry*, 46–47.

92. MC, Box—Ledgers, File—Student-Faculty Senate Minutes 1960–1967, October 28, 1960; MC, Box—Ledgers, File—Student-Faculty Senate Minutes 1960–1967, November 25, 1960; MC, Box—Ledgers, File—Student-Faculty Senate Minutes 1960–1967, December 9, 1960.

93. MC, Box—Ledgers, File—Student-Faculty Senate Minutes 1960–1967, December 9, 1960.

94. University of Tennessee Special Collections (UTSC), Carl and Anne Braden Papers (MS.0425) (CABP), SSOC—Southern Student Organizing Committee, "Klan Responds to Student Conference," *The New Rebel* 1, no. 2, October 1964. The Southern Regional Council's 1960 "Intimidation Reprisal and Violence in the South's Racial Crisis" document mentions occasions of Klan activity in Tennessee, but the state's number was considerably less than other southern states, particularly in the Deep South. See "Intimidation Reprisal and Violence in the South's Racial Crisis," Southeastern Office, American Friends Service Committee, Department of Racial and Cultural Relations, National Council of the Churches of Christ in the United States of America, and Southern Regional Council (SRC), 1960, in possession of the author.

95. UTSC, CABP, SSOC—Southern Student Organizing Committee, "Klan Responds to Student Conference," *The New Rebel* 1, no. 2, October 1964. It is possible that this was part of a weekly series of discussions between the three schools by Highlander. See Blum, "Everyone You Don't Like," 64–65.

96. UTSC, CABP, SSOC—Southern Student Organizing Committee, "Klan Responds to Student Conference," *The New Rebel* 1, no. 2, October 1964.

97. Cunningham, *Klansville, U.S.A.*

98. Jackson, "White Liberal Intellectuals," 101; Badger, *New Deal/New South*, esp. chapter 11.

99. See University of Memphis Special Collections (UMSC), Dr. Cecil C. Humphreys Collection (PO-HUMP) (CCHC), Box 7, Folders 5–7, 13, 14, and 24.

100. See Black and Black, *Politics and Society in the South*, 9–11.

101. UMSC, CCHC, Box 7, Folder 6, Memorandum from J. M. Smith, President of Memphis State University, to State Board of Education, August 8, 1958.

102. The "Memphis Eight," as they are commonly called, were: Bertha Rogers Looney, Marvis LaVerne Kneeland Jones, Rose Blakney-Love, Sammie Burnett-Johnson, Luther McClellan, John Simpson, Eleanor Gandy, and Ralph Prater. See Elizabeth Jane Walker, "Eight who changed history," *University of Memphis Magazine*, n.d., and "The Memphis State Eight," The Historical Marker Database, https://www.hmdb.org/m.asp?m=86685; Sorrels, *The Exciting Years*, 23; Tucker, *Memphis Since Crump*, 118–19.

103. Sorrels, *The Exciting Years*, 24.

104. Green, "The Rural-Urban Matrix in the 1950s South," in *From the Grassroots to the Supreme Court*, ed. Lau, 281; Wallenstein, "Black Southerners and Nonblack Universities," in *Higher Education and the Civil Rights Movement*, ed. Wallenstein, 34; Beck Cultural Exchange Center (BCEC), Civil & Human Rights, Slavery & Oral History, Desegregation in Knoxville (CHR), "Stony the Road: Desegregating America's Schools: The Story of East Tennessee," published by Beck Cultural Exchange Center, Inc. and produced by Knox County Public Library, n.d.

105. Houston, *The Nashville Way*, 55.

106. Ibid.

107. Lovett, *The Civil Rights Movement*, 60.

108. Houston, *The Nashville Way*, 55.

109. Ibid.

110. Wright quoted in LC, "Fisk Seeks to Attract More White Students," *Southern School News* 8, issue 7, January 1962.

111. Lovett, *The Civil Rights Movement*, 60.

112. Houston, *The Nashville Way*, 57.

113. LC, "In The Colleges: Formerly All-Negro University Enrolls Half-Dozen Whites," *Southern School News* 9, issue 6, December 1962.

114. There seems to be disagreement between sources on how many Black students were admitted at this time, but this account uses Lovett's figure. See Lovett, *The Civil Rights Movement*, 347; BCEC, CHR, "Stony the Road: Desegregating America's Schools: The Story of East Tennessee"; Wallenstein, "Black Southerners and Nonblack Universities", 35.

115. UTSC, Office of the University Historian Collection, 1819–1997 (bulk 1870–1997), Series V—Race Relations (OUHCV), Box 22, Folder 16: Desegregation-Undergraduate Experience, 1900–1995 (bulk 1950–1953), Letter from Herman E. Spivey to Andrew Holt, May 22, 1961.

116. See the following chapter's discussion of Students for Equal Treatment (SET) and Forum for Racial Equality, Etc. (FREE).

117. Hess, *Lincoln Memorial University*, 203, 233–34.

118. A Chinese instructor had worked at Lincoln Memorial in 1946, but Kincaid argued that this was because he had been a scholar of Abraham Lincoln and had nothing to do with his race. See Hess, *Lincoln Memorial University*, 203.

119. Wallenstein, "Introduction," in *Higher Education and the Civil Rights Movement*, ed. Wallenstein, 6–8.

120. Hess, *Lincoln Memorial University*, 203.

121. Ibid.

122. The first Black student to attend classes at Lincoln Memorial after *Brown* was Mattie Babb, during the summer of 1966, with a handful of other students doing the same after her, and four Black students were admitted in the fall semester of 1968. See Hess, *Lincoln Memorial University*, 214.

123. Haynes, *The Last Segregated Hour*, 124–25.

124. SUASC, UR, Box 100, Folder—Segregation correspondence, Letter to President Peyton N. Rhodes, Southwestern at Memphis, from Edward McCrady on November 14, 1962. For Clemson University's usage of test scores in determining the applicability of Black students, see Burton, "Dining With Harvey Gantt," in *Matthew J. Perry*, eds. Burke and Gergel, 183–220.

125. Roberson, "The Problem of the Twentieth Century," 503.

126. Italics in original. SUASC, UR, Box 100, Folder—Segregation correspondence, Letter to President Peyton N. Rhodes, Southwestern at Memphis, from Edward McCrady on November 14, 1962.

127. Ibid. The college has since been renamed Randolph College.

128. Kean, *Desegregating Private Higher Education in the South*, 12.

129. Ibid.

130. Ibid., 59. This incident will be further discussed in chapter 2

131. MC, RBD, "The President's Annual Report, Part II, October 15, 1954"; BCEC, CHR, "Stony the Road: Desegregating America's Schools: The Story of East Tennessee."

132. MC, Board Min. 1951–1974 (BM), Board of Directors Minutes 1951–1964, "A Report and Recommendation by the President to the Directors of Maryville College, May 19, 1954."

133. Later, the remaining four ballots were received, with three votes for accepting Black students that year and one against the proposal. MC, RBD, "The President's Annual Report, Part II, October 15, 1954."

134. Ibid.

135. The students were Shirley Carr Clowney, Nancy Smith Wright, Queen Crossing, Louise Hill Gilmore, Leo Valentine, and Freeman Wyche. See "2 crossed color line quietly in '54," *Knoxville News-Sentinel*, February 28, 2011.

136. Jimmie Baxter, interview by Jamie Roberts, December 2, 1993. Transcript held in UTSC, OUHCV, Box 22, Folder 10: Blacks—Faculty at UT.

137. Elizabeth Jane Walker, "Eight who changed history," *University of Memphis Magazine*, n.d., and "The Memphis State Eight," The Historical Marker Database, https:// www.hmdb.org/m.asp?m=86685.

138. William Gatewood Sibley, letter to the editor, "Sewanee Has Basic Conflict," *Sewanee Purple* 65, no. 13, February 13, 1957.

139. Williams returned to Fisk after the incident. See Williamson Jr., *Sewanee Sesquicentennial History*, 312. Whether a deliberate omission or not, the *Sewanee Purple* did not mention a cross burning at any point that year.

140. Ibid., 306, 319.

141. The Fisk student who was involved in the Nashville sit-ins was Angeline Butler. See Roberson, "The Problem of the Twentieth Century," 512–13; Lee, "The Nashville Civil Rights Movement," 153.

142. Williamson Jr., *Sewanee Sesquicentennial History*, 306.
143. Ibid.
144. Shirley Carr Clowney, Interview U-0618, interviewed by Joey Fink, May 20, 2011, SOHP, University of North Carolina at Chapel Hill; Shirley Carr Clowney, oral history conducted by the author, August 12, 2014.
145. Nancy Smith Wright, oral history conducted by the author, August 6, 2014; Karen Beaty, "Opening MC doors; Woman was first black to graduate from MC in 60 years back in 1960," *Daily Times*, February 1, 2000.
146. Clowney, oral history, August 12, 2014; Wright, oral history, August 6, 2014.
147. Clowney, oral history, August 12, 2014.
148. Wright, oral history, August 6, 2014.
149. Clowney, SOHP oral history, May 20, 2011.
150. Ibid.
151. Wright, oral history, August 6, 2014.
152. Ibid.; Clowney, oral history, August 12, 2014.
153. Roberson, "The Problem of the Twentieth Century," 508.

Chapter 2. Kneel, Sit, or Stand

1. Turner, *Sitting In and Speaking Out*, 47.
2. Ibid. Quote is from Claude Sitton writing for the *New York Times*.
3. Ibid., 44.
4. deGregory, "Raising a Nonviolent Army," ix; Hogan, "Freedom Now," in *Civil Rights History from the Ground Up*, ed. Crosby, 174; Doyle, *Nashville Since the 1920s*, 244–45; Whittington, "Interracial Dialogue and the Southern Student Human Relations Project," in *Rebellion in Black and White*, 90; Turner, "The Rise of Black and White Student Protest in Nashville," in *Rebellion in Black and White*, 131; Rogers, *The Black Campus Movement*, 62.
5. Turner, *Sitting In and Speaking Out*, 44–45.
6. Harris, "Unfamiliar Streets," 13–14; Lovett, *The Civil Rights Movement*, 149–51.
7. UTSC, CABP, Student Movement, Special Report by the Southern Regional Council, "The Student Protest Movement—A Recapitulation," September 1961.
8. Ibid.
9. Chafe, *Civilities and Civil Rights*, 42.
10. Ibid., 8.
11. Italics in original. Houston, *The Nashville Way*, 4.
12. Ibid., 5.
13. Turner, *Sitting In and Speaking Out*, 50.
14. Houston, *The Nashville Way*, 85.
15. Ibid., 85.
16. Lovett, *The Civil Rights Movement*, 119–20; Doyle, *Nashville Since the 1920s*, 245; Houston, *The Nashville Way*, 86.
17. Houston, *The Nashville Way*, 83, 87.
18. Lovett, *The Civil Rights Movement*, 122; Houston, *The Nashville Way*, 87.
19. The Lawson and Smith workshops ended by the spring of 1961. See Hogan, "Freedom Now," 173; Turner, "The Rise of Black and White Student Protest," 135.
20. NPL, CROHP, Carawan, oral history, January 17, 2003.
21. Lovett, *The Civil Rights Movement*, 121.
22. Ibid., 122. For more on the beginning of the sit-ins, see Rogers, *The Black Campus Movement*, 63.

23. Houston, *The Nashville Way*, 87–88; Turner, *Sitting In and Speaking Out*, 51.
24. Turner, *Sitting In and Speaking Out*, 51–52.
25. Ibid., 52.
26. Ibid., 53.
27. Ibid.; Sumner, "The Local Press and the Nashville Student Movement, 1960," 72–76.
28. Houston, *The Nashville Way*, 95–96; Lewis, *Walking With the Wind*, 100.
29. Houston, *The Nashville Way*, 96–99.
30. Lovett, *The Civil Rights Movement*, 127.
31. Turner, *Sitting In and Speaking Out*, 54.
32. Houston, *The Nashville Way*, 99–100.
33. Lawson was first asked to withdraw from the Divinity School, but he refused. See Turner, *Sitting In and Speaking Out*, 84.
34. Lovett, *The Civil Rights Movement*, 143.
35. The article was from March 4, 1960, and referred to the university's Divinity School. See Turner, *Sitting In and Speaking Out*, 84.
36. For more on Branscomb, please see Kean, *Desegregating Private Higher Education in the South*.
37. "Celebrating Change: Courage, Determination and Inclusion," Vanderbilt University, n.d., http://www.vanderbilt.edu/celebratingblackhistory/.
38. Houston, *The Nashville Way*, 117.
39. Ibid., 114–15.
40. Ibid., 115; Halberstam, *The Children*, 232.
41. Houston, *The Nashville Way*, 115–16.
42. Ibid., 114; Lovett, *The Civil Rights Movement*, 139–40.
43. Quotation is from J. Metz Rollins. See Lovett, *The Civil Rights Movement*, 159–60. For more on the Freedom Rides, see Arsenault, *Freedom Riders*.
44. Lovett, *The Civil Rights Movement*, 160; VUSCUA, Nelson and Marian D. Fuson Collection, Box 2, Folder 5, "Without Your Help Our Hands Are Chained," n.d.
45. LC, "In The Colleges: Disciplinary Action Against Students At A&I Considered," *Southern School News* 7, issue 12, June 1961; LC, "In The Colleges: A&I Places 'Freedom Riders' On Probation," *Southern School News* 8, issue 1, July 1961; LC, "In The Colleges: Expelled Students Win Readmission. Committee Hearing." *Southern School News* 8, issue 7, January 1962. For information on a similar situation concerning Louisiana's State Board of Education, see Fairclough, *Race & Democracy*, 265–71, quotations are from 268; Bailey and Easson, *The Education of a Black Radical*, 41–42, 47–43.
46. Lovett, *The Civil Rights Movement*, 172.
47. LC, "Legal Action: A&I Allows 'Riders' To Remain Students," *Southern School News* 8, issue 8, February 1962.
48. Zagumny, "Sit-Ins in Knoxville, Tennessee," 45.
49. Cities experiencing similar forms of protest and community reaction included Dallas, Texas, Louisville, Kentucky, Tampa, Florida, Greensboro, North Carolina, and Little Rock, Arkansas. For more on Dallas, Louisville, and Tampa, see Brophy, "Active Acceptance–Active Containment," in *Southern Businessmen and Desegregation*, eds. Jacoway and Colburn; Wright, "Desegregation of Public Accommodations in Louisville," in *Southern Businessmen and Desegregation*; Lawson, "From Sit-In to Race Riot," in *Southern Businessmen and Desegregation*. For additional information on Greensboro, see Chafe, *Civilities and Civil Rights*. For more on Little Rock, see Kirk, "Another Side of the Sit-Ins," in *From Sit-Ins to SNCC*.
50. Zagumny, "Sit-Ins in Knoxville," 45. For more on this concept in relation to

Knoxville, see Wheeler, *Knoxville, Tennessee*, 92. Historian Clive Webb has argued that "authorities in many communities exercised considerable restraint, and there were relatively few serious outbreaks of violence" in sit-ins across the South. See Webb, "Breaching the Wall of Resistance," in *From Sit-Ins to SNCC*, 61.

51. The speech was given on May 30, 1960. See Wheeler, *Knoxville, Tennessee*, 92; Zagumny, "Sit-Ins in Knoxville, Tennessee," 52. For an account that argues Black disaffection, with the pace of racial change within 1950s southern biracial politics, led to the direct-action phase of the civil rights movement, see Badger, *New Deal/New South*, chapter 7.

52. Proudfoot, *Diary of a Sit-In*, xlii.

53. Ibid., 2–3, 5.

54. Robert J. Booker, oral history conducted by the author, December 12, 2013.

55. WHS, HRECC, Subject File, Box 65, Folder 8, Nashville Sit-Ins, 1960, Margaret Price, "Toward a Solution of the Sit-In Controversy," SRC-16 [probably Southern Regional Council], May 31, 1960.

56. The variety stores Duncan visited in New York are unknown. See Proudfoot, *Diary of a Sit-In*, 4; WHS, HRECC, Subject Files, Box 65, Folder 8, Nashville Sit-Ins, 1960, Margaret Price, "Toward a Solution of the Sit-In Controversy," SRC-16 [probably Southern Regional Council], May 31, 1960.

57. John F. Kennedy Presidential Library (JFKPLM), Burke Marshall Personal Papers (#161) (BMP), Series 1, Assistant Attorney General Files, 1958–1965, Alabama 1964, Virginia Prince Edward County 1963, Box 21, Folder 10, Tennessee-Highlander Folk School, 1961–1963, Letter from Myles Horton to Burke Marshall, January 11, 1962.

58. Proudfoot, *Diary of a Sit-In*, 4; Booker, oral history, December 12, 2013; Wheeler, *Knoxville, Tennessee*, 125. Memphis businessmen and city officials similarly attempted to negotiate with New York chain owners, but in 1961, not 1960. The secretary of commerce in Kennedy's administration, Luther H. Hodges, was in communication with Robert F. Kennedy and Burke Marshall in these efforts. See JFKPLM, White House Central Subject Files (#6.1) (WHCSF), Series 31, Local Governments (LG), Box 504, MART-MEMZ, Letter from Luther H. Hodges to Robert F. Kennedy, August 17, 1961.

59. Booker, oral history, December 12, 2013. For more on this process see Zagumny, "Sit-Ins in Knoxville," 45–54.

60. UT students included Harry Wiersema Jr., Lee Butler, Pete Benson, and Mike Kennedy. See BCEC, Civil & Human Rights, Slavery & Oral History, University of Tennessee and the Civil Rights Movement (CHRUT), "UTK and the Civil Rights Movement," historical vignette prepared by the Office of the University Historian, March 29, 1996.

61. Ibid.

62. Ibid.; BCEC, African Americans, B thru C, Reverend William T. Crutcher (AAWC), "Rev. Dr. W. T. Crutcher," unknown publication, November 7, 1989.

63. BCEC, AAWC, "Rev. Dr. W. T. Crutcher," unknown publication, November 7, 1989.

64. The downtown Woolworth's, Kress's, McClellan's, Grant's, and Walgreen's lunch counters opened, leaving only Miller's and Cole's segregated. See Proudfoot, *Diary of a Sit-In*, 137.

65. BCEC, CHRUT, "UTK and the Civil Rights Movement," historical vignette prepared by the Office of the University Historian, March 29, 1996.

66. Ibid.

67. BCEC, Civil & Human Rights, Slavery & Oral History, Civil Rights (Movement) (CHRM), "51 Theater Pickets Jailed," *Knoxville News-Sentinel*, October 10, 1961.

68. BCEC, Newspapers Collection, Mount Zionite, Beardsley Crimson Caravan, Times Herald, "Stand Ins," *Times-Herald*, 11, no. 50, December 17, 1961.

69. BCEC, CHRM, "Knoxville's Greatest Story: A Reunion and Retelling of the Knoxville Civil Rights Movement, 1960–1965," March 9, 2006.

70. Avon Rollins, oral history conducted by the author, December 27, 2013.

71. BCEC, Newspapers Collection, Knoxville Flashlight-Herald, 1963/06/08, "'Theater Stand Ins,'" *Knoxville Flashlight-Herald*, June 8, 1963.

72. Booker, oral history, December 12, 2013.

73. Proudfoot, *Diary of a Sit-In*, 102–3; Wiersema Sr. in *Fifty Years of Social Activism at the Tennessee Unitarian Universalist Church*, ed. Yarbro, 21–22; Proudfoot, *Diary of a Sit-In*, 74.

74. BCEC, CHRM, "2 Charged in Attempt To Eat at Byerley's," *Knoxville News-Sentinel*, n.d. [October 1962 is clear] and "Trespassing Charged To Two In Cafeteria," *Knoxville News-Sentinel*, n.d. [October 1962].

75. BCEC, Newspapers Collection, Knoxville Flashlight-Herald, 1963/01/12, "KCIC To Gather Clothing For Needy Mississippi Families," *Knoxville Flashlight-Herald* 32, no. 2, January 12, 1963. For more on KCIC's role in integrating Knoxville, see Zagumny, "Sit-Ins in Knoxville, Tennessee," 50.

76. Harry Wiersema Jr., oral history conducted by the author, August 7, 2014; BCEC, CHRUT, "UTK and the Civil Rights Movement," historical vignette prepared by the Office of the University Historian, March 29, 1996; Rollins, oral history, December 27, 2013. For more on Wiersema's parents and their role in the Knoxville sit-ins, see Proudfoot, *Diary of a Sit-In*, 58–61.

77. BCEC, CHRUT, "UTK and the Civil Rights Movement," historical vignette prepared by the Office of the University Historian, March 29, 1996.

78. Marion Barry and Harry Wiersema reportedly led SET and FREE as either president and vice-president or chairman and vice-chairman (accounts differ in the terminology). See Wiersema Jr., oral history, August 7, 2014.

79. WHS, Carl and Anne Braden Papers, 1928–2006 (MSS 6) (CABP), Part 1, Subseries: Southern Conference Educational Files, 1954–1972, Box 56, Folder 8 Nashville, Tennessee, 1958–1964, report on the status of southern student activism by Ed Hamlett, n.d. This is almost certainly from early 1964, when Hamlett and Sam Shirah visited various southern campuses in order to gauge their readiness for activism organization. See Michel, "Building the New South," 51

80. BCEC, Civil & Human Rights, Slavery & Oral History, Segregation (Restaurants) (CHRS), "Local Restaurants Segregated," n.d.

81. BCEC, CHRUT, "UTK and the Civil Rights Movement," historical vignette prepared by the Office of the University Historian, March 29, 1996.

82. Ibid.

83. BCEC, CHRS, "Local Restaurants Segregated," n.d.; Wiersema Jr., oral history, August 7, 2014; BCEC, CHRUT, "UTK and the Civil Rights Movement," historical vignette prepared by the Office of the University Historian, March 29, 1996.

84. BCEC, CHRUT, "UTK and the Civil Rights Movement," historical vignette prepared by the Office of the University Historian, March 29, 1996.

85. BCEC, CHRS, "Local Restaurants Segregated," n.d.

86. The arrests of the three UT students occurred in spring 1962. Jones had the charges against him dropped while Rollins was fined $25. See BCEC, CHRS, "Local Restaurants Segregated," n.d.; BCEC, CHRM, "2 Charged in Attempt To Eat at Byerley's," *Knoxville News-Sentinel*, n.d. [October 1962 is clear]; BCEC, CHRM, Notice of Motion to Dissolve

Injunction in *Byerley v. Wiersema et al.*, February 26, 1963; Wiersema Jr., oral history, August 7, 2014.

87. Zagumny, "Sit-Ins in Knoxville, Tennessee," 50.

88. Wiersema Jr., oral history, August 7, 2014; BCEC, CHRM, "UTK and the Civil Rights Movement," historical vignette prepared by the Office of the University Historian, March 29, 1996. Harry Wiersema Sr. was the head of the Tennessee Valley Unitarian Universalist Church public relations committee at the time of the sit-ins. See Yarbro, *Fifty Years of Social Activism*, 21; Oral History of the Tennessee Valley Authority: Interview with Harry Wiersema, September 24, 1969, by Charles W. Crawford, Oral History Research Office, Memphis State University, https://archive.org/details/oralhistoryoftenoowier.

89. BCEC, CHRUT, "UTK and the Civil Rights Movement," historical vignette prepared by the Office of the University Historian, March 29, 1996.

90. Wiersema Jr., oral history, August 7, 2014.

91. BCEC, CHRUT, "UTK and the Civil Rights Movement," historical vignette prepared by the Office of the University Historian, March 29, 1996.

92. Ibid.

93. Ibid.

94. JFKPLM, BMP, Series 1. Assistant Attorney General Files, 1958–1965, Attorney General, July 1961–March 1963 White House Referrals, Box 8, Folder 2, Special Correspondence, Attorney General, April–June 1963, Memorandum to the Attorney General from Burke Marshall, May 22, 1963.

95. The party was hosted by Malcolm Ottaway, a former UT graduate student. See BCEC, CHRUT, "UTK and the Civil Rights Movement," historical vignette prepared by the Office of the University Historian, March 29, 1996; BCEC, Newspapers Collection, Knoxville Flashlight-Herald, 1963/06/08, "Party Too Informal," *Knoxville Flashlight-Herald* 32, no. 18, June 8, 1963.

96. BCEC, CHRUT, "UTK and the Civil Rights Movement," historical vignette prepared by the Office of the University Historian, March 29, 1996; BCEC, Newspapers Collection, Knoxville Flashlight-Herald, 1963/06/08, "Party Too Informal," *Knoxville Flashlight-Herald* 32, no. 18, June 8, 1963.

97. BCEC, CHRUT, "UTK and the Civil Rights Movement," historical vignette prepared by the Office of the University Historian, March 29, 1996.

98. WHS, CABP, Part 1, Subseries: Southern Conference Educational Files, 1954–1972, Box 62, Folder 8, Tennessee Voting Project, 1960–1964, SNCC News Release, "Tennessee Students Protest Jim Crow Athletics," April 30, 1964.

99. Ibid.

100. Ibid.

101. Martin, "Hold That (Color) Line!," in *Higher Education and the Civil Rights Movement*, ed. Wallenstein, 171; C. J. Schexnayder, "The Integration of Football in the Southeastern Conference," SB Nation (Vox Media), May 9, 2012, http://www.teamspeedkills.com/2012/5/9/3008248/the-integration-of-football-in-the-southeastern-conference.

102. Interview of Theotis Robinson Jr., Appendix 9 in Wallenstein, *Higher Education and the Civil Rights Movement*, 275–79.

103. Booker, oral history, December 12, 2013.

104. Trotter, "The Memphis Business Community and Integration," in *Southern Businessmen and Desegregation*, 282–83. See also Strub, "Black and White and Banned All Over," 696.

105. Lovett, *The Civil Rights Movement*, 189.

106. Strub, "Black and White and Banned All Over," 701.
107. Green, *Battling the Plantation Mentality*, 134–35.
108. Ibid., 112.
109. There was also an earlier attempt at interracial politics, the Memphis Commission on Interracial Cooperation. It was established in June 1940 and similarly collapsed (in 1942) from inability to push through reform. See Trotter, "The Memphis Business Community and Integration," 285–86.
110. Lovett, *The Civil Rights Movement*, 114–17, 188–89, 193.
111. Trotter, "The Memphis Business Community and Integration," 282–83.
112. Lovett, *The Civil Rights Movement*, 117, 192–93. Vasco would later be a county commissioner and Maxine, in addition to serving as the executive secretary from 1962 to 1995, later served on the Memphis Board of Education as the first Black member elected to the board and on the Tennessee Board of Regents. See "Celebrating The Life Of Maxine A. Smith," 2013, https://naacp.org/resources/celebrating-life-maxine-smith; Kinchen, *Black Power in the Bluff City*, 20–21.
113. Lovett, *The Civil Rights Movement*, 192.
114. Ibid., 117.
115. Haynes, *The Last Segregated Hour*, 55.
116. Lovett, *The Civil Rights Movement*, 189; Trotter, "The Memphis Business Community and Integration," 286–87; Haynes, *The Last Segregated Hour*, 25; Green, *Battling the Plantation Mentality*, 232–41.
117. Barry graduated from LeMoyne in 1958 and Lawson had moved to Memphis in 1962. See Haynes, *The Last Segregated Hour*, 25.
118. Lovett, *The Civil Rights Movement*, 189.
119. Green, *Battling the Plantation Mentality*, 234.
120. Ibid., 235.
121. Ibid., 236.
122. Ibid., 238–39.
123. Kinchen, *Black Power in the Bluff City*, 32.
124. These students were arrested and considered leaders of the movement: Ronald S. Anderson, Claree Avant, Rosetta J. Bonds, Jean F. Brown, James Cleaves, Frank Cole, Mattie M. Daniels, Charles Gregory, Bernice Hightower, Carol A. Hooks, Rose Lee Ingram, Jo Iris, Willie Jamerson, Bernie Bay Johnson, Ernestine Lee ("Miss LeMoyne"), Johnnie Naylor, Virginia Owens, Harold O. Ransom, Kathy J. Robinson, Darnell L. Thomas, Dorothy Truitt, and Curtis Williams. See Lovett, *The Civil Rights Movement*, 189–90.
125. Haynes, *The Last Segregated Hour*, 25.
126. The McLellan store was part of a national chain of five-and-dime stores. See Lovett, *The Civil Rights Movement*, 190.
127. Ibid.
128. Ibid.
129. Ibid.
130. Ibid., 191.
131. Ibid.
132. Ibid., 192. For more on WDIA and its role in the civil rights movement, see Ward, *Radio and the Struggle for Civil Rights in the South*.
133. Tucker, *Memphis Since Crump*, 120; Kinchen, "'We Want What People Generally Refer to as Black Power,'" 37; Green, *Battling the Plantation Mentality*, 220.
134. The NAACP members of the MCCR were Vasco Smith, Russell Sugarmon Jr., Jesse

H. Turner, and A. W. Willis Jr. See Tucker, *Memphis Since Crump*, 120–21; Lovett, *The Civil Rights Movement*, 194–95.

135. Trotter, "The Memphis Business Community and Integration," 287.

136. Lovett, *The Civil Rights Movement*, 194–95.

137. Ibid., 197.

138. Ibid., 56.

139. They were affiliated with the Presbyterian Church of the United States (PCUS). See Haynes, *The Last Segregated Hour*, 64.

140. Green, *Battling the Plantation Mentality*, 255.

141. Haynes, *The Last Segregated Hour*, 124.

142. Green, *Battling the Plantation Mentality*, 240–41, 247–49.

143. The other location in Tennessee where kneel-in campaigns took place was Jackson. See Haynes, *The Last Segregated Hour*, 26–29.

144. The NAACP members included Vasco and Maxine Smith, James Lawson, and Carl Pritchett. See Haynes, *The Last Segregated Hour*, 57, 148.

145. Ibid., 64.

146. Rhodes College Archives and Special Collections (RCASC), File—Second Presbyterian Church, Letter from President Peyton Rhodes to George M. Russell, June 29, 1964. For more on Southwestern's position, see RCASC, File—Second Presbyterian Church, Alfred O. Canon, Dean of Alumni and Development, "From the Ivy-Covered Tower," *Southwestern News*, June 1964.

147. Haynes, *The Last Segregated Hour*, 69.

148. Ibid., 69–70.

149. For more on this concept in Nashville, see Houston, *The Nashville Way*.

150. The exception are the Communists. See Kazin, *The Populist Persuasion*, 198–99.

151. For more on Hayden, see Hayden, *The Port Huron Statement*.

152. For additional information on Savio, see Cohen, *Freedom's Orator*. For further information about the grassroots experience of activists during Freedom Summer, please see Marshall, *Student Activism and Civil Rights in Mississippi*.

153. Turner, *Sitting In and Speaking Out*, 131.

154. See chapter 1 of this book for more on 1930s youth radicalism. Michel, "Building the New South," in *The New Left Revisited*, eds. McMillian and Buhle, 51–52.

155. This agreement between SSOC and SDS will be further discussed in chapter 3.

156. Rogers, *The Black Campus Movement*, 70.

157. Bailey, *The Education of a Black Radical*, 58.

158. Ibid., 63.

159. Lewis, *Walking With the Wind*, 244.

160. Constance Curry was director from 1960 to 1963. For more information on Curry, please see Curry, *Silver Rights*; Whittington, "Interracial Dialogue"; Raines, *My Soul Is Rested*, 103–8. In her list, Curry also included Georgia's Students for Human Rights, Duke University's Core [sic] Chapter, Kentucky's Students for Social Action, New Orleans's Liberal's Club, and Florida's Student Group for Equal Rights. See Emory University, Robert W. Woodruff Library, Manuscript, Archives, and Rare Book Library, Online Manuscript Resources in Southern Women's History, Constance W. Curry Papers, "SSOC role, goals, organizational structure," https://findingaids.library.emory.edu/documents/curry818/.

161. Turner, "The Rise of Black and White Student Protest," 139. PROD was led by Vanderbilt student Ron Parker. Interestingly, former student activist Lee Frissell could

not recall whether this group's name, PROD, was an acronym; Turner similarly mentions the possibility of this. Instead, the group's name could simply be the capitalized form of the verb "to prod," to suggestively encourage others to follow in one's beliefs, and to push others towards reform. See Lee Frissell, correspondence conducted by historian Jeffrey Turner, emails in possession of the author, April 2011.

162. Turner, "The Rise of Black and White Student Protest," 139.

163. Thrasher does not name the restaurant, only referring to it as "the local greasy spoon restaurant." See Thrasher, "Circle of Trust," 220.

164. Thrasher, "Circle of Trust," 228.

165. Michel, *Struggle For a Better South*, 90–92.

166. Stefani, *Unlikely Dissenters*, 190.

167. Lee Frissell, correspondence with author, March 6, 2013.

168. Stefani, *Unlikely Dissenters*, 197.

169. Rossinow, *The Politics of Authenticity*; Frissell, correspondence with author, May 26, 2016.

170. For more on Anne Braden, see Fosl, *Subversive Southerner*. For connections between SNCC and SCEF, see Stefani, *Unlikely Dissenters*, 148–49.

171. Fosl, *Subversive Southerner*, 280; Michel, *Struggle For a Better South*, 13.

172. Michel, *Struggle For a Better South*, 65; VUSCUA, Edwin Hamlett Papers (MSS188) (EHP), Box 48, Folder 4, 'Proposal to the SCEF Board,' n.d. [likely spring 1964–spring 1965]. The grant from SNCC of $300 was for SSOC's organizational meeting in May 1964 in Atlanta, while the grant from SCEF of $100 was for SSOC's founding meeting in April 1964 in Nashville.

173. Stefani, *Unlikely Dissenters*, 210.

174. Fosl, *Subversive Southerner*, 291; Stefani, *Unlikely Dissenters*, 156–57, 179.

175. Michel, *Struggle For a Better South*, 77.

Chapter 3. Waging the Labor Struggle in Tennessee

1. Chude Allen, "Why Struggle? Why Care?," Interdisciplinary Lecture Series, "Letters From Mississippi and Social Justice," Western College, Miami University, September 20, 2005, http://www.crmvet.org/comm/chude05.htm.

2. For more on Robb Burlage and his time at the University of Texas, see Rossinow, *The Politics of Authenticity*, 165.

3. Hobson, "Henry Louis Mencken, 1880–1956," in *Encyclopedia of Southern Culture*, Wilson and Ferris, eds., available at: https://docsouth.unc.edu/southlit/mencken/bio.html. For more on the Agrarians, see Houston, *The Nashville Way*, 52.

4. Michel, "Building the New South," 52–53.

5. Michel, *Struggle For a Better South*, 21.

6. VUSCUA, S.S.O.C. Reunion—2002—Box (MSS 411) (SSOC), SSOC Reunion, July 2002, Wells, Hudson Biographical Sketch, July 4, 2002, "The Southern Student Organizing Committee: Looking Back From Here."

7. Levy, *The New Left and Labor in the 1960s*, 138.

8. NPL, CROHP, oral history of Archie Allen, interviewed by Kathy Bennett, September 30, 2003.

9. Michel, *Struggle For a Better South*, 154.

10. Kiffmeyer, *Reformers to Radicals*, 18.

11. Anderson, "The New American Revolution," in *The Sixties*, ed. Farber, 177.

12. Michel, *Struggle for a Better South*, 154; WHS, Social Action Vertical File (MSS 577)

(SAVF), Box 45—Southern Student Organizing Committee, Folder—Research and Education Workshop, 1968, Dec. 14–15, SSOC Workshop on Research and Education, Highlander Center, Knoxville, Tennessee, December 14–15, 1968.

13. WHS, SAVF, Box 46, SNCC Publications (1), "Working Paper: SNCC and the Southern Campus," n.d. [c. 1964].

14. Michel, *Struggle for a Better South*, 199.

15. For more on the SSOC–SDS relationship in the South, see Michel, *Struggle for a Better South* and Billingsley, *Communists on Campus*.

16. See Lorenzini, "'Power concedes nothing'"; Billingsley, *Communists on Campus*; Rossinow, *Politics of Authenticity*. Shirletta Kinchen contends that the Memphis SDS chapter was in fact connected with the city, not Memphis State University. See Kinchen, *Black Power in the Bluff City*, 129. There were SDS chapters by 1969 at Clemson University in South Carolina, the University of Alabama, Florida State University, and the University of Miami. Another variation on the SDS–SSOC organizing approach were joint chapters, which existed at the University of Georgia, University of Florida, and Duke University in North Carolina.

17. UMSC, President's Office Files III, Reading File, June 1967–Feb. 1972, 1968/10/01–1968/12/31, Letter from President C. C. Humphreys to Mrs. E. D. Ware, October 31, 1968; UMSC, President's Office Files III, Reading File, June 1967–Feb. 1972, 1969/01/02–1969/03/03, Letter from President C. C. Humphreys to Mr. Lewis C. Callow, January 22, 1969; UTSC, Office of the University Historian Collection, Series VI (OUHCVI), Box 23, File 11, Anti-War Protests (1 of 2), John H. Bond, Letter to the editor, "Visions of Reform, Justice Fade With Rise of SDS," *The Daily Beacon*, May 9, 1969.

18. UTSC, OUHCVI, Box 23, File 11, Anti-War Protests (1 of 2), "Communications Gap Alive and Well at UT," *Daily Beacon*, March 7, 1969.

19. VUSCUA, SSOC, SSOC Reunion, July 2002, Wells, Hudson Biographical Sketch, "The Southern Student Organizing Committee: Looking Back From Here," July 4, 2002.

20. Michel, *Struggle for a Better South*, 64.

21. VUSCUA, SSOC, Folder SSOC, Lynn Wells, "Draft Proposal to SSOC," March 30, 1967.

22. Guerrero was succeeded by Howard Romaine in November 1964. See Michel, *Struggle for a Better South*, 98.

23. Levy, *The New Left and Labor*, 138–39.

24. Hamlett mentioned the work of "some decent labor guys," a reference to Guerrero and SSOC organizers Lynn Wells, and Sue Thrasher, among others. See Yale University, Sterling Library, University Archives (YUMA), C. Vann Woodward Papers (MS 1436) (CVWP), Box 24, Folder 275, Letter from Ed Hamlett to C. Vann Woodward, March 25, 1967.

25. Michel, *Struggle for a Better South*, 154.

26. The textile workers were employed by Kayser-Roth, and the meat cutters worked for Frosty-Morn. See WHS, David Nolan Papers, 1960–1987 (MSS 773) (DNP), Box 5, Folder 19: (SSOC) Southern Student Organizing Committee General Papers, "Introduction," unknown author, n.d.

27. Ibid.

28. Michel, *Struggle For a Better South*, 159.

29. Carson, *In Struggle*.

30. VUSCUA, S.S.O.C. Box (SSOCB), Sue Thrasher, "Students Reach Out to White Mississippi," *Southern Patriot*, October 1964. For more on the White Community Project, see Michel, *Struggle For a Better South*, 64–74 (quote from 65); Spencer and Hogan,

"Telling Freedom Stories from the Inside Out," in *Civil Rights History from the Ground Up*, edited by Crosby, 343.

31. Michel, *Struggle For a Better South*, 70.

32. Ibid., 161.

33. Michel, *Struggle For a Better South*, 163; Levy, *The New Left and Labor*, 138–39; WHS, SAVF, Box 45—Southern Student Organizing Committee, Folder—1967, May 5–7, "The New SSOC," Membership Mailing Number Eight, May 17, 1967.

34. Michel, *Struggle For a Better South*, 161.

35. Egerton, *Speak Now Against the Day*, 35.

36. Michel, *Struggle For a Better South*, 161.

37. NPL, CROHP, oral history of Bernard LaFayette and James Bevel, interviewed by Kathy Bennett, January 17, 2003.

38. Michel, *Struggle For a Better South*, 165; WHS, SAVF, Box 45—Southern Student Organizing Committee, Folder—Conf. on Poverty and Labor in Tenn., 1968, Oct. 25–27, n.d.; Levy, *The New Left and Labor*, 137.

39. VUSCUA, SSOC, Dave and Renda Kotelchuck / Dec 2000 Acquisition, "A Preliminary Prospectus for / SLAM: SOUTHERN LABOR ACTION MOVEMENT/ Toward New, Militant Workers Action in the South / ROOTS"; WHS, SAVF, Box 45, Southern Student Organizing Committee, Folder—1967, May 5–7, "The New SSOC," Membership Mailing Number Eight, May 17, 1967.

40. Kiffmeyer, *Reformers to Radicals*, 17–18.

41. Ibid., 37.

42. Ibid., 23.

43. Michel, *Struggle For a Better South*, 153–60 (quote from 153). The North Nashville Project remains largely absent from the historiography of Nashville student activism, mostly because studies focus on 1960–63. See Houston, *The Nashville Way*, 164, 174; Michel, "Building the New South," 56–57. For more on the area of North Nashville, see Erickson, *Making the Unequal Metropolis*.

44. Houston, *The Nashville Way*, 220.

45. See, for instance, Lyndon Baines Johnson Library and Museum (LBJLM), White House Central Files, 1963–1969 (WHCF), Human Rights (HU), Box 41, Folder HU 2/ST 34, Telegram from James C. Gardner, N.C. Congressman, to LBJ, July 20, 1967; LBJLM, WHCF, Human Rights (HU), Box 27, Folder HU 2/ST 33–ST 42, *Associated Press* article, no title given, August 3, 1967.

46. Sonnie and Tracy, *Hillbilly Nationalists*, 27. For more on ERAP, see Hall, *Peace and Freedom*, 23; Tracy, "Rising Up" in *The Hidden 1970s*, 214–30; Frost, "An Interracial Movement of the Poor"; Isserman, *If I Had a Hammer*; Isserman, "The Not-So-Dark and Bloody Ground"; Evans, *Personal Politics*; Breines, *Community and Organization in the New Left, 1962–1968*.

47. Frost, "An Interracial Movement of the Poor," 3.

48. Sonnie and Tracy, *Hillbilly Nationalists*, 14.

49. Ibid., 11. Other organizations similar to JOIN include Rising Up Angry (Chicago), White Lightning (Bronx, New York), and October 4th Organization (Philadelphia).

50. Sonnie and Tracy, *Hillbilly Nationalists*, chapter 1.

51. Kiffmeyer, *Reformers to Radicals*, 18.

52. Ibid., 18–19 (quote from 19).

53. William "Preacherman" Fesperman, "Young Patriots at the United Front Against Fascism Conference," *Viewpoint Magazine*, August 10, 2015, https://viewpointmag.com/2015/08/10/young-patriots-at-the-united-front-against-facsism-conference/.

54. VUSCUA, SSOCB, "MS. ST. SOV. Com. Files, Jackson, Etc.," Carl Bloice, "Accent Labor in Project To Organize White Poor," *The Worker*, February 28, 1967.

55. YUMA, CVWP, Box 24, Folder 275, Letter from Ed Hamlett to C. Vann Woodward, March 25, 1967; VUSCUA, SSOCB, SSOC Reunion, July 2002, Wells, Hudson Biographical Sketch, July 4, 2002, "The Southern Student Organizing Committee: Looking Back From Here." For more on the work of college-age organizers in Durham, North Carolina, see Greene, *Our Separate Ways*.

56. Michel, *Struggle For a Better South*, 180.

57. Anderson, "The New American Revolution," 186.

58. Ibid., 178.

59. Turner, *Sitting In and Speaking Out*, 251.

60. Michel, *Struggle For a Better South*, 221, 218. For more on the differences in opinion between SSOC and SDS over economic initiatives, see WHS, SAVF, Box 45, Southern Student Organizing Committee, Folder—SDS Meeting, 1969, Apr. 5, "Build SDS in the South," *New Left Notes*, April 4, 1969; WHS, SAVF, Box 45, Southern Student Organizing Committee, Folder—SDS Meeting, 1969, Apr. 5, Letter to Bernardine [sic—Bernadine] Dohrn (inter-organizational Secretary for SDS) from Steve Wise (SSOC), March 14, 1969; WHS, SAVF, Box 45—Southern Student Organizing Committee, Folder—SDS Meeting, 1969, Apr. 5, "SDS Severs Ties With SSOC," *Kudzu*, April 5, 1969.

61. John Lewis describes turning to the global anti-colonial struggle in SNCC from 1964. See Lewis, *Walking With the Wind*, 297; Hall, "The Sit-Ins, SNCC, and Cold War Patriotism," 140–41.

62. WHS, SAVF, Box 45—Southern Student Organizing Committee, Folder—Dissolution, 1969, June 8, Edwards, Miss., "Resolution: To Dissolve SSOC," adopted at Edwards, Mississippi, June 8, 1969. For more on Black and white student activists and their views of imperialism, see Levy, *The New Left and Labor*, 118.

63. Levy, *The New Left and Labor*, 117.

64. Ibid., 81.

65. WHS, SAVF, Box 45—Southern Student Organizing Committee, Folder—Dissolution, 1969, June 8, Edwards, Miss., "Resolution: To Dissolve SSOC," adopted at Edwards, Mississippi, June 8, 1969.

66. Ibid.

67. Taylor, "Turn to the Working Class," 61.

68. NPL, CROHP, Allen oral history, September 30, 2003.

69. Kiffmeyer, *Reformers to Radicals*, 11.

70. The terms "pluralistic" and "nationalistic" come from Van Deburg, *New Day in Babylon*, 25–26.

71. More recent scholarship including the youth activity during the strike includes Green, *Battling the Plantation Mentality*, Lorenzini, "'Power concedes nothing,'" Kinchen, "'We want what people,'" and Kinchen, *Black Power in the Bluff City*.

72. Turner, "The Rise of Black and White Student Protest in Nashville," 135.

73. Honey, *Going Down Jericho Road*, 3.

74. Pohlmann and Kirby, *Racial Politics at the Crossroads*, 57.

75. Greene, "'Someday . . . the Colored and White Will Stand Together'", in *The War On Poverty*, eds. Orleck and Hazirjian, 161.

76. Green, "Saving Babies in Memphis" in *The War On Poverty*, 133; Kinchen, "'We want what people,'" 16, 57, 63, 146; Green, *Battling the Plantation Mentality*, 257. Alongside MAP-South, Memphis Area Project-North was a similar program established in a poor

neighborhood in North Memphis around 1967. See Murray, "Taming the War on Poverty." For more on the Invaders, see Strub, "Black and White and Banned All Over," 702.

77. Murray, "Taming the War on Poverty," 4. For more on Memphis and its anti-poverty organizations, see Green, *Battling the Plantation Mentality*, 268–75.

78. Murray, "Taming the War on Poverty," 2, 5. Youth were also involved in VISTA programs in Memphis. For more on the NOP, see Kinchen, "'We want what people,'" 95–97.

79. Green, "Saving Babies in Memphis," 142.

80. Ibid., 134.

81. Smith was one of the first two Black students to integrate Southwestern. See Honey, *Going Down Jericho Road*, 85. Smith and Cabbage were later investigated by the U.S. Senate's Judiciary Committee, led by Mississippi Senator James Eastland, as it attempted to determine the cause of urban riots in 1967. See Green, "Saving Babies in Memphis," 152.

82. Murray, "Taming the War on Poverty," 5; Kinchen, "'We want what people,'" 95, 62. The NOP was organized in the summer of 1968. See Kinchen, *Black Power in the Bluff City*, 83. See also, Honey, *Going Down Jericho Road*, 231; Murray, "Taming the War on Poverty".

83. Kinchen, "'We want what people,'" 97.

84. Murray, "Taming the War on Poverty," 9.

85. On the general sympathy of young NAACP members towards Black Power ideologies, see Hall, "The NAACP, Black Power, and the African American Freedom Struggle," 72–74.

86. Kinchen, "'We want what people,'" 59–60.

87. Ibid., 63–64.

88. Ibid., 64.

89. Kinchen, *Black Power in the Bluff City*, 154.

90. Ibid., 156.

91. UMSC, CCHC, Box 4, Folder 29, David Vincent, "MSU Negroes Seek Campus Unity," *Commercial Appeal*, March 7, 1968.

92. Ibid.

93. Lorenzini, "'Power concedes nothing,'" 190–91. According to Lorenzini, the mention of "blowing shit up" refers to the SDS protests at Columbia University and the University of Wisconsin-Madison

94. Lorenzini, "'Power concedes nothing,'" 181, 178. Letters from the Memphis State President Dr. Cecil C. Humphreys to department chairs urging them to hire more African Americans supports this point. See UMSC, CCHC, Box 4, Folder 32.

95. UMSC, CCHC, Box 4, Folder 29, David Vincent, "MSU Negroes Seek Campus Unity," *Commercial Appeal*, March 7, 1968.

96. Kinchen, "'We want what people,'" 66–67.

97. Ibid., 67.

98. Ibid., 58.

99. Green, *Battling the Plantation Mentality*, 257; Murray, "Taming the War on Poverty," 6; Memphis Public Library (MPL), Memphis and Shelby County Room, The Everett R. Cook Oral History Collection, Box 60, Thomas Faist Interviews (Conducted 1982 [sic–1983]), Folder 2, Interview Summaries (Faist), Summary of oral history of Coby Smith, conducted by Thomas Faist, September 19, 1983; Kinchen, *Black Power in the Bluff City*, 55–56.

100. Kinchen, *Black Power in the Bluff City*, 175.

101. Kinchen, "'We want what people,'" 69.

102. UMSC, The Memphis Multi-Media Archival Project, The 1968 Sanitation Workers Strike (MS.178) (MMMAP), Box 5, Folder 21, Black Students' Militancy And Organization, Memphis, Analysis on Coby Smith in "American Radicalism in the 1960s" by Clifford Karchmer, 1968, for Humanities Class, Princeton University, May 7, 1968; Kinchen, "'We want what people,'" 48.

103. Honey, *Going Down Jericho Road*, 50–53.

104. Ibid., 1–4. For more on the Memphis Sanitation Strike, see *The Encyclopedia of Strikes in American History*, eds. Brenner, Day, and Ness, 231–32; Strub, "Black and White and Banned All Over," 702; Tucker, *Memphis Since Crump*, 152–59; Levy, *The New Left and Labor*, 141–45; Green, *Battling the Plantation Mentality*, 275–87.

105. Honey, *Going Down Jericho Road*, 4; Murray, "Taming the War on Poverty," 5–6.

106. Honey, *Going Down Jericho Road*, 64.

107. Ibid., 105.

108. McCann L. Reid, "New Kind Of Militancy In Memphis: Citizen Support In Sanitation Strike Puzzles Authorities," *Chicago Defender*, March 25, 1968.

109. *At The River I Stand*, 1993 documentary directed by David Appelby, Allison Graham, and Steven John Ross, https://newsreel.org/video/AT-THE-RIVER-I-STAND.

110. McCann L. Reid, "New Kind Of Militancy In Memphis: Citizen Support In Sanitation Strike Puzzles Authorities," *Chicago Defender*, March 25, 1968.

111. Kinchen, "'We want what people,'" 54.

112. The teenager's name was Larry Payne. See "Mayor of Memphis Shuns Labor Plan in Garbage Crisis," *Lewiston Daily Sun*, February 14, 1968; Lorenzini, "'Power concedes nothing,'" 157; Tucker, *Memphis Since Crump*, 159.

113. Tucker, *Memphis Since Crump*, 159.

114. Kinchen, "'We want what people,'" 53, 58.

115. Kinchen, *Black Power in the Bluff City*, 1.

116. Lorenzini, "'Power concedes nothing,'" 3.

117. Honey, *Going Down Jericho Road*, 89.

118. "*At The River I Stand*," 1993 documentary directed by David Appelby, Allison Graham, and Steven John Ross, https://newsreel.org/video/AT-THE-RIVER-I-STAND.

119. MPL, Smith oral history, September 19, 1983.

120. "*At The River I Stand*," 1993 documentary directed by David Appelby, Allison Graham, and Steven John Ross, https://newsreel.org/video/AT-THE-RIVER-I-STAND.

121. Michel, *Struggle For a Better South*, 113–14.

122. UMSC, MMMAP, Box 5, Folder 23, Student Responses to Strike, LeMoyne College, 1968, "E. W."

123. Italics in original. UMSC, MMMAP, Box 5, Folder 21, Black Students' Militancy And Organizations, Memphis, "An Ode To Memphis: The City Built On A Bluff," *Liberator*, August 31, 1968.

124. UMSC, MMMAP, Box 5, Folder 21, Black Students' Militancy And Organizations, Memphis, "Call for picketing of East Memphis Shopping Centers on March 9, 1968," *The Apex*, n.d.; Lorenzini, "'Power concedes nothing,'" 147.

125. UMSC, MMMAP, Box 7, Folder 46, Student Surveys from Dr. Jack Hurley's class on American Economic History (Hist. 3822), n.d.

126. Honey, *Going Down Jericho Road*, 457–58; Lorenzini, "'Power concedes nothing,'" 164.

127. "Henry Loeb, 71, Memphis Mayor At Time of King's Assassination," *New York Times*, September 10, 1992.

128. Honey, *Going Down Jericho Road*, 461. The carnival had an affiliated event, the Cotton Makers' Jubilee, for Memphis blacks; the two coexisted separately until 1981 when they merged. For more on the Jubilee, see Sadler, "'On Parade'" in *Tennessee Women*, eds. Bond and Freeman, 147; Kinchen, *Black Power in the Bluff City*, 34–35.

129. Lorenzini, "'Power concedes nothing,'" 161.

130. The relevant section of the Internal Revenue Code was Title 42, section 1855–1855g. See LBJLM, WHCF, HU, Box 41, Gen HU 2/ST 32–ST 50, Folder HU 2/ST 42, May 1968 Correspondence between LBJ's administration and Henry Loeb, Mayor of Memphis; LBJLM, WHCF, HU, Box 41, Gen HU 2/ST 32–ST 50, Folder HU 2/ST 42, Telegram from Buford Ellington to Marvin Watson, White House, April 15, 1968.

131. LBJLM, WHCF, HU, Box 41, Gen HU 2/ST 32–ST 50, Folder HU 2/ST 42, Letter from Washington Butler, Executive Director of War on Poverty Committee of Memphis—Shelby County to LBJ, April 29, 1968.

132. Rogers, *The Black Campus Movement*, 95.

133. Honey, *Going Down Jericho Road*, 465.

134. Ibid., 490–92.

135. Ryan Poe, "Memphis pledges $900K to surviving 1968 sanitation strikers," *Commercial Appeal*, July 6, 2017, https://eu.commercialappeal.com/story/news/government/city/2017/07/06/memphis-offers-grants-retirement-make-sanitation-workers-whole/454852001/.

Chapter 4. Reforming Administrative Policies

1. Fry, *The American South and the Vietnam War*, 290.

2. See Slaughter and Rhoades, *American Capitalism and the New Economy*, 1.

3. Ruth Anne Thompson's article on protests at the University of Tennessee makes a similar point, but gives credit to student government leaders, not student activists. Thompson sees the elected officers of the SGA from 1965 on as more representative of the student body, and "more politicized" than previous years as officers were previously elected by fraternities and sororities on campus. Thompson, "'A Taste of Student Power'", 84–85, in particular (quote from 84).

4. Wright, oral history, August 6, 2014.

5. Bruce S. Keenan, "Gentlemen, (I hope) . . . ," *Sewanee Purple* 76, no. 3, October 22, 1958.

6. Williamson Jr., *Sewanee Sesquicentennial History*, 325.

7. "Ferment on Other Campuses," *New York Times*, February 28, 1969. For more on UT dormitory curfews, see interview of Rev. Al Minor, "A Sense of Revolution," *The Vietnam War: East Tennessee*, East Tennessee Public Broadcasting Service (PBS), February 10, 2017.

8. UTSC, OUHCVI, Box 24, File 1, Open Speakers Controversy (1 of 2), Ben Taylor, "Rain Fails To Cool Hot Issues at Rally," *Daily Beacon*, February 7, 1969.

9. FBI Records: The Vault (FBI), Letter from SAC in Knoxville, to Director, FBI, COINTELPRO-New Left, Bureau File xx-100-3687, June 13, 1968; "College Coeds Are Dismissed," *Kingsport News*, May 13, 1968, 8. Before it closed in 1994, Morristown College was one of two HBCUs in East Tennessee, the other being Knoxville College.

10. "College Coeds Are Dismissed," *Kingsport News*, May 13, 1968, 8.

11. "Morristown Pastor Resigns Board Post," *Kingsport News*, May 15, 1968, 13.

12. Obituary of Elmer P. Gibson, June 10, 1994, http://www.greensboro.com/obituaries/article_308d0a34-b2aa-530e-bcbc-a5570b5c2aa8.html; Robert Cohen, introduction to *Rebellion in Black and White*, 3–4.

13. The 1969 Lane College protests primarily concerned Black student rights. See later in this chapter.

14. UMSC, CCHC, Box 4, Folder 29, Letter to Dr. Cecil C. Humphreys from Associate Dean of Students Student Life Clarence Hampton, n.d.

15. "Maryville Miss, WSGA Handbook For Resident Women, 1963–64," in possession of the author.

16. Crossroads to Freedom, Oral History Archive, Rhodes College, Interview with Bill Short, July 27, 2007, http://www.crossroadstofreedom.org/detail.collection?max=64&page=3&oid=16&order=oid&dir=asc.

17. RCASC, "Dorm Board Considers Rules Revision," *Sou'wester*, October 18, 1968.

18. The Vanderbilt students opposed the rule banning women from men's dormitories. See Fry, *The American South and the Vietnam War*, 290–91; "Sit-in in Tennessee," *New York Times*, December 13, 1969.

19. For more on the YAF nationally, see Scanlon, *The Pro-War Movement*, 246; Anderson, *The Movement and the Sixties*, 108–9.

20. Congressman John Ashbrook, on March 17, 1969, 91st Cong., 1st sess., *Congressional Record*, 115, Part 5 – Extensions of Remarks, 6648.

21. Short, oral history, July 27, 2007; Williamson Jr., *Sewanee Sesquicentennial History*, 320; "Maryville Miss, WSGA Handbook For Resident Women, 1963–64."

22. Williamson Jr., *Sewanee Sesquicentennial History*, 320–21; "D.C. changes gown-wearing, coat-tie rules," *Sewanee Purple* 76, no. 17, April 8, 1959; Laura Shin, "Cloak and Swagger," *New York Times*, December 24, 2008, http://www.nytimes.com/2009/01/04/education/edlife/sewanee-t.html?_r=0.

23. First mention appears in Ken Kinnett, "Our Fading Tradition," *Sewanee Purple* 76, no. 16, March 7, 1956.

24. Haynes, *The Last Segregated Hour*, 80. One Southwestern student recalled that chapel attendance policies continued to be negotiated until 1971. See Short, oral history, July 27, 2007.

25. Maryville College and Rhodes College (formerly Southwestern College) are both affiliated with the Presbyterian Church (U.S.A.) and are within the Synod of Living Waters.

26. "Maryville Miss, WSGA Handbook For Resident Women, 1963–64."

27. John Friedel, "Comment," *Sewanee Purple* 85, no. 4, October 13, 1966; "Faculty Passes Amended Resolution," *Sewanee Purple* 85, no. 5, October 20, 1966; John Friedel, "Comment," *Sewanee Purple* 85, no. 6, October 27, 1966.

28. Akins and Wiggins, *Keeping the Faith*, 121–22.

29. Williamson Jr., *Sewanee Sesquicentennial History*, 256.

30. RCASC, "Sign-Out Revision Curfews, Parietals Ruled On By SRC," *Sou'wester*, September 12, 1969.

31. RCASC, File—Residence Hall For Women (RHFW), Claude Stayton, "Women Miss the Point," *Sou'wester*, December 4, 1970; RCASC, RHFW, Wilda Dodson, "Open Dorms Not Likely," *Sou'wester*, April 23, 1971.

32. Akins and Wiggins, *Keeping the Faith*, 122.

33. Letters to the Editor, *Sewanee Purple* 80, no. 17, March 14, 1963; Bill Grimball, "A Continuation of the History Of Student-Faculty Relations," *Sewanee Purple* 85, no. 6, October 27, 1966.

34. "Gailor Behavior Two Sided Coin," *Sewanee Purple* 85, no. 11, December 8, 1966.

35. "First Demonstration Erupts Over Bad Gailor Situation," *Sewanee Purple* 85, no. 16,

March 2, 1967. For more on this episode, see Williamson Jr., *Sewanee Sesquicentennial History*, 320–21.

36. WHS, Robert S. Gabriner, 1961–1981 (MSS 575) (RSG), Subject Files, Sub-series: African Americans, Box 11, Folder 5: Southern Student Organizing Committee, 1964–1965, *The Newsletter: Southern Student Organizing Committee* II, no. 2, "SOS From Students at Knoxville College," February 1965.

37. UTSC, OUHCVI, Box 23, File 13, The Boling Appointment Controversy, October 5, 1970, Annual Message; UTSC, OUHCVI, Box 23, File 20, Nixon-Graham Crusade 1970, "UT scene of political activism, rapid expansion in recent years," *Daily Beacon*, May 9, 1977.

38. VUSCUA, SSOC, Dave and Ronda Kotelchuck/Dec. 2000 Acquisition, *Vanderbilt Hustler*, February 28, 1967.

39. Italics in original. MC, Box—Ledgers, File—Student-Faculty Senate Minutes 1960–1967, February 18, 1966.

40. Jim Showalter, comment, *Highland Echo* 54, no. 20, May 15, 1969.

41. MC, BM, File—Board of Directors Minutes 1965–1974, Spring Meeting of the Directors of Maryville College, April 29, 1971.

42. Cohen, *Freedom's Orator*, 1.

43. Levy, *The New Left and Labor in the 1960s*, 117.

44. Sorrels, *The Exciting Years*, 112.

45. See WHS, SAVF, Box 45, Southern Student Organizing Committee, Folder—Executive Committee Meetings, Lynn Wells, "Some Ideas On My Generation," June 8, 1967. Berkeley's activists also included the Vietnam War in their descriptions of this machine, but anti-war sentiment would not gain a significant foothold on Tennessee campuses until 1969. For Tennessee's anti-war protests see chapter 5.

46. Ben Taylor, "Presidential Race On: SGA Office Attracts Candidates," *Daily Beacon*, April 2, 1969; "Warner, Baxter in SGA Race," *Daily Beacon*, April 22, 1969; "SGA Eligibles Announced," *Daily Beacon*, April 26, 1969.

47. UTSC, OUHCVI, Box 23, File 16, Election Controversy—1969 (SGA), "Two Withdraw From SGA Race," *Daily Beacon*, May 22, 1969.

48. "Our Party. Does it really work?," Challenge '69 ad, *Daily Beacon*, April 24, 1969; "Baxter Enters Presidential Race," *Daily Beacon*, April 29, 1969; Pete Bishop, "UP Platform Stresses Communication," *Daily Beacon*, April 30, 1969.

49. "Hager Charges Opponents Exerting 'Clique Control,'" *Daily Beacon*, May 1, 1969.

50. James Baxter, "No Real Government At UT," *Daily Beacon*, May 1, 1969.

51. John R. Long, "Election '69 Leadership Election's Issue," *Daily Beacon*, May 1, 1969; "Sure We're Running a Big Campaign," Challenge '69 ad, *Daily Beacon*, May 1 1969.

52. UTSC, OUHCVI, Box 23, File 16, Election Controversy—1959 (SGA), "Tribunal Listens to Ballot Testimony," *Daily Beacon*, May 9, 1969.

53. UTSC, OUHCVI, Box 23, File 16, Election Controversy—1969 (SGA), "Tribunal Rules SGA Elections 'Invalid,'" *Daily Beacon*, May 10, 1969.

54. Ibid.

55. UTSC, OUHCVI, Box 23, File 16, Election Controversy—1969 (SGA), "Long Wins Narrow Victory Over Hager," *Daily Beacon*, May 8, 1969.

56. UTSC, OUHCVI, Box 23, File 16, Election Controversy—1969 (SGA), "UT Students Take Second Trip To Polls," *Daily Beacon*, May 23, 1969; UTSC, OUHCVI, Box 23, File 16, Election Controversy—1969 (SGA), "Two Withdraw From SGA Race," *Daily Beacon*, May 22, 1969.

57. James Lessenberry, "Presidential Candidates Hurl Charges, Countercharges," *Daily Beacon*, May 2, 1969.

58. Ibid.

59. "Eliot To Run With Baxter," *Daily Beacon*, May 22, 1969.

60. Wallenstein, "Black Southerners and Nonblack Universities," 51.

61. UTSC, OUHCVI, Box 23, File 16, Election Controversy—1969 (SGA), "'Common Sense': Baxter Approach," *Daily Beacon*, May 27, 1969.

62. UTSC, OUHCVI, Box 23, File 16, Election Controversy—1969 (SGA), "Long Wins Narrow Victory Over Hager," *Daily Beacon*, May 8, 1969; UTSC, OUHCVI, Box 23, File 16, Election Controversy—1969 (SGA), "'Common Sense': Baxter Approach," *Daily Beacon*, May 27, 1969.

63. UTSC, OUHCVI, Box 23, File 16, Election Controversy—1969 (SGA), "'Common Sense': Baxter Approach," *Daily Beacon*, May 27, 1969.

64. UTSC, OUHCVI, Box 23, File 16, Election Controversy—1969 (SGA), "Baxter: 'Reorganization, Practicality, Reason,'" *Daily Beacon*, May 30, 1969.

65. Ibid.; Thompson, "'A Taste of Student Power,'" 86.

66. Baxter, interview, 2 December 1993.

67. Coye Baker, "Baxter Explains 'Student Power,'" *Daily Beacon*, May 3, 1969.

68. Baxter, interview, 2 December 1993.

69. UTSC, OUHCVI, Box 23, File 16, Election Controversy—1969 (SGA), "Reinstating Baxter," *Daily Beacon*, May 23, 1969.

70. Ibid.

71. Correspondence between Barry Bozeman and the author, June 19, 2014.

72. Joseph, "Black Studies, Student Activism, and the Black Power Movement," in *The Black Power Movement*, ed. Joseph, 263–64.

73. Rogers, *The Black Campus Movement*, 71.

74. Joseph, "Black Studies, Student Activism, and the Black Power Movement," 263–64.

75. Rogers, *The Black Campus Movement*, 113.

76. See especially Cohen, *Freedom's Orator*.

77. Jacobs, *Across the Line*, 42.

78. On this process at Memphis State, see UMSC, CCHC, Box 4, Folder 29, David Vincent, "Identity Is Hard For All At MSU," *Commercial Appeal*, March 8, 1968; Kinchen, *Black Power in the Bluff City*, 149.

79. 1,152 Black students were enrolled at Memphis State and 342 at UT. UMSC, CCHC, Box 4, Folder 29, David Vincent, "Huge Negro Enrollment At MSU Has Produced Few Real Problems," *Commercial Appeal*, March 6, 1968.

80. Ibid. For a comparative description of life for Black students at Maryville College in 1954, see chapter 2.

81. University of Memphis, Office of Multicultural Affairs, http://www.memphis.edu/multiculturalaffairs/organizations/index.php.

82. UMSC, CCHC, Box 4, Folder 29, "Statement of Dr. C. C. Humphreys [to] Students, Faculty and Friends of Memphis State University," April 29, 1969.

83. Ibid. See Tuck, *We Ain't What We Ought To Be*, 228–29, 329.

84. UTSC, OUHCVI, Box 24, File 1, Open Speakers Controversy (1 of 2), "1968–69: UT's Year of Changes," *Daily Beacon*, September 25, 1969.

85. UMSC, CCHC, Box 4, Folder 29, "Statement of Dr. C. C. Humphreys [to] Students, Faculty and Friends of Memphis State University," April 29, 1969; Sorrels, *The Exciting Years*, 173–78.

86. UMSC, CCHC, Box 4, Folder 29, "Statement of Dr. C. C. Humphreys [to] Students, Faculty and Friends of Memphis State University," April 29, 1969.

87. Ibid.

88. Sorrels, *The Exciting Years*, 174. For earlier discussion on COME, see chapter 3.

89. The two administrative officials at the meeting were Dr. Jess Parrish, dean of students, and Dr. Ronald Carrier, provost, both from the Dean of Students' office. See UMSC, CCHC, Box 4, Folder 29, "Statement of Dr. C. C. Humphreys [to] Students, Faculty and Friends of Memphis State University," April 29, 1969.

90. Ibid.

91. Ibid.

92. Ibid.

93. Sorrels, *The Exciting Years*, 176; Rogers, *The Black Campus Movement*, 138; Kinchen, *Black Power in the Bluff City*, 164–65.

94. UMSC, CCHC, Box 4, Folder 29, "Statement of Dr. C. C. Humphreys [to] Students, Faculty and Friends of Memphis State University," April 29, 1969.

95. Rogers, *The Black Campus Movement*, 123; Lorenzini, "'Power Concedes Nothing,'" 177.

96. Van Deburg, *New Day in Babylon*, 66.

97. UMSC, CCHC, Box 4, Folder 35, Petition signed by 873 students in support of Humphreys and Memphis State administration, April 25, 1969.

98. UMSC, CCHC, Box 4, Folders 37–40; Sorrels, *The Exciting Years*, 178.

99. Hine, "Civil Rights and Campus Wrongs."

100. Kinchen, *Black Power in the Bluff City*, 57.

101. RCASC, "Black Campus Erupts In Turmoil; Protest Molds LeMoyne Reform," *Sou'wester*, December 6, 1968; Rogers, *The Black Campus Movement*, 120.

102. Kinchen, *Black Power in the Bluff City*, 125–26. The UT account will be discussed later in this chapter.

103. Ibid., 123–41.

104. RCASC, "Black Campus Erupts In Turmoil; Protest Molds LeMoyne Reform," *Sou'wester*, December 6, 1968; Rogers, *The Black Campus Movement*, 120; Kinchen, *Black Power in the Bluff City*, 124.

105. "Lane College Trustees discuss school reopening," *Johnson City Press*, March 6, 1969, 18; "Lane College Will Close Dormitories," *Jackson Sun*, March 3, 1969, 1, 7.

106. "Lane College Group Is Given Ultimatum," *Jackson Sun*, March 2, 1969, 3. For more on the BLF at North Carolina A&T, see Favors, *Shelter in a Time of Storm*, 217.

107. UMSC, CCHC, Box 4, Folder 29, Statement to Parents of Students, Alumni, Supporters and Friends of Lane College from C. A. Kirkendoll, President of Lane College, April 4, 1969; "Lane College Trustees discuss school reopening," *Johnson City Press*, March 6, 1969, 18; "Lane Campus Is Calm Again," *Jackson Sun*, March 4, 1969, 7; "Lane College Will Close Dormitories," *Jackson Sun*, March 3, 1969, 1 and 7.

108. "Lane College Group Is Given Ultimatum," *Jackson Sun*, March 2, 1969, 3.

109. "Lane College Will Close Dormitories," *Jackson Sun*, March 3, 1969, 1, 7.

110. "Lane Campus Is Calm Again," *Jackson Sun*, March 4, 1969. 7 (quote from this source); "Lane College Will Close Dormitories," *Jackson Sun*, March 3, 1969, 1, 7.

111. "Mayor Conger Sets Curfews Around Lane," *Jackson Sun*, March 23, 1969, 1; John Parish, "Lane Disorder Is Quelled," *Jackson Sun*, March 23, 1969, 1, 10; "Lane College Disorders Cost Taxpayers $32,000,'" *Daily News-Journal*, April 10, 1969, 1.

112. "Weather Helps Put Lid On Restive Campus," *Jackson Sun*, March 24, 1969, 1; John

Parish, "'A Lasting Peace' For Lane Campus Is Being Sought," *Jackson Sun*, March 24, 1969, 1, 9; UMSC, CCHC, Box 4, Folder 29, Statement to Parents of Students, Alumni, Supporters and Friends of Lane College from C. A. Kirkendoll, President of Lane College, April 4, 1969; Rogers, *The Black Campus Movement*, 31, 122; Kinchen, *Black Power in the Bluff City*, 160; "Fear More Violence At Lane College," *Chicago Defender*, March 24, 1969; Miles, *The Radical Probe*, 236; Lorenzini, "'Power Concedes Nothing,'" 178.

113. "Weather Helps Put Lid On Restive Campus," *Jackson Sun*, March 24, 1969, 1; John Parish, "'A Lasting Peace' For Lane Campus Is Being Sought," *Jackson Sun*, March 24, 1969, 1, 9.

114. Rogers, *The Black Campus Movement*, 107; Kinchen, *Black Power in the Bluff City*, 150. For more on the student experience in the BSU (as well as the UT SSOC chapter), see interview of James "Sparky" Rucker, "A Sense of Revolution," *The Vietnam War: East Tennessee*, East Tennessee Public Broadcasting Service (PBS), February 17, 2017.

115. UTSC, OUHCV, Box 22, Folder 8, Black Student Union and Black Studies Office, "Blacks Consider Class Boycott," *Daily Beacon*, September 25, 1969.

116. Modern Political Archive, University of Tennessee (MPA), William Emerson Brock Collection (MPA.106) (WEBC), Box 31, Folder 9, Correspondence, Fisk Univ. Visit, Discussion between Brock and Rep. Buchanan re Fisk and Vanderbilt visits, n.d.

117. Larry McDowell, "Integrated: Who are you kidding man?!," *Highland Echo*, February 13, 1970, 1.

118. UTSC, OUHCVI, Box 23, File 15, Demonstration Clippings, "Officials Hear Demands of Picketing Black Students," *Daily Beacon*, May 9, 1969.

119. UTSC, OUHCV, Box 22, Folder 8, Black Student Union and Black Studies Office, "[Aldmon] Says Understanding Came From BSU Meetings," *Daily Beacon*, May 16, 1969.

120. UTSC, OUHCV, Box 22, Folder 8, Black Student Union and Black Studies Office, "BSU Continues Demonstration," *Daily Beacon*, May 10, 1969.

121. UTSC, OUHCV, Box 22, Folder 8, Black Student Union and Black Studies Office, "[Aldmon] Says Understanding Came From BSU Meetings," *Daily Beacon*, May 16, 1969.

122. BCEC, CHRUT, "SGA Tribunal To Hear Case: Former Cheerleaders Charge Pep Club With 'Bias,'" *Daily Beacon*, May 1, 1969.

123. BCEC, CHRUT, "Black Coed Says Pep Club Unfair," *Daily Beacon*, May 3, 1969.

124. UTSC, OUHCV, Box 22, Folder 8, Black Student Union and Black Studies Office, "Follow-up to BSU's Recommendations Presented in the Spring Quarter 1969," n.d. Middle Tennessee State University had also witnessed a controversy about the playing of "Dixie" at football games in the 1968–69 academic year. This will be further discussed in the conclusion. Middle Tennessee State University, Albert Gore Research Center, Forrest Hall Protest Collection, (FHPC) "'Dixie' and Confederate Flag," *Sidelines*, October 23, 1969, 5.

125. UTSC, OUHCV, Box 22, Folder 8, Black Student Union and Black Studies Office, "BSU Votes Unified Black Studies," *Daily Beacon*, January 22, 1970.

126. In contrast with UT and Memphis State, the BSA at Southwestern was recognized as an official college organization in November 1969. See RCASC, Black Student Association, Box 2, Black Student Charter 1969, November 12, 1969.

127. MPA, WEBC, Box 31, Folder 9, Correspondence—Fisk Univ. Visit, Letter from Congressman Lawrence Coughlin to Congressman William Brock, May 27, 1969.

128. UTSC, OUHCVI, Box 23, File 13, The Boling Appointment Controversy, "Speculation Running Rampant On UT President's Successor," June 27, 1969.

129. Ibid.; Thompson, "'A Taste of Student Power,'" 86.

130. Barry Bozeman, "40 Year Flashback—Nixon & Graham at Tennessee," May 28,

2010, http://www.dailykos.com/story/2010/05/28/864563/-40-YEAR-FLASHBACK-NIXON-GRAHAM-at-TENNESSEE. Bozeman was the twenty-second protestor arrested on the felony charge of inciting a riot following the January 15, 1970, protest.

131. Italics in original. UTSC, OUHCVI, Box 23, File 13, The Boling Appointment Controversy, "Will The Board Ever Learn?," *Daily Beacon*, August 22, 1969.

132. UTSC, OUHCVI, Box 23, File 13, The Boling Appointment Controversy, "Students Set Stage For Protest Today," *Daily Beacon*, January 15, 1970. For more on this incident, see Wheeler, *Knoxville, Tennessee*, 226n36; Fry, *The American South and the Vietnam War*, 298; interview of Gary Heatherly, "A Sense of Revolution," *The Vietnam War: East Tennessee*, East Tennessee Public Broadcasting Service (PBS) 2017, n.d.

133. Barry Bozeman, "40 Year Flashback—Nixon & Graham at Tennessee," May 28, 2010, http://www.dailykos.com/story/2010/05/28/864563/-40-YEAR-FLASHBACK-NIXON-GRAHAM-at-TENNESSEE.

134. Ibid.

135. Thompson, "'A Taste of Student Power,'" 87.

136. UTSC, OUHCVI, Box 23, File 13, The Boling Appointment Controversy, "UT Student Demonstration Subsides," *Daily Beacon*, January 16, 1970.

137. "U.T. Goes Wild," *The Highland Echo* 55, no. 2, April 10, 1970.

138. FBI, Letter, from SAC in Knoxville, to Director, FBI, February 19, 1970, COINTELPRO—New Left, Bureau File xx-100-3687.

139. Interview of James "Sparky" Rucker, "A Sense of Revolution," *The Vietnam War: East Tennessee*, East Tennessee Public Broadcasting Service (PBS), February 17, 2017.

140. UTSC, OUHCVI, Box 23, File 13, The Boling Appointment Controversy, "21 Arrested: Rebel Students Call for Vote, Strike at U-T," *Knoxville News-Sentinel*, January 16, 1970.

141. Ibid.

142. UTSC, OUHCVI, Box 23, File 13, The Boling Appointment Controversy, "Demonstration Conducted Peacefully," *Daily Beacon*, February 12, 1970.

143. UTSC, OUHCVI, Box 23, File 13, The Boling Appointment Controversy, "Several Students Protest Selection Of Boling," *Daily Beacon*, January 9, 1970.

144. UTSC, OUHCVI, Box 23, File 15, Demonstration Clippings "UTC Leftists Stir Anger Of State's Legislators," *Chattanooga News–Free Press*, January 18, 1970.

145. UTSC, OUHCVI, Box 23, File 13, The Boling Appointment Controversy, "UTC Students Protest Selection Of Boling," *Daily Beacon*, January 9, 1970.

146. UTSC, OUHCVI, Box 23, File 13, The Boling Appointment Controversy, "Strike Worse Than Nixon Protest," *Daily Beacon*, May 30, 1970.

147. UTSC, OUHCVI, Box 23, File 20, Nixon-Graham Crusade—1970, "UT scene of political activism, rapid expansion in recent years," *Daily Beacon*, May 9, 1977.

148. For a more detailed examination of the May 1970 Graham-Nixon incident, see chapter 5.

149. UTSC, OUHCVI, Box 23, File 16, Election Controversy—1969 (SGA), "Baxter: 'Reorganization, Practicality, Reason,'" *Daily Beacon*, May 30, 1969.

150. Similar conflicts over speaker policies also occurred at University of North Carolina—Chapel Hill, University of South Carolina, Louisiana State University, and Western Kentucky University. See Fry, *The American South and the Vietnam War*, 291.

151. Carmichael had given numerous campus tours during the 1966–67 academic year. See Rogers, *The Black Campus Movement*, 78.

152. Lovett, *The Civil Rights Movement*, 205.

153. WHS, CABP, Part 1, Sub-series: Southern Conference Educational Files, 1954–1972,

Box 56, Folder 8, Nashville, Tennessee, 1958–1964, document about the status of southern student activism written by Ed Hamlett, n.d. [c. 1964].

154. Lovett, *The Civil Rights Movement*, 206.

155. LBJLM, National Advisory Commission on Civil Disorders (RG 220) (NACCD), Series E08, Material Pulled From Commission Files, Box E37, Chapter II Supplemental Working Arrest Records to Chapter II Supplemental Working The Background of Disorder, Folder—Chapter II Supplementary Working Materials, "Cities in Which Racial Disorders Have Occurred This Year," Vol. II, August 1, 1967; Rogers, *The Black Campus Movement*, 93–94.

156. Lovett, *The Civil Rights Movement*, 208–12.

157. LBJLM, NACCD, Series E04, Office of Investigation City Files, Box E24, Jackson—General to New Brunswick—Newspaper Clippings, Folder Nashville—FBI Reports, May 2, 1967, report from Memphis; and April 9, 1967, report from Memphis.

158. Quote is from a memorandum, not a direct quote from Sorace. See LBJLM, NACCD, Series E08– Material Pulled From Commission Files, Box E24, Folder Nashville—General, Memorandum from Kathy Adler to M. C. Miskovsky, n.d., "McClellan Hearings—Continuation of Nashville Hearings"; LBJLM, NACCD, Series E08, Material Pulled From Commission Files, Box E24, Folder Nashville—FBI Reports, April 15, 1967, from Memphis.

159. The editorial was from 1982. Doyle, *Nashville Since the 1920s*, 162.

160. Houston, *The Nashville Way*, 173.

161. Heard, *Speaking of the University*, 92.

162. For more on the impact of the riots following Carmichael's speech in Nashville, see chapter 5 of Houston, *The Nashville Way*; Miles, *The Radical Probe*, 234–35.

163. Ramsey, "'We Will Be Ready Whenever They Are,'" 46.

164. LBJLM, NACCD, Series E08, Material Pulled From Commission Files, Box E37, Chapter II Supplemental Working Arrest Records to Chapter II Supplemental Working The Background of Disorder, Folder—Chapter II Supplementary Working Materials, "Cities in Which Racial Disorders Have Occurred This Year" Vol. II, August 1, 1967. The three Tennessee judges who formed the court were Judges William Miller, Frank Gray, and Harry Phillips. See LBJLM, NACCD, Series E04, Office of Investigation City Files, Box E24, Jackson—General to New Brunswick Newspaper Clippings, Folder—Nashville—General, Memorandum from Kathy Adler to M. C. Miskovsky, "McClellan Hearings—Nashville," November 8, 1967. For more on the McClellan Committee related to Tennessee, see Houston, *The Nashville Way*, 181.

165. Houston, *The Nashville Way*, 181.

166. LBJLM, NACCD, Series E07, Material Received From Other Agencies, Box E36, Labor Department to Disturbances for 1967 (Current List), Folder—Disturbances for 1967 (Current List), "List of Sources For Disturbances Of 1967," n.d.

167. "Report of The National Advisory Commission on Civil Disorders," National Criminal Justice Reference Service, https://www.ncjrs.gov/pdffiles1/Digitization/8073NCJRS.pdf.

168. LBJLM, Papers of Lyndon Baines Johnson, Office Files of Fred Panzer, 1963–1968, Box 412, Folder—Riots 1965–1967, "At Any Cost: Law And Order Must Be Preserved," *Nashville Banner*, July 25, 1967.

169. Maraniss, *Strong Inside*, 207.

170. Jacobs, *Across the Line*, 29.

171. Powell was also the subject of a speaker controversy at Memphis State University in 1969. See UTSC, OUHCVI, Box 24, File 1, Open Speakers Controversy (1 of 2), "The

Speaker Ban Controversy: A Statement of Fact and Principle by the Student Government Association."

172. Ibid.; Thompson, "'A Taste of Student Power,'" 85. Despite the invitation of Leary—renowned for his LSD experiments—to campus, there were no significant instances in Tennessee of campus counterculture, two underground newspapers in Memphis notwithstanding. For southern campus counterculture, see Nicholas G. Meriwether, "The Counterculture as Local Culture in Columbia, South Carolina" in *Rebellion in Black and White*, ed. Cohen and Snyder, 218–52, and regional underground newspapers like *Kudzu*, published by a group of SSOC activists in Jackson, Mississippi, and *Rodent* and *Logos* produced in Memphis. For more on *Rodent* and *Logos*, see Lorenzini, "'Power Concedes Nothing'"; UMSC, University Publications–Student Publications. For more on *Root and Branch*, a southern journal focused on radical labor organizing, see Levy, *The New Left and Labor in the 1960s*, 124.

173. Janda, *Prairie Power*, 51, 57, 53.

174. UTSC, OUHCVI, Box 24, File 1, Open Speakers Controversy (1 of 2), "The Speaker Ban Controversy: A Statement of Fact and Principle by the Student Government Association." In Ibram X. Kendi's research, Dick Gregory reportedly made the highest number of speeches in the Black Campus Movement, reportedly five hundred in one account. See Rogers, *The Black Campus Movement*.

175. UTSC, OUHCVI, Box 24, File 1, Open Speakers Controversy (1 of 2), "Board Considers Speaker Policy," *Daily Beacon*, February 1, 1969.

176. UTSC, OUHCVI, Box 24, File 1, Open Speakers Controversy (1 of 2), "Speaker's Policy for the University of Tennessee," Board of Trustees, Executive Session, October 18, 1968.

177. UTSC, OUHCVI, Box 24, File 1, Open Speakers Controversy (1 of 2), "1968–69: UT's Year of Changes," *Daily Beacon*, September 25, 1969.

178. Ibid.

179. Ibid.

180. "Judge Says U. of Tennessee Violates Freedom of Speech," *New York Times*, April 19, 1969; UTSC, OUHCVI, Box 24, File 1, Open Speakers Controversy (1 of 2), "Speaker Policy 'Null and Void,'" *Daily Beacon*, May 2, 1969.

181. UTSC, OUHCVI, Box 24, File 1, Open Speakers Controversy (1 of 2), "New UT Speaker Policy Approved," *Summer Beacon*, June 20, 1969.

182. Anderson, *The Movement and the Sixties*; Farber, *Chicago '68*; Tracy, *Direct Action*.

183. "Columnist to Speak," *Knoxville News-Sentinel*, March 31, 1970; "Kunstler Dislikes 'Progress,'" *Knoxville News-Sentinel*, April 11, 1970. The other speakers scheduled as part of the "Man and His Environment" series at UT with Kunstler were Karl Hess, Dick Gregory, and psychologist B. F. Skinner. Kunstler's speech was originally set for the Alumni Memorial Auditorium, but the organizers moved it at the last minute to the Stokely Athletics Center, a larger campus venue. See "Kunstler To Speak at Stokely Tonight," *Knoxville News-Sentinel*, April 2, 1970.

184. "Kunstler To Arrive in Knox Thursday," *Knoxville News-Sentinel*, March 31, 1970.

185. "Our Neighbors Speak; 'Attorney Kunstler and UT,'" *Knoxville News-Sentinel*, March 17, 1970.

186. "ACLU Criticizes Anti-Kunstler Talk," *Knoxville News-Sentinel*, March 18, 1970.

187. Fred A. Peters, "Says City Dump Should Be Site of Kunstler's Speech," Letter to the Editor, *Knoxville News-Sentinel*, March 26, 1970.

188. Lois Reagan Thomas, "May Be Rescheduled; Kunstler Grounded, Cancels UT Speech," *Knoxville News-Sentinel*, April 3, 1970.

189. "Kunstler Tells Students To 'Resist,'" *Knoxville News-Sentinel*, 5 April 1970; "Kunstler Allowed To Speak at UK," *Knoxville News-Sentinel*, April 4, 1970.

190. "Demonstration Planned April 12," *Knoxville News-Sentinel*, March 31, 1970.

191. "At Nashville's Centennial Park; Jerry Rubin To Speak at April 12 Rally," *Knoxville News-Sentinel*, April 2, 1970. For more on Joe Paisley, see Honey, *Going Down Jericho Road*, 122. Rubin's speech at the University of Alabama in May 1970 was met with similar consternation. See Turner, *Sitting In and Speaking Out*, 1.

192. FBI, Memo, Knoxville, to Director, FBI, William Moses Kunstler, Bureau File xx-100-3811, May 15, 1970.

193. Lois Reagan Thomas, "Carroll Bible Planning; Kunstler Urges All-Out UT Strike," *Knoxville News-Sentinel*, May 15, 1970.

194. Ibid.

195. Ibid.

196. MPA, Richard Nixon/Billy Graham Episode Tapes, 1987 (MPA.190) (RNBG), Interview #21, Dr. Charles Weaver, June 1, 1987.

197. Ibid.

198. Ibid.

199. UTSC, Office of the University Historian Collection, 1819–1997 (bulk 1870–1997), AR.0015, Series XII: Chancellor's/President's Reports (OUHCXII), Box 29, File 17, President's Report 1966[sic–1968]–1970; UTSC, OUHCVI, Box 23, File 13, The Boling Appointment Controversy, Statement for Student Disruption, January 15, 1970.

200. Lovett, *Civil Rights Movement*, 354–55.

201. UTSC, OUHCVI, Box 23, File 11, Anti-War Protests (1 of 2), James Lessenberry, "SGA Studies Assembly Bill," *Daily Beacon*, April 2, 1969.

202. UTSC, OUHCVI, Box 23, File 13, The Boling Appointment Controversy, "Recent Legislation Concerning Campus Operations," September 19, 1969.

203. UTSC, OUHCXII, Box 29, File 17, President's Report 1966[sic–1968]–1970.

204. Ibid.

205. UTSC, OUHCVI, Box 23, File 15, Demonstration Clippings.

206. UTSC, OUHCXII, Box 29, File 18, President's Report 1970–71.

207. MPA, WEBC, Box 17, Folder 14, Campus Unrest Report to the President, June 17, 1969 (for release on June 19).

208. MPA, WEBC, Box 17, Folder 15, Campaign Position Papers—1970, Brock News Release, October 6, 1970.

209. MPA, WEBC, Box 17, Folder 18, Brock News Release, "Brock Discusses Campus Disorder On Statewide Radio," July 8, 1970.

210. UTSC, OUHCVI, Box 23, File 20, Nixon-Graham Crusade—1970, Memo to the University Regarding the Visit of Dr. Billy Graham, June 9, 1970; MPA, WEBC, Box 17, Folder 18, Brock News Release, "Brock Discusses Campus Disorder On Statewide Radio," July 8, 1970.

211. MC, BM, File—Board of Directors Minutes 1965–1974, Spring Meeting of the Directors of Maryville College, May 8, 1969; MC, BM, File—Board of Directors Minutes 1965–1974, Fall Meeting of the Directors of Maryville College, October 16, 1969.

212. Ibid.

213. Ibid.

214. MC, BM, File—Board of Directors Minutes 1951–1964, A Report and Recommendation by the President to the Directors of Maryville College, May 19, 1954.

Chapter 5. "Deep Division"

1. For a discussion of antiwar activism on other southern campuses, see Fry, *The American South and the Vietnam War*, 286.
2. UMSC, CCHC, Box 4, Folder 25, Scott Hill, "10 Years After Kent State, A Memory," *Commercial Appeal*, April 27, 1980.
3. Fry, *The American South and the Vietnam War*, 319. That said, there were smaller campus-based protests in Tennessee after May 1970, such as the Morristown College shooting and the Middle Tennessee State University effigy burning protests discussed in the next chapter.
4. FBI COINTELPRO, Memorandum to FBI Director from SAC Knoxville, XX 100-3687, June 24, 1969.
5. FBI COINTELPRO, Memorandum to SAC Knoxville, XX 100-3687, from FBI Director, July 8, 1969.
6. Michel, *Struggle for a Better South*, 110, cited in Fry, *The American South and the Vietnam War*, 293.
7. Fry, *The American South and the Vietnam War*, 306.
8. Michel, *Struggle For a Better South*, 112. Campus groups similar to this group existed across the country, including at Kent State University in Ohio and the University of Texas in Austin. For more, see Rossinow, *The Politics of Authenticity*, 215 Heineman, *Campus Wars*, 70.
9. The SCCEWV Atlanta event took place in early 1966 and included forty protesters who had opposed the Affirmation Vietnam Rally. The latter group featured as speakers Georgia Senator Richard Russell and Secretary of State Dean Rusk. In Richmond, 125 people gathered for a forum on Vietnam featuring anti-war speakers. See Michel, *Struggle For a Better South*, 113-14 This event is described in more detail in Turner, *Sitting In and Speaking Out*, 231-32. The rally also featured Atlanta's mayor, Ivan Allen, as well as Senator Herman Talmadge Turner states that the rally was preceded by SSOC efforts from Gene Guerrero and Jody Palmour with Thomas J. J. Alitzer (a divinity professor at Emory University) to organize the South's first Vietnam teach-in in October 1965. Additionally, Jody Palmour was mentioned by Ed Hamlett in his correspondence with C. Vann Woodward in December 1966, when Hamlett said he wanted to speak with Woodward about Palmour "and I propose to do so on southern nationalism." See YUMA, CVWP, Box 24, Folder 275, letter to C. Vann Woodward from Ed Hamlett, December 12, 1966. In a letter to SDS's national council, Hamlett argued Hayden's visit could reinvigorate SSOC and SDS's anti-war and southern poverty initiatives. See VUSCUA, EHP, Box 48, Folder 4, "Proposals to the National Council From the Southern Caucus," n.d.
10. Michel, *Struggle For a Better South*, 104. This is likely the same event historian Don Doyle termed "one of the few demonstrations on campus" during this period. See Doyle, *Nashville Since the 1920s*, 162.
11. Lovett, *The Civil Rights Movement*, 203; Westheider, *Fighting on Two Fronts*, 18.
12. Hershberger, *Traveling to Vietnam*, 76-77; Lovett, *The Civil Rights Movement*, 203.
13. WHS, SAVF, Box 6, Black Power, Statement by Diane Nash Bevel, n.d.
14. See Carson, *In Struggle*, 182.
15. Estes, *I Am a Man!*, 12.
16. Westheider, *Fighting on Two Fronts*.
17. Fry, *The American South and the Vietnam War*, 156.
18. Westheider, *Fighting on Two Fronts*, 20.
19. Ibid., 23.

20. Ibid.

21. This quotation was Westheider's summation of the activists' argument. Ibid., 20.

22. This memo was published by SDS in the January 1967 edition of *New Left Notes*. Appy, *American Reckoning*, 135.

23. Appy, *American Reckoning*, 136.

24. For more on draft boards and concerns of racial injustice, see Westheider, *Fighting on Two Fronts*, 24; Hall, *Peace and Freedom*, 9; Sellers, *The River Of No Return*, 189; Rollins, oral history, December 27, 2013; Michel, *Struggle For a Better South*, 114.

25. "Draft Test Date Nears," *Stanford Daily*, April 21, 1966, 1. On SSOC and SDS's opposition to the Selective Service College Qualifications Test, and on the test's racially discriminatory effect, see WHS, SAVF, Box 45, Southern Student Organizing Committee, Folder—Unsorted Material, "Call to Action," n.d.

26. Grace, *Kent State*, 77.

27. WHS, SAVF, Box 45, Southern Student Organizing Committee, Folder—Unsorted Material, "Call to Action," n.d.

28. Sellers, *The River of No Return*, 189–90.

29. Brick and Phelps, *Radicals In America*, 137.

30. Smith had earlier written to Johnson about there not being any Blacks on the local draft boards in January 1966. See LBJLM, WHCF, HU, Box 41, Gen HU 2/ST 32–ST 50, Folder—HU 2/ST 42, Letter from Maxine A. Smith, Executive Secretary, Memphis Branch NAACP, to LBJ, September 6, 1966.

31. LBJLM, WHCF, HU, Box 41, Gen HU 2/ST 32–ST 50, Folder—HU 2/ST 42, Letter to Maxine A. Smith, Executive Secretary, Memphis Branch NAACP, from Lewis B. Hershey, Director of Selective Service System, September 14, 1966.

32. Westheider, *Fighting on Two Fronts*, 28–29. Selective Service officials introduced a lottery system in 1969.

33. VUSCUA, SSOCB, Dave and Ronda Kotelchuck/Dec. 2000 Acquisition, SSOC press release, "Stopping the Man" or "The Ides of March," n.d. For more on this incident, see Michel, "Building the New South," 56; Ernst and Baldwin, "The Not So Silent Minority," 120.

34. VUSCUA, SSOCB, Dave and Ronda Kotelchuck/Dec. 2000 Acquisition, SSOC press release, "Stopping the Man" or "The Ides of March," n.d.; Michel, "Building the New South," 56.

35. Ernst and Baldwin, "The Not So Silent Minority," 120.

36. Ibid., 122.

37. YUMA, CVWP, Box 24, Folder 275, Letter from Ed Hamlett to C. Vann Woodward, March 25, 1967.

38. Grace, *Kent State*, 95, 101.

39. "Percent in Different Age Groups Who Consider American Intervention in the Vietnam War a Mistake 1965–1971," Gallup Poll released June 6, 1971, in Lipset, *Rebellion in the University*, 39.

40. Fry, *The American South and the Vietnam War*, 296–97.

41. FBI, COINTELPRO Memorandum 100-449698-24-3, "New Left Activity, University of Tennessee, Knoxville, Tennessee," July 2, 1968.

42. WHS, Students for a Democratic Society (SDS) Records, 1958–1970 (MSS 177) (SDS), Series 3, Subseries—Locality File, Box 43, Folder 1—Rhode Island, South Carolina, Tennessee, 1965–1968, Roger S. Zimmerman, William G. Smith, and James H. Koplan, "The Student Movement Flies South: Dow at Vanderbilt," n.d. [approx. November 10, 1967].

43. Grace, *Kent State*, 98.

44. Student protestors also carried coffins in demonstrations at Kent State University,

on November 4, 1968, and at the University of Kentucky after the Kent State tragedy. Grace, *Kent State*, 128; Hall, "'A Crack in Time,'" 48.

45. WHS, SDS, Series 3, Subseries—Locality File, Box 43, Folder 1, Rhode Island, South Carolina, Tennessee, 1965–1968, "The Student Movement Flies South: Dow at Vanderbilt' by Roger S. Zimmerman, William G Smith, and James H. Koplan, n.d. [approx. November 10, 1967]; WHS, SDS, Series 3, Subseries—Locality File, Box 43, Folder 1, Rhode Island, South Carolina, Tennessee, 1965–1968, "Nashville, Tennessee," *New Left Notes*, December 25, 1967.

46. Grace, *Kent State*, 101.

47. Lipset, *Rebellion in the University*, 49.

48. LBJLM, WHCF, Confidential File, Box 56 HU 2/FG 216 (2 of 2), Folder—HU 2 Equality of Races (1967–) (1 of 5), Army intelligence briefing, September 11, 1968.

49. Turner, *Sitting In and Speaking Out*, 229.

50. UMSC, CCHC, Box 4, Folder 29, William Bennett, "State Board Charts Policy To Stop Campus 'Takeover,'" *Commercial Appeal*, September 19, 1968.

51. UMSC, CCHC, Box 4, Folder 29, Michael Lollar, "Activists: Where are they now?," *Commercial Appeal Mid-South Magazine*, January 6, 1985.

52. Heard, *Speaking of the University*, 113–15.

53. Ibid., 133. From a speech Heard gave at the Johns Hopkins University School of Medicine in Baltimore, Maryland, December 6, 1968.

54. WHS, SAVF, Box 45, Southern Student Organizing Committee, Folder—Unsorted Material, "Worklist Mailing," n.d.

55. UTSC, OUHCVI, Box 23, File 11, Anti-War Protests (1 of 2), "500 Participate in Anti-War Demonstration," *Daily Beacon*, March 29, 1968.

56. "Students Await Trial For Flag Burning," *Sou'wester*, December 6, 1968.

57. Scott Bomboy, "Inside the Supreme Court's flag burning decision," *Constitution Daily*, June 14, 2015, https://constitutioncenter.org/blog/inside-the-supreme-courts-flag-burning-decision/.

58. The Circuit Court case took place in May 1969. "Desegregation, Riots Were Top News Events," *Jackson Sun*, December 31, 1969, 1-A, 2-A (quote from 2-A).

59. VUSCUA, EHP, Box 52, Folder 14, "Because of the Need For Us to Have a Clearly Unique and Identifiably Southern Role in National Mobilizations We Propose a 'Southern Days of Secession' (April 20–30th)"; WHS, SAVF, Box 45, Southern Student Organizing Committee, Folder—Unsorted Material, "We Secede: Call to Southern Days of Secession, April 20–30," April 20–30, 1968.

60. Italics in original. WHS, SAVF, Box 45, Southern Student Organizing Committee, Folder—Unsorted Material, "We Secede: Call to Southern Days of Secession, April 20–30", April 20–30, 1968.

61. Ibid.

62. UTSC, OUHCVI, Box 23, File 11, Anti-War Protests (1 of 2), letter to "Friends of the University of Tennessee" from the officers of the UT-Knoxville Chapter of the AAUP (Professors H. W. Fuller, Richard C. Marius, Kermit J. Blank, Louis E. Dotson, Forrest W. Lacey, George A. Spiva, A. M. Johnston), March 17, 1969.

63. Ibid.

64. UTSC, OUHCVI, Box 23, File 11, Anti-War Protests (1 of 2), Thomas E. Humphrey, "Moratorium Plans Arouse Tennesseans," *Daily Beacon*, October 11, 1969.

65. Ibid.

66. UTSC, OUHCVI, Box 23, File 11, Anti-War Protests (1 of 2), "Moratorium—To War Or Not To War," *Daily Beacon*, October 15, 1969.

67. For complaints about student apathy at Fisk, see Turner, "The Rise of Black and White Student Protest," 143.

68. Jim Daugherty, "Viet Nam Moratorium To Confront College Community," *Highland Echo* 55, no. 5, October 9, 1969. Maryville also tried to organize a group for the national moratorium in D.C. on November 14–15, 1969. See "November 14–15 Moratorium Organized," *Highland Echo* 55, no. 7, October 24, 1969. For more on apathy at Maryville, see Sue Forman, letter to the editor, *Highland Echo* 50, no. 14, March 6, 1965; "Up From Silence," *Highland Echo* 54, no. 14, March 6, 1969.

69. "Points to Ponder," *Highland Echo* 53, no. 5, October 27, 1967.

70. Law Wilson, "Gownsmen Support Vietnam Observance," *Sewanee Purple* 88, no. 3, October 9, 1969; Leland Howard, "Moratorium Is Observed Here," *Sewanee Purple* 88, no. 4, October 17, 1969; Williamson Jr., *Sewanee Sesquicentennial History*, 325; "This Week In Vanderbilt History," *Vanderbilt Hustler*, October 3, 1969, and October 15, 1969, reproduced in *Vanderbilt Register*, https://www.jstor.org/site/vanderbilt/vanderbilt-hustler/; Bob Tigert and Kirk Hadaway, "Moratorium Yields Day of Peace," *Sou'wester*, October 17, 1969; Akins and Wiggins, *Keeping The Faith*, 123; Fry, *The American South and the Vietnam War*, 304.

71. Ernst and Baldwin, "The Not So Silent Minority," 121–22; Bob Tigert and Kirk Hadaway, "Moratorium Yields Day of Peace," *Sou'wester*, October 17, 1969; Bob Tigert, "Moratorium Activities Quelled In Deference To Local Strike Issue," *Sou'wester*, November 14, 1969.

72. UTSC, OUHCVI, Box 23, File 11, Anti-War Protests (1 of 2), Thomas E. Humphrey, "Moratorium Plans Arouse Tennesseans," *Daily Beacon*, October 11, 1969.

73. UTSC, OUHCVI, Box 23, File 11, Anti-War Protests (1 of 2), Thomas E. Humphrey, "Moratorium Plans Arouse Tennesseans," *Daily Beacon*, October 11, 1969; UTSC, OUHCVI, Box 23, File 12, Anti-War Protests (2 of 2), "YAF Seeks Disruption Curb," *Daily Beacon*, October 4, 1969.

74. UTSC, OUHCVI, Box 23, File 11, Anti-War Protests (1 of 2), Thomas E. Humphrey, "Moratorium Plans Arouse Tennesseans," *Daily Beacon*, October 11, 1969.

75. UTSC, OUHCVI, Box 23, File 11, Anti-War Protests (1 of 2), Frank Gibson, "YAF To Burn Vietnamese Flag," *Daily Beacon*, October 15, 1969.

76. On YAF's mobilization to oppose anti-war and New Leftist activism on college campuses, see Scanlon, *The Pro-War Movement*, 242.

77. Congressman John Ashbrook, on March 17, 1969, 91st Cong., 1st sess., *Congressional Record*, 115, Part 5 – Extensions of Remarks, 6648. UT's Majority Coalition was also referenced in FBI, COINTELPRO Memorandum to FBI Director from SAC Knoxville, XX 100-3687, March 25, 1969.

78. Rogers, *The Black Campus Movement*, 101.

79. Blumenthal, "Children of the 'Silent Majority,'" 350.

80. Appy, *American Reckoning*, 190; Hall, "A Crack in Time," 60.

81. Other campuses with National Guard presence and curfews included Southern Illinois University in Carbondale, Ohio University in Athens, Eastern Michigan University in Ypsilanti, Northwestern University in Evanston, Northern Michigan University in Marquette, and University of Denver. See "Guardsmen at Work; Some Students Still Protest Violently," *Knoxville News-Sentinel*, May 14, 1970.

82. Conflicts over lowering the flag to half-mast also took place at the University of Kentucky after Kent State. See Hall, "A Crack in Time," 56.

83. Sorrels, *The Exciting Years*, 199–200; UTSC, OUHCVI, Box 23, File 12, Anti-War Protests (2 of 2), "Fights Break Out At Memphis State," *Daily Beacon*, May 6, 1970.

84. Sorrels, *The Exciting Years*, 200.
85. Ibid.
86. UMSC, CCHC, Scott Hill, "10 Years After Kent State, A Memory," *Commercial Appeal*, April 27, 1980.
87. Sorrels, *The Exciting Years*, 201.
88. UMSC, University Archives, President's Office Files III, Reading File, June 1967–Feb. 1972, 1970/04/01–1970/08/31, letter from President Humphreys to Mrs. Harriet Verrell of Memphis, June 3, 1970.
89. MPA, RNBG, Weaver, interview, June 1, 1987.
90. Appy, *American Reckoning*, 193–96.
91. UTSC, OUHCVI, Box 23, File 20, Nixon-Graham Crusade—1970, *Volunteer Moments: Vignettes of the History of The University of Tennessee, 1794–1994*, prepared by the Office of the University Historian, The University of Tennessee, Knoxville, 1994, 78. According to this source, the strike was called for Wednesday through Friday, while other accounts say it took place from Thursday through Saturday. See UTSC, OUHCVI, Box 23, File 11, Anti-War Protests (1 of 2), Jane McEacher, "UT Classes Less Than Half Full," *Daily Beacon*, May 9, 1970; UTSC, OUHCVI, Box 23, File 11, Anti-War Protests (1 of 2), "Strike Three—And Then What?," *Daily Beacon*, May 12, 1970. See also interview of James "Sparky" Rucker, "A Sense of Revolution," *The Vietnam War: East Tennessee*, East Tennessee Public Broadcasting Service (PBS), February 17, 2017.
92. UTSC, OUHCVI, Box 23, File 12, Anti-War Protests (2 of 2), "Baxter Calls 3-Day Student Strike," *Daily Beacon*, May 6, 1970.
93. UTSC, OUHCVI, Box 23, File 11, Anti-War Protests (1 of 2), "War Comes Home," *Daily Beacon*, May 8, 1970.
94. UTSC, OUHCVI, Box 23, File 11, Anti-War Protests (1 of 2), Jane McEacher, "UT Classes Less Than Half Full," *Daily Beacon*, May 9, 1970.
95. "On UT Property; Arson-Linked Fire Hits Army Reserve Building," *Knoxville News-Sentinel*, May 5, 1970; Fry, *The American South and the Vietnam War*, 300.
96. Rucker, interview, February 17, 2017.
97. Interview with Cynthia Fleming, "A Sense of Revolution," *The Vietnam War: East Tennessee*, East Tennessee Public Broadcasting Service (PBS) 2017.
98. RCASC, Presidents Papers, 70-62 Campus Unrest—1970, press release, May 8, 1970.
99. "ACC Discusses National—International Crises," *Highland Echo* 55, no. 6, May 8, 1970.
100. Judith Warren, "Strike," *Sou'wester* 51, no. 23, May 15, 1970.
101. Lipset, *Rebellion in the University*, 5.
102. UTSC, OUHCVI, Box 23, File 20, Nixon-Graham Crusade—1970, Billy Graham Crusade at Neyland Stadium Program, May 30, 1970; UTSC, OUHCVI, Box 23, File 20, Nixon-Graham Crusade—1970, *Volunteer Moments: Vignettes of the History of The University of Tennessee, 1794–1994*, prepared by the Office of the University Historian, The University of Tennessee, Knoxville, 1994, 78.
103. MPA, RNBG, Interview Number 2, Kathleen Anderson, May 7, 1987; MPA, RNBG, Interview Number 7, Zoe Hoyle, May 12, 1987.
104. Miller, *Billy Graham and the Rise of the Republican South*, 141, 155; Miller, "Billy Graham, Civil Rights, and the Changing Postwar South" in *Politics and Religion in the White South*, ed. Feldman, 161.
105. MPA, RNBG, Tape Number 12, Dr. Kenneth Newton, April 27, 1987.
106. UTSC, Baxter, interview, December 2, 1993.
107. MPA, RNBG, Weaver, interview, June 1, 1987; RNPLM, WHCF, States-Territories

(ST), Box 16, Ex ST 41 South Dakota to Gen ST 45 Vermont, Folder Gen ST 42 Tennessee, Letter to Governor Buford Ellington from Dwight L. Chapin, Special Assistant to the President, July 12, 1969.

108. RNPLM, WHCF, States-Territories (ST), Box 16, Ex ST 41 South Dakota to Gen ST 45 Vermont, Folder Gen ST 42 Tennessee [1969–1974], Letters dated July 12, 1969, and July 21, 1969, from Dwight L. Chapin, Special Assistant to the President, to Governor Buford Ellington.

109. RNPLM, WHCF, Staff Member Office Files (SMOF), Series III, Inter-Office Memoranda, Sub-Series A, House of Representatives, Box 89, Folder Duncan, John J., Memorandum for Dwight Chapin from William E. Timmons, May 23, 1970.

110. Perlstein, *Nixonland*, 500.

111. MPA, RNBG, Interview No. 19, Dr. William Verplanck, May 20, 1987, MS–1330. For other faculty views in line with Verplanck, see MPA, RNBG, Interview No. 8, Dr. Forrest Lacey, May 26, 1987, MS–1330; MPA, RNBG, Interview No. 15, Dr. Howard Pollio, May 7, 1987.

112. MPA, RNBG, Weaver, interview, June 1, 1987.

113. Italics in original. RNPLM, White House Central Files, Trips (TR), Box 38 Ex TR 48-1 Knoxville, Tenn., to speak at Billy Graham's "Crusade," Univ. of Tenn., 5/28/70 to Gen TR 50-3 San Clemente, California, 6/25/70, Folder Ex TR 48-1 Knoxville, Tenn., to speak at Billy Graham's "Crusade," Univ. of Tenn., 5/28/70, confidential memo for Harry Dent, Murray Chotiner, and Bill Timmons from Dwight L. Chapin, February 20, 1970.

114. Ibid.

115. RNPLM, White House Central Files, Trips (TR), Box 38 Ex TR 48-1 Knoxville, Tenn., to speak at Billy Graham's "Crusade," Univ. of Tenn., 5/28/70 to Gen TR 50-3 San Clemente, California, 6/25/70, Folder Ex TR 48-1 Knoxville, Tenn., to speak at Billy Graham's "Crusade," Univ. of Tenn., 5/28/70, confidential memo for Dwight Chapin from Murray Chotiner and Harry Dent, February 20, 1970; RNPLM, White House Central Files, Trips (TR), Box 38, Ex TR 48-1 Knoxville, Tenn., to speak at Billy Graham's "Crusade," Univ. of Tenn., 5/28/70 to Gen TR 50-3 San Clemente, California, 6/25/70, Folder Ex TR 48-1 Knoxville, Tenn., to speak at Billy Graham's "Crusade," Univ. of Tenn., 5/28/70, memo from Dwight L. Chapin to H. R. Haldeman, May 27, 1970.

116. RNPLM, White House Central Files, Trips (TR), Box 38 Ex TR 48-1 Knoxville, Tenn., to speak at Billy Graham's "Crusade," Univ. of Tenn., 5/28/70 to Gen TR 50-3 San Clemente, California, 6/25/70, Folder Ex TR 48-1 Knoxville, Tenn., to speak at Billy Graham's "Crusade," Univ. of Tenn., 5/28/70, memo from Dwight L. Chapin to H. R. Haldeman, May 26, 1970.

117. RNPLM, The White House Communications Agency Sound Recording Collection, WHCA SR #P 700516, Neyland Stadium, Knoxville, Tennessee 5/28/1970.

118. RNPLM, WHCF, Trips (TR), Box 38, Ex TR 48-1 Knoxville, Tenn., to speak at Billy Graham's "Crusade," Univ. of Tenn., 5/28/70 to Gen TR 50-3 San Clemente, California, 6/25/70, Folder Ex TR 48-1 Knoxville, Tenn., to speak at the Billy Graham's "Crusade," Univ. of Tenn., 5/28/70, memo from Dwight L. Chapin to James Keogh, May 25, 1970; RNPLM, WHCF, Trips (TR), Box 38 Ex TR 48-1 Knoxville, Tenn., to speak at Billy Graham's "Crusade," Univ. of Tenn., 5/28/70 to Gen TR 50-3 San Clemente, California, 6/25/70, Folder Ex TR 48-1 Knoxville, Tenn., to speak at Billy Graham's "Crusade," Univ. of Tenn., 5/28/70, memo from Dwight L. Chapin to H. R. Haldeman, May 25, 1970. May 24, 1970, was the crusade's first Youth Night, making the night of Nixon's speech on May 28 the second Youth Night. See RNPLM, WHCF, Trips (TR), Box 38, Ex TR 48-1 Knoxville, Tenn., to speak at Billy Graham's "Crusade," Univ. of Tenn., 5/28/70 to Gen TR 50-3 San Clem-

ente, California, 6/25/70, Folder Ex TR 48-1 Knoxville, Tenn., to speak at Billy Graham's "Crusade," Univ. of Tenn., 5/28/70, "East Tennessee Billy Graham Crusade," n.d.

119. RNPLM, WHCF, Trips (TR), Box 38, Ex TR 48-1 Knoxville, Tenn., to speak at Billy Graham's "Crusade," Univ. of Tenn., 5/28/70 to Gen TR 50-3 San Clemente, California, 6/25/70, Folder Ex TR 48-1 Knoxville, Tenn., to speak at the Billy Graham's "Crusade," Univ. of Tenn., 5/28/70, memo from Dwight L. Chapin to James Keogh, May 25, 1970.

120. RNPLM, WHCF, Trips (TR), Box 38, Ex TR 48-1 Knoxville, Tenn., to speak at Billy Graham's "Crusade," Univ. of Tenn., 5/28/70 to Gen TR 50-3 San Clemente, California, 6/25/70, Folder Ex TR 48-1 Knoxville, Tenn., to speak at the Billy Graham's "Crusade," Univ. of Tenn., 5/28/70, memo from Dwight L. Chapin to H. R. Haldeman, May 25, 1970. This is a paraphrasing of Graham, quoted from the memorandum.

121. RNPLM, WHCF, Trips (TR), Box 38, Ex TR 48-1 Knoxville, Tenn., to speak at Billy Graham's "Crusade," Univ. of Tenn., 5/28/70 to Gen TR 50-3 San Clemente, California, 6/25/70, Folder Ex TR 48-1 Knoxville, Tenn., to speak at Billy Graham's "Crusade," Univ. of Tenn., 5/28/70, memo related to May 27, 1970 telegram to Nixon from the UT Student Steering Committee (received by the White House on May 28).

122. RNPLM, WHCF, Staff Member Office Files (SMOF), Series II, Inter-Office Memoranda, Sub-Series A, House of Representatives, Box 89, Folder Duncan, John J., Memorandum for Dwight Chapin from William E. Timmons, 27 May 1970; RNPLM, White House Central Files, Trips (TR), Box 38, Ex TR 48-1 Knoxville, Tenn., to speak at Billy Graham's "Crusade" Univ. of Tenn., 5/28/70 to Gen TR 50-3 San Clemente, California, 6/25/70, Folder Ex TR 48-1 Knoxville, Tenn., to speak at Billy Graham's "Crusade," Univ. of Tenn., 28/5/70, Memorandum for Dwight Chapin from William E. Timmons, May 27, 1970.

123. RNPLM, WHCF, Trips (TR), Box 38, Ex TR 48-1 Knoxville, Tenn., to speak at Billy Graham's "Crusade," Univ. of Tenn., 28/5/70 to Gen TR 50-3 San Clemente, California, 25/6/70, "On Board Plane Meeting," n.d.; Thompson, "'A Taste of Student Power,'" 89.

124. Italics in original. RNPLM, White House Central Files, Trips (TR), Box 38, Ex TR 48-1 Knoxville, Tenn., to speak at Billy Graham's "Crusade," Univ. of Tenn., 5/28/70 to Gen TR 50-3 San Clemente, California, 6/25/70, Folder Ex TR 48-1 Knoxville, Tenn., to speak at Billy Graham's "Crusade," Univ. of Tenn., 5/28/70, Letter from President Richard Nixon to John Smith, June 5, 1970; RNPLM, The Haldeman Diaries, May 28, 1970.

125. Robert B. Semple Jr., "Nixon Counting On Time To Ease Twin Crises," *New York Times*, May 31, 1970, 115.

126. Smith was traveling to Washington with Joseph Zvanut and Mike Haynes (fellow UT students). See RNPLM, WHCF, Federal Government Organizations (FG), Box FG 288, President's Commission on Campus Unrest, Folder Gen FG 288 President's Commission on Campus Violence, Begin—7/31/70, Letter to Congressman John Duncan from Hugh W. Sloan Jr., Staff Assistant to the President, July 7, 1970.

127. Thompson, "'A Taste of Student Power,'" 90.

128. See RNPLM, WHCF, Trips (TR), Box 38, Ex TR 48-1 Knoxville, Tenn., to speak at Billy Graham's "Crusade," Univ. of Tenn., 5/28/70 to Gen TR 50-3 San Clemente, California, 6/25/70, Folder Ex TR 48-1 Knoxville, Tenn., to speak at Billy Graham's "Crusade," Univ. of Tenn., 5/28/70, "East Tennessee Billy Graham Crusade," n.d.; RNPLM, WHCF, Trips (TR), Box 38, Ex TR 48-1 Knoxville, Tenn., to speak at Billy Graham's "Crusade," Univ. of Tenn., 5/28/70 to Gen TR 50-3 San Clemente, California, 6/25/70, Folder Ex TR 48-1 Knoxville, Tenn., to speak at Billy Graham's "Crusade," Univ. of Tenn., 5/28/70, memo from Dwight L. Chapin to H. R. Haldeman, May 26, 1970; MPA, RNBG, Newton, interview, April 27, 1987; UTSC, OUHCVI, Box 23, File 20, Nixon-Graham

Crusade—1970, *Volunteer Moments: Vignettes of the History of The University of Tennessee, 1794–1994*, prepared by the Office of the University Historian, The University of Tennessee, Knoxville, 1994, 80; RNPLM, WHCF, Trips (TR), Box 38, Ex TR 48-1 Knoxville, Tenn., to speak at Billy Graham's "Crusade," Univ. of Tenn., 5/28/70 to Gen TR 50-3 San Clemente, California, 6/25/70, Folder Ex TR 48-1 Knoxville, Tenn., to speak at Billy Graham's "Crusade," Univ. of Tenn., 5/28/70, letter to Nixon from J. H. Gammon, May 29, 1970; RNPLM, White House Central Files, Trips (TR), Box 38, Ex TR 48-1 Knoxville, Tenn., to speak at Billy Graham's "Crusade," Univ. of Tenn., 5/28/70 to Gen TR 50-3 San Clemente, California, 6/25/70, Folder Gen TR 48-1 Knoxville, Tenn., to speak at Billy Graham's "Crusade," Univ. of Tenn., 5/28/70; John Jiran and Guy L. Smith IV, "Record Knox Crowd Gives Tumultuous Welcome To ET Crusade," *Knoxville News-Sentinel*, May 29, 1970; RNPLM, WHCF, Trips (TR), Box 38, Ex TR 48-1 Knoxville, Tenn., to speak at Billy Graham's "Crusade," Univ. of Tenn., 5/28/70 to Gen TR 50-3 San Clemente, California, 6/25/70; Bruce Hight, "Nixon Stresses Problems Of Youth," *Daily Beacon*, May 29, 1970; RNPLM, The White House Communications Agency Sound Recording Collection (WHCASRC), WHCA SR #P 700516, Neyland Stadium, Knoxville, Tennessee 5/28/1970; Independent Voices: An Open Access Collection of an Alternative Press, *Great Speckled Bird* 3, no. 23, June 8, 1970, 3.

129. MPA, RNBG, Tape Number 16, Dr. Charles H. Reynolds, April 27, 1987; RNPLM, The White House Communications Agency, Weekly News Summaries (WHCAWNS), File ID: 3737, May 29, 1970—Reports of Nixon's speech at UT.

130. Fry, *The American South and the Vietnam War*, 331.

131. MPA, RNBG, Newton, interview, April 27, 1987.

132. Barry Bozeman, correspondence with author, May 23, 2014.

133. Ibid.

134. MPA, RNBG, Reynolds, interview, April 27, 1987.

135. RNPLM, WHCF, Trips (TR), Box 38, Ex TR 48-1 Knoxville, Tenn., to speak at Billy Graham's "Crusade," Univ. of Tenn., 5/28/70 to Gen TR 50-3 San Clemente, California, 6/25/70, "Dr. Billy Graham's Introduction of The President," May 28, 1970.

136. RNPLM, The Haldeman Diaries, May 28, 1970.

137. RNPLM, WHCAWNS, File ID: 3737, May 29, 1970—Reports of Nixon's speech at UT.

138. RNPLM, WHCF, Speeches (SP), Box 121, Ex SP 3-86/PRO 6/23/70–6/24/70 to Ex SP 3-88 Radio & T.V. Address by the President on the Cambodian Sanctuary Operation 6/3/70 (3 of 3), Folder Ex SP 3-87 "Billy Graham Crusade" Univ. of Tenn. Neyland Stadium Knoxville, Tenn., 5/28/70, Remarks of the President at Dr. Billy Graham's East Tennessee Crusade, Neyland Stadium, University of Tennessee, May 28, 1970.

139. Waters's comments transcribed in dialect. RNPLM, WHCASRC, WHCA SR #P 700516, Neyland Stadium, Knoxville, Tennessee 5/28/1970, also quoted in RNPLM, WHCF, Trips (TR), Box 38 Ex TR 48-1 Knoxville, Tenn., to speak at the Billy Graham's "Crusade," Univ. of Tenn., 5/28/70 to Gen TR 50-3 San Clemente, California, 6/25/70, John Jiran and Guy L. Smith IV, "Record Knox Crowd Gives Tumultuous Welcome to ET Crusade," *Knoxville News-Sentinel*, May 29, 1970.

140. RNPLM, The Haldeman Diaries, May 28, 1970.

141. Miller, *Billy Graham and the Rise of the Republican South*, 142.

142. RNPLM, WHCAWNS, File 3737, May 29, 1970—Reports of Nixon's speech at UT.

143. MPA, RNBG, Interview No. 18, Michael Tomlinson, May 22, 1987.

144. UTSC, OUHCVI, Box 23, File 15, Demonstration Clippings, Statement from Chancellor Weaver regarding his involvement in bringing Graham's Crusade to campus, June 5, 1970.

145. UTSC, OUHCVI, Box 23, File 20, Nixon-Graham Crusade—1970, *Volunteer Moments: Vignettes of the History of The University of Tennessee, 1794–1994*, prepared by the Office of the University Historian, University of Tennessee, Knoxville, 1994, 82; Jack Neely, "The World Was Watching," *Metro Pulse*, May 22, 2000; Wheeler, *Knoxville, Tennessee*, 146.

146. Barry Bozeman, "40 Year Flashback—Nixon & Graham at Tennessee," May 28, 2010, http://www.dailykos.com/story/2010/05/28/864563/-40-YEAR-FLASHBACK -NIXON-GRAHAM-at-TENNESSEE.

147. RNPLM, WHCF, Trips (TR), Box 38, Ex TR 48-1 Knoxville, Tenn., to speak at Billy Graham's "Crusade," Univ. of Tenn., 5/28/70 to Gen TR 50-3 San Clemente, California, 6/25/70, letter from Leonard Garment to Reverend Frank R. Erickson, June 30, 1970; Wheeler, *Knoxville, Tennessee*, 146. For an account about UT police from the Chief of Police for the University of Tennessee, Ed Yovella, see MPA, RNBG, Interview Number 24, Ed Yovella, May 26, 1987.

148. For more on this, please see chapter 4. FBI, COINTELPRO Memorandum to FBI Director from SAC Knoxville, XX 100-3687, July 19, 1970; FBI, COINTELPRO Memorandum to FBI Director from SAC Knoxville, XX 100-3687, January 20, 1971.

149. Jackson State College expanded in 1974 to become Jackson State University. For more on the commission, see Grace, *Kent State*, 243–44.

150. RNPLM, WHCF, Staff Member and Office Files, Robert H. Finch, Campus Unrest File, Box 26, Prepared Testimony to Scranton Commission—Personnel, Folder—The Report of the President's Commission on Campus Unrest, n.d.

151. RNPLM, WHCF, Staff Member and Office Files, Robert H. Finch, Campus Unrest File, Box 26, Prepared Testimony to Scranton Commission—Personnel, Folder—The Report of the President's Commission on Campus Unrest, n.d.; Fry, *The American South and the Vietnam War*, 314–15.

152. One of the few who spoke against Heard was the Vanderbilt trustee and editor of the newspaper the *Nashville Banner*, Jimmy Stahlman.

153. "Alexander Heard, Vanderbilt's fifth chancellor, dies," *Vanderbilt News*, July 25, 2009, http://news.vanderbilt.edu/2009/07/ alexander-heard-vanderbilts-fifth-chancellor-dies-85205/.

154. Italics in original. Fry, *The American South and the Vietnam War*, 315–16.

155. Ibid., 316–17.

156. Ibid., 316.

157. Ibid., 317.

158. RNPLM, WHCF, Staff Member and Office Files, Robert H. Finch, Campus Unrest File, Box 27, Scranton Commission, Presentation to Special Report—The Kent State Tragedy, Folder—Scranton Commission Report, Press release, November 5, 1970. For more on the relationship between the commission and the White House, see RNPLM, WHCF, Staff Member and Office Files, Robert H. Finch, Campus Unrest File, Box 27, Scranton Commission, Presentation to Special Report—The Kent State Tragedy, Folder—Scranton Commission Presentation and Folder—Scranton Commission Confidential.

159. RNPLM, WHCF, Staff Member and Office Files, Robert H. Finch Campus Unrest File, Box 27, Scranton Commission, Presentation to Special Report—The Kent State Tragedy, Folder—Scranton Commission Presentation, Scranton to Nixon, September 26, 1970.

160. RNPLM, WHCF, Staff Member and Office Files, Robert H. Finch, Campus Unrest File, Box 27, Scranton Commission, Presentation to Special Report—The Kent State Tragedy, Folder—Scranton Commission Report, Press release, November 5, 1970.

161. Ibid.

162. RCASC, President's Papers, 70–62 Campus Unrest—1970, Scranton Commission Survey.

Conclusion

1. Hall, "'Guerrilla Theater,'" 123; Bill Mason, "Dean nixes PBC demonstration; defiance planned," *Sidelines* 49, no. 23, October 31, 1975, 1.

2. Bill Mason, "Dean nixes PBC demonstration; defiance planned," *Sidelines* 49, no. 23, October 31, 1975, 1; Bill Mason, "Dean backs down; Cook effigy to burn Thursday," *Sidelines* 49, no. 24, November 4, 1975, 2.

3. Editorial and column about the PBC, *Sidelines* 49, no. 23, October 31, 1975, 4.

4. "ASB acts wisely on controversy," *Sidelines* 49, no. 24, November 4, 1975, 4.

5. Hall, "'Guerrilla Theater,'" 114–36.

6. Hall, Abstract, "'Guerrilla Theater,'" 114.

7. Hall, "'Guerrilla Theater,'" 117.

8. Ibid.

9. The 1972 trade agreement between the Soviet Union and the United States entailed the American government receiving $700 million from the USSR for 440 million bushels of wheat. Gina Jeter, "Comment: PBC battles monopolies, corporate tyranny," *Sidelines*, 49, no. 1, July 2, 1975, 4; Hall, "'Guerrilla Theater,'" 123.

10. Bill Mason, "Dean nixes PBC demonstration; defiance planned," *Sidelines* 49, no. 23, October 31, 1975, 1.

11. Hall, "'Guerrilla Theater,'" 123; Gina Jeter, "Comment: PBC battles monopolies, corporate tyranny," *Sidelines*, 49, no. 1, July 2, 1975, 4.

12. Hall, "'Guerrilla Theater,'" 123–24.

13. Simon Hall made a similar argument in his analysis of the gay rights movement and the anti-busing campaign of the 1970s, as did Timothy Reese Cain in his work on students and labor activism. See Hall, "Protest Movements in the 1970s;" Cain, "Student Activists and Organized Labor," in *Rethinking Campus Life*, eds. Ogren and VanOverbeke, 181–82.

14. "Morristown College Quiet After Shooting," *Kingsport News*, October 10, 1970, 1.

15. Middle Tennessee State University, Albert Gore Research Center, FHPC, "Cross burning initates [sic] protest by blacks at president's home," *Sidelines*, No. 28, December 11, 1970, 1; Middle Tennessee State University, Albert Gore Research Center, FHPC, *Sidelines*, No. 44, March 12, 1971, 1–2; "President M. G. Scarlett discusses Race Relations at MTSU," Albert Gore Research Center, n.d., https://www.youtube.com/watch?t=299&v=ghCzfUgoWA0&feature=youtu.be.

16. Middle Tennessee State University, Albert Gore Research Center, FHPC, *Sidelines*, No. 44, March 12, 1971, 1.

17. Middle Tennessee State University, Albert Gore Research Center, FHPC, Dylan Skye Aycock, "Understanding the controversy: A brief history of Nathan Bedford Forrest," *Sidelines* Special Issue, "De-Forrestation," 90, no. 5, March 21, 2016, 4; Tonyaa Weathersbee, "Anonymous no more: Honoring African-American Fort Pillow victims," *Commercial Appeal*, April 13, 2017, https://eu.commercialappeal.com/story/news/columnists/2017/04/12/anonymous-no-more-ceremony-honors-african-american-ft-pillow-victims/100281168/.

18. Middle Tennessee State University, Albert Gore Research Center, FHPC, Devin Ross, "The Evolution of MT's Mascot," *Sidelines* Special Issue, "De-Forrestation," 90, no. 5,

March 21, 2016, 6–7; Middle Tennessee State University, Albert Gore Research Center, Holland Bratten, "MTSC Nickname And Colors Date Back To Old 'Normal,'" *Sidelines*, March 30, 1960, 2.

19. Middle Tennessee State University, Albert Gore Research Center, Homer Pittard, *The First Fifty Years: Middle Tennessee State College, 1911–1961* (Murfreesboro, TN: Middle Tennessee State College, 1961), 149–51 (quote from 150).

20. Italics in original. Middle Tennessee State University, Albert Gore Research Center, "Blue Raider Mystic Symbol Appears," *Sidelines*, November 8, 1961, 2.

21. Middle Tennessee State University, Albert Gore Research Center, FHPC, Devin Ross, "The Evolution of MT's Mascot," *Sidelines* Special Issue, "De-Forrestation," 90, no. 5, March 21, 2016, 6–7; Josh Howard, "A Confederate on Campus: Nathan Bedford Forrest as MTSU's Mascot," August 25, 2015, https://digital.mtsu.edu/digital/collection/p15838coll11/id/122/. For more on Confederate memory, see Cook, *Civil War Memories*.

22. Student activists beginning in 2006 protested for the renaming of the ROTC building on campus known as Forrest Hall; efforts to rename the building have continued into 2018. Sarah Calise, "Protesting the Confederacy on Campus," *Activist History Review*, July 25, 2018, https://activisthistory.com/2018/07/25/protesting-the-confederacy-on-campus/.

23. Middle Tennessee State University, Albert Gore Research Center, FHPC, Devin Ross, "The Evolution of MT's Mascot," *Sidelines* Special Issue, "De-Forrestation," 90, no. 5, March 21, 2016, 6–7 (quote from 6); Middle Tennessee State University, Albert Gore Research Center, FHPC, Devin Ross, "The Evolution of MT's Mascot," *Sidelines* Special Issue, "De-Forrestation," 90, no. 5, March 21, 2016, 6–7; Jerry Manley, "So where did the 'Blue Raiders' come from?," *Sidelines*, February 4, 1975, 5; Albert Gore Research Center, Middle Tennessee State University, John Potts, "Keckley explains PR stance on logo issue," *Sidelines* 48, no. 33, January 31, 1975, 1–2; Middle Tennessee State University, Albert Gore Research Center, FHPC, Devin Ross, "The Evolution of MT's Mascot," *Sidelines* Special Issue, "De-Forrestation," 90, no. 5, March 21, 2016, 6–7.

24. RCASC, Black Student Association, Box 1 of 2, Black Student Association, 1970–1979, "Suspension Stirs Protest By Blacks," *Commercial Appeal*, April 24, 1972.

25. Southwestern's president was William B. Bowden. The other institutions participating in the track meet were Fisk University, LeMoyne-Owen College, and David Lipscomb College in Tennessee, and Hendrix College in Arkansas. RCASC, Black Student Association, Box 1 of 2, Black Student Association, 1970–1979, "Suspension Stirs Protest By Blacks," *Commercial Appeal*, April 24, 1972; RCASC, President's Papers, 72-62 Campus Unrest—1972, Memo from Coach Bill Bretherick to William Bowden, April 26, 1972.

26. RCASC, Black Student Association, Box 1 of 2, Black Student Association, 1970–1979, Letter to BSA from Dean Robert G. Patterson, May 24, 1972; RCASC, Black Student Association, Box 1 of 2, Black Student Association, 1970–1979, Letter from Dean Robert G. Patterson to BSA members on academic probation, May 24, 1972; RCASC, Black Student Association, Box 1 of 2, Black Student Association, 1970–1979, Letter from Dean Robert G. Patterson to Miss Eva Thurman, May 9, 1972 [quotes from this source]; RCASC, President's Papers, 72-62 Campus Unrest—1972, Letter from Susan L. Smith, President of the Social Regulations Council, to Dean Robert G. Patterson, 3 May 1972; RCASC, President's Papers, 72-62 Campus Unrest—1972, Memo from the BSA to Dean Robert G. Patterson, May 18, 1972; RCASC, President's Papers, 72-62 Campus Unrest—1972, Memo from William L. Bowden to Executive Committee Board of Trustees, "Policy on Campus Disorder," May 16, 1972.

27. "Women's Rights Rally," *Daily News Journal*, April 30, 1970, 7.

28. "Editorial: Women's Rights Noticed," *Highland Echo* 57, no. 6, October 22, 1971, 2; Sorrels, *The Exciting Years*, 213.

29. "Editorial: Women's Rights Noticed," *Highland Echo* 57, no. 6, October 22, 1971, 2.

30. Linda Lou Blomeke, "MC's Emancipated Women," *Highland Echo* 56, no. 2, September 25, 1970, 3.

31. Gary Fields, "The New Feminism On Campus: Has Women's Liberation Come To Tennessee?," *Kingsport Times-News*, October 11, 1970, 67.

32. *Highland Echo* 61, no. 23, 1976 primary poll, May 3, 1976, 6; Emerson Henderson, "Echo Primary results," *Highland Echo* 61, no. 25, May 14, 1976, 3.

33. Emerson Henderson, "Echo Primary results," *Highland Echo* 61, no. 25, May 14, 1976, 3.

34. Gilmore, "The Dynamics of Second-Wave Feminist Activism in Memphis, 1971–1982"; Allured, *Remapping Second-Wave Feminism*. For more on the national movement over gender equality, see also Spruill, *Divided We Stand* and Spruill, "Gender and America's Right Turn" in *Rightward Bound*.

35. Italics in original. [No first name given] Cherrington '74, "Guest editorial: 'Does it really matter whom we choose to love . . .?'" *Highland Echo* 58, no. 8, November 3, 1972, 2.

36. "Our Unorthodox Junior Class Does it Again," *Highland Echo*, no. 7, February 28, 1970, 1; "Spring Cleaning," *Highland Echo*, no. 8, March 6, 1970, 5; "Why April 22 is Important to You," *Highland Echo*, no. 3, April 17, 1970, 1.

37. "Everybody's talking about pollution. Woodsy Owl has 104 ways to stop it," *Highland Echo* 58, no. 1, September 8, 1972, 4.

38. Italics in original. Rick Mitz, "It's the right time: The Relevancy of relevance," *Highland Echo* 57, no. 24), May 5, 1972, 2.

39. Albert Gore Research Center, Middle Tennessee State University, Jim Baskin, "Baskin suggests alternative symbol," *Sidelines*, December 14, 1971, 7.

40. Susan E. Carver, "Readers' Forum: Defends U-T Student Action," *Kingsport Times*, March 13, 1969, 25.

41. Carter, "Deep South Campus Memories and the World the Sixties Made," foreword in *Rebellion in Black and White*, eds. Cohen and Snyder, viii–ix. The full title of the book was *Masters of Deceit: The Story of Communism in America and How to Fight It*, published in 1958. For more on Hoover's concerns, see Gerstle, *American Crucible*, 243–45.

42. Fairclough, *Race & Democracy*, 410.

BIBLIOGRAPHY

Archival Collections

Austin, Texas

Lyndon Baines Johnson Library and Museum
    National Advisory Commission on Civil Disorders
    Office Files of Frederick Panzer
    White House Central Files, 1963-69

Boston, Massachusetts

John F. Kennedy Presidential Library and Museum
    Burke Marshall Personal Papers
    White House Central Subject Files

Knoxville, Tennessee

The Beck Cultural Exchange Center
Modern Political Archives, University of Tennessee
    Richard Nixon/Billy Graham Episode Tapes, 1987
    William Emerson Brock Collection
Special Collections, John C. Hodges Library, University of Tennessee
    Carl and Anne Braden Papers
    Office of the University Historian Collection, 1819-1997

Madison, Wisconsin

Archives Division, Wisconsin Historical Society
    Carl and Anne Braden Papers, 1928-2006
    David Nolan Papers, 1960-87
    Highlander Research and Education Center Collection
    Students for a Democratic Society (SDS) Records, 1958-70

Maryville, Tennessee

Lamar Memorial Library and Archives, Maryville College
    Board Minutes and Recorder Copies 1956-61
    Reports of Board of Directors, 1946-50, 1950-57

Memphis, Tennessee

Memphis and Shelby County Room, Memphis Public Library
    The Everett R. Cook Oral History Collection
Rhodes College Archives and Special Collections
    President's Papers
    Student Handbooks

Special Collections, Ned R. McWherter Library, University of Memphis
    Dr. Cecil C. Humphreys Presidential Collection
    The Memphis Multi-Media Archival Project, The 1968 Sanitation Workers' Strike
    University Archives

Murfreesboro, Tennessee

Albert Gore Research Center, Middle Tennessee State University
    Forrest Hall Protest Collection
    Sidelines Collection

Nashville, Tennessee

The Nashville Room, Nashville Public Library
    The Civil Rights Periodicals Collection
Special Collections and Archives, Fisk University
    Arna Wendell Bontemps Collection, 1934–65
Special Collections and University Archives, Jean and Alexander Heard Library, Vanderbilt University
    Edwin (Ed) Hamlett Papers
    Nelson and Marian D. Fuson Papers
    Box S.S.O.C. Reunion—2002

New Haven, Connecticut

Manuscripts and Archives, Sterling Memorial Library, Yale University
    C. Vann Woodward Papers

Sewanee, Tennessee

University Archives and Special Collections, Sewanee: The University of the South
    University Records, Executive Offices, Vice-Chancellor
    Edward McCrady, 1951–71

Washington, District of Columbia

The Library of Congress
    Southern School News Collection

Yorba Linda, California

Richard Nixon Presidential Library and Museum
    H. R. Haldeman Diaries
    White House Central Files
    White House Communications Agency Sound Recording Collection

Online Archival Materials

Constance W. Curry Papers, Manuscript, Archives, and Rare Book Library, Robert W. Woodruff Library, Emory University. http://pid.emory.edu/ark:/25593/8z61z.
Eleanor Roosevelt Papers Project, George Washington University. https://www2.gwu.edu/~erpapers/myday/1938/. https://erpapers.columbian.gwu.edu/.
FBI Records: The Vault. http://vault.fbi.gov/.
Freedom Summer Digital Collection, Wisconsin Historical Society. http://content.wisconsinhistory.org/cdm/landingpage/collection/p15932coll2.
MTSU Collection, MTSU Miscellaneous, Albert Gore Research Center, Middle Tennessee State University. http://www.mtsu.edu/gorecenter/.

Oral History Interviews Conducted by Author

Booker, Robert J., December 12, 2013.
Clowney, Shirley Carr, August 12, 2014.
Rollins, Avon, December 27, 2013.
Wiersema Jr., Harry, August 7, 2014.
Wright, Nancy Smith, August 6, 2014.

Published Oral History Interviews

Civil Rights Oral History Project, Nashville Room, Nashville Public Library
    Allen, Archie Eugene, interviewed by Kathy Bennett, September 30, 2003.
    Bevel, Rev. James, and Rev. Bernard Lafayette Jr. with Rip Patton, interviewed by Kathy Bennett, January 17, 2003.
    Carawan, Guy, and Candie Carawan, interviewed by Kathy Bennett, January 17, 2003.
    Vivian, Dr. C. T., and Octavia Vivian, interviewed by Kathy Bennett, May 12, 2003.
    Walker Jr., Matthew, interviewed by Kathy Bennett, September 3, 2004.
Crossroads To Freedom, Oral History Collection, Rhodes College. http://hdl.handle.net/10267/33498
    Short, Bill, interviewed by Joshua Jeffries, July 27, 2007.
Civil Rights Oral Histories, The Everett R. Cook Oral History Collection, Memphis and Shelby County Room, Memphis Public Library
    Smith, Coby, interviewed by Thomas Faist, September 19, 1983.
Eyes on the Prize: The Complete Series, Henry Hampton Collection, Washington University Film and Media Archive
    Campbell, Reverend Will D., interviewed by Orlando Bagwell, November 3, 1985. http://mavisweb.wulib.wustl.edu:81/mavisDetail/TitleWork/key/1033.
Oral History of the Tennessee Valley Authority, Oral History Collection, Special Collections Department, University Libraries, The University of Memphis
    Wiersema Sr., Harry, interviewed by Charles W. Crawford, September 24, 1969.
Richard Nixon/Billy Graham Episode Tapes, 1987, Modern Political Archives, University of Tennessee (MPA.190)
    Anderson, Kathleen, May 7, 1987, #2.
    Hoyle, Zoe, May 12, 1987, #7.
    Lacey, Dr. Forrest, May 26, 1987, #8.
    Newton, Dr. Kenneth, April 27, 1987, #12.
    Pollio, Dr. Howard, May 7, 1987, #15.
    Reynolds, Dr. Charles H., April 27, 1987, #16.
    Tomlinson, Michael, May 22, 1987, #18.
    Verplanck, Dr. William, May 20, 1987, #19.
    Weaver, Dr. Charles, June 1, 1937, #21.
    Yovella, Ed, May 26, 1987, #24.
"A Sense of Revolution," *The Vietnam War: East Tennessee*, East Tennessee Public Broadcasting Service (PBS), 2017. Transcripts in possession of author.
    Alspaugh, JoAnn, n.d. (video)
    Fleming, Cynthia, n.d. (video)
    Heatherly, Gary, n.d.
    Minor, Al, February 10, 2017.
    Rucker, James "Sparky," February 17, 2017.

Southern Oral History Program Collection, University of North Carolina at Chapel Hill
> Clowney, Shirley Carr, Interview U-0618, interviewed by Joey Fink, May 20, 2011.
> West, Don, Interview E-0016, interviewed by Jacquelyn Hall, January 22, 1975.

University of Tennessee Special Collections and Archives
> Baxter, Jimmie, interviewed by Jamie Roberts, December 2, 1993.

Correspondence Conducted by Author

Bible, Carroll, May, June, and November 2014.
Bozeman, Barry, March and June 2014.
Carawan, Candie, February 2013.
Frissell, Lee, April 2011. Conducted by historian Jeffrey Turner, emails in possession of author.
Frissell, Lee, March 2013 and May 2016.

Periodicals

The Apex
Brotherhood
The Chattanooga News-Free Press
The Chicago Defender
The Commercial Appeal
The Commercial Appeal Mid-South Magazine
Congressional Record
The Daily Beacon
The Daily News-Journal
The Daily Times
Fisk News
The Highland Echo
Highlander Reports
Kingsport Times-News
Knoxville Flashlight-Herald
The Knoxville News-Sentinel
Kudzu
The Liberator
Logos
Memphis Press-Scimitar
The Metro Pulse
The Nashville Banner
The Nation
National Review
New Left Notes
The New Rebel
The New York Times
The Newsletter: Southern Student Organizing Committee
Rodent
Root and Branch
The Sewanee Purple
Sidelines
The Southern Patriot
Southern School News
Southwestern News
The Sou'wester
The Stanford Daily
The Summer Beacon
The Tennessean
The Times-Herald
The University of Memphis Magazine
The Vanderbilt Hustler
Vanderbilt Register
Viewpoint Magazine
The Voice of the Movement

PhD Dissertations

Broadhurst, Christopher James. "The Silent Campus Speaks: North Carolina State University and the National Student Protest, May 1970." PhD diss., North Carolina State University, 2012.
deGregory, Crystal A. "Raising a Nonviolent Army: Four Nashville Black Colleges and the Century-Long Struggle For Civil Rights, 1830s–1930s." PhD diss., Vanderbilt University, 2011.
Favors, Jelani Manu-Gowon. "Shelter in a Time of Storm: Black Colleges and the Rise of Student Activism in Jackson, Mississippi." PhD diss., Ohio State University, 2006.

Kinchen, Shirletta Jeanette. "'We Want What People Generally Refer to as Black Power': Youth and Student Activism and the Impact of the Black Power Movement in Memphis, Tennessee, 1965–1975." PhD diss., University of Memphis, 2011.

Lee, Barry Everett. "The Nashville Civil Rights Movement: A Study of the Phenomenon of Intentional Leadership Development and its Consequences for Local Movements and the National Civil Rights Movement." PhD diss., Georgia State University, 2010.

Lorenzini, Jack Brian. "'Power Concedes Nothing Without a Demand': Student Activism at Memphis State University in the 1960s." PhD diss., University of Memphis, 2014.

Mariner, Nicholas Scott. "'People Who Look Like Me': Community Space and Power in a Segregated East Tennessee School." PhD diss., University of Tennessee, 2010.

Parr, Stephen Eugene. "The Forgotten Radicals: The New Left in the Deep South, Florida State University, 1960–1972." PhD diss., Florida State University, 2000.

Saunders, Richard L. "Encouraged By a Little Progress: Voting Rights and the Contests Over Social Place and Civil Society in Tennessee's Fayette and Haywood Counties, 1958–1964." PhD diss., University of Memphis, 2012.

Sumner, David E. "The Local Press and the Nashville Student Movement, 1960." PhD diss., University of Tennessee, 1989.

Taylor, Kieran Walsh. "Turn to the Working Class: The New Left, Black Liberation, and the U.S. Labor Movement (1967–1981)." PhD diss., University of North Carolina at Chapel Hill, 2007.

Visser-Maessen, Laura. "A *Lot* of Leaders? Robert Parris Moses, SNCC, and Leadership in the Production of Social Change during the American Civil Rights Movement, 1960–1965." PhD diss., Universiteit Leiden, 2013.

Master's Theses

Duke, Kira Virginia. "To Disturb the People as Little as Possible: The Desegregation of Memphis City Schools." Master's thesis, University of Tennessee, 2005.

Harris, Jessie. "Unfamiliar Streets: The Chattanooga Sit-Ins, the Local Press, and the Concern for Civilities." Master's thesis, Virginia Commonwealth University, 2011.

Online Materials and Press Releases

"Alexander Heard, Vanderbilt's fifth chancellor, dies." Last modified July 25, 2009. http://news.vanderbilt.edu/2009/07/alexander-heard-vanderbilts-fifth-chancellor-dies-85205/.

Bozeman, Barry. "40 Year Flashback—Nixon & Graham at Tennessee." *Daily Kos* Online news site. May 28, 2010. http://www.dailykos.com/story/2010/5/28/864563/-.

Calise, Sarah. "Protesting the Confederacy on Campus." *The Activist History Review*. July 25, 2018. https://activisthistory.com/2018/07/25/protesting-the-confederacy-on-campus/.

"Celebrating Change: Courage, Determination and Inclusion." Vanderbilt University. n.d. http://www.vanderbilt.edu/celebratingblackhistory/.

Howard, Josh. "A Confederate on Campus: Nathan Bedford Forrest as MTSU's Mascot." Online blog included in the Forrest Hall Protest Collection, Albert Gore Research Center, Middle Tennessee State University. August 25, 2015. https://digital.mtsu.edu/digital/collection/p15838coll11/id/122/.

Lorence, James J. "Don West (1906–1992)." New Georgia Encyclopedia. December 17, 2015. http://www.georgiaencyclopedia.org/articles/arts-culture/don-west-1906-1992.

"The Movement and Its Legacy: A Panel Discussion with Civil Rights Veterans." Wisconsin Historical Society. April 17, 2014. https://vimeo.com/92429752.

NAACP Resolution. "Celebrating The Life Of Maxine A. Smith." 2013. https://naacp.org/resources/celebrating-life-maxine-smith.

Report of the National Advisory Commission on Civil Disorders. National Criminal Justice Reference Service. 1967. https://www.ncjrs.gov/pdffiles1/Digitization/8073NCJRS.pdf.

Schexnayder, C. J. "The Integration of Football in the Southeastern Conference." SB Nation (Vox Media). May 9, 2012. http://www.teamspeedkills.com/2012/5/9/3008248/the-integration-of-football-in-the-southeastern-conference.

Statistical Abstract of the United States: 1938. http://www.census.gov/library/publications/1939/compendia/statab/60ed.html.

Weathersbee, Tonyaa. "Anonymous no more: Honoring African-American Fort Pillow victims." *Commercial Appeal*. April 13, 2017. https://eu.commercialappeal.com/story/news/columnists/2017/04/12/anonymous-no-more-ceremony-honors-african-american-ft-pillow-victims/100281168/.

Materials in Possession of the Author

Intimidation Reprisal and Violence in the South's Racial Crisis. Southeastern Office, American Friends Service Committee, Department of Racial and Cultural Relations, National Council of the Churches of Christ in the United States of America, and Southern Regional Council, 1960.

"Leadership award at Maryville College named for alumna Nancy Smith Wright." Maryville College Office of Communications press release, May 23, 2006.

The Maryville College Miss: WSGA Handbook for Resident Women, 1963–64.

School Desegregation in Tennessee: 12 Districts Released from Desegregation Orders, 17 Districts Remain Under Court Jurisdiction. Tennessee Advisory Committee to the United States Commission on Civil Rights, April 2008.

Yarbro, Karen, ed. *Fifty Years of Social Activism at the Tennessee Valley Unitarian Universalist Church*, March 2001.

Published Books

Adams, Frank, and Myles Horton. *Unearthing Seeds of Fire: The Idea of Highlander*. Winston-Salem, N.C.: John F. Blair Publisher, 1975.

Akins, Bill, and Genevieve Wiggins. *Keeping The Faith: A History of Tennessee Wesleyan College, 1857–2007*. Athens, Tenn.: Tennessee Wesleyan College, 2007.

Alinsky, Saul. *Rules for Radicals: A Practical Primer for Realistic Radicals*. New York: Random House, 1971.

Allured, Janet. *Remapping Second-Wave Feminism: The Long Women's Rights Movement in Louisiana, 1950–1997*. Athens: University of Georgia Press, 2016.

Altbach, Philip G. *Student Politics in America: A Historical Analysis*. New York: McGraw Hill, 1974.

Altman, Jake. *Socialism before Sanders: The 1930s Moment from Romance to Revisionism*. Cham, Switzerland: Palgrave Macmillan, 2019.

Anderson, Karen. *Little Rock: Race and Resistance at Central High School*. Princeton: Princeton University Press, 2010.

Anderson, Terry H. *The Movement and the Sixties*. Oxford: Oxford University Press, 1995.

Andrew III, John A. *The Other Side of the Sixties: Young Americans for Freedom and the Rise of Conservative Politics*. London: Rutgers University Press, 1997.

Appy, Christian G. *American Reckoning: The Vietnam War and Our National Identity*. New York: Penguin, 2015.

Arsenault, Raymond. *Freedom Riders: 1961 and the Struggle for Racial Justice.* Oxford: Oxford University Press, 2006.
Avorn, Jerry L. *University In Revolt: A History of the Columbia Crisis.* London: Macdonald, 1969.
Badger, Anthony J. *New Deal/New South: An Anthony J. Badger Reader.* Fayetteville: University of Arkansas Press, 2007.
Bailey, Beth. *Sex in the Heartland.* Cambridge, Mass.: Harvard University Press, 1999.
Bailey, D'Army, and Roger Easson. *The Education of a Black Radical: A Southern Civil Rights Activist's Journey, 1959-1964.* Baton Rouge: Louisiana State University Press, 2009.
Bartley, Numan V. *The Rise of Massive Resistance: Race and Politics in the South During the 1950's.* Baton Rouge: Louisiana State University Press, 1969.
Billingsley, William J. *Communists on Campus: Race, Politics, and the Public University in Sixties North Carolina.* Athens: University of Georgia Press, 1999.
Biondi, Martha. *The Black Revolution on Campus.* Berkeley: University of California Press, 2012.
Black, Earl, and Merle Black. *Politics and Society in the South.* Cambridge, Mass.: Harvard University Press, 1989.
Booker, Robert J. *200 Years of Black Culture in Knoxville, Tennessee: 1791-1991.* Virginia Beach: Donning, 1993.
Borstelmann, Thomas. *The Cold War and the Color Line.* Cambridge, Mass.: Harvard University Press, 2003
Braden, Anne. *The Wall Between.* Knoxville: University of Tennessee Press, 1999.
Branch, Taylor. *Pillar of Fire: America in the King Years, 1963-1965.* New York: Simon & Schuster, 1998.
Breines, Wini. *Community and Organization in the New Left, 1962-1968: The Great Refusal.* New York: Praeger, 1982
———. *The Trouble Between Us: An Uneasy History of White and Black Women in the Feminist Movement.* Oxford: Oxford University Press, 2006.
Brenner, Aaron, Benjamin Day, and Immanuel Ness, eds. *The Encyclopedia of Strikes in American History.* New York: Routledge, 2015.
Brick, Howard, and Christopher Phelps. *Radicals in America: The US. Left Since the Second World War.* Cambridge: Cambridge University Press, 2015.
Brisbane, Robert H. *Black Activism: Racial Revolution in the United States, 1954-1970.* Valley Forge, Penn: Judson Press, 1974.
Brown, Sarah Hart. *Standing Against Dragons: Three Southern Lawyers in an Era of Fear.* Baton Rouge: Louisiana State University Press, 1998.
Carson, Clayborne. *In Struggle: SNCC and the Black Awakening of the 1960s.* Cambridge, Mass.: Harvard University Press, 1981.
Carson, Clayborne, David J. Garrow, Gerald Gill, Vincent Harding, and Darlene Clark Hine, eds. *Eyes On the Prize Civil Rights Reader: Documents, Speeches, and Firsthand Accounts from the Black Freedom Struggle, 1954-1990.* New York: Penguin, 1991.
Chafe, William H. *Civilities and Civil Rights: Greensboro, North Carolina, and the Black Struggle for Freedom.* Oxford: Oxford University Press, 1980.
Chappell, David L. *Inside Agitators: White Southerners in the Civil Rights Movement.* Baltimore: Johns Hopkins University Press, 1994.
Charron, Katherine Mellen. *Freedom's Teacher: The Life of Septima Clark.* Chapel Hill: University of North Carolina Press, 2009.

Cobb, James C. *The Selling of the South: The Southern Crusade for Industrial Development, 1936–1990*. 2nd ed. Urbana: University of Illinois Press, 1993.
———. *The South and America Since World War II*. Oxford: Oxford University Press, 2011.
Cohen, Robert. *Freedom's Orator: Mario Savio and the Radical Legacy of the 1960s*. Oxford: Oxford University Press, 2009.
———. *When the Old Left Was Young: Student Radicals and America's First Mass Student Movement, 1929–1941*. Oxford: Oxford University Press, 1993.
Cook, Robert J. *Civil War Memories: Contesting the Past in the United States since 1865*. Baltimore: Johns Hopkins University Press, 2017.
Cotham, Perry C. *Toil, Turmoil, & Triumph: A Portrait of the Tennessee Labor Movement*. Franklin, Tenn.: Hillsboro Press, 1995.
Cunningham, David. *Klansville U.S.A.: The Rise and Fall of the Civil Rights-era Ku Klux Klan*. Oxford: Oxford University Press, 2012.
Dittmer, John. *Local People: The Struggle for Civil Rights in Mississippi*. Urbana: University of Illinois Press, 2003.
Doyle, Don H. *Nashville Since the 1920s*. Knoxville: University of Tennessee Press, 1985.
Draper, Alan. *Conflict of Interests: Organized Labor and the Civil Rights Movement in the South, 1954–1968*. Ithaca, N.Y.: ILR Press, 1994.
Dudziak, Mary L. *Cold War Civil Rights: Race and the Image of American Democracy*. Princeton: Princeton University Press, 2000.
Durr, Virginia Foster. *Outside the Magic Circle: The Autobiography of Virginia Foster Durr*. Tuscaloosa: University of Alabama Press, 1985.
Egerton, John. *Speak Now Against the Day: The Generation Before the Civil Rights Movement in the South*. Chapel Hill: University of North Carolina Press, 1995.
Erickson, Ansley T. *Making the Unequal Metropolis: School Desegregation and Its Limits*. Chicago: The University of Chicago Press, 2016.
von Eschen, Penny M. *Race Against Empire: Black Americans and Anticolonialism, 1937–1957*. Ithaca, N.Y.: Cornell University Press, 2014.
Estes, Steve. *I Am a Man! Race, Manhood, and the Civil Rights Movement*. Chapel Hill: University of North Carolina Press, 2005.
Evans, Sara. *Personal Politics: The Roots of Women's Liberation in the Civil Rights Movement*. New York: Knopf, 1980.
Fairclough, Adam. *Race & Democracy: The Civil Rights Struggle in Louisiana, 1915–1972*. 2nd ed. Athens: The University of Georgia Press, 2008.
Farber, David. *Chicago '68*. Chicago: The University of Chicago Press, 1988.
———, ed. *The Sixties: From Memory to History*. Chapel Hill: The University of North Carolina Press, 1994.
Farrell, James. *The Spirit of the Sixties: Making Postwar Radicalism*. London: Routledge, 1997.
Favors, Jelani M. *Shelter in a Time of Storm: How Black Colleges Fostered Generations of Leadership and Activism*. Chapel Hill: University of North Carolina Press, 2019.
Fleming, Cynthia. *Soon We Will Not Cry: The Liberation of Ruby Doris Smith Robinson*. Lanham, Md.: Rowman & Littlefield, 1998.
Foley, Michael S. *Confronting the War Machine: Draft Resistance During the Vietnam War*. Chapel Hill: University of North Carolina Press, 2003.
———. *Front Porch Politics: The Forgotten Heyday of American Activism in the 1970s and 1980s*. New York: Hill and Wang, 2013.

Fosl, Catherine. *Subversive Southerner: Anne Braden and the Struggle for Racial Justice in the Cold War South*. Lexington: University of Kentucky Press, 2006.
Franklin, Sekou M. *After the Rebellion: Black Youth, Social Movement Activism, and the Post-Civil Rights Generation*. New York: New York University Press, 2014.
Freeman, Margaret L. *Women of Discriminating Taste: White Sororities and the Making of American Ladyhood*. Athens: University of Georgia Press, 2020.
Frost, Jennifer. *"An Interracial Movement of the Poor": Community Organizing and the New Left in the 1960s*. New York: New York University Press, 2001.
Fry, Joseph A. *The American South and the Vietnam War: Belligerence, Protest, and Agony in Dixie*. Lexington: University Press of Kentucky, 2015.
Garrow, David J. *Protest At Selma: Martin Luther King, Jr., and the Voting Rights Act of 1965*. New Haven: Yale University Press, 1978.
Gerstle, Gary. *American Crucible: Race and Nation in the Twentieth Century*. 2nd ed. Princeton: Princeton University Press, 2017.
Gildea, Robert, James Mark, and Anette Warring, eds. *Europe's 1968 Voices of Revolt*. Oxford: Oxford University Press, 2013.
Gilmore, Glenda. *Defying Dixie: The Radical Roots of Civil Rights, 1919-1950*. New York: Norton, 2008.
Gilpin, Patrick J., and Marybeth Gasman. *Charles S. Johnson: Leadership Beyond the Veil in the Age of Jim Crow*. Albany: State University of New York Press, 2003.
Gitlin, Todd. *The Sixties: Years of Hope, Days of Rage*. New York: Bantam, 1987.
Glen, John M. *Highlander: No Ordinary School, 1932-1962*. Lexington: University Press of Kentucky, 1988.
Gosse, Van. *The Movements of the New Left, 1950-1975: A Brief History with Documents*. New York: Bedford/St. Martin's, 2005.
———. *Rethinking the New Left: An Interpretative History*. New York: Palgrave Macmillan, 2005.
Goudsouzian, Aram, and Charles W. McKinney, Jr., eds. *An Unseen Light: Black Struggles for Freedom in Memphis, Tennessee*. Lexington: University Press of Kentucky, 2018.
Grace, Thomas M. *Kent State: Death and Dissent in the Long Sixties*. Boston: University of Massachusetts Press, 2016.
Graham, Hugh Davis. *Crisis in Print: Desegregation and the Press in Tennessee*. Nashville: Vanderbilt University Press, 1967.
Green, Laurie B. *Battling the Plantation Mentality: Memphis and the Black Freedom Struggle*. Chapel Hill: University of North Carolina Press, 2007.
Greene, Christina. *Our Separate Ways: Women and the Black Freedom Movement in Durham, North Carolina*. Chapel Hill: University of North Carolina Press, 2005.
Halberstam, David. *The Children*. New York: Ballantine Books, 1999
Hall, Simon. *American Patriotism, American Protest: Social Movements Since the Sixties*. Philadelphia: University of Pennsylvania Press, 2010.
———. *Peace and Freedom: The Civil Rights and Antiwar Movements in the 1960s*. Philadelphia: University of Pennsylvania Press, 2005.
———. *Rethinking the American Anti-War Movement: American Social and Political Movements of the Twentieth Century*. Abingdon-on-Thames: Routledge, 2012.
Hamburger, Robert, ed. *Our Portion of Hell: Fayette County, Tennessee: An Oral History of the Struggle for Civil Rights*. New York: Links, 1973.
Hartman, Andrew. *A War for the Soul of America: A History of the Culture Wars*. Chicago: University of Chicago Press, 2015.

Hayden, Tom. *The Port Huron Statement: The Visionary Call of the 1960s Revolution*. New York: Thunder's Mouth, 2005.
Haynes, Stephen B. *The Last Segregated Hour: The Memphis Kneel-Ins and the Campaign for Southern Church Desegregation*. Oxford: Oxford University Press, 2012.
Haynie, Aeron, and Timothy S. Miller, eds. *A Memoir of the New Left: The Political Autobiography of Charles A. Haynie*. Knoxville: University of Tennessee Press, 2009.
Heard, Alexander. *Speaking of the University: Two Decades at Vanderbilt*. Nashville: Vanderbilt University Press, 1995.
Heineman, Kenneth J. *Campus Wars: The Peace Movement at American State Universities in the Vietnam Era*. New York: New York University Press, 1993.
Hershberger, Mary. *Traveling to Vietnam: American Peace Activists and the War*. Syracuse: Syracuse University Press, 1998.
Hess, Earl J. *Lincoln Memorial University and the Shaping of Appalachia*. Knoxville: University of Tennessee Press, 2011.
Hoffschwelle, Mary S. *The Rosenwald Schools of the American South*. Gainesville: University Press of Florida, 2006.
Holt, Len. *The Summer That Didn't End*. London: Heinemann, 1966.
Honey, Michael K. *Black Workers Remember: An Oral History of Segregation, Unionism, and the Freedom Struggle*. Berkeley: University of California Press, 2002.
———. *Going Down Jericho Road: The Memphis Strike, Martin Luther King's Last Campaign*. London: Norton, 2007.
Horton, Aimee Isgrig. *The Highlander Folk School: A History of Its Major Programs, 1932–1961*. New York: Carlson, 1989.
Horton, Myles, and Judith and Herbert Kohl. *The Long Haul: An Autobiography*. New York: Teachers College Press, 1997.
Houston, Benjamin. *The Nashville Way: Racial Etiquette and the Struggle for Social Justice in a Southern City*. Athens: University of Georgia Press, 2012.
Isserman, Maurice. *If I Had a Hammer ... The Death of the Old Left and the Birth of the New Left*. New York: Basic Books, 1987.
Isserman, Maurice, and Michael Kazin. *America Divided: The Civil War of the 1960s*. 4th ed. Oxford and New York: Oxford University Press, 2011.
Janda, Sarah Eppler. *Prairie Power: Student Activism, Counterculture, and Backlash in Oklahoma, 1962–1972*. Norman: University of Oklahoma Press, 2018.
de Jong, Greta. *You Can't Eat Freedom: Southerners and Social Justice after the Civil Rights Movement*. Chapel Hill: University of North Carolina Press, 2016.
Joseph, Peniel E., ed. *The Black Power Movement: Rethinking the Civil Rights–Black Power Era*. London: Routledge, 2006.
Kazin, Michael. *The Populist Persuasion: An American History*. Ithaca, N.Y.: Cornell University Press, 1995.
Kean, Melissa. *Desegregating Private Higher Education in the South: Duke, Emory, Tulane, and Vanderbilt*. Baton Rouge: Louisiana State University Press, 2008.
Kieran, David. *Forever Vietnam: How a Divisive War Changed American Public Memory*. Amherst: University of Massachusetts Press, 2014.
Kiffmeyer, Thomas. *Reformers to Radicals: The Appalachian Volunteers and the War on Poverty*. Lexington: The University Press of Kentucky, 2009.
Kinchen, Shirletta J. *Black Power in the Bluff City: African American Youth and Student Activism in Memphis, 1965–1975*. Knoxville: University of Tennessee Press, 2016.
Klatch, Rebecca E. *A Generation Divided: The New Left, the New Right, and the 1960s*. Berkeley: University of California Press, 1999.

Korstad, Robert. *Civil Rights Unionism: Tobacco Workers and the Struggle for Democracy in the Mid-Twentieth-Century South.* Chapel Hill: University of North Carolina Press, 2003.
Kruse, Kevin M. *White Flight: Atlanta and the Making of Modern Conservatism.* Princeton: Princeton University Press, 2007.
Kruse, Kevin M., and Stephen Tuck, eds. *Fog of War: The Second World War and the Civil Rights Movement.* Oxford: Oxford University Press, 2012.
Lamis, Alexander P. *The Two-Party South.* 2nd ed. Oxford: Oxford University Press, 1990.
——, ed. *Southern Politics in the 1990s.* Baton Rouge: Louisiana State University Press, 1999.
Lassiter, Matthew, and Joseph Crespino, eds. *The Myth of Southern Exceptionalism.* Oxford: Oxford University Press, 2009.
Lawson, Steven F., and Charles M. Payne. *Debating the Civil Rights Movement: 1945–1968.* Lanham, Md.: Rowman & Littlefield, 2006.
Lawson, Steven F. *Running for Freedom: Civil Rights and Black Politics in America since 1941.* Chichester: Wiley-Blackwell, 2009.
Lesene, Henry H. *A History of the University of South Carolina, 1940–2000.* Columbia: University of South Carolina Press, 2001.
Levy, Peter B. *The New Left and Labor in the 1960s.* Champaign: University of Illinois Press, 1994.
Lewis, George. *Massive Resistance: The White Response to the Civil Rights Movement.* New York: Oxford University Press, 2006.
Lewis, John, and Michael D'Orso. *Walking With the Wind: A Memoir of the Movement.* New York: Simon & Schuster, 1998.
Lichtenstein, Nelson. *State of the Union: A Century of American Labor.* Princeton: Princeton University Press, 2003.
Lieberman, Robbie. *Prairie Power: Voices of 1960s Midwestern Student Protest.* Columbia: University of Missouri Press, 2004.
Lipset, Seymour Martin. *Rebellion in the University: A History of Student Activism in America.* Abingdon-on-Thames: Routledge and K. Paul Press, 1972.
Little, Kimberly K. *You Must Be From the North: Southern White Women in the Memphis Civil Rights Movement.* Jackson: University Press of Mississippi, 2009.
Lovett, Bobby L. *The Civil Rights Movement in Tennessee: A Narrative History.* Knoxville: University of Tennessee Press, 2005.
Lucks, Daniel S. *Selma to Saigon: The Civil Rights Movement and the Vietnam War.* Lexington: University Press of Kentucky, 2014.
Marshall, J. Stanley. *The Tumultuous Sixties: Campus Unrest and Student Life at a Southern University.* Tallahassee, Fla.: Sentry Press, 2006.
Marwick, Arthur. *The Sixties: Cultural Revolution in Britain, France, Italy, and the United States, c. 1958–c. 1974.* Oxford: Oxford University Press, 1998.
Maxwell, Angie, and Todd G. Shields, eds. *Unlocking V. C. Key, Jr.: Southern Politics for the Twenty-First Century.* Fayetteville: University of Arkansas Press, 2011.
McAdam, Doug. *Freedom Summer.* New York: Oxford University Press, 1988.
——. *Political Process and the Development of Black Insurgency, 1930–1970.* 2nd ed. Chicago: University of Chicago Press, 1999.
Michel, Gregg. *Struggle For a Better South: The Southern Student Organizing Committee, 1964–1969.* New York: Palgrave McMillan, 2004.
Miles, Michael W. *The Radical Probe: The Logic of Student Rebellion.* New York: Atheneum, 1973.

Miller, Steven P. *Billy Graham and the Rise of the Republican South*. Philadelphia: University of Pennsylvania Press, 2009.

Mills, Kay. *This Little Light of Mine: The Life of Fannie Lou Hamer*. Lexington: University of Kentucky Press, 2007.

Mills, Nicolaus. *Like a Holy Crusade: Mississippi 1964—The Turning of the Civil Rights Movement in America*. Chicago: Ivan R. Dee, 1992.

Minchin, Timothy J. *The Color of Work: The Struggle For Civil Rights in the Southern Paper Industry*. Chapel Hill: University of North Carolina Press, 2001.

Minton, John Dean. *The New Deal in Tennessee, 1932–1938*. New York: Garland, 1979.

Morris, Aldon D. *The Origins of the Civil Rights Movement: Black Communities Organizing for Change*. New York: Free Press, 1984.

Nash, Diane. *Diane Nash: The Fire of the Civil Rights Movement: A Biography*. Miami: Barnhardt & Ashe, 2007.

Nasstrom, Kathryn L. *Everybody's Grandmother and Nobody's Fool: Frances Freeborn Pauley and the Struggle for Social Justice*. Ithaca, N.Y.: Cornell University Press, 2000.

Nelson, Bruce. *Divided We Stand: American Workers and the Struggle for Black Equality*. Princeton: Princeton University Press, 2001.

Ogren, Christine A., and Marc A. VanOverbeke, eds. *Rethinking Campus Life: New Perspectives on the History of College Students in the United States*. London: Palgrave Macmillan, 2018.

Parsons, Sara M. *From Southern Wrongs to Civil Rights: The Memoir of a White Civil Rights Activist*. Tuscaloosa: University of Alabama Press, 2000.

Patterson, James T. *The Eve of Destruction: How 1965 Transformed America*. New York: Basic Books, 2012.

———. *Grand Expectations: The United States, 1945–1974*. New York: Oxford University Press, 1996.

Payne, Charles M. *I've Got the Light of Freedom: The Organizing Tradition and the Mississippi Freedom Struggle*. Berkeley: University of California Press, 1997.

Perlstein, Rick. *Nixonland: The Rise of a President and the Fracturing of America*. New York: Scribner, 2008.

Pittard, Homer. *The First Fifty Years: Middle Tennessee State College, 1911–1961*. Murfreesboro: Middle Tennessee State College, 1961.

Pohlmann, Marcus D., and Michael P. Kirby. *Racial Politics at the Crossroads: Memphis Elects Dr. W. W. Herenton*. Knoxville: University of Tennessee Press, 1996.

Proudfoot, Merrill. *Diary of a Sit-In*. 2nd ed. New Haven: College and University Press, 1990.

Raines, Howell. *My Soul Is Rested: Movement Days in the Deep South Remembered*. New York: G. P. Putnam's Sons, 1977.

Reed, Linda. *Simple Decency & Common Sense: The Southern Conference Movement, 1938–1963*. Bloomington: Indiana University Press, 1991.

Roberts, Gene, and Hank Klibanoff. *The Race Beat: The Press, the Civil Rights Struggle, and the Awakening of a Nation*. New York: Vintage, 2006.

Rogers, Ibram H. *The Black Campus Movement: Black Students and the Racial Reconstitution of Higher Education, 1965–1972*. New York: Palgrave MacMillan, 2012.

Rossinow, Doug. *The Politics of Authenticity: Liberalism, Christianity, and the New Left in America*. New York: Columbia University Press, 1998.

———. *Visions of Progress: The Left-Liberal Tradition in America*. Philadelphia: University of Pennsylvania, 2008.

Scanlon, Sandra. *The Pro-War Movement: Domestic Support for the Vietnam War and the

Making of Modern American Conservatism. Amherst: University of Massachusetts Press, 2013.

Schulman, Bruce J. *From Cotton Belt to Sunbelt: Federal Policy, Economic Development, and the Transformation of the South, 1938–1980*. Durham: Duke University Press, 1994.

———. *The Seventies: The Great Shift in American Culture, Society, and Politics*. Boston: Da Capo, 2001.

Schulman, Bruce J., and Julian E. Zelizer, eds. *Rightward Bound: Making America Conservative in the 1970s*. Cambridge, Mass.: Harvard University Press, 2008.

Sellers, Cleveland. *The River Of No Return: The Autobiography of a Black Militant and the Life and Death of SNCC*. Jackson: University Press of Mississippi, 1990.

Shafer, Byron E., and Richard Johnston. *The End of Southern Exceptionalism: Class, Race, and Partisan Change in the Postwar South*. Cambridge, Mass.: Harvard University Press, 2009.

Sitkoff, Harvard. *The Struggle for Black Equality, 1954–1980*. New York: Hill and Wang, 1981.

Slaughter, Sheila, and Gary Rhoades. *American Capitalism and the New Economy: Markets, State, and Higher Education*. Baltimore: Johns Hopkins University Press, 2004.

Smith, Gerald L. *A Black Educator in the Segregated South: Kentucky's Rufus B. Atwood*. Lexington: University Press of Kentucky, 1994.

Sonnie, Amy, and James Tracy. *Hillbilly Nationalists, Urban Race Rebels, and Black Power*. New York: Melville, 2011.

Sorrels, William. *The Exciting Years: The Cecil C. Humphreys Presidency of Memphis State University, 1960–1972*. Memphis: Memphis State University Press, 1987.

Spruill, Marjorie J. *Divided We Stand: The Battle Over Women's Rights and Family Values That Polarized American Politics*. New York: Bloomsbury Press, 2017.

Stefani, Anne. *Unlikely Dissenters: White Southern Women in the Fight for Racial Justice, 1920–1970*. Gainesville: University Press of Florida, 2015.

Stoper, Emily. *The Student Nonviolent Coordinating Committee: The Growth of Radicalism in a Civil Rights Organization*. Brooklyn: Carlson, 1989.

Street, Joe. *The Culture War in the Civil Rights Movement*. Gainesville: University Press of Florida, 2007.

Sullivan, Patricia. *Days of Hope: Race and Democracy in the New Deal Era*. Chapel Hill: University of North Carolina Press, 1996.

Thornton, J. Mills. *Dividing Lines: Municipal Politics and the Struggle for Civil Rights in Montgomery, Birmingham, and Selma*. Tuscaloosa: University of Alabama Press, 2002.

Tracy, James. *Direct Action: Radical Pacifism From the Union Eight to the Chicago Seven*. Chicago: University of Chicago Press, 1996.

Trouillot, Michel-Rolph. *Silencing the Past: Power and the Production of History*. Boston: Beacon, 1995.

Tuck, Stephen. *We Ain't What We Ought To Be: The Black Freedom Struggle From Emancipation to Obama*. Cambridge, Mass.: Harvard University Press, 2010.

Tucker, David M. *Memphis Since Crump: Bossism, Blacks, and Civic Reformers, 1948–1968*. Knoxville: University of Tennessee Press, 1980.

Turner, Jeffrey A. *Sitting In and Speaking Out: Student Movements in the American South, 1960–1970*. Athens: University of Georgia Press, 2010.

Tyler, Pamela. *Silk Stockings and Ballot Boxes: Women and Politics in New Orleans, 1920–1963*. Athens: University of Georgia Press, 1996.

Tyson, Timothy B. *Radio Free Dixie: Robert F. Williams and the Roots of Black Power*. Chapel Hill: University of North Carolina Press, 1999.

Van Deburg, William L. *New Day in Babylon: The Black Power Movement and American Culture, 1965–1975.* Chicago: University of Chicago Press, 1992.

Walker, Anders. *The Ghost of Jim Crow: How Southern Moderates Used Brown v. Board of Education to Stall Civil Rights.* New York: Oxford University Press, 2009.

Ward, Brian, and Tony Badger, eds. *The Making of Martin Luther King and the Civil Rights Movement.* New York: New York University Press, 1996.

Ward, Brian. *Radio and the Struggle for Civil Rights in the South.* Gainesville: University Press of Florida, 2004.

Webb, Clive. *Rabble Rousers: The American Far Right in the Civil Rights Era.* Athens: University of Georgia Press, 2010.

Weisbrot, Robert. *Freedom Bound: A History of America's Civil Rights Movement.* New York: Plume, 1990.

Wells, JoVita, ed. *A School For Freedom: Morristown College and Five Generations of Education for Blacks, 1868–1985.* Morristown, Tenn.: Morristown College, 1986.

Wells, Tom. *The War Within: America's Battle Over Vietnam.* Oakland: University of California Press, 1994.

Westheider, James E. *Fighting on Two Fronts: African Americans and the Vietnam War.* London: New York University Press, 1997.

Wheeler, William Bruce. *Knoxville, Tennessee: A Mountain City in the New South.* 2nd ed. Knoxville: University of Tennessee Press, 2005.

Wilkerson, Jessie. *To Live Here, You Have to Fight: How Women Led Appalachian Movements for Social Justice.* Champaign: University of Illinois Press, 2019.

Williamson, Joy Ann. *Radicalizing the Ebony Tower: Black Colleges and the Black Freedom Struggle in Mississippi.* New York: Teachers College Press, 2008.

Williamson Jr., Samuel R. *Sewanee Sesquicentennial History: The Making of the University of the South.* Sewanee, Tenn.: University of the South, 2008.

Woodard, Komozi. *A Nation within a Nation: Amiri Baraka (LeRoi Jones) & Black Power Politics.* Chapel Hill: University of North Carolina Press, 1999.

Published Articles and Chapters in Edited Volumes

Altbach, Philip G. "From Revolution to Apathy: American Student Activism in the 1970s." *Journal of Higher Education* 8, no. 6 (November 1979): 609–26.

Altbach, Philip G., and Robert Cohen. "American Student Activism: The Post-Sixties Transformation." *Journal of Higher Education* 61, no. 1 (January-February 1990): 32–49.

Anderson, Terry. "The New American Revolution: The Movement and Business." In *The Sixties: From Memory to History,* edited by David Farber, 175–205. Chapel Hill: University of North Carolina Press, 1994.

Anderson, Terry H. "Vietnam Is Here: The Antiwar Movement." In *The War That Never Ends: New Perspectives on the Vietnam War,* edited by David L. Anderson and John Ernst, 245–64. Lexington: University Press of Kentucky, 2007.

Arnesen, Eric. "Reconsidering the 'Long Civil Rights Movement.'" *Historically Speaking* 10, no. 2 (2009): 31–34.

Badger, Tony. "Lyndon Johnson and Albert Gore: Southern New Dealers and the Modern South." In *Poverty and Progress in the U.S. South Since 1920,* edited by Suzanne W. Jones and Mark Newman, 99–118. Amsterdam: VU University Press, 2006.

Blum, Michael. "'Everyone You Don't Like is a Communist': The Highlander Center and the Civil Rights Movement in Knoxville, 1961–1971." *Journal of East Tennessee History* 86 (2014): 57–76.

Blumenthal, Seth E. "Children of the 'Silent Majority': Richard Nixon's Young Voters for the President, 1972." *Journal of Policy History* 27, no. 2 (2015): 337–63.

Borden, Richard J., and Stuart P. Taylor. "The Social Instigation and Control of Physical Aggression." *Journal of Applied Social Psychology* 3, no. 4 (1973): 354–61.

Brauer, Carl M. "Women Activists, Southern Conservatives, and the Prohibition of Sex Discrimination in Title VII of the 1964 Civil Rights Act." *Journal of Southern History* 49 (1983): 37–56.

Brophy, William. "Active Acceptance—Active Containment: The Dallas Story." In *Southern Businessmen and Desegregation*, edited by Elizabeth Jacoway and David R. Colburn, 137–50. Baton Rouge: Louisiana State University Press, 1982.

Burton, Orville Vernon. "Dining With Harvey Gantt." In *Matthew J. Perry: The Man, His Times, and His Legacy*, edited by W. Lewis Burke and Belinda F. Gergel, 183–220. Columbia: University of South Carolina Press, 2004.

Carter, Dan T. "Deep South Campus Memories and the World the Sixties Made." Foreword in *Rebellion in Black and White: Southern Student Activism in the 1960s*, edited by Robert Cohen and David J. Snyder, vii–xviii. Baltimore: Johns Hopkins University Press, 2013.

———. "More than Race: Conservatism in the White South since V. O. Key Jr." In *Unlocking V. O. Key Jr.: Southern Politics for the Twenty-First Century*, edited by Angie Maxwell and Todd G. Shields, 129–60. Fayetteville: The University of Arkansas Press, 2011.

Cha-Jua, Sundiata Keita, and Clarence Lang. "The 'Long Movement' as Vampire: Temporal and Spatial Fallacies in Recent Black Freedom Studies." *Journal of African American History* 92, no. 2 (2007): 265–88.

Cohen, Robert. "Prophetic Minority versus Recalcitrant Majority: Southern Student Dissent and the Struggle for Progressive Change in the 1960s." Introduction in *Rebellion in Black and White: Southern Student Activism in the 1960s*, edited by Robert Cohen and David J. Snyder, 1–39. Baltimore: Johns Hopkins University Press, 2013.

Doggett, David. "*The Kudzu*: Birth and Death in Underground Mississippi." In *Insider Histories of the Vietnam Era Underground Press, Part 2*, edited by Ken Wachsberger, 121–52. East Lansing: Michigan State University Press, 2012.

Duhé, Gregory. "The FBI and Students for a Democratic Society at the University of New Orleans, 1968–1971." *Louisiana History* 43 (2002): 53–74.

van Dyke, Nella. "Hotbeds of Activism: Locations of Student Protest." *Social Problems* 45 (1998): 205–20.

Edelson, Elihu. "*Both Sides Now* Remembered: Or, The Once and Future Journal." In *Insider Histories of the Vietnam Era Underground Press, Part 2*, edited by Ken Wachsberger, 369–84. East Lansing: Michigan State University Press, 2012.

Edwards, Laura F. "Southern History as U.S. History." *Journal of Southern History* 75, no. 3 (August 2009): 533–64.

Ernst, John, and Yvonne Baldwin. "The Not So Silent Minority: Louisville's Antiwar Movement, 1966–1975." *Journal of Southern History* 73, no. 1 (2007): 105–42.

Farber, David. "Building the counterculture, creating right livelihoods: the counterculture at work." *The Sixties: A Journal of History, Politics and Culture* 6, no. 1 (2013): 1–24.

Few, April L., Dionne P. Stephens, and Marlo Rouse-Arnett. "Sister-to-Sister Talk: Transcending Boundaries and Challenges in Qualitative Research with Black Women." *Family Relations* 52 (2003): 205–15.

Franklin, V. P. "Patterns of Student Activism at Historically Black Universities in the

United States and South Africa, 1960–1977." *Journal of African American History* 88, no. 2 (Spring 2003): 204–17.

Frederickson, Mary E. "'Each One Is Dependent on the Other': Southern Churchwomen, Racial Reform, and the Process of Transformation, 1880–1940." In *Visible Women: New Essays on American Activism*, edited by Nancy A. Hewitt and Suzanne Lebsock, 296–324. Urbana-Champaign: Board of Trustees of the University of Illinois, 1993.

Fry, Joseph A. "Unpopular Messengers: Student Opposition to the Vietnam War." In *The War That Never Ends: New Perspectives on the Vietnam War*, edited by David L. Anderson and John Ernst, 219–45. Lexington: The University Press of Kentucky, 2007.

Gabb, Sally. "A Fowl in the Vortices of Consciousness: The Birth of the *Great Speckled Bird*." In *Insider Histories of the Vietnam Era Underground Press, Part 1*, edited by Ken Wachsberger, 91–107. East Lansing: Michigan State University Press, 2011.

Gilmore, Stephanie. "The Dynamics of Second-Wave Feminist Activism in Memphis, 1971–1982: Rethinking the Liberal/Radical Divide." *NWSA Journal* 15, no. 1 (Spring 2003): 94–117.

Graham, Hugh Davis. "On Riots and Riot Commissions: Civil Disorders in the 1960s." *The Public Historian* 2, no. 4 (1980): 7–27.

Green, Laurie B. "Saving Babies in Memphis: The Politics of Race, Health, and Hunger during the War on Poverty." In *The War On Poverty: A New Grassroots History, 1964–1980*, edited by Annelise Orleck and Lisa Gayle Hazirjian, 133–58. Athens: University of Georgia Press, 2011.

———. "The Rural-Urban Matrix in the 1950s South: Rethinking Racial Justice Struggles in Memphis." In *From the Grassroots to the Supreme Court: Brown v. Board of Education and American Democracy*, edited by Peter F. Lau, 270–99. Durham, N.C.: Duke University Press, 2004.

Greene, Christina. "'Someday . . . the Colored and White Will Stand Together': The War on Poverty, Black Power Politics, and Southern Women's Interracial Alliances." In *The War On Poverty: A New Grassroots History, 1964–1980*, edited by Annelise Orleck and Lisa Gayle Hazirjian, 159–83. Athens: University of Georgia Press, 2011.

Griffin, Larry J. "'Generations and Collective Memory' Revisited: Race, Region, and Memory of Civil Rights." *American Sociological Review* 69 (2004): 544–57.

Hall, Jacquelyn Dowd. "The Long Civil Rights Movement and the Political Uses of the Past." *Journal of American History* 91 (2005): 1233–63.

Hall, Mitchell K. "'A Crack in Time': The Response of Students at the University of Kentucky to the Tragedy at Kent State, May 1970." *Register of the Kentucky Historical Society* 83, no. 1 (1985): 36–63.

Hall, Ronald E. "White Women as Postmodern Vehicle of Black Oppression: The Pedagogy of Discrimination in Western Academy." *Journal of Black Studies* 37 (2006): 69–82.

Hall, Simon. "Civil Rights Activism in 1960s Virginia." *Journal of Black Studies* 38 (2007): 251–67.

———. "'Guerrilla Theater . . . in the Guise of Red, White, and Blue Bunting': The People's Bicentennial Commission and the Politics of (Un-)Americanism," *Journal of American Studies* 52, no. 1 (February 2018): 114–36.

———. "The NAACP, Black Power, and the African American Freedom Struggle, 1966–1969." *The Historian* 69, no. 1 (2007): 49–82.

———. "Protest Movements in the 1970s: The Long 1960s." *Journal of Contemporary History* 43, no. 4 (2008): 655–72.

———. "The Sit-Ins, SNCC, and Cold War Patriotism." In *From Sit-Ins to SNCC: The*

Student Civil Rights Movement in the 1960s, edited by Iwan Morgan and Philip Davies, 135–52. Gainesville: University Press of Florida, 2012.

Heclo, Hugh. "The Sixties' False Dawn: Awakenings, Movements, and Postmodern Policy-making." *Journal of Policy History* 8, no. 1 (1996): 34–63.

Hine, William C. "Civil Rights and Campus Wrongs: South Carolina State College Students Protest, 1955-1968." *South Carolina Historical Magazine* 97, no. 4 (October 1996): 310–31.

Hoelscher, Steven. "Making Place, Making Race: Performances of Whiteness in the Jim Crow South." *Annals of the Association of American Geographers* 93 (2003): 657–86.

Hogan, Wesley. "Freedom Now: Nonviolence in the Southern Freedom Movement, 1960–1964." In *Civil Rights History from the Ground Up: Local Struggles, a National Movement*, edited by Emilye Crosby, 172–93. Athens: University of Georgia Press, 2011.

Houston, Benjamin. "A Conversation with Will D. Campbell." *Journal of Southern Religion* 10 (2007). http://jsr.fsu.edu/Volume10/Houston.htm.

———. "'The Aquinas of the Rednecks': reconciliation, the Southern character, and the bootleg ministry of Will D. Campbell." *The Sixties: A Journal of History, Politics and Culture* 4, no. 2 (2011): 135–50.

Hunt, Andrew. "How New Was the New Left?: Re-Thinking New Left Exceptionalism." In *The New Left Revisited*, edited by John McMillian and Paul Buhle, 139–55. Philadelphia: Temple University Press, 2003.

Irons, Jenny. "The Shaping of Activist Recruitment and Participation: A Study of Women in the Mississippi Civil Rights Movement." *Gender and Society* 12 (1998): 692–709.

Isaac, Larry W., Daniel B. Cornfield, Dennis C. Dickerson, James M. Lawson Jr., and Jonathan S. Coley. "'Movement Schools' and the Dialogical Diffusion of Nonviolent Praxis: Nashville Workshops in the Southern Civil Rights Movement." *Research in Social Movements, Conflicts and Change* 34 (2012): *Nonviolent Conflict and Civil Resistance*, 155–84.

Isserman, Maurice, and Michael Kazin. "The Failure and Success of the New Radicalism." In *The Rise and Fall of the New Deal Order, 1930–1980*, edited by Steve Fraser and Gary Gerstle, 212–42. Princeton: Princeton University Press, 1990.

Isserman, Maurice. "The Not-So-Dark and Bloody Ground: New Works on the 1960s." *American Historical Review* 94, no. 4 (1989): 990–1010.

Jackson, Walter A. "White Liberal Intellectuals, Civil Rights and Gradualism, 1954–1960." In *The Making of Martin Luther King and the Civil Rights Movement*, edited by Brian Ward and Tony Badger, 96–114. New York: New York University Press, 1996.

Jones, Antwan. "Race and the 'I Have A Dream' Legacy: Exploring Predictors of Positive Civil Rights Attitudes." *Journal of Black Studies* 37 (2006): 193–208.

Joseph, Peniel E. "Black Studies, Student Activism, and the Black Power Movement." In *The Black Power Movement: Rethinking the Civil Rights-Black Power Era*, edited by Peniel E. Joseph, 251–78. London: Routledge, 2006.

Kiffmeyer, Thomas. "Looking Back to the City in the Hills: The Council of the Southern Mountains and a Longer View of the War on Poverty in the Appalachian South, 1913–1970." In *The War On Poverty: A New Grassroots History, 1964–1980*, edited by Annelise Orleck and Lisa Gayle Hazirjian, 359–86. Athens: University of Georgia Press, 2011.

King, Randall E. "When Worlds Collide: Politics, Religion, and Media at the 1970 East Tennessee Billy Graham Crusade." *Journal of Church and State* 39 (1997): 273–95.

Kirk, John. "Another Side of the Sit-Ins: Nonviolent Direct Action, the Courts, and the

Constitution." In *From Sit-Ins to SNCC: The Student Civil Rights Movement in the 1960s*, edited by Iwan Morgan and Philip Davies, 23–40. Gainesville: University Press of Florida, 2012.

Kirk, John A. "'Massive Resistance and Minimum Compliance': The Origins of the 1957 Little Rock School Crisis and the Failure of School Desegregation in the South." In *Massive Resistance: Southern Opposition to the Second Reconstruction*, edited by Clive Webb, 76–98. Oxford: Oxford University Press, 2005.

Kornbluh, Felicia. "Food as a Civil Right: Hunger, Work, and Welfare in the South after the Civil Rights Act." *Labor Studies in Working-Class History of the Americas* 12, issues 1–2 (2015): 135–58.

Korstad, Robert R., and James L. Leloudis. "Citizen Soldiers: The North Carolina Volunteers and the War on Poverty." *Law and Contemporary Problems* 62, no. 4 (1999): 177–97.

Lamon, Lester C. "The Black Community in Nashville and the Fisk University Student Strike of 1924–1925." *Journal of Southern History* 40, no. 2 (1974): 225–44.

Lassiter, Matthew, and Kevin Kruse. "The Bulldozer Revolution: Suburbs and Southern History Since World War II." *Journal of Southern History* 75, no. 3 (2009): 691–706.

Lawson, Steven F. "From Sit-In to Race Riot: Businessmen, Blacks, and the Pursuit of Moderation in Tampa, 1960–1967." In *Southern Businessmen and Desegregation*, edited by Elizabeth Jacoway and David R. Colburn, 257–81. Baton Rouge: Louisiana State University Press, 1982.

Levine, Arthur, and Keith R. Wilson. "Student Activism in the 1970s: Transformation Not Decline." *Higher Education* 8, no. 6 (November 1979): 627–40.

Lewis, George. "The Impact of the Sit-Ins on the Ideology of Southern Segregationists." In *From Sit-Ins to SNCC: The Student Civil Rights Movement in the 1960s*, edited by Iwan Morgan and Philip Davies, 41–57. Gainesville: University Press of Florida, 2012.

Lichtenstein, Alex. "The Other Civil Rights Movement and the Problem of Southern Exceptionalism." *Journal of The Historical Society* 11, no. 3 (2011): 351–76.

Lieberman, Robbie, and David Cochran. "'It Seemed a Very Local Affair': The Student Movement at Southern Illinois University at Carbondale." In *The New Left Revisited*, edited by John McMillian and Paul Buhle, 11–27. Philadelphia: Temple University Press, 2003.

Ling, Peter. "SNCCs: Not One Committee, but Several." In *From Sit-Ins to SNCC: The Student Civil Rights Movement in the 1960s*, edited by Iwan Morgan and Philip Davies, 81–96. Gainesville: University Press of Florida, 2012.

Martin, Charles H. "Hold That (Color) Line!: Southeastern Conference Football." In *Higher Education and the Civil Rights Movement: White Supremacy, Black Southerners, and College Campuses*, edited by Peter Wallenstein, 166–98. Gainesville: University Press of Florida, 2008.

Michel, Gregg L. "Building the New South: The Southern Student Organizing Committee." In *The New Left Revisited*, edited by John Campbell McMillian and Paul Buhle, 48–66. Philadelphia: Temple University Press, 2003.

———. "It Even Happened Here: Student Activism at Furman University, 1967–1970." *South Carolina Historical Magazine* 109, no. 1 (January 2008): 38–57.

———. "Surveilling the Memphis Movement: Police Spying in Memphis, 1968–1976." *Journal of Southern History* 87 (2021): 673–710.

Miller, Steven P. "Billy Graham, Civil Rights, and the Changing Postwar South." In *Politics and Religion in the White South*, edited by Glenn Feldman, 157–86. Lexington: The University Press of Kentucky, 2005.

———. "Whither Southern Liberalism in the Post–Civil Rights Era? The Southern Regional Council and its Peers, 1965–1972." *Georgia Historical Quarterly* 90 (2006): 547–68.

Murray, Gail Schmunk. "Taming the War on Poverty: Memphis as a Case Study." *Journal of Urban History* 43, no. 1 (2015): 1–21.

Nasstrom, Kathryn L. "Beginnings and Endings: Life Stories and the Periodization of the Civil Rights Movement." *Journal of American History* 86 (1999): 700–711.

Park, Laurel. "Planting the Seeds of Academic Excellence and Cultural Awareness: The Michigan–Tuskegee Exchange Program." *Michigan Historical Review* 30, no. 1 (2004): 117–31.

Perlstein, Daniel. "Teaching Freedom: SNCC and the Creation of the Mississippi Freedom Schools." *History of Education Quarterly* 30, no. 3 (1990): 297–324.

Pierce, Michael. "Odell Smith, Teamsters Local 878, and Civil Rights Unionism in Little Rock, 1943–1965." *Journal of Southern History* 84, no. 4 (November 2018): 925–58.

Ramsey, Sonya. "'We Will Be Ready Whenever They Are': African American Teachers' Responses to the Brown Decision and Public School Integration in Nashville, Tennessee, 1954–1966." *Journal of African American History* 90 (2005): 29–51.

Roberson, Houston. "The Problem of the Twentieth Century: Sewanee, Race and Race Relations." In *Sewanee Perspectives: On the History of the University of the South*, edited by Gerald L. Smith and Samuel R. Williamson, 485–518. Sewanee, Tenn.: The University Press, 2008.

Robertson, Suzanne Craig. "When 'Courage Superseded Fear.'" *Tennessee Bar Journal* 46, no. 5 (2010): 12–19.

Rogers, Ibram H. "The Black Campus Movement and the Institutionalization of Black Studies, 1965–1970." *Journal of African American Studies* 16, no. 1 (2012): 21–40.

———. "The Black Campus Movement: the case for a new historiography." *The Sixties: A Journal of History, Politics and Culture* 4, no. 2 (2011): 171–86.

Rogers, Kim L. "Life Questions: Memories of Women Civil Rights Leaders." *Journal of African American History* 87 (2002): 355–68.

Rudwick, Elliott, and August Meier. "The Kent State Affair: Social Control of a Putative Value-Oriented Movement." *Sociological Inquiry* 42, no. 2 (1972): 81–86.

Sadler, Cynthia. "'On Parade': Race, Gender, and Imagery in the Memphis Mardi Gras, Cotton Carnival, and Cotton Makers' Jubilee." In *Tennessee Women: Their Lives and Times*, Vol. 2, edited by Beverly Greene Bond and Sarah Wilkerson Freeman, 125–51. Athens: The University of Georgia Press, 2015.

Sarvis, Will. "Leaders in the Court and Community: Z. Alexander Looby, Avon N. Williams, Jr., and the Legal Fight for Civil Rights in Tennessee, 1940–1970." *Journal of African American History* 88, no. 1 (Winter 2003): 42–58.

Spencer, Robyn C., and Wesley Hogan "Telling Freedom Stories from the Inside Out: Internal Politics and Movement Cultures in SNCC and the Black Panther Party." In *Civil Rights History from the Ground Up*, edited by Emilye Crosby, 330–65. Athens: The University of Georgia Press, 2011.

Sprayberry, Gary S. "Student Radicalism and the Antiwar Movement at the University of Alabama." In *Rebellion in Black and White: Southern Student Activism in the 1960s*, edited by Robert Cohen and David J. Snyder, 148–70. Baltimore: Johns Hopkins University Press, 2013.

Spruill, Marjorie J. "Gender and America's Right Turn." In *Rightward Bound: Making America Conservative in the 1970s*, edited by Bruce J. Schulman and Julian E. Zelizer, 71–89. Cambridge, Mass.: Harvard University Press, 2008.

Street, Joe. "From Beloved Community to Imagined Community: SNCC's Intellectual Transformation." In *From Sit-Ins to SNCC: The Student Civil Rights Movement in the 1960s*, edited by Iwan Morgan and Philip Davies, 116-34. Gainesville: University Press of Florida, 2012.

Strub, Whitney. "Black and White and Banned All Over: Race, Censorship, and Obscenity in Postwar Memphis." *Journal of Social History* 40, no. 3 (2007): 685-715.

Thrasher, Sue. "Circle of Trust." In *Deep in Our Hearts: Nine White Women in the Freedom Movement*, edited by Constance Curry, Joan C. Browning, Dorothy Dawson Burlage, Penny Patch, Theresa Del Pozzo, Sue Thrasher, Elaine DeLott Baker, Emmie Schrader Adams, and Casey Hayden, 209-51. Athens: University of Georgia Press, 2000.

Thompson, Ruth Ann. "'A Taste of Student Power': Protest at the University of Tennessee, 1964-1970." *Tennessee Historical Quarterly* 57, no. 1 (Spring/Summer 1998): 80-97.

Tracy, James. "Rising Up: Poor, White, and Angry in the New Left." In *The Hidden 1970s: Histories of Radicalism*, edited by Dan Berger, 214-30. New Brunswick, N.J.: Rutgers University Press, 2010.

Trotter, Anne. "The Memphis Business Community and Integration." In *Southern Businessmen and Desegregation*, edited by Elizabeth Jacoway and David R. Colburn, 282-300. Baton Rouge: Louisiana State University Press, 1982.

Turner, Jeffrey A. "The Rise of Black and White Student Protest in Nashville." In *Rebellion in Black and White: Southern Student Activism in the 1960s*, edited by Robert Cohen and David J. Snyder, 129-47. Baltimore: Johns Hopkins University Press, 2013.

Wallenstein, Peter. "Black Southerners and Nonblack Universities: The Process of Desegregating Southern Higher Education, 1935-1965." In *Higher Education and the Civil Rights Movement: White Supremacy, Black Southerners, and College Campuses*, edited by Peter Wallenstein, 17-59. Gainesville: University Press of Florida, 2008.

———. "Introduction: Higher Education, Black Access, and the Civil Rights Movement." In *Higher Education and the Civil Rights Movement: White Supremacy, Black Southerners, and College Campuses*, edited by Peter Wallenstein, 1-16. Gainesville: University Press of Florida, 2008.

Walmsley, Mark Joseph. "Tell It Like It Isn't: SNCC and the Media, 1960-1965." *Journal of American Studies* 48, no. 1 (2014): 291-308.

Webb, Clive. "Breaching the Wall of Resistance: White Southern Reactions to the Sit-Ins." In *From Sit-Ins to SNCC: The Student Civil Rights Movement in the 1960s*, edited by Iwan Morgan and Philip Davies, 58-80. Gainesville: University Press of Florida, 2012.

Weyant, Thomas. "'We Will Be Heard': Student Citizenship and Ohio University in the 1960s." *Ohio Valley History* 19, no. 2 (Summer 2019): 23-48.

Whittington, Erica L. "Interracial Dialogue and the Southern Student Human Relations Project." In *Rebellion in Black and White: Southern Student Activism in the 1960s*, edited by Robert Cohen and David J. Snyder, 83-105. Baltimore: John Hopkins University Press, 2013.

Wright, George C. "Desegregation of Public Accommodations in Louisville: A Long and Difficult Struggle in a 'Liberal' Border State." In *Southern Businessmen and Desegregation*, edited by Elizabeth Jacoway and David R. Colburn, 191-210. Baton Rouge: Louisiana State University Press, 1982.

Yow, Ruth Carbonette. "Shadowed Places and Stadium Lights: An Oral History of Integration and Black Student Protest in Marietta, Georgia." *Oral History Review* 42, no. 1 (2015): 70-95.

Zagumny, Lisa L. "Sit-Ins In Knoxville, Tennessee: A Case Study of Political Rhetoric." *Journal of Negro History* 86 (2002): 45-54.

INDEX

Locators in italics indicate a figure.

Acey, David, 121
Adawayhi Pep Club elections, 103–4
Afro-American Association (Vanderbilt), 110–11
Aldmon, Howard, 103, 104
Altbach, Philip, 17
American Association of University Professors (AAUP), 24, 130
American Federation of Labor and Congress of Industrial Organizations (AFL-CIO), 65, 67, 70
American Federation of State, County, and Municipal Employees (AFSCME), 79, 114
Anderson, Terry, 70
anti-war movement in Tennessee: division over, 120–22; draft and, 124–25; earlier conflicts and, 143; flag burning and, 129; Graham Crusade and, 1–2, 135–40; Johnson speech and, 126; national movement compared to, 121; opposition to, 126–27; Southern Days of Secession and, 130; university administrators and, 128–29; Vanderbilt, Dow Chemical, and, 127
apathy among student bodies, 19, 76, 91–92, 120, 131
Appalachian Volunteers (AV), 67–68
aptitude test (Selective Service System), 124–25
armed self-defense, 72–73
Armer, Mike, 22
Asbury, Beverly, 111
Ayer, Perley, 6

Barnett, Ross, 27
Barry, Marion, 39, 47, 48
Bates, Scott, 24–25
Baxter, James "Jimmie," 32, 93–96, 106, 108, 134–35
Berkeley Free Speech Movement, 57, 70, 90, 92
Bible, Carroll, 114, 138
Black Liberation Front (BLF), 101
Black Organizing Project (BOP), 74–75, 77, 79
Black Power: Afro-American Student Movement and, 96–97; armed self-defense, 72–73; Black students and, 76–77; Black Tennessee student radicals and, 72–74; BOP and, 75; increasing influence of, 8, 10, 62; Memphis Sanitation Strike and, 80; MLK and, 80; NOP and, 75; Tennessee student activism and, 62
Black Student Association (BSA), 74, 75–77, 98–100, 104
Black studies programs, 76, 83, 96–98, 102–4
Blake, Eugene Carson, 26
Blue Raiders (MTSU), 147
Boling, Edward J., 105–6, 115, 117–18
Bontemps, Arna, 25
Booker, Robert, 44–46
Bowden, William L., 142–43
Braden, Anne, 59–60
Branscomb, Harvie, 31, 41
Brehm, C. E., 28
Brock, William, 102, 105, 117–18, 131–32
Brosi, George, 67
Brotherhood, the, 14–17
Brown v. Board of Education of Topeka, 3, 18–19, 27, 32–33, 118, 152. *See also* desegregation
Burgess, Ernest W., 18
Burlage, Dorothy, 65
Burlage, Robb, 63, 65
Butler, Washington, 82

Cabbage, Charles, 75
Campbell, Will D., 22
campus unrest: in 1970s, 146; anti-war movement and, 128; Brock report on, 117; "Declaration on Campus Unrest" and, 118; Graham Crusade and, 1–2, 135–40; Lane College and, 100, 101–2; LeMoyne-Owen College and, 100–101; MLK assassination and, 81; Scranton Commission on, 8, 140–43; student apathy and, 19, 76, 91–92, 120, 131; university administrators and, 105–6, 128; university handling of, 115–19. *See also* in *loco parentis* protests; student activism; student power; university administrators; *individual universities*
Cantrell, Paul, 144

219

capitalism and grassroots programs, 71
Carawan, Candie, 20, 39
Carawan, Guy, 19, 41
Carmichael, Stokely, 108–10
Carson, Clayborne, 123
Carter, Asa, 33
Carver, Susan, 151
Chafe, William, 21–22, 38
Chattanooga sit-ins, 40
Cheek, James E., 141–42
Chicago and white southern migration, 69
Christianity and The Brotherhood, 16–17
citizenship, 6
civil rights movement: Afro-American Student Movement conference and, 96; Highlander Folk School and, 19; Memphis Sanitation Strike and, 74, 80; southern student activism and, 36–37, 50–52, 92; SSOC and, 61–63, 71; white student participation in, 57–59. *See also* desegregation; Knoxville sit-ins; Memphis sit-ins; Nashville sit-ins; sit-in movement in Tennessee
class-based organizing, 66–69
Clowney, Shirley Carr, 33–34
Cohen, Robert, 7, 92
Cole, Echol, 78
Colston, James, 46
Committee on the Move for Equality (COME), 74, 79
Communism, 17–18, 60
community-focused approach, 3
community organizing, white, 62, 66–69
Confederate flag, 61, 69, 71, 147
Congress of Industrial Organizations (CIO), 13, 18
Cook, Ned, 145
Coughlin, Lawrence, 105
Council of the Southern Mountains (CSM), 67–68
Counter Intelligence Program of the FBI (COINTELPRO), 74, 86, 121, 140
Crawford, Gary, 115
Cronkite, Walter, 128
cross burning (MTSU), 146–47
Crusade in Knoxville (Billy Graham), 1–2, 135–40
Cunningham, David, 26
curfew protests, 84–85

Davis, W. S., 29
desegregation: higher education and, 27–35, 43, 96, 152; Knoxville and, 43; Memphis and, 52–54, 62; Nashville, 58; Tennessee public schools and, 21–22. *See also* civil rights movement
Diggs, Charles, 100–101
Dillard, Godfrey, 111
Dombrowski, James, 13–14
Dow Chemical Company, 127
draft for Vietnam War, 124–26
Du Bois, W. E. B., 10, 11
Dunbar, Leslie, 60
Duncan, John, Sr., 44–45, 113, 132, 136–37
Duncan, John "Jimmy," Jr., 88

East Tennessee State University, *xii*, 149
Economic Opportunity Act, 73
Economic Research Action Project (ERAP), 68
Edmondson, Rick, 145
Edwards, Gerald, 146–47
effigy burning (MTSU), 144–46
Ellington, Buford, 82, 101, 107, 113
Equal Rights Amendment (ERA), 149
Estes, Steve, 123
Evans, Stanton, 87

Farber, David, 7
Federal Bureau of Investigation (FBI), 18, 74, 86, 121, 140
Fellowship of Reconciliation (FOR), 38
Fisk University: Afro-American Student Movement conference at, 96–97; Du Bois speech at, 11; five "liabilities" at, 23; integration and, 29; interracial exchange program at, 21–22; location of, *xii*; McKenzie and, 11–12; Nashville sit-ins and, 39–41; private-college similarities in protests at, 11; Social Action Committee at, 23; Stokely Carmichael and, 108–9; student power and, 10; student strike at, 11–12
Flag Desecration Act, 129
force, use of, 116
Forrest, Nathan Bedford, 147
Forum for Racial Equality, Etc. (FREE), 47
Fosl, Catherine, 60
Fowler, James Henry, 33
"freedom of choice" desegregation policy, 27
Freedom Riders, 42
Freedom Songs, 19
Freedom Train, 52
Frissell, Lee, 59, 171n161
Frost, Jennifer, 68
Fulton, Hazel, 12

Gaines v. Canada, 29
Gibson, Elmer, 86

220 INDEX

Gitlin, Todd, 2
Glen, John, 158n46
Gordon, Frank R., 33
Gosse, Van, 155n3
Graham, Billy, 1, 135–39
Graham Crusade in Knoxville, 1–2, 135–40
Gray v. University of Tennessee, 28
Greater Memphis Race Relations Committee (GMRRC), 52
Green, Laurie, 77
Grundy County, Tennessee, 14, 16
Guerrero, Gene, 65

Hager, Jim, 93–96, 132
Halberstam, David, 41
Haldeman, Bob, 136–37
Hall, Simon, 145
Hamlett, Ed, 47, 69, 122, 126
Hanson, Ray, 73
Hayden, Tom, 57, 122
Heard, Alexander, 109, 129, 141–42
Heard Report, 141–42. *See also* Scranton Commission
Hershey, Lewis B., 125, 129
Highlander Folk School: The Brotherhood and, 14–17; civil rights and interracialism at, 18; college workshops at, 19, 21; Communism and, 18; Horton and support of student groups at, 18–20; link for intergenerational and interracial activism and, 14; Nashville sit-ins and, 19–21; origins of, 13–14; role in student movement of, 7, 10, 35; SNCC and, 20; Summerville Community Council and, 16–17; threats to, 17–18
Holloway, Harry, 73
Holt, Andrew D., 49, 112, 116
Honey, Michael, 78
Hooks, Benjamin L., 51
Hoover, J. Edgar, 121
Horton, Aimee Isgrig, 20
Horton, Myles, 13–14, 16, 18–20, 44
Houston, Benjamin, 29, 38, 39
Humphreys, Cecil C., 28, 81, 86, 98–100, 128–29, 133

in loco parentis protests: chapel attendance and, 88–89; conservative students and, 87–88; curfew protests and, 84–85, 87; dormitory policies and, 86; dress codes and, 88; female students and, 84, 86, 89; student power and, 5; tradition of, 83; visitation policies and, 85–86
integration: Black university student experiences with, 32–35; Highlander Folk School and, 19; Jim Crow, Asian students, and, 30; KCIC and, 46; Memphis and, 51–53; SET and, 48; Tennessee universities and, 21, 24–35, 76; tokenism and, 102; university athletics and, 50
interracial exchange programs, 22–26
interracialism, 16, 18, 63
Invaders (BOP), 75, 77–80
Issues lecture series, 111–12
I. T. Watson et al. v. City of Memphis et al., 54
Ivy, Ronald, 76, 77

Jackson, H. Ralph, 99
Jackson State shooting, 2
Jobs or Income Now (JOIN), 68–69
Johnson, Lyndon B., 126
Joint University Council on Human Relations (JUC), 58
Jones, T. O. 78–79
Joseph, Peniel, 96

Kami, Peter, 106, 114
Kasper, John, 39
Kazin, Michael, 56
Kean, Melissa, 31
Kefauver, Estes, 14
Kendi, Ibram X, 11, 96 155n3
Kent State shooting, 1, 2, 3, 107–8, 132–34
Kerner Commission (National Advisory Commission on Civil Disorders), 110
Kiffmeyer Thomas, 64, 72
Kincaid, Robert L., 30
King, Martin Luther, Jr., 43–44, 80, 81, 108
King, Russell, 107
Kirkendoll, Chester A., 101
Knoxville: as "All-American City," 48; integration efforts in, 44; police responses to student protests in, 49–50; race relations in, 43–44; resident responses to sit-ins in, 45; restaurant demonstrations in, 47–49; student activism and, 50–51
Knoxville 22, 106, 113; Knoxville crusade and, 1–2
Knoxville Civic Improvement Committee (KCIC), 46–47
Knoxville College: exchange program with Maryville College, 26; Knoxville sit-ins and, 44–46; library hours and, 90; location of, xii
Knoxville sit-ins, 43–46, 50–51
Ku Klux Klan (KKK), 26
Kunstler, William, 113–14

labor organizing and SSOC, 64–67, 72
Labor's Political Conference of Grundy County, 16
Lamis, Alexander P., 4
Lamon, Lester, 11
Lancaster, Robert S., 24
Lane College, 100–102
LaPrad, Paul, 23, 40
Lawson, James M., Jr., 23, 38–39, 41, 74, 80
LeMoyne College, *xii*, 51, 53–54,
LeMoyne-Owen College, *xii*, 100–101
Lewis, John, 38–40
Libby, Jean, 130
Lincoln Memorial University, *xii*, 11–13, 30–31
local organizing, 14–17
Loeb, Henry, 52, 79, 81–82
Long, John, 93–96
Looby, Z. Alexander, 41
Looby bombing, 41–42
Lovett, Bobby, 13, 39

Majority Coalition (UT), 87–88
Majors, Shirley, 103
Marius, Richard, 86
Maryville College: campus policy organizing and, 87, 88; exchange program Knoxville College, 26; integration and, 32–35; location of, *xii*; managing student unrest and, 118; student apathy and, 91–92; tokenism and, 102–3; women's rights gains and, 148–49
Massive Resistance, 39
McCarthyism, 7
McClellan, Frank D., 26
McCrady, Edward, 25, 31, 34–35
McDowell, Larry, 102–3
McKenzie, Fayette Avery, 11
Memphis: activism groups in, 73–75; church service kneel-ins in, 55–56; community support for sit-ins in, 53; convergence of forces in, 78; generational differences in activism in, 77–78; integration tensions in, 28; MCCR and, 54–55; MLK assassination and, 81–82; pre-sit-in integration initiatives in, 52; racial politics in, 51–52; sanitation strike in, 62, 73–74, 78–82; sit-in movement and, 51; Vietnam War draft and, 80
Memphis and Shelby County Improvement League, 51
Memphis Area Project-South (MAP-South), 74–75
Memphis Committee on Community Relations (MCCR), 54–55
Memphis Community Relations Committee (MCRC), 52

Memphis Freedom Movement, 53
Memphis Sanitation Strike, 62, 73–74, 78–82
Memphis sit-ins, 51, 53–55, 57
Memphis State University: apathy and, 76; Black inclusion and, 97–98, 104–5; BSA 109 and, 98–99; BSA of, 75–77; flagpole fight at, 132–33; integration tensions and, 28; location of, *xii*; Memphis Sanitation Strike and, 81; NSA chapter at, 57
Michel, Gregg, 66
Middlebrook, Harold, 79
Middle Tennessee State University (MTSU), *xii*, 144–46, 147
migration of white southerners, 69
military service and African Americans, 123–24
Miller, Steven P., 135
"moderation" as racial stance, 38
Moon, Dick, 81
Moratorium to End the War in Vietnam, 130–31
Morison, James Henderson Stuart, 12
Morristown College, *xii*, 86
Moynihan, Daniel Patrick, 142
Murphy, Charles, 2, 139

napalm, 127
Nash, Diane, 41, 42, 123
Nashville Christian Leadership Council (NCLC), 39
Nashville riot, 109–10
Nashville sit-ins: centrality of, 38; Fisk exchange program and, 23; Highlander Folk School and, 19–21; influence on student movement of, 38–43; Looby bombing and, 41–42; NSM and, 39; Tennessee sit-in movement context of, 7; white participation in, 23; white student participation in, 58–59; Wright speech and, 40–41
Nashville Student Movement (NSM), 39
National Advisory Commission on Civil Disorders (Kerner Commission), 110
National Association for the Advancement of Colored People (NAACP): intercollegiate chapter, 53, Memphis chapter, 51–54, 125
National Student Association (NSA), 57
Negro Board of Trade (Nashville), 12
Neighborhood Organizing Project (NOP), 74–75
New Left: anti-war movement and, 125, 130; Black students and, 5–6; campus subversion and, 110, 121; Highlander Folk School and, 7, 35; labor and, 70; Old Left and, 35, 56, 59; PBC and, 145; Tennessee and, 2, 3; white southerners in Chicago and, 69
Nixon, Richard M., 1–2, 8, 135–41

nonviolent protest workshops at Highlander Folk School, 19–21, 23, 35, 39
North Nashville Project (SSOC), 68

October League, 72
Old Left, 2, 7, 9–10, 20, 56, 60
open speaker policies, 108–15
Owen Junior College, *xii*, 51, 53. *See also* LeMoyne-Owen College

People's Bicentennial Commission (PBC), 144–46
personal autonomy and student power, 5 *See also in loco parentis* protests
Pierce, Johnny, 104
"politics of authenticity," 6
politics of moderation, 37–38
Populists, 63–64
Powell, Adam Clayton, 98
prairie power, 6
President's Commission on Campus Unrest (Scranton Commission), 8, 140–43
Prince, Hollis, 100–101
PROD, 58, 171n161
progressivism in the South, 22
prophetic minority, 7
Proudfoot, Merrill, 44

"qualified" students and integration, 30
Quillen, James, 151

race and the draft, 124–25
Radical Vocations in the White Community (conference), 69
recalcitrant majority, 7
religion and activism, 55, 59, 68
Rhodes, Peyton N., 31, 55–56
Robinson, Theotis, Jr., 29, 50
Rogers, Leonard, 140
Rollins, Avon, 46–48, 50
Roop, Hervin U., 12
Rossinow, Doug, 6, 59
Rowan, Carl T., 42
Rucker, James "Sparky," 106

"Sahara of the Bozart" (Mencken), 63
sanctuary of university, 117–18
Savio, Mario, 57, 92
Scarritt College for Christian Workers, *xii*, 28–29
Scarlett, M. G., 146
Scranton, William, 140
Scranton Commission (President's Commission on Campus Unrest), 8, 140–43

Students for a Democratic Society (SDS), 57, 59; draft exam and, 125; ERAP and, 63; Humphrey in Austin and, 126; participatory democracy and, 56; SDS/SSOC exam and, 125; SSOC and, 57, 64–65, 70, 124–25, 130
SDS/SSOC exam, 125
Second Presbyterian Church (SPC), 55–56
Selective Service System, 124–25
Sewanee: The University of the South: campus life protests and, 88; Gailor Hall protests and, 89–90; integration and, 23–25, 28, 31, 33–35; location of, *xii*
Shirah, Sam, 67
sip-ins, 58
sit-in movement in Tennessee, 36–38, 40, 43–46, 50–51, 60. *See also* Knoxville sit-ins, Memphis sit-ins; Nashville sit-ins
Smith, Coby, 75, 80
Smith, J. Millard, 28
Smith, John, 137–38
Smith, Kelly Miller, 38–40, 42
Smith, Maxine, 52–54, 99, 125
Student Nonviolent Coordinating Committee (SNCC): formation of, 20; Nashville riots and, 109; southern universities and, 64; Vietnam War and, 123; white student activists and, 57, 59
Sorace, John, 109–10
Southern Agrarians, 63
Southern Christian Leadership Conference (SCLC), 38–39
Southern Conference Education Fund (SCEF), 59
Southern Conference for Human Welfare (SCHW), 14
Southern Coordinating Committee to End the War in Vietnam (SCCEWV), 122
Southern Days of Secession protest (SSOC), 130
Southern Labor Action Movement (SLAM), 66–67
Southern Regional Council (SRC), 50
southern student activism. *See* student activism, southern
Southwestern at Memphis, *xii*, 52, 55–56, 87, 88, 148
Spivey, Herman E., 29–30, 47–48, 49
Southern Student Organizing Committee (SSOC): appeal to poorer white Southerners by, 66–68; class-based organizing and, 66–68; dissolution of, 70–72; draft and, 124–25, 126; emblem and mission of, 61, 71; formation of, 57–58; funding of, 59–60; influence of previous social movements on, 63–64; internal conflict and, 67;

INDEX 223

SSOC (*continued*)
   interracialism and membership of, 62, 71–72, 82; labor and interracialism goals of, 64; labor organizing and, 61–62, 65–66; North Nashville Project of, 68; Populist references by, 63; purpose of, 59; radical considerations of, 70; as regional organization, 64; SDS and, 57, 64–65, 70, 124–25, 130; Southern Days of Secession protest and, 130; southern goals of, 65; Vietnam War and, 122, 127; "We'll Take a Stand" statement of, 63; white community organizing and, 66–69
Stahlman, James, 41, 109
Stefani, Anne, 60
Streator, George, 12
Strickland, Jim, 82
strikes, 11–13, 65–66, 96–97, 134–35. *See also* Memphis Sanitation Strike
student activism, interracial: collaboration and divergence in, 152–53; division and, 145–46; labor organizing and, 8, 61–62; NSA and, 57; Old Left and New Left in, 56; separation and, 5–6, 82; student power and, 6; in Tennessee, 2–3
student activism, national: Baby Boomer enrollments and, 84; community-focused approach to, 3; community *vs.* campus organizing and, 71; JOIN and, 68–69; political diversity in, 6–7; radicalizing ideology and, 70; Tennessee as distinctive experience of, 3, 9; working-class whites and, 68; World War II and, 17
student activism, southern: minority of student bodies and, 151–52; political order and, 5; Populism, community organizing, and, 72; *prophetic minority* and *recalcitrant majority* in, 7; role of, 4; SET and, 50; similarities with national movements of, 92; Southern Days of Secession and, 130; Vietnam War and, 126. *See also* Southern Student Organizing Committee (SSOC)
student activism in Tennessee: absence of counterculture in, 185n172; anti-war movement and, 1–2, 120–21, 124–30, 135–40, 143; apathy among student bodies and, 19, 76, 91–92, 120, 131; Black Power and, 62, 72–73; Black students, armed self-defense, and, 73; Black-white collaboration in, 152–53; campus unrest and, 8; changing nature of, 150–51; community-focused approach to, 3; community interactions during Memphis Sanitation Strike and, 74; Confederate imagery and, 147; conservatism and, 132;

curfew protests and, 84–85; denunciations of apathy and, 91; early efforts of, 35; environmental movement and, 150; focus on campus circumstances at, 11; gay rights and, 149–50; Highlander Folk School and, 7; interracial exchange programs and, 21–22; Kent State shootings and, 132–34; labor organizing and, 61–62; Lane College unrest and, 101–2; linking anti-war protests and campus efforts in, 130; *in loco parentis* protests and, 5, 83–89; long trajectory of, 2–3, 153; Memphis church service kneel-ins and, 55–56; Memphis colleges and, 76; Memphis sit-ins and, 51–56; MTSU effigy burning and, 144–46; Nixon, Graham Crusade, and, 135–40; nonviolent protest workshops and, 39; open speaker policies and, 108–15; post-1970s, 146; post-Kent State strikes and, 134–35; regional variations of, 4; as representative of national trends, 151; scope of, 2–4, 9–10; sit-in movement and, 36–37, 40; southern context of, 4–5; Southwestern BSA and, 148; split of interracial initiatives in, 5–6; student power and, 83, 148, 151, 153; UT presidential appointment demonstrations and, 105–7; UT's SGA election and, 93–96; Vietnam War and, 8, 120–21, 131; white students, Christianity, and, 59; women's rights and, 148–49. *See also individual groups*
student power: autonomy and, 12; *in loco parentis* protests and, 83–84; MTSU effigy burning and, 144; pre-1960s, 11; demands for, 6; racial inequalities and, 104–5; racial justice and, 96; reach of concept of, 13; SGA (UT) election and, 93–96; Tennessee sit-in movement and, 60; unifying theme of, 5; as unifying theme of student activism, 151, 153; UT presidential appointment demonstration and, 106; Vietnam War and, 122
students, Black: armed self-defense and, 73; Black Power and, 75–77; campus life inclusion and, 97–98; consequences of activism for, 5; differences in experience and activism of, 152; draft and, 124–25; Fisk University and, 10; inclusion at Memphis State and, 97–98; Memphis Sanitation Strike and, 73, 81; post-1970 fight for racial equality by, 146; racial "machine" and, 5–6; southern context and, 4–5; student power and, 5; tokenism and, 102–3; university athletics and, 50
students, female, 11, 84–89, 101, 146, 148–50
students, white: Christianity and activism of,

59; civil rights movement participation by, 57–58; draft and, 124–26; labor organizing focus of, 8; southern context and, 5; student power and, 5. *See also individual groups*
Students for Equal Treatment (SET), 47–50
Sugarmon, R. B., Jr., 51
Summerfield Community Council, 16
Sweatt v. Painter, 29

Taylor, Calvin, 77, 79
Taylor, Isaac, 98
Taylor, Maxwell, 127
Tennessee: development of student activism in, 3; fear of interracial exchange programs in, 23–24, 26; "freedom of choice" to desegregate in, 27; Highlander Folk School charter and, 18; interracialism and, 16; Kunstler UT speech responses in, 113–14; legislative opposition to integration in, 21; map of colleges and universities in, *xii*; politics of moderation in, 37–38; regional variation of, 4; riots in, 110; significance of study of, 3–4; source bases and study of, 6. *See also* sit-in movement in Tennessee
Tennessee State Board of Education, 42
Tennessee State University, *xii*, 39, 41–43, 108–109
Tennessee Wesleyan College, *xii*, 88
Tet Offensive, 127–29
Thompson, Ruth Anne, 177n3
Thrasher, Sue, 58–60, 66
Thurmond, Strom, 108
Timmons, William E., 136
tokenism, 102–3, 125
Turner, Charles C., Jr., 89

university administrators: anti-war movement and, 128–29; Baby Boomer influx and, 84; campus policies and, 86–87; campus unrest and, 83–84, 97, 115–19; congressional impressions of, 105; Knoxville sit-ins and, 44–50, 51; and efforts to address racial discrimination, 103–4; *in loco parentis* and liability concerns for, 90–91; pro-war locals and, 133–34; resignation of university presidents and, 99–100; Scranton Commission and, 141–43; SCS and SSOC seen as threats by, 64–65; sit-in movement and, 40–43, 53–54; university as sanctuary and, 117–18; UT Chattanooga incident and, 107; UT presidential appointment demonstrations and, 105–7
University of Tennessee, Knoxville: Adawayhi Pep Club elections and, 103–4; addressing Black student demands at, 103–4; administrators and, 90–91; anti-war demonstrations at, 107; BSU demands and, 103–5; campus policy unrest and, 85–86; Hershey speech protest and, 129; integration of, 29–30; integration of athletics at, 50; *Issues* lecture series and, 111–12; Knoxville sit-ins and, 44–47; linking anti-war protests and campus efforts at, 130; location of, *xii*; managing student unrest and, 115–17; Nixon protest at, 135–40; open speaker policy considerations and, 111–13; post-Kent State strike and, 134–35; presidential appointment demonstrations and, 105–7; responses to student protesters by, 49–50; SGA election at, 93–96; student restaurant protests and, 47–49; Taylor visit, 127; tokenism and, 102; Vietnam Moratorium and, 130–31; William Kunstler speech and, 113–14; Women's Action Movement and, 148
University of Tennessee, Chattanooga, *xii*, 107

Vanderbilt University: Afro-American Association and, 110–11; Dow Chemical and, 127; integration and, 31–32; JUC and SSOC at, 58–59; location of, *xii*; Nashville sit-ins and, 39, 40–41; sit-in response of administrators at, 41; Stokely Carmichael and, 108–9; tokenism and, 102; Vietnam War and, 122–23
Vanderbilt Vietnam Action Committee (VVAC), 127
Vietnam War: draft and, 124–25; interracial student activism and, 8; Memphis and draft for, 80; military enlistment, African Americans, and, 123–24; public opinion and, 127–28. *See also* anti-war movement in Tennessee
Vivian, Cordy Tindell, 20–21

Walker, Robert, 78
Wallace, George, 27
Walters, Herbert, 55
War on Poverty, 72–75
War on Poverty Committee (WOPC), 74–75
Waters, Ethel, 139
WDIA (Memphis radio station), 54–55
Weaver, Charles, 90, 106–7, 112, 115–18, 133–35, 139
Webb, John Maurice, 90
Weber, Blanchard, 33
Weissman, Steve, 92
Wells, Lynn, 63, 92

INDEX 225

"We'll Take a Stand" (SSOC), 63
West, Ben, 41
West, Don, 13–14
Westheider, James E., 123
Westmoreland, William, 126–27
Weyant, Thomas, 6
White Community Project (SSOC), 66
Whitmore, Terry, 123
Whittle, Chris, 86
Wiersema, Harry, 47, 49, 106
Wilkins, Roy, 23
Williams, Avon, 109–10

Williams, Calvin Kendall, 33
Williams, Nat D., 78
women's rights on campus, 148–49
Woodward, C. Vann, 69, 126
World War II, 17
Wright, Nancy Smith, 33–34, 85
Wright, Stephen J., 29, 40
Wyche, Freeman, 34

Young Patriots, 69
youth activism, 7, 17, 50–51

POLITICS AND CULTURE IN THE TWENTIETH-CENTURY SOUTH

A Common Thread: Labor, Politics, and Capital Mobility in the Textile Industry
BY BETH ENGLISH

"Everybody Was Black Down There": Race and Industrial Change in the Alabama Coalfields
BY ROBERT H. WOODRUM

Race, Reason, and Massive Resistance: The Diary of David J. Mays, 1954–1959
EDITED BY JAMES R. SWEENEY

The Unemployed People's Movement: Leftists, Liberals, and Labor in Georgia, 1929–1941
BY JAMES J. LORENCE

Liberalism, Black Power, and the Making of American Politics, 1965–1980
BY DEVIN FERGUS

Guten Tag, Y'all: Globalization and the South Carolina Piedmont, 1950–2000
BY MARKO MAUNULA

The Culture of Property: Race, Class, and Housing Landscapes in Atlanta, 1880–1950
BY LEEANN LANDS

Marching in Step: Masculinity, Citizenship, and The Citadel in Post–World War II America
BY ALEXANDER MACAULAY

Rabble Rousers: The American Far Right in the Civil Rights Era
BY CLIVE WEBB

Who Gets a Childhood?: Race and Juvenile Justice in Twentieth-Century Texas
BY WILLIAM S. BUSH

Alabama Getaway: The Political Imaginary and the Heart of Dixie
BY ALLEN TULLOS

The Problem South: Region, Empire, and the New Liberal State, 1880–1930
BY NATALIE J. RING

The Nashville Way: Racial Etiquette and the Struggle for Social Justice in a Southern City
BY BENJAMIN HOUSTON

Cold War Dixie: Militarization and Modernization in the American South
BY KARI FREDERICKSON

Faith in Bikinis: Politics and Leisure in the Coastal South since the Civil War
BY ANTHONY J. STANONIS

Womanpower Unlimited and the Black Freedom Struggle in Mississippi
BY TIYI M. MORRIS

New Negro Politics in the Jim Crow South
BY CLAUDRENA N. HAROLD

Jim Crow Terminals: The Desegregation of American Airports
BY ANKE ORTLEPP

Remaking the Rural South: Interracialism, Christian Socialism, and Cooperative Farming in Jim Crow Mississippi
BY ROBERT HUNT FERGUSON

The South of the Mind: American Imaginings of White Southernness, 1960–1980
BY ZACHARY J. LECHNER

The Politics of White Rights: Race, Justice, and Integrating Alabama's Schools
BY JOSEPH BAGLEY

The Struggle and the Urban South: Confronting Jim Crow in Baltimore before the Movement
BY DAVID TAFT TERRY

Massive Resistance and Southern Womanhood: White Women, Class, and Segregationist Resistance
BY REBECCA BRUCKMANN

I Lay This Body Down: The Transatlantic Life of Rosey E. Pool
BY LONNEKE GEERLINGS

Partners in Gatekeeping: How Italy Shaped U.S. Immigration Policy Over Ten Pivotal Years, 1891–1901
LAUREN BRAUN-STRUMFELS

Radical Volunteers: Dissent, Desegregation, and Student Power in Tennessee
KATHERINE J. BALLANTYNE

www.ingramcontent.com/pod-product-compliance
Lightning Source LLC
Chambersburg PA
CBHW031748230426
43669CB00007B/543